Modern Governments
GOVERNING GERMANY

MODERN GOVERNMENTS

General Editor
GILLIAN PEELE
Fellow and Tutor in Politics, Lady Margaret Hall, Oxford

Consulting Editor
MAX BELOFF
Former Gladstone Professor of Government and Public
Administration in the University of Oxford

Titles already published

ITALY: Republic Without Government
P. A. Allum

**THE GOVERNMENT OF THE UK: Political Authority in a
Changing Society**
Max Beloff and Gillian Peele

**GOVERNING FRANCE: The One and Indivisible Republic
(Second Edition)**
J. E. S. Hayward

GOVERNMENT OF CANADA
Thomas A. Hockin

JAPAN: Divided Politics in a Growth Economy (Second Edition)
J. A. A. Stockwin

Modern Governments

Governing Germany

WILLIAM E. PATERSON
and
DAVID SOUTHERN

Basil Blackwell

Copyright © William E. Paterson and David Southern 1991

First published 1991

Basil Blackwell Ltd
108 Cowley Road, Oxford, OX4 1JF, UK

Basil Blackwell Inc.
3 Cambridge Center,
Cambridge, MA 02142, USA

British Library Cataloguing in Publication Data

A CIP catalogue record for this book is available from the British Library.

Library of Congress Cataloging in Publication Data

Paterson, William E.
    Governing Germany/William E. Paterson and David Southern.
       p.   cm. — (Modern governments)
    Bibliography: p.
    Includes index.
    ISBN 0–631–17099–5
    ISBN 0–631–17101–0 (pbk.)
    1. Germany—Politics and government.   I. Southern, David.
II. Title. III. Series.
  JN3971.A2P38   1991
320.943—dc20
                                               89–33264
                                                 CIP

Typeset in 10 on 11½ pt Baskerville by Wearside Tradespools, Fulwell, Sunderland
Printed in Great Britain by Billing and Sons Ltd., Worcester

Contents

General Editor's Introduction   vii

Preface   ix

Maps   x

Abbreviations   xv

1   Introduction   1

2   The Origins of Modern Germany   18

3   The Constitutional Dimension   53

4   The Executive Dimension   77

5   The Legislative Dimension   111

6   The Federal Dimension   141

7   Political Parties   172

8   The Political Economy of the Federal Republic   225

9   The Federal Republic and the West   258

10   *Ostpolitik, Deutschlandpolitik* and the Two Germanies   280

11   Conclusion   302

Appendix: Statistical Tables   307

Notes   312

Further Reading   320

Index   325

General Editor's Introduction

The series of which this volume forms a part is intended as a contribution to the study of comparative government. It aims to provide clear and comprehensive analyses of the political systems of major countries selected either because of their intrinsic importance or because their pattern of government is of special interest to students of political science. Although the series is primarily aimed at students in higher education, it is hoped that the style and presentation of the individual volumes will make them accessible to a wider readership and of use to anyone who might need to acquire an understanding of that country for practical purposes.

All study of government must be comparative in the sense that the questions one asks of a particular political system will be generated by one's knowledge of another; and the distinctive features of any given system will only be highlighted by reference to a range of other political systems which work differently Yet the generalizations to which political scientists aspire need to be based on the secure foundations of knowledge of the history, institutions and culture of a country and how its policy-making processes have been formed.

Government is not of course something carried out for its own sake – much less something undertaken for the amusement of academics. It is an important practical activity and ultimately the criterion of success is to be found in its impact on the lives of individual citizens. And here two vital questions need to be asked: how does a government conduct itself in regard to the citizen and what protection has he through the courts or in other ways against the possibility of arbitrary action or maladministration? In this series special attention has been focused on these issues which are sometimes neglected in general texts. Increasingly also the decisions of one government are not autonomous. The international arena places constraints on a country's leaders and more decisions are taken jointly with a group of other governments rather than as an exercise of sovereign power. The volumes in the series therefore take account of the extent to which much decision-making is multi-lateral and pay special attention to the interaction of foreign and domestic policy.

Although some themes figure prominently in all the volumes in the series, no attempt has been made to impose uniformity of treatment on the authors. Each writer is an authority on his or her particular country or group of countries and will have a different perspective on the problems of the area in question. However, this volume by Professor Paterson and Dr Southern in many ways exemplifies the principles of the series. Their examination of Germany is written in a way which will be of interest not merely to those studying that country as part of a course but also to many general readers anxious to understand the political institutions and dynamics of a major European power. It will be relevant also to those interested in the role of Germany within the European Community and the NATO Alliance at a time of profound change and uncertainty in the wider international arena. In this context the authors' discussion of the political economy of Germany and of the tensions surrounding its foreign policy are timely and pertinent. For, as the authors suggest, economic success is in many ways the motor force of the German political system while foreign policy constitutes the most serious question-mark over the future of the state.

The editor of any series is heavily dependent on others for the successful operation of the venture. Here I record two major debts. Lord Beloff initiated the series and then continued as joint editor until other obligations made it necessary for him to hand on the responsibility for it. Fortunately he has agreed to continue as a Consulting Editor and this volume benefited greatly from his breadth of scholarship and judgement. I owe a deep debt of gratitude to Sean Magee of Basil Blackwell whose professional advice and personal encouragement have been of immense assistance, and my thanks also go to Bridget Jennings and the other staff at Blackwell's who make the production process smooth, friendly and efficient.

Gillian Peele

Preface

This book has been some years in gestation and the authors would like to thank the editors, Lord Beloff and Gillian Peele, for their inexhaustible patience as well as their editorial labours. David Southern wrote chapters 3, 4, 5 and 6. William Paterson was responsible for chapters 1, 7, 8, 9 and 10, and the conclusion, while chapter 2 was shared.

William Paterson would like to thank Dr Klaus Günther (Bonn University) and Dr Eckhard Jesse (Trier University) with whom he has often discussed aspects of West German politics. He would also like to thank Mrs Dorothy Foster for her patience in translating illegible drafts into a final manuscript.

David Southern would like to thank Dr Klaus Kirschbaum of Kirschbaum Verlag for his inexhaustible knowledge and unfailing hospitality over the years; Ministerialrat, Dr Hermann Pabel of the Federal Health Ministry; colleagues and students at Kent University; colleagues in the Inland Revenue Solicitor's Office, for their intellectual stimulation and insights into the nature of – in the best Weberian sense – bureaucracy; and the Leverhulme Foundation for a Faculty Fellowship in European Studies, which enabled him to spend a study year in the law department of Bonn University.

W.E.P
D.B.S.

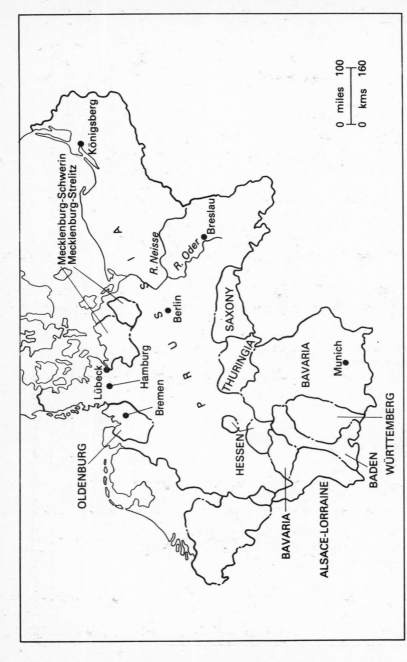

Map 1 Germany 1871–1914, showing the principal federal states.

x

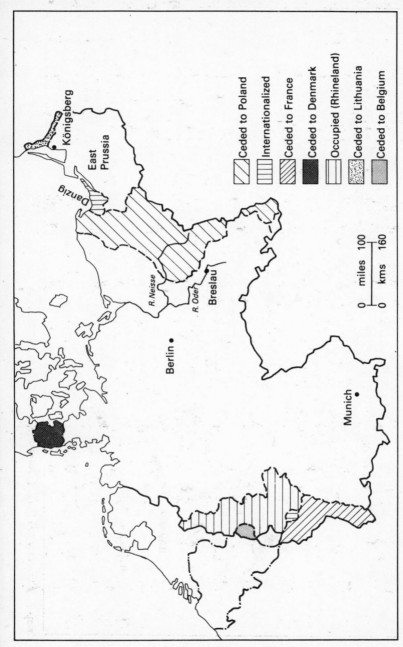

Map 2 Germany 1919, after the Treaty of Versailles.

Ceded to Poland
Internationalized
Ceded to France
Ceded to Denmark
Occupied (Rhineland)
Ceded to Lithuania
Ceded to Belgium

Königsberg

East Prussia

Danzig

R. Neisse

R. Oder

Breslau

Berlin

Munich

miles   100
kms   160

xi

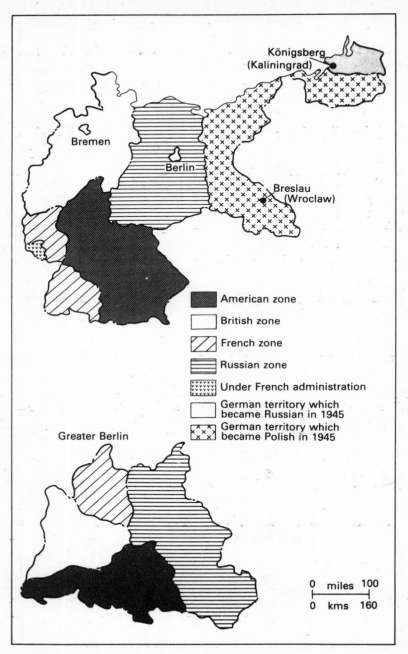

Königsberg
(Kaliningrad)

Bremen

Berlin

Breslau
(Wroclaw)

■ American zone

□ British zone

▨ French zone

☰ Russian zone

▩ Under French administration

□ German territory which
became Russian in 1945

▨ German territory which
became Polish in 1945

Greater Berlin

| 0 | miles | 100 |
| 0 | kms | 160 |

Map 3 Occupation zones, 1945–1949.

Map 4 The West German *Länder* (from 1957).

Map 5 The Laender of the Federal Republic, 3 October 1990.

Abbreviations

APO	*Ausserparlamentarische Opposition* (Extra Parliamentary Opposition)
BDA	*Bundesvereinigung der Deutschen Arbeitgeberverbände* (Federation of German Employers' Associations)
BDI	*Bundesverband der Deutschen Industrie* (Federation of German Industry)
BGBI	*Bundesgesetzblatt* (Federal Law Record)
BP	*Bayern Partei* (Bavarian Party)
BRD	*Bundesrepublik Deutschland* (Federal Republic of Germany)
BVerfG	*Bundesverfassungsgericht* (Federal Constitutional Court)
BVP	*Bayerische Volkspartei* (Bavarian People's Party)
BVerfGE	*Entscheidungen des Bundesverfassungsgerichts* (Decisions of the Federal Constitutional Court)
BVerfGG	*Gesetz über das Bundesverfassungsgericht* (Law on the Federal Constitutional Court)
CDU	*Christlich Demokratische Union* (Christian Democratic Union)
CSU	*Christlich-Soziale Union* (Christian Social Union)
DAG	*Deutsche Angestellten-Gewerkschaft* (Union for Employees)
DBB	*Deutscher Beamtenbund* (German Officials League)
DBV	*Deutscher Bauernverband* (German Farmers Union)
DDR	*Deutsche Demokratische Republik* (German Democratic Republic)
DGB	*Deutscher Gewerkschaftsbund* (Federation of German Trade Unions
DIHT	*Deutscher Industrie und Handelstag* (Diet of German Industry and Commerce)
DKP	*Deutsche Kommunistische Partei* (German Communist Party after 1969)
DP	*Deutsche Partei* (German Party)
DRP	*Deutsche Reichspartei* (German Reich Party)
EC	European Community
EDC	European Defence Community

Abbreviations

EMS	European Monetary System
EVG	*Europäische Verteidigungsgemeinschaft* (European Defence Community)
FDP	*Freie Demokratische Partei* (Free Democratic Party)
FRG	Federal Republic of Germany
GDR	German Democratic Republic
GG	*Grundgesetz* (Basic Law)
GDP/BHE	*Gesamtdeutsche Partei/Block der Heimatvertriebenen und Entrechteten*
KPD	*Kommunistische Partei Deutschlands* (German Communist Party before 1956)
MDB	*Mitglied des Bundestages* (Member of the Bundestag)
NATO	North Atlantic Treaty Organization
NDP	*Nationaldemokratische Partei Deutschland* (National Democratic Party)
NSDAP	*National Sozialistische Deutsche Arbeiterpartei* (National Socialist German Workers Party, Nazi Party)
OECD	Organization for Economic Cooperation and Development
PDS	*Partei Demokratisches Socialismus* (Party of Democratic Socialism)
SED	*Sozialistische Einheitspartei Deutschlands* (Social Unity Party)
SPD	*Sozialdemokratische Partei Deutschlands* (Social Democratic Party)
WAV	*Wirtschaftsaufbau Verein* (Economic Reconstruction League)

1 Introduction

For the past century Britain, France and Germany have been clearly the most powerful European states. The contrast in their political development is equally striking. Britain and France emerged as consolidated states around a central core in early modern times. With the notable exception of the great caesura of the French Revolution, continuity is a central theme in both systems.

The political history of Germany provides a notable contrast – it is a history of discontinuity and fragmentation. Before 1815 Germany was a patchwork of principalities. It was united under Prussian hegemony after 1871 but did not include the German lands of the Habsburgs. Large tracts of territory were lost after 1918. Under Hitler the German state underwent a huge territorial expansion and included Alsace and Austria and the Sudetenland. With the defeat of the Third Reich, Alsace returned to France, the lands beyond the Oder–Neisse were occupied by Poland and the USSR, Sudetenland was reincorporated in Czechoslovakia and its German population expelled. The three Western zones of occupied Germany formed the Federal Republic in 1949 and the Soviet zone became the German Democratic Republic in the same year. Austria regained its independence in 1945.

These rapid changes in the territorial area of the German state were paralleled by equally dramatic changes in political regimes. The authoritarian Imperial period of 1871–1918 was succeeded by the democracy of Weimar which lasted until 1933. The Third Reich dominated by Hitler and the National Socialist German Workers Party was replaced by the Allied occupation only to be replaced by the rival regimes of the Western-oriented representative democracy of the Federal Republic and the communist state of East Germany.

All observers looking at German development in the early post-war period were struck by the obvious contrast between German success in economic and technological development and its tragic political history. The failure of the Weimar Republic had been, and remained, a particularly traumatic episode for German democrats and foreign observers who found it hard to come to terms with the rejection of democracy by the citizens of an advanced industrial state. The conclusion that most came to was that democracy could only be established on a secure footing if the Allied occupation authorities were able to bring about a profound change in the leadership of German social and economic institutions and if they were able to bring about similarly far-reaching changes in German political culture, i.e. the underlying attitudes of German citizens towards political objects. The circumstances of the Allied occupation and its short duration undermined the achievement of both goals. With the onset of the Cold War the United States became less concerned about change and more concerned with stabilizing the Western zones of Germany in order to meet what they perceived as a Soviet challenge. This necessarily implied playing down large-scale societal change and its replacement by a strategy of collaboration with established elites who were, however, expected to endorse the principles of liberal representative democracy. The short duration of the occupation regime and the Germans' position as subjects was a very unpromising platform on which to instil democratic political attitudes.

The nature of the German political past and the initially uncertain prospects of democracy has meant that both the political leadership of the Federal Republic and outside observers have been preoccupied with the question of the political stability of the Federal Republic, i.e. would the newly established democratic regime, contrary to all historical experience, root itself firmly on German soil?

WHITHER THE WEST GERMAN POLITY?

The traumatic political history of the successive German states, the cataclysm of the Third Reich, the apparent destruction of German industry and the enforced division of Germany by external powers scarcely suggested a stable future for the newly created Federal Republic in 1949. Despite these handicaps, the stability of the Federal Republic was never seriously challenged and it rapidly emerged as an immensely prosperous liberal democratic polity. In chapter 2 we identify a number of factors which made this more likely than a concentration on the obvious and undoubted difficulties would have suggested. The Third Reich and its collapse had brought about the end of the political role of the Prussian aristocratic elite and the army. The breakup of the Third Reich and the flood of refugees into the Federal Republic as a result of expulsion and flight did much to undermine the sectional loyalties which had underpinned a deeply fragmented party system. The economy was in a less parlous state than it appeared and economic recovery really predated the establishment of the Federal Republic, though it took some time for full employment to appear.

The Federal Republic reflected and was a creation of the global bipolarity, often called the Cold War, which characterized the early post-war years. Not surprisingly, therefore, a major contribution to the stability of the Federal Republic was made by the deeply held anti-communist sentiments of its citizens, one-quarter of whom had fled from areas under communist rule. The fruits of the economic recovery which had begun in 1948 really began to be apparent in the 1950s as the outbreak of the Korean War set off a long and sustained boom in the western economies. A major innovation was also made with the foundation of the Christian Democratic Party (CDU/CSU) as a *Volkspartei* (people's party). German parties had traditionally been identified with a particular class, region or confession and the creation of a party which aimed at and actually achieved in 1957 a majority on the basis of a cross-class, biconfessional appeal represented a very important advance. The success of the CDU/CSU as a *Volkspartei* impelled the Social Democratic Party (SPD) to weaken its identification with the working class and explicitly to adopt the people's party model in 1959 in the Bad Godesberg Programme. The result of these developments was a polity dominated by the two great people's parties which emphasized stability at the price of ideological choice.

By the 1970s the West German polity, after two decades of industrial peace, economic growth and political stability, was beginning to be seen both in the Federal Republic itself and abroad as the West German model, a highly consensually oriented, liberal, democratic polity, conducive to, and dependent on, a very high rate of economic growth. As Paterson and Smith wrote,

Underpinning all else is a massively prosperous economy, insulated from direct politicisation by its rational framework for economic policy-making, and by its continued success. This sustained performance led in turn to the development of a supportive political culture, now no longer exclusively dependent on a high level of economic growth, but closely related to the political institutions as well. This effect is strengthened by factors which together encourage the successful functioning of these institutions: the absence of deeply divisive social cleavages, the orientation of the major political parties towards the winning and exercise of governmental power, and the resources provided in the office of Federal Chancellor for the exercise of political leadership. The internal stability is buttressed by a network of international relationships which guarantee security, assure the freedom of West Berlin, and provide outlets for an export-oriented economy.[1]

THE ROAD TO UNITY

The celebrations which marked the fortieth anniversary of the Basic Law in May 1989 reflected the satisfaction of the political class and the citizens of the Federal Republic with this stability. They were celebrating, rightly as foreign observers believed, a major success story. The political miracle of the Federal Republic, a stable liberal-democratic German state, which had proved itself to be a reliable ally and model Community partner had been if anything a greater achievement than the earlier economic miracle. German unity was, of course, referred to but it remained a distant aspiration and a growing number of intellectuals and academics, especially on the centre-left, called for a constitutional patriotism based on the Federal Republic and its constitution.

Three hundred miles to the east, however, the Hungarian government began gradually to dismantle the barbed-wire fence that divided it from Austria. The implications of this step for overcoming German division were not immediately clear but a trickle of East Germans began to slip across the Hungarian border into Austria from May 1989. As the holiday season drew to a close in August the trickle turned into a flood of over 5,000 East Germans a week with thousands more camping in Hungary awaiting permission to leave. On 10 September, the Hungarian government relaxed its border controls and over 12,000 East Germans left through Austria for the Federal Republic. This mass exodus was a vivid demonstration of the lack of legitimacy of the GDR. It had often been argued that what East Germans really wanted was the opportunity merely to travel to the West, not to leave the GDR. This wish had largely been conceded by the Honecker regime. The flight made it clear that rejection of the regime, especially by young people who had been brought up in it, was total.

Within the GDR itself mass demonstrations began on 25 September in Leipzig and were quickly emulated in other towns and villages. Dissent, hitherto confined to a number of intellectuals, became a mass phenomenon with the Protestant Church playing a leading role. The activists who organized themselves in 'the New Forum' thought strictly in terms of democratizing and reforming the East German system. Gradually, however, democratic political parties emerged. The Christian Democrats and the Liberals prized themselves free from control of the Socialist Unity Party (SED) and the SPD, which had been merged with the SED in 1946, re-emerged as an individual party.

The East German regime responded with difficulty to these pressures. President Gorbachev indicated his preference for reform during his visit to the fortieth birthday celebrations of the GDR on 7 October. The problem was that all the reforms desired by the East German population would have reduced the differences between the two regimes and thus further undermined what legitimacy the regime still possessed. The Politburo sacked Erich Honecker on 18 October and replaced him with Egon Krenz. Krenz made some faltering attempts at reform and opened up 'the wall' on 9 November. He did not, however, abolish the hated 'Stasi' (Secret Police) and his position became unviable due to revelations of past Communist corruption and the inexorable tide of refugees to the West. The Politburo resigned on 3 December 1989 and an interim government under Hans Modrow took office.

The East German Election

In a speech to the Bundestag on 28 November 1989, Chancellor Kohl made it clear that the unity of the two German states was not a distant aspiration, but rather a goal that could and should be achieved in the short term although the form of unity suggested in the ten-point programme was comparatively loose. In East Germany the tone of the mass demonstrations had changed from calls for reform to demands for immediate unity. The mass demonstrations and the continued mass exodus of GDR citizens made it abundantly clear that the GDR had passed the point of no return. Chancellor Kohl kept up a relentless pressure on the GDR government by his refusal to grant large-scale help to the interim government of Hans Modrow. To do so, in Kohl's view, would have entailed shoring up a government totally lacking in any sort of electoral legitimacy. Under this pressure the Modrow government set an election date of 18 March 1990.

The election campaign was, to a great degree, a proxy election campaign with most of the resources and themes provided by the large West German parties. The West German Social Democrats (SPD) appeared to be in the best position in the early phase. A new party was formed which held its founding conference in Leipzig in February 1990. This new party was expected to benefit from lack of association with the despised Socialist Unity Party State of the preceding forty years and from the popularity of Willy Brandt, its Honorary President.

The Christian Democrats had a more difficult task intially since the East German CDU had been a faithful ally of the Socialist Unity Party throughout the history of the German Democratic Republic. The CDU/CSU therefore spread its support between the Christian Democratic Union (CDU), the German Social Union (DSU) and the Democratic Awakening (DA) who were loosely coordinated in the Alliance for Germany grouping. The Free Democrats sponsored a similar arrangement known as the Alliance of Free Democrats, which grouped together three small Liberal parties, the alliance of German Forum Party (DFP), the Liberal Democratic Party (LDP) and the Free Democratic Party (FDP). The West German Greens gave some support to the Green Party and the independent Women's League. The Socialist Unity Party changed its name to the Party of Democratic Socialism (PDS).

Most of the running was made by Chancellor Kohl who made six major appearances during the campaign. A key feature of his appeal was a strong indication that the Deutschmark and Ostmark could be changed at 1:1. His overwhelming emphasis was on speedy unification and the prospect he held out was that the GDR could join the Federal Republic through Article 23. If this procedure were followed, unity would simply result in the addition of five extra Länder to the Federal Republic with the Basic Law remaining in force. The entry of the new Länder would, however, have to secure two-thirds support in the Bundestag and Bundesrat. The Social Democrats, who started out very well in the opinion polls, fought a lacklustre campaign with Oskar Lafontaine, the Chancellor candidate, especially ill at ease since part of his appeal in West Germany had been to play up the costs of unity. The Social Democrats favoured the negotiation of a new constitution under Article 146 of the Basic Law; a procedure that was bound to drag out the unity negotiations as it would involve establishing a joint constituent assembly and referendum on both sides of the border. Hans-Dietrich Genscher, a native of Halle, also made a number of appearances but the FDP campaign failed to capitalize on its incumbency status in Bonn since the advantages to be derived from that position had been fully exploited by Chancellor Kohl.

The election results were, for the most part, a surprise (table 1.1). The very convincing victory for the Alliance for Germany illustrated Chancellor Kohl's wisdom in spreading the CDU's support between three East German parties, following the revelation that Wolfgang Schnur, the leader of the Democratic Awakening, was associated with the Stasi (State Security Police). Schnur resigned before the election with a subsequent transfer of votes from his party to the other two Alliance members. There was thus no measurable damage to the Alliance. The central message of the Alliance victory was the endorsement of speedy unification. The CDU's overwhelming victory in the first GDR Länder elections on 14 October 1990 indicates that the Alliance will probably dominate the normal politics of that part of Germany.

The SPD result was a disaster. The party had hoped to use the expected triumph in the East German election as a springboard for the Federal Election of 2 December and Lafontaine's adoption as Chancellor candidate was planned for 19 March in Bonn. In the event it was completely overshadowed by the poor result in East Germany and the campaign got off to the worst possible start. The SPD's strategy of proceeding more slowly to unity was clearly the major reason for its failure. It was especially disappointed by its poor showing in the industrial south of the GDR where the workers, tired of poor equipment and inadequate salaries, largely voted for the Alliance – a case of 'Deutschmark, Deutschmark über alles'.

The other parties and groupings performed largely as expected. The Alliance of Free Democrats polled 5.28 per cent and the Alliance 90, a loose grouping of those who had brought about the peaceful revolution in East Germany, polled 2.90 per

Introduction

Table 1.1   The Voting: East German Election (18 March 1990)

Party	Votes	%	Seats
Alliance for Germany (conservative coalition of):	5,524,647	48.14	193
Christian Democratic Union (CDU)	(4,694,636)	(40.91)	(164)
German Social Union (DSU)	(724,760)	(6.32)	(25)
Democratic Awakening (DA)	(105,251)	(0.92)	(4)
Social Democratic Party (SDP)	2,506,151	21.84	87
Party of Democratic Socialism (PDS) (communist)	1,873,666	16.33	65
Alliance of Free Democrats (Liberal alliance of German Forum Party (DFP), Liberal Democratic Party (LDP) and Free Democratic Party (FDP))	606,283	5.28	21
Alliance 90 (Left-wing coalition of New Forum, Democracy Now and Peace and Human Rights initiative)	333,005	2.90	12
Democratic Farmers Party (DED)	250,943	2.19	9
Green Party and Independent Women's League	225,234	1.96	8
National Democratic Party (NDPD)	44,435	0.39	2
Democratic German Women's League (DFD)	38,088	0.33	1
Action Alliance United Left (AVL)	20,180	0.18	1
Alternative Youth List (AJL)	14,573	0.13	1
Christian League	10,699	0.90	—
German Communist Party (KPD)	8,836	0.08	—
European Federalist Party (EFP)	3,690	0.03	—
Independent Socialist Democratic Party (USPD)	3,891	0.03	—
Independent People's Party (UVP)	2,999	0.03	—
German Beerdrinkers Union (DBU)	2,534	0.02	—
Unity Now	2,356	0.02	—
German Spartacist Workers Party (SPAD)	2,296	0.02	—
League of Socialist Workers (BSA/ Trotskyite)	374	0	—
Union of Work Groups for Workers Policy and Democracy (VAA)	373	0	—
European Union of East Germany	n/a	n/a	—

cent after a campaign which had been marked by hesitation and incoherence. Paradoxically the members of Alliance 90 who had been the most bitter critics of the GDR regime were strongly committed to preserving elements of a GDR identity in the new German state. As members of a relatively privileged intelligentsia they fared less badly than workers and were therefore able to contemplate a reform of the GDR rather than its complete abolition.

Alongside the magnitude of the Alliance for Germany victory, another major surprise of the results was the relatively good performance of the PDS. There had been a massive haemorrhage of support from the SED in the last months of 1989 but some ground was recovered after it had changed its name to the PDS. Hans Modrow was an impressive governmental leader in impossible circumstances and Grygor Gysi, the party leader, was a very effective campaigner. Support for the PDS was also especially marked in the East Berlin area where many former employees of the regime were concentrated. The unexpected vitality of the PDS means that it will probably continue to be a factor in all-German elections.

The Unity Negotiations

The only real function of the new government headed by Lothar de Maizière (CDU) was to negotiate unity. The election had determined that this would take place according to Article 23 of the Basic Law. Article 23 concludes with the words that the Basic Law is 'to be put into force in other parts of Germany after their joining'. 'Other parts of Germany' means those parts of Germany within its borders of 1937 which did not form West Germany in 1949. This provision gave West Germany the right to admit these other areas to the Federation. It did not confer an entrance ticket to the Federation. The conditions which an entrant would have to satisfy were laid down both in the Basic Law itself and as further stipulated by the Federal Government. It was under this provision that the Saarland joined the Federal Republic as an additional Land in 1957.

The real aim of part 2 of Article 23 was to keep open – alongside Article 146 – a 'second way' to achieve German unification. While Article 23 contemplated an extension of the Basic Law to other parts of Germany which voluntarily acceded to the Federation as an additional Land or new Länder, Article 146 provided for the entire supersession of the Basic Law by a new 'constitution' – the word so sedulously avoided in 1948–9. Both these provisions appeared to be merely symbolic and rhetorical until 1989, when the question of unification changed overnight from impossibility to inevitability.

East Germany had passed its own constitution on 7 October 1949. Superficially it resembled the Basic Law and showed the same ancestry. While verbally compatible with the pluralist parliamentary principle, however, the constitution was superimposed upon incompatible political theories and realities, namely, the vanguard, hegemonic role of the SED as a fraternal Marxist-Leninist party within the Soviet bloc. The 1974 constitution contained the provision that the German Democratic Republic was 'forever and irrevocably ... united with the Union of Soviet Socialist Republics'. Article 144(2) stated that the law of the constitution was subordinate to 'subsequent measures to overcome National Socialism and militarism' – a provision which relativized the whole paper constitutional order. Under the terms of the 1949 constitution East Germany had been divided into five Länder: Saxony, Mecklenburg, Brandenburg, Saxony-Anhalt and Thuringia. In 1958 these were abolished and replaced by fourteen administrative districts.

The 1974 constitution became effectively obsolete through the revolution of November 1989. East Germany was left in a constitutional vacuum. While some contemplated a more thorough-going reformation via Article 146 of the Basic Law, it was easier to adapt an existing political framework rather than form a new one, especially when the system of government established under the Basic Law enjoyed the support of most Germans East and West. The most realistic and practical way of filling the vacuum in the East and bringing about unification in a reasonably swift and painless manner was by means of Article 23. In July 1990 the two states became economically unified: as with the establishment of the United Economic Region in 1948, political unification followed logically. In East Germany the Länder were reconstituted by means of elections for their individual parliaments. The political institutions of West Germany were modified to accommodate the new entrants to the union, in accordance with the state treaty between the two governments. Having carried through its role as liquidator of the state which it had inherited, the East German government exited noiselessly from the stage of history. Germany, it seemed, had finally come home to itself.

THE POLITICAL CONTOURS OF THE UNIFIED GERMANY

The political structures of the unified Germany are simply the Federal Republic writ large. The Basic Law remains in force and the institutions, i.e. Bundesbank, Federal Constitutional Court, Bundestag, Bundesrat, have simply been enlarged. In the Bundestag 16 West Berlin members were joined by 144 members from the GDR on 3 October so that the Bundestag after 3 December has 656 new members.

The allocation of votes in the Bundesrat had to be modified, to take account of the accession with effect from 3 October 1990 under Article 23(2) of the Basic Law of the newly reconstituted Laender which represented the former East German state, to the area of application of the Basic Law. Article 51(2) of the Basic Law was amended to produce a revised system for distributing votes in the Bundesrat. Each Land has at least three votes; Laender with over two and up to six million inhabitants have four votes; Laender with a population of over six million have six votes.

As a result of these changes the number of votes in the Bundesrat has increased from 41 votes distributed amongst 10 Laender pre-unification to 69 votes shared by 16 Laender post-unification. The members of the expanded Bundesrat, and the number of votes which each enjoys, are as follows:

	Votes in Bundesrat	Population (m)
North Rhine-Westphalia	6	16.7
Bavaria	6	10.9
Baden-Württemberg	6	9.3
Lower Saxony	6	7.2
Hessen	4	5.5
Rhineland-Palatinate	4	3.6
*Berlin	4	3.3
*Saxony	4	5.0
Schleswig-Holstein	4	2.6
*Mecklenburg-Lower Pomerania	4	2.1
*Thuringia	4	2.5

	Votes in Bundesrat	Population (m)
*Saxony-Anhalt	4	3.0
*Brandenburg	4	2.7
Saarland	3	1.1
Hamburg	3	1.5
Bremen	3	0.7
	69	77.7

*Land includes former East German territory.

The Laender which comprised or included former East German territory are excluded for a transitional period from the system of financial equalisation. Instead they receive direct grants-in-aid from the Federation, as part of the costs of unification, together with a share of VAT receipts, initially set at 1.5 milliard DM.

GERMAN ECONOMIC AND MONETARY UNION

The key priority for the Bonn government was to halt the flow of refugees from the GDR. Chancellor Kohl quickly endorsed the idea of a currency union on the grounds that only the prospect of earning hard, convertible currency would persuade GDR citizens to remain at the workplace in the GDR. During the campaign for the East German election he indicated strongly that the Deutschmark and Ostmark would be exchanged at 1:1. This was calculated to consolidate the electoral appeal of the CDU, whilst not damaging the interests of the middle-class supporters of his FDP coalition partners. Bundesbank President Pöhl, concerned about inflation and the further undermining of the competitiveness of the GDR, suggested a 2:1 rate with a DM 2000 concession for small savers. In the final effect the Bundesbank won on savings, though Chancellor Kohl was able to increase the amounts that could be transferred at a privileged rate, especially by the potentially electorally important pensioners.

In setting the final rates of conversion, a distinction was made between graduated levels of personal savings and assets and liabilities. Assets and liabilities denominated in Ostmarks will be exchanged into Deutschmarks at 2:1. All East Germans between the ages of 15 and 60 are allowed to exchange (E)M 4000 of cash or savings at parity and the rest at 2 : 1. Children under 15 can exchange only (E)M 2000 at parity but retired persons over 60 can exchange (E)M 6000 at parity. Wages and prices were converted at parity. These rates are clearly a trade-off between economic logic and political expediency.

The State Treaty on Economic and Monetary Union entered into force on 30 June 1990. Its central provision was the currency union of 1 July 1990, but it contained a number of other important provisions. Article 16 addressed the vital environmental issue and committed the GDR government to aligning its laws with those of the FRG. The appalling condition of the environment in the GDR will continue to create serious problems with the European Community however. The Federal Government has consistently pushed for a very high level of Community-wide environmental regulation and is in a weak position to argue that EC environmental regulation should not apply to what will soon become a significant part of its territory. This is therefore an area in which the German authorities will have to rely on the EC Commission to display a considerable amount of understanding of German difficulties. The Treaty also provided for a social union extending the social benefits enjoyed by citizens of the FRG to the GDR. The conclusion of the State Treaty was the major achievement of the de Maizière government. It had been attended by contention from its inception with the SPD only agreeing to participate after some delay. As the true costs of unity became apparent and as unemployment soared in the GDR, the coalition partners became preoccupied with pinning the blame on their rivals. The Liberals withdrew from the coalition in midsummer and the SPD pulled out after de Maizière had sacked the Agriculture and Finance Ministers both of whom were SPD members.

The de Maizière government was able to continue with the tacit support of the Liberals. Unification of the two Germanies took place on 3 October 1990, two months before the Federal election of 2 December 1990. The election date had been subject to intense interparty wrangling. Initially the SPD, especially its Chancellor candidate Oskar Lafontaine, had wanted to extend the period before the election in order to give the East German government the maximum chance to influence the negotiations. As the pains of the unity process became ever more apparent, the SPD pressed for immediate unification in order to saddle

Chancellor Kohl's government with the difficulties in the run-up to the all-German election on 2 December. The priorities of the CDU/CSU were, of course, the reverse. It was very convenient to have an East German government on whose lack of experience many of the difficulties could be blamed.

The electoral system under which the first post-war all-German elections were to be held also occasioned acute controversy. Differences centred on the 5 per cent 'barrier clause' applicable to West German elections, under which a party must obtain five per cent of the national total of votes, in order to win any seats in parliament. The question was, single barrier clause or separate barrier clauses (one for West Germany, one for East Germany)? The SPD and FDP wanted the whole of Germany to be treated as a single election area with a single set of voting rules. This would have blotted out the smaller East German parties, which might satisfy the 5 per cent rule in East Germany alone but would not secure enough votes to meet the threshold requirement in Germany as a whole. The SPD calculated that this would remove their left-wing rivals, the PDS (Party of Democratic Socialism, made up of ex-Communists). The FDP reckoned on eliminating the DSU (German Social Union, and East German helpmate of the CSU). A dilution of the relative strength of the CSU within the CDU/CSU party group would augment the influence of the FDP in a coalition. The CDU/CSU in West Germany, and CDU and DSU in East Germany, wanted separate barrier clauses.

On 1 August 1990 a formula was agreed, which provided for the 5 per cent clause to be applied throughout Germany, but gave the small East German parties a chance of winning seats in the all-German Bundestag. Candidates of smaller parties were to be allowed – for this election only – to have places on the lists of larger, allied parties. By this means some of the smaller parties would be able to 'piggy-back' their way into the Bundestag. While this helped the DSU and East German Greens, it was of no use to those small East German parties which had no natural associates in the West.

The PDS and other small parties took their complaint to the Federal Constitutional Court. In a surprise judgment of 29 September 1990 the Court upset the careful political calculations by rejecting the common electoral law passed by the West German Bundestag and East German Volkskammer, on the grounds that it failed to ensure the requisite degree of equality of opportunity for political parties. The decision dealt a further blow to the declining fortunes of the SPD, and revived in the PDS the hope of securing parliamentary representation. On 5 October 1990 the Bundestag enacted a revised electoral law, which provided for separate 5 per cent barrier clauses to be applied in the December election in the former areas of West and East Germany respectively. The law completed all its parliamentary stages by 16 October.

THE EXTERNAL TRACK

The speed with which unity negotiations took place between the two German states was not totally surprising, since both governments were agreed on the desirability of unification and one of the negotiating partners (the Federal Government) was in a relatively much stronger position. The negotiations with external powers were expected to be much more difficult. Conventional wisdom had held that the Soviet Union could not agree to German unity since it meant ceding the GDR, the base from which it could in the last analysis control Eastern Europe militarily. It was also assumed that a strong Germany was so obviously not in the interest of the Soviet Union that it would never agree to a unified Germany aligned with the West. The Western powers were ostensibly committed to supporting the Federal Government's position on German unity, but there were real doubts about how much they actually wished it to take place. The views of all four powers were clearly going to be crucial in the unification process. This was most obviously true in relation to the Soviet Union which would have to agree to abandon its dominant position in the GDR. It was also true, however, of the Western allies who also possessed important residual legal rights, especially in relation to Berlin. They were extremely unlikely to agree to cede these rights unless the new Germany was to remain firmly enclosed in the Atlantic alliance. They were resolutely opposed to the prospect of an unaligned Germany which they feared would be a loose canon in the centre of Europe.

Chancellor Kohl's 'Ten Point' plan at the end of November 1989 alerted the four powers to the determination of the Federal Government in relation to achieving unification. The Western governments were concerned by the lack of consultation and the British and Soviet governments expressed doubts about the immediate prospect of unification. This opposition began to soften in early 1990. Both governments had to register the strength of German feeling on the matter and the unsustainability of the GDR regime once Chancellor Kohl had made it clear that the Federal Government would not support the GDR before free elections had taken place. The British government found themselves relatively isolated in the European Community and NATO in their reservations about German unity and this had a softening effect on British policy. The Soviet Union was so weak economically and so dependent upon actual and potential German aid that Gorbachev was not in a position to resist. The weakness of the Soviet position was partially counterbalanced by the fear that too obvious a demonstration of this weakness might lead to the toppling of Gorbachev and his replacement by hardliners.

The acceptance by external powers of German unity was temporarily shaken by a dispute over the finality of the Oder–Neisse line as Germany's Eastern border. Chancellor Kohl, sensitive to the prospect of the electoral gains by the Republicans, publicly raised the legal status of the Oder–Neisse line as an issue. This provoked intense alarm in Poland and dismayed friendly governments, and Chancellor Kohl was eventually forced to climb down. The Oder–Neisse episode demonstrated the potential that external and border issues possessed in calling into question the unification process. The Allied governments and the Federal Government were both relieved when it was agreed at a Conference in Ottawa on 13 February 1990, to handle the issues in a so-called two-plus-four formula, i.e. the two German governments would negotiate with each other and simultaneously hold joint meetings with the four powers. In this way it was hoped to prevent the two tracks drifting apart and to ensure that they moved at the same speed.

NATO

The most difficult question to resolve was the relationship of a unified Germany to the alliance system. The Soviet Union was for a long time unwilling to accept that a unified Germany in its entirety would be a NATO member. The Federal Government was equally insistent on NATO membership since it needed the backing of its Western allies and it genuinely believed that security issues were best handled collectively. It was prepared to make some concessions, however, and quite early on Hans-Dietrich Genscher floated the idea that although a unified Germany should remain in NATO, the NATO front line should remain as at present with the East German area being held by German rather than NATO forces. Despite both the annoyance of the British government at what they saw as Foreign Minister Genscher's premature sacrifice of what should have been a common Western position and determined Soviet resistance, the final Kohl/Gorbachev agreement on 16 July 1990 was along these lines with Soviet forces being allowed to remain in the GDR until 1994. The East German Army (NVA) was integrated into the Bundeswehr on 3 October 1990 and there will be a very steep reduction in German and Allied forces stationed in Germany in the period up to 1994.

The European Community

Potential conflicts between German unity and European integration were headed off by the policies of the EC Commission and the French government. The Commission and the French government were agreed that a united Germany was a very strong argument in favour of speeding up integration. A unified Germany outside an integrated Europe would be a source of instability and inside a highly integrated Europe it would not be so dominant as to overpower the other members. The British Prime Minister and government were very concerned about German hegemony but wanted a wider and looser Europe. The incoherence of its position left it without influence on events.

East Germany will not sign a Treaty of Accession to the EC but will become part of the EC in uniting with the Federal Republic. For a transitional period the EC will allow wide discretion in the application of EC policy in relation to subsidies, environmental law and agriculture.

In general, despite very profound problems of economic transition in East Germany, the new Germany has every chance of political and economic success. German unity has been achieved with the agreement of the other powers and the structures and values of the new state will be based on those of the enormously successful Federal Republic.

2 The Origins of Modern Germany

> The Germans are of the day before yesterday and the day
> after tomorrow – they have as yet no today.
>
> Nietzsche, *Beyond Good and Evil*

Germans have long had a sense of cultural identity and pride in
being German but they have lacked political unity. Traditionally
Germans had two competing focuses of potential loyalty: their
immediate form of state; and a wider, shadowy entity called
'Germany'. The appeal of the wider unity of the nation tended
to destabilize the political and social status quo, and this in turn
helps to explain the unevenness of German development which
presented a curious blend of backwardness and modernity.
What Konrad Adenauer, the first Chancellor of West Germany,
forced Germans to decide was the choice between the form of
statehood which was on offer and reunification – between
statehood and nationality. The establishment of West Germany
in 1949 marked the long-delayed triumph of modernist assimi-
lationist forces in German politics over the reactionary isolation-
ist forces. After the dramatic and finally cataclysmic development of modern Germany, West Germany joined the societies
and political system of the West. To understand the significance
of this step, we need to put the foundation of West Germany in
its historical context.

THE NATION AND THE STATE

The official name of the state created in 1949 is 'the Federal
Republic of Germany' (*Bundesrepublik Deutschland*, BRD). The
remarkable feature of this designation is the use of the name
'Germany' because West Germany was not, nor has there ever
been, a German national state.

Germany had a sense of nationhood but could develop no
corresponding state form. In the tenth century the German

nation meant an association of West German nobles. Around that time there was an eastwards migration of peasants into the territories east of the Elbe. After the failure of the Crusades the crusading orders conquered and colonized Slav lands east of the Oder. An extensive area grew up in which widely divergent dialects were spoken. The Electors of Saxony and Brandenburg adopted a common form of German as a diplomatic language which was disseminated through the German-speaking world by Luther's Bible.

Lutheranism established that the German nation was the German people (*Volk*), a term which escapes perfect definition. Its identity rested not on common statehood but on linguistic and cultural affinities. As a result of the French occupation of Germany by Napoleon, the population became aware of being German in a political sense. Napoleon began the unification of Germany by abolishing the Holy Roman Empire in 1806 and sharply reducing the number of political units into which Germany was divided.

The War of Liberation (1812–14), which led to the expulsion of Napoleon from Germany, was accompanied by a great upsurge of national sentiment. The peace-makers of Europe sought in the Vienna Settlement of 1815 to reinstate the legitimist, dynastic principle rather than to give expression to the new political forces of nationalism and liberalism. The Federal Acts of 6 June 1815 created in Germany a confederation of sovereign states – the German Bund – consisting of thirty-five monarchical states and four free cities.

Throughout much of continental Europe in 1848 there occur-red a widespread revolt against the Vienna Settlement – 'the Metternich system' – in the name of political and national liberation. In Germany the first national parliament was elected – the Frankfurt National Assembly. The liberal nationalists enacted the Paul's Church Constitution of 1849, which envis-aged a Greater Germany, including Austria, united on a liberal, democratic and federal basis.

The members of the Frankfurt Assembly proved unequal to the task. No coherent majority emerged, and alarmed by insur-rection among the lower classes and trouble on the eastern borders the Assembly eventually turned to the King of Prussia for help. The failure of the Frankfurt Assembly was a defeat both for German liberalism and the bourgeoisie and ensured that unification would be brought about not on the basis of a

19

self-confident liberal bourgeoisie but by Prussia.

The Frankfurt liberals were unarmed prophets, lacking the power to introduce a new political order in a national Germany. The leading members of the confederation were Prussia in the north and the Austrian Empire in the south. Since 1748 Silesia had belonged to Prussia. Prussia had continued its territorial expansion as a result of the Vienna Settlement, when the Rhineland was given to Prussia in order to create a counter-weight to France in the east and so help to keep France within her borders. The Rhineland contained the Ruhr Basin. With the advent of the industrial revolution Silesia and the Ruhr with their coal and iron became the leading industrial areas of Germany. In 1865 Prussia possessed 15,000 steam engines with 800,000 horsepower; Austria had only 3,400 steam engines with 100,000 horsepower. Prussia had a railway network of 11,000 kilometres; Austria's totalled 6,600 kilometres. 'The industrial revolution enabled Prussia to develop from a nominal into a real great power' (F. L. Carsten).

On the surface the modernization process in Germany and Austria assumed the same form as in western Europe: industrialization, the refinement of industrial techniques, urbanization. But there was a lag in value changes. Membership of the political and social elite was largely confined to pre-industrial classes who adhered to and maintained pre-industrial values and political forms. A hybrid type of society emerged, in which archaic social forces were harnessed to modern industrial techniques. Germany's industrial revolution failed to produce a liberal industrial middle class. Germany became an industrial state with feudal institutions and attitudes. Economical and political development proved to be asymmetrical. Germany was incompletely liberalized. The profound social changes wrought by the industrial revolution were not adequately heeded or reflected in the political structure. The widespread demands for constitutional reform and national unification were distorted and deflected rather than answered.

German liberals and democrats sought both national unity and democratic political change. Only the use or threatened use of force could promote the former goal; those who controlled the resources of the state were determined to ensure the survival of their order. Ultimately, political modernization was sacrificed for the sake of conservative support for the national cause.

As a result of the upheavals of 1848–9 the Prussian monarchy became a constitutional state in the sense that the king no longer ruled absolutely. In 1850 the monarch granted a constitution which established a bicameral parliament alongside the royal executive but failed to delimit their respective responsibilities. Legislation required the assent of both chambers and the king. In 1861–2 a constitutional crisis arose, whose outcome fundamentally affected subsequent developments. The Progressive majority was hostile to the status quo, and advocated national self-determination and political liberalism. Bismarck was appointed to uphold conservative interests but he was not a conservative in the conventional mould. He had two aims: to assert Prussia's right to be treated as a great power and to maintain the conservative ruling order in Prussia. He believed that the forces of change had to be met both by resistance and by accommodation. Revolution from below was to be counteracted by revolution from above on the principle 'better to make a revolution than to suffer one'. He was, in Lothar Gall's phrase, 'a white revolutionary'.[1]

Liberals assumed that the liberal and nationalist elements of their programme were complementary. Bismarck made them choose by offering them a united Germany excluding the Austrian Empire – the 'little German' (*kleindeutsch*) solution – in return for their acceptance and endorsement of a modifed form of the existing legitimist–dynastic state structure. By 'placing the Prussian army at the head of the German national cause' he built his 'golden bridge to the liberals'. This was the price which Bismarck required Prussian conservatives to pay in order to retain their power, position and privilege.

Bismarck's immediate action in 1862 was to continue the collection of taxes not voted by the chambers. Notions of popular consent to government were not yet firmly planted in Prussia. Bismarck successfully called the liberals' bluff by taking advantage of Prussia's undeveloped constitutionalism. At the same time he appeased their nationalist aspirations. In Bismarck's three Wars of Unification (1864, 1866 and 1870–1) Prussia first crushed Austrian political influence in Germany and then supported the national cause to establish the German Reich of 1871. The liberal position was undermined and most Progressives were prepared to support the Prussian state as the instrument of achieving national self-determination. Bismarck hoped that the traditional Prussian state would thenceforward be secure in a *klein Deutschland* blessed by the liberals.

BISMARCK'S GERMANY

The 1871 Constitution set the pattern of government until 1916. Parliament was composed of the Bundesrat and the Reichstag. The Bundesrat was an appointed assembly, consisting of delegations from the federal states (*Freistaaten*) which constituted the new Reich. The Reichstag was directly elected by universal manhood suffrage. The free states retained their own heads of state, executives and parliaments. The efficient secret of Bismarck's constitution was that while there was a Reich parliament, there was no Reich cabinet. The Reich government comprised the Reich Chancellor alone. For two reasons Bismarck unshakeably opposed the strengthening of the central institutions of government, which would have resulted from the establishment of a Reich cabinet. First, the Reichstag would have sought a measure of influence over any cabinet; given the nature of the Reichstag franchise, this would have been a step towards parliamentary government unthinkable for conservatives. Secondly, it would have undermined the Bundesrat, which was the instrument of conservative interests at national level and had a veto over measures passed by the Reichstag. This veto was effectively in the hands of the Prussian Foreign Minister, which post Bismarck also held, in addition to his roles as Prussian Prime Minister and Reich Chancellor. The government of Germany remained in conservative hands; the Reichstag was – in Liebknecht's words – 'the fig-leaf of absolutism'.

Nevertheless, the government needed support in the Reichstag. In the Reichstag two political parties emerged which – unlike the conservatives and liberals who had hitherto dominated parliaments – were highly organized and represented mass movements with permanent bases: the Centre Party and the Social Democratic Party of Germany (SPD). The Centre Party, formed in 1868, became the political vehicle of German Catholicism by reason of Bismarck's anti-Catholic policies of 1871–8 (the *Kulturkampf*). The SPD, founded in 1875, represented the new urban working class, not a revolutionary class but one seeking recognition of its position as an estate of the nation. Whilst Bismarck had won wars and forged a united Germany, he could only avert or distort the problem of how to adopt old forms to a changed world.

The brief liberal phase of German political development which had produced unification, a parliamentary system, economic and social modernization came to an end in 1879, with the replacement of the Liberal/Progressive governmental grouping in the Reichstag by a majority centred on the most authoritarian elements in German industry and society, the alliance of 'iron and rye', the old agrarians and heavy industry.

Bismarck used two issues to divide the liberals and unite his new majority: protectionism and the suppression of the Social Democrats. The political changes of 1878–9 constituted 'a second foundation of the Reich'. The decisive switch in policy affected German political, economic and social life fundamentally. It marked the end of the ruling classes' limited attempts to meet change by adaptation and the emergence of a dogmatic and ultimately degenerate conservatism, which believed that general war would be less hostile to the ruling classes' interests than a change in the status quo. A decade after unification it became clear that no political consensus had emerged about the state and society. Unification had been imposed from above, without fundamentally altering the existing state and political system.

Yet the growing social conservatism needs to be contrasted with the increasing urbanization and industrialization of Germany. Between 1880 and 1914 Germany overtook Britain in the three classic indicators of industrial power: coal, pig-iron and steel. Germany led the world in the classic industries of the second industrial revolution: the chemical and electrical industries. A unified and industrialized Germany rose to continental hegemony.

The chief political beneficiary of urban and industrial expansion was the SPD. Domestically the outstanding feature of the first decade of the twentieth century was the growth of this party. The rise of the SPD was both cause and symptom of the difficulties of governing Germany. The SPD was not only the chief spokesman of the working class, it was also the principal constitutional opposition, standing for the democratization of the system. The electoral system for the Reichstag was weighted against the SPD by retaining the constituency boundaries of 1871, notwithstanding the huge shift of population from the country to the town. Nevertheless, in the Reichstag election of 1912 the Social Democrats became the largest single party in the Reichstag, with 110 out of 397 seats.

Faced with the growing disparity between the composition of the Reichstag and the basis of political power, and the difficulty of embodying any compromise arrangement in institutional form, the last pre-1914 Chancellor, Bethmann-Hollweg, sought to govern without reference to parties and interests, steering a middle course, resisting and repressing parliamentarization, and seeking to pacify public opinion by piecemeal reforms without thereby activating the veto of the Emperor or the Prussian government. The assumptions of his government were intensely conservative, its policies moderately liberal. This style of government was justified as being the rule of the 'state above the parties', whereby the state apparatus acted as a broker between political groups and formulated policy in the public interest. This theory of government rested on the fallacy that there can be impartial, disinterested solutions to political questions. Usually, it was simply a cloak for and rationalization of conservative interests and could not have been sustained indefinitely.

THE FIRST WORLD WAR

The years 1870–1914 were ones of exceptional stability. Indeed the outbreak of the First World War was greeted throughout Germany with a feeling of profound release from political divisions at home. Yet the stability produced by the European balance of power allowed great domestic, social and economic change and created a corresponding degree of political tension. On 1 August 1914 Kaiser Wilhelm II for once found words to express the national mood, when in the most popular words he ever uttered he declared: 'I no longer know any parties, I know only Germans' (*ich kenne keine Parteien mehr, ich kenne nur Deutsche*).

The proclamation of a political truce among the parties (*Burgfrieden*) brought about the superficial integration of the SPD into German society. Like the liberals in the 1860s, the Social Democrats felt obliged in an emergency to subordinate internal reform to external national considerations. There was general recognition that a national war, which made such extraordinary demands upon each individual, would necessarily have a democratic effect upon German society. One could not simply go back to the old ways and the old system, which had already lost their power of conviction. Among right-wing circles this perception simply intensified their existential feeling of

Angst, of having lost their bearings. Idealizing the past, but despairing of preserving it, they took refuge in the concept of an expansionary, annexationist peace, in which their order would continue to rule Germany and Germany would rule central Europe. It was a question of 'world domination or world downfall'.

Faced with the strains of total war and the ideological gulf between different sections of German society, Bismarck's system of government, based on a Chancellor dependent on the confidence of the Kaiser, broke down. On 12 July 1917, the military leadership – Hindenburg and Ludendorff – forced the resignation of Bethmann-Hollweg by threatening their own resignations. Unconstitutional, authoritarian, prerogative government triumphed. As long as Ludendorff thought Germany could win, there would be no peace. It is difficult to trace the exact moment at which he decided that the military situation was hopeless. It was certainly much later than the military situation justified. Ludendorff was also aware of the growing agitation at home, fanned by the near famine of the winter of 1917 and the example of the Russian Revolution. The German leadership faced the nightmare of a squeeze between overwhelming attack in the west and a political collapse at home.

Two military events above all seem to have driven Ludendorff to sue for peace: the Allied breakthrough on 8 August 1918 – 'the black day of the German army' he called it – and the collapse of the least considerable of all the central powers, Bulgaria, on 25 September, which exposed the whole south-east flank of the central powers and threatened oil supplies from Rumania. The combination of actual or potential disasters forced Ludendorff to inform the Chancellor on 29 September 1918 that Germany must seek an armistice.

Conservatives believed that they owed it to themselves and their order not to be left with responsibility for the disaster into which they had plunged their country. Such was the power of the High Command that they were able to install a parliamentary government by a few sharp memoranda. As a result of Ludendorff's 'revolution from above' a Reich cabinet formed of the representatives of the majority parties in the Reichstag – including the Social Democrats – was formed under the Chancellorship of Prince Max von Baden. In October 1918 the constitutional reforms so long demanded came in a rush, apparently as gifts from above. German political life was democratized – but not because of the inherent strength of democratic forces.

As soon as the hypnotic spell of victory was broken social cohesion and respect for authority disintegrated. As in Russia the revolution was sparked off by the Navy. The Kiel mutinies were then followed by upheaval in most German cities.

General Groener – Ludendorff's successor – realized three things: peace had to be made under any conditions before the Allies broke through into Germany; the Kaiser had to go; and the only people capable of riding the storm and creating some sort of national consensus were the members of the centre–left coalition in the Reichstag, above all the SPD. On 9 November 1918 the German Republic was proclaimed and Max von Baden handed over power to the Council of People's Representatives headed by Friedrich Ebert. On 11 November 1918 the Armistice Agreement was signed and came into effect. Hindenburg was later to write: 'Our exhausted front collapsed, like Siegfried under the treacherous spearthrust of grim Hagen.' Thereby he lent his massive authority to a destructive myth of vast proportions. By assuming office when they did, the democratic parties were saddled with responsibility for the German surrender.

THE WEIMAR REPUBLIC

It was the fate of the German left to come to power at a time when it was bitterly divided. In 1916 the SPD had split into the Majority Social Democrats (MPSD), who supported the continuance of the war, and the leftist Independent Social Democrats (USPD), who opposed it. To the left of the Independents was the Spartacist League, headed by Karl Liebknecht and Rosa Luxemburg. On 1 January 1919 the Spartacists formally seceded from the Independents and constituted themselves as the Communist Party of Germany (KPD). The Council of People's Representatives consisted of three representatives of the Majority Socialists and three Independents. The Spartacists attacked the Independents for entering into partnership with the Majority Socialists. Amongst the Independents ideology was stronger than the will to power and on 29 December 1918 they gratefully found a pretext to resign from the government, leaving the Majority Socialists to confront the problems of a time so out of joint that nobody could see how to go forward. The Majority Socialists had no friends – and many enemies – both at home and abroad and they lacked any political programme or strategy of their own. They also lacked any governmental experience and their immediate goal was simply to hold Germany together in the face of internal dissolution and external collapse until a National Assembly could be elected. This Assembly would take the long-term decisions on the future government of Germany, and provide for an orderly transfer of power. The leaders of the Majority Socialists regarded the revolutionary legitimation of their authority not as a springboard but as a stigma. In his opening speech to the Weimar National Assembly on 6 February 1919, Ebert declared:

Germany must never again succumb to the old misery of fragmentation and contraction ... the provisional government inherited a desperate situation ... We were the liquidators of the old regime ... Supported and encouraged by the Central Council of the Workers' and Soldiers' Councils we have employed our best endeavours to fight the dangers and misery of the transitional period. We have not pre-empted the National Assembly.

The German Revolution of 1918 marked the opening of a tumultuous phase of German history, which only began to subside after 1920. In this period the new democratic rulers of Germany cooperated with elements of the right to prevent anarchy, disorder and revolution at home. With the wisdom of hindsight the policy of Ebert and his colleagues has been condemned as excessively pragmatic. Despite the major shortcomings of government in these early years the Republic was not doomed irrevocably by 1920. Its final ousting by the National Socialists is not attributable to the course which the German Revolution assumed in 1920, fateful though that may have been, but to subsequent and independent developments.

The elections for the Weimar National Assembly of 19 January 1919 gave three-quarters of the seats to the 'Weimar Coalition' of the three parties who proved the most consistent and stable supporters of the Republic: the SPD, the Centre and the German Democratic Party (DDP – a small progressive liberal party). The tasks of the National Assembly were to establish a new government to take the place of the Council of the People's Representatives, to draft a constitution and to accept the Allies' peace terms.

The Assembly set to work with a draft constitution prepared by Hugo Preuss. The final version of the Weimar Constitution was passed into law on 11 August 1919. The shortcomings of constitutional arrangements have often been held responsible for the political weakness of the Weimar Republic, both at the time and subsequently. But as Gladstone observed: 'The manufacture of a constitution is always the easiest thing in the world. The question is whether the people concerned will work it.'

The most widely criticized feature of the formal political arrangements which emerged was the pure party list system of proportional representation used in elections, whereby votes were cast exclusively for parties and – in principle – each party received one deputy for every 60,000 votes it received. This system was the product not of the Constitution but of the Electoral Law of 27 April 1920. Moreover, the voting system did not create but merely perpetuated the fragmentation of the party system, which pre-dated the First World War and derived from the deliberate exclusion of the parties from governmental responsibility in Bismarck's system of government.[2] In any case, the Weimar party system proved capable until 1930 of producing at least three viable government coalitions: the Weimar coalition; the bourgeois coalition stretching from the Centre on the left to the German National People's Party (DNVP) on the right; and the Grand Coalition running from the SPD to the German People's Party (DVP) on the right.

The Constitution has also been criticized for retaining a federal system with its peculiar Reich–Prussia dualism, whereby forty out of Germany's seventy million inhabitants belonged to Prussia, while the remainder belonged to the other seventeen *Länder*. But political arrangements cannot correspond to some tidy mathematical formula. In the Weimar context the influence of Reich–Prussia dualism was largely benign. In Prussia the Weimar coalition retained its majority until 1932. In the Reich the Weimar coalition lost its majority irrevocably after 1920. The continuity of the Prussian government counteracted the discontinuity of the Reich government. The Weimar system was, moreover, much more centralistic than it might appear. The second chamber of Parliament – the Reichsrat – possessed, unlike the former Bundesrat, only a suspensory instead of an absolute power of veto over bills passed by the Reichstag. In 1919 Erzberger, in the most creative and effective institutional reforms of the Weimar Republic, established a centralized Reich

Finance Ministry which raised and distributed tax revenues throughout the Reich.

Another feature of the Constitution which has been widely condemned – particularly by the founders of the Federal Republic – was its provision of a double executive, of President and Chancellor. The President was an Ersatz–Kaiser, elected for seven years by the whole nation and endowed with extensive powers and intended to counteract the dangers of a leaderless democracy. The Chancellor headed the cabinet and was responsible to the Reichstag, but was both appointed by and could be dismissed by the President. For all the criticisms that have been made, the system proved until 1930, under the Reich Presidencies both of Ebert up to 1925 and Hindenburg thereafter, quite workable. If Weimar Reichstags had been able to produce stable majorities, the extension and abuse of presidential power after 1930, arising from the vacuum of parliamentary authority, would never have been possible.

Where the system failed was not in its formal political arrangements but in achieving the substantive legitimation of the new order. In January and March 1919 the Spartacists launched uprisings in Berlin, which were repressed by hastily organized formations of ex-soldiers known as the Freikorps. In the early summer of 1919 and March and April of 1920 a wave of putschist actions and mass strikes of enormous proportions shattered German society and convulsed the Ruhr, Berlin and Central Germany. The government's response was to use the Freikorps and other repressive means to assert its authority. It seems clear that there occurred in this period a spontaneous radicalization of the working masses, to which the parties of the left – both in and outside government – failed to react adequately.[3]

The forces of the right had been ready to join with the republican governments in opposing what they saw as anarchy and social revolution. The government, however, did not thereby gain the allegiance of the higher social groups to the Republic. German conservatives did not recognize the German Republic as their legitimate government and either contested or ignored its claim to rule. The revolution of 1918 was a political revolution but not a social or economic revolution. The possessing classes were most favourably treated by the new order. But with a few distinguished exceptions, members of the German right proved unable to adapt rigid attitudes, ingrained in them before 1914, to changed political circumstances. They remained irreconcilably divided from the Republic and its principal bastion the Social Democrats by ideology which blinded them to their own self-interest and even to the basic decencies of organized society.

Thus the Republic emerged from its early traumas with a fragmented political culture and no national consensus. Nevertheless the years from 1920 to 1930 marked a period of substantial political, economic and social achievement.

German workers and managers applied themselves to the rebuilding of the economy to such effect that within a few years the economy had risen from the ruins of defeat and dissolution to even higher levels of production. In 1925 unemployment fell below 200,000. In 1926 German foreign trade moved strongly into surplus. Despite Germany's great loss of territory and resources, pre-war levels of production were surpassed in 1929.

In May 1921 Josef Wirth (Centre Party) became Chancellor. He held the post until November 1922 – the longest period for which a Weimar Chancellor had yet survived. He adopted a consistent and honest policy towards the Treaty of Versailles: the policy of fulfilment. Like it not, he argued, Germany had been defeated and could not reverse the result of the war. Britain and France held the upper hand and were resolute to enforce the terms of the peace treaty. In Germany's immediate situation, the only way forward was to seek some form of working arrangement with Britain and France, and that could only be attained by accepting and implementing the terms of the Treaty.

The Nationalists, who would have faced the same dilemma if they had served in what statesmen called 'the trenches of responsibility', stigmatized this as 'national suicide'. Their hostility was directed almost entirely against their fellow countrymen. In 1921 Erzberger was hounded from public life by the right and assassinated. In June 1922 the Foreign Minister Rathenau was also murdered. Wirth found words to match the occasion and also to express his fundamental convictions and policy:

With Nationalist demonstrations you do not solve any problem in Germany. Therefore patience, more patience and yet more patience with one's nerves screwed up and held firm, even in the times when it would be easier for oneself and one's party to sneak away into the woods.

The Reichstag enacted the Law for the Defence of the Republic. Its central provision was to establish new political offences and a Court for the Defence of the Republic to try them. This was sabotaged by the Bavarian government. Since 1919, when a nationalist–particularist government had come to power there, Bavarian authorities had deliberately made the state a haven for right-wing extremists from all parts of Germany, including Hitler and the nascent National Socialist German Workers Party (NSDAP). The Bavarian government refused to implement the Law for the Defence of the Republic in Bavaria and in particular insisted that political offenders in Bavaria should be tried by Bavarian People's Courts (*Volksgerichte*) and not by the Court for the Defence of the Republic.

In an attempt to secure the reparations due under the Versailles Treaty the French occupied the Ruhr in January 1923. Chancellor Cuno's government proclaimed a policy of passive resistance, which entailed unlimited subsidies to the population of the Ruhr. During and after the First World War German governments had incurred enormous and uncontrolled budget deficits. The increase in the amount of money in circulation relative to the volume of goods and services caused inflation. The 'discount happy signature' of the Cuno government now turned inflation into hyperinflation.[4] By October 1923 the position had been reached in which the only way in which monetary stability could be restored was by the wholesale replacement of the old paper mark currency by a new currency. On the outbreak of the First World War one paper mark was worth one gold mark. On 15 November 1923 the mark had stabilized on the basis of 1 Rentenmark=1 gold mark=0.42 dollars=1 billion (10^{12}) paper marks. The German hyperinflation had been called 'the grave of the middle classes' and by forcing down some members of the middle class into the working class, it stored up discontent which contributed to the rise of National Socialism. Yet it is clear that the social identity, expectations and habits of thought of the bulk of the middle class survived the inflation.

The stabilization of the currency overnight was a remarkable achievement. It was overshadowed, however, by Hitler's Beer Hall Putsch in Munich on 8/9 November 1923. Hitler attempted to force his protectors in the Bavarian government to join with him in overthrowing the Republic and marching on Berlin. Instead, he frightened them into suppressing his putsch through the use of the Bavarian state police. The prospect of Hitler's trial in the aftermath of the failed putsch caused the Bavarian authorities acute embarrassment. The Bavarian government wished to conceal its own role in fostering the Nazi movement. The fateful consequences of the Bavarian government's failure to uphold the Law of the Defence of the Republic now became manifest. By law Hitler's trial should have taken place before the Court for the Defence of the Republic. The Bavarian government – for its own protection – would only allow his trial to take place before the Munich *Volksgerichte*. The *Volksgerichte* had long been a thorn in the flesh of the administration of justice in the Reich. The Reich government, still uncertain how far they could go against Bavaria, did a deal: the Bavarian government could keep control of Hitler's trial, if thereafter the *Volksgerichte* were abolished. The *Volksgerichte* ultimately sentenced Hitler to five years' fortress confinement. But the most significant part about the sentence was an omission: because Hitler had – in the Bavarian tribunal's view – acted out of 'honourable motives', it did not order his deportation to his native Austria. If his trial had taken place before a Reich court, it is almost certain that Hitler would have been deported. The consequences of his removal from Germany might have been incalculable.

As soon as Hitler's trial was over, the blaze of publicity surrounding him vanished. In the ten *Landtag* elections between 1923 and 1928 the NSDAP could not muster even 4 per cent of the vote. In the 1928 Reichstag election his party won only 2.6 per cent of the vote, which gave them twelve out of 491 seats.

The two Reichstag elections of 1924 were a victory for the traditional right, above all the DNVP. The MSPD and USPD had reunited in 1922. This merger, however, had produced a disunited and unwieldy party, more comfortable in opposition than in government. It was also in competition on the left with the KPD. In this situation the pragmatic wing of the DNVP gained a temporary preponderance over the ideological wing of the party, and entered the government of the Republic. Throughout this period, the dominating political figure was the foreign minister, Gustav Stresemann, who essentially continued the policy of Wirth: pacification at home, reconciliation with the west.

The years of political and monetary stability, however, did not alter the fundamental fragility of the Republic, Ideologically, middle class voters remained unreconciled to the Republic. They regarded the stabilization of the Republic as proof of the ascendancy of the left, and became more prone to turn to extremist parties. There occurred in this period a fundamental breakdown of voter identification with the established parties both of the bourgeois centre and of the right. This proved to be the critical intermediate step in the electoral realignment that ended with the Nazi triumph of 1930–2, which was achieved at the expense of the existing parties of the right.

The dissolution of the bourgeois right was shown by the split in the DNVP which followed Hugenberg's election as party leader in 1928. Hugenberg's election marked the triumph of those in the party who were implacably anti-system. Hugenberg wanted to demonstrate the enhanced radicalism of the party by taking the lead on a national issue. He seized upon the Young Plan, which the government was in the course of negotiating as the latest attempt to achieve a long-term solution to the problem of reparations. Hugenberg wished to inaugurate a national campaign against acceptance of the Plan. But for all his populist aspirations, he was no demagogue. Nor was the DNVP anything more than the political organization of the most reactionary sections of the possessing classes. He needed an ally with popular credentials and his own disregard of consequence. He intuitively recognized that Hitler and the National Socialists were the coming force in German politics.

The great depression made its impact first and most devastatingly in the sphere of German agriculture. In the Prussian local elections of 17 November 1929 the NSDAP showed remarkable gains over its results in the Prussian *Landtag* elections of 20 May 1928, above all in the agricultural areas of Schleswig–Holstein and East Prussia. The National Socialists now obtained the benefit of all the press and financial resources and respectability of the German conservative establishment.

Under the impact of the depression the Grand Coalition which had come to office as a result of the 1928 Reichstag election began to fall apart. But before it had suffered any parliamentary defeat, President Hindenburg's advisers and confidants persuaded him to dismiss Chancellor Müller and appoint in his place Heinrich Brüning.

According to 'the Brüning myth' Brüning was the Chancellor who struggled heroically against overwhelming odds to save the doomed republican system and who was removed from office –

in his own words – 'a hundred yards from the finishing post'. In fact Brüning's Chancellorship marked the first stages in an authoritarian transformation of the Republic which led via the Presidential Chancellors to Hitler. Far from wishing to rescue the Republic, he sought to be its liquidator and install in its place some authoritarian system of government which constituted a third way between democracy and dictatorship.[5]

The Presidential Chancellors relied for their authority not on the Reichstag but on the President. Quite consciously, no attempt was made to form a parliamentary government, because this would entail bringing together representatives of various political parties – especially the Social Democrats – in order to find common solutions to practical problems. The whole rationale of presidential regimes was to avoid this option. The only alternative was to seek the support of the National Socialists. Given a choice between the Social Democrats and the National Socialists the German centre and right unhesitatingly preferred the latter.

Brüning's policies appeared to be specifically designed to work to the political advantage of the National Socialists. He adopted the view that the prime aim of German government should be to reject the Treaty of Versailles. To that end he deliberately intensified the impact of the depression on Germany in order to demonstrate the unworkability of the Versailles settlement. Devoted to public order and financial stability, he presided over and accelerated the collapse of both.

The Nazis were given their chance to press their advantage by the successive ill-timed and unnecessary elections at a time of economic crisis. When the Reichstag, in a last gesture of self-assertion, rejected the emergency decree enacting Brüning's budget, Brüning dissolved the Reichstag rather than seek an accommodation with the parliamentary parties. In the elections of September 1930 the Nazis obtained 18.3 per cent of the votes and 107 seats. Thereafter they became a mass force in German politics; their party army took over the streets and assaulted the very principle of authority. By 1932 Brüning had learned that no accommodation with Hitler was possible except on his terms. Brüning's better instincts reasserted themselves. On 13 April 1932 he successfully carried through a measure to ban the Nazis' private armies. Hitler was not prepared to defy the state outright; overnight, tranquillity and public order returned to the streets of Germany. But the one successful act of Brüning's

Chancellorship cost him his office. The President's advisers were alarmed: if Brüning had turned against the National Socialists, to whom could he now turn, except the Social Democrats?

Von Papen relaced Brüning, withdrew the ban on Nazi organizations and proclaimed new elections, which in July 1932 gave the Nazis 37.4 per cent of votes and 230 seats. Hitler demanded the Chancellorship. Hindenburg regarded such a prospect with abhorrence. Papen, motivated chiefly by vanity, refused to budge and prepared to break with the Nazis. The elections of November 1932 showed that Hitler's movement was far from unstoppable: the party lost two million votes as compared with July, gaining 33.1 per cent of the vote and 196 seats. Papen wanted to capitalize on the situation by breaking the mould of the Constitution and ruling by force against right and left. At the crucial moment, Schleicher withdrew the support of the German army from Papen's movement. He now tried his hand at being Chancellor, having been instrumental in removing his three predecessors. He sought to gain support of the left and the trade unions and to split up the NSDAP.

In January 1933 the only alternatives were: dictatorial powers for Schleicher against right and left extremists in breach of the Constitution, or the appointment of a Hitler–Papen–Hugenberg government without an open breach of the Constitution. Papen, determined to have his revenge on Schleicher, oblivious to Hitler's recent enmity and frivolously overestimating his own powers, persuaded President Hindenburg, whose long and honourable days were slipping into an inglorious twilight, to adopt the latter course. Hitler became Chancellor on 30 January 1933, the post for which he had held out since 1930.

There was no inevitability about the installation of the National Socialists in power. They had always been parasitic on economic distress and the support of the German establishment. Although Hitler had mass support, he needed the help of the elites to carry him across the threshold of power. Like the Bavarian government in 1923, Hugenberg in 1929 and Brüning and Papen in 1931–2, the conservative members and backers of the new government believed that they could use Hitler as a cat's paw for their own ends. Successive experience to the contrary failed to disabuse them of this illusion.

NATIONAL SOCIALISM

Alfred Rosenberg – the so-called philosopher of National Socialism – began *The Myth of the Twentieth Century* with a quotation from Goethe: 'From here and now there begins a new epoch in the history of the world.' In twelve tumultuous years the Thousand Year Reich tore the world apart and caused a revision of basic ideas about the nature of human society which went back to the dawn of civilization.

In coming to a judgement on this period two questions can be posed: were Hitler's actions improvised or premeditated? Was National Socialism an opportunist or an ideological movement? The novelty of Hitler's approach to politics lay in his capacity to formulate policies and solutions in terms which were simultaneously dogmatic and manipulative. Germany, in Hitler's view, faced two problems. The first was the perennial problem of the two-front war. In order to have any prospect of victory, it had always been necessary for the Prussian army to be the hammer rather than the anvil, so that it could knock out one opponent and then turn its full weight against the other. Only by taking the offensive could the problem of the two-front war be resolved. The Schlieffen Plan as implemented in 1914 had been the most grandiose product so far of this cast of thought. The second problem was the economic vulnerability of Germany, which the British blockade in the First World War had revealed. For oil, iron ore and other vital raw materials Germany was totally dependent on imports. The revelation of Germany's economic vulnerability governed Hitler's thought.

From Hitler's speeches, writings and actions both before and after 30 January 1933 a consistent pattern of thought emerges: to create an autarchic, self-sufficient Germany, which was not dependent on any outside sources for raw material. To this he added the fashionable concept of over-population and the consequent need for living space (*Lebensraum*). The third element of his grand strategy was the unification of a racially pure and politically monolithic German *Volk* by the elimination of the *Anti-Volk*, above all the Jews but also the Slavs. The natural theatre in which to realize these aims lay in eastern Europe, stretching to the Urals and the Caucasus. 'If, however, we talk today of new territory and soil in Europe,' wrote Hitler in *Mein Kampf*, 'we can think in the first place only of Russia and its neighbouring satellite states. Fate itself seems to want to beckon us.'

There is then compelling evidence that Hitler had a dream of a single, autarchic, racially pure German state stretching through Eastern Europe to the Urals. This was to be achieved, first by neutralizing the west; secondly, by a war of race annihilation in the east. It was this racial ideological element in Hitler's thought which distinguished his policy from the most wildly expansionist dreams of the Second Reich. Nevertheless, what was called national conservatism shared an undoubted ideological affinity with National Socialism. Both had in common eastern imperialism, the traumatic fear of Bolshevism, the internalized equating of Jews with socialism, and a consequent uncontrolled anti-Semitism. In so far as conservative ideology coincided with conservative interests, National Socialism was the most extreme expression of the resistance of sections of German society to the twin forces of capitalist economic development and democratization.

Traditional elites in Germany, however, had lost their bearings. They had ceased to believe in the idols which they worshipped, without ceasing to worship them. They sacrificed their material interests to ideology. The corruption of traditional elites was the precondition not only of the Nazi rise to power but of the crimes of National Socialism. Consciously or unconsciously they recognized that they could not resist evil because the evil was already within themselves, as well as co-existent in the universe.

National Socialism was never a mere vehicle of conservative class interests. The most important single feature was its progressive radicalization. The regime became cumulatively more extreme in its goal and methods. With their undisguised ruthlessness of purpose the Nazis combined a blind belief in the righteousness of their will against all mankind, so that Hitler could regard himself – like Tamburlaine – as the scourge of God:

> Come, let us march against the powers of heaven,
> And set black streamers in the firmament,
> To signify the slaughter of the gods.

In an analysis of National Socialism published in 1938 under the title *The Revolution of Nihilism*, Herman Rauschning observed that the movement was 'permanent revolution, without any possibility of resolving or ending it'. National Socialism, he argued, created only to destroy in the name of a higher creativeness. It had no fixed goals or aims. Its objects were infinite, not finite. It was simply the gospel of force. As Orwell put it in *1984*:

Power is not a means, it is an end. One does not establish a dictatorship in order to safeguard a revolution; one makes a revolution in order to establish the dictatorship. The object of persecution is persecution. The object of torture is torture. The object of power is power.[6]

Yet the very incoherence of National Socialist aims makes it difficult to contend that everything was planned in advance. Hitler's projects were too vague to form a programme of action and had only been conceived in grandiose outline. Their concrete realization required several intermediary stages. The process of implementation had a large role in determining the ultimate outcomes. Rather than thinking things through in advance, Hitler relied on trial and error. He improvised, but the improvisations were premeditated; National Socialism was a doctrine of power, but the pursuit of power for its own sake is itself an ideology.

On 30 January 1933 the characteristic crimes of National Socialism still lay in the future. There was no inexorable train of logic which led from that day to the Holocaust. The fate of the world was not written in the stars. Hitler had a simple programme: power for himself, his party and the nation (*Volk*) with which he identified himself. How and how far he was to carry it out depended on the circumstances which he found and the actions of others.

He exploited the fortuitous burning of the Reichstag to excite a state of hysteria and obtain a grant of arbitrary and unlimited police powers by the Reichstag Fire Decree of 28 February 1933, powers that were used to suppress his enemies and intimidate the general population. The formal end of the Weimar Republic was marked by the Enabling Law of 24 March 1933, by which the Reichstag transferred its powers to the Cabinet, so freeing Hitler from dependence upon emergency presidential decrees. The subsequent establishment of a one-party state would have achieved the same result. The only party to vote against the Enabling Law was the SPD, which had been the major support of a number of Weimar coalitions but had no convincing response to the recession and the crisis of government after the Müller cabinet had broken up in 1930 over the issue of unemployment payments. When it was too late to alter the course of events, the party's leaders found the courage to assert themselves. Otto Wels bid farewell to the fading epoch of human rights and humanity in words which echoed down the corridors of future years: 'Life and freedom can be taken from us, but not honour.'

The basis of National Socialist domestic rule thereafter was the abolition of unemployment, the creation of an illusion of prosperity, the use of massive repression against the opponents of the regime. Above all, there occurred a political mobilization of society, animated by a collective purpose and quickened by mass emotion, which produced a collective *élan* of awesome proportions.

When the Nazis came to power, the number of unemployed totalled six million, although this had already begun to fall. Through work creation, investment-led growth, rearmament and a prices and wages freeze, full employment had been achieved by 1937–8, which brought with it enhanced economic security, self-respect and a rise in average living standards.[7] The Strength Through Joy movement organized holidays and recreations on a mass scale for workers.

Hitler – in contrast to his predecessors and Western neighbours – appeared to have got the economy right, and people assumed that he could do nothing else wrong. In foreign policy Hitler found himself pushing on open doors. The Russians had withdrawn from European affairs to concentrate on building Socialism in One Country. Stalin trusted Hitler, though he trusted no one else, inside or outside the Soviet Union. In the Western democracies the will to enforce the Treaty of Versailles had evaporated, because people had come to believe that the settlement was neither wise nor just. Having resisted when they should have yielded, the Western powers now yielded when they should have resisted. Hitler embarked upon his extraordinary series of bloodless diplomatic triumphs. In 1938–9 Austria and the whole of Czechoslovakia were incorporated into the Reich. Appeasement simply fuelled Hitler's ambitions and augmented his resources. Only belatedly did Britain and France call a halt to a process which had already gone much too far.

THE SECOND WORLD WAR AND THE FINAL SOLUTION

Up to the outbreak of the Second World War when Germany invaded Poland on 1 September 1939, Hitler employed diplomacy backed by threats. On both the diplomatic and military fronts he was triumphantly and invariably successful up to the invasion of Russia on 22 June 1941. This was the turning-point in the history of his Empire, as it had been in that of Napoleon's. How did it come to pass?

A modest programme of rearmament had begun in 1933–4. Hitler did not seek rearmament in depth. He wanted forces capable of quick, decisive victories against diplomatically isolated opponents. Hence he pressed for rearmament in width, not depth. By 1938–9 Germany had an impressive Wehrmacht, but little was behind the shopwindow.

This has provided support for A. J. P. Taylor's view that Hitler did not want war.[8] He certainly did not want a war of attrition on two fronts, because that way disaster lay. But Hitler and certain senior officers believed their armed forces were suitable for a certain type of war: *Blitzkrieg*, a lightning war. This proved irresistible wherever it was applied. But the key to the creation of the Third Reich lay in Russia. Why did Hitler attack Russia, before disposing of Britain, thereby producing a war on two fronts?

Hitler felt safe in attacking Russia since Britain was not in a position to mount a continental invasion and few doubted the capacity of the Wehrmacht to knock out Russia in six weeks. Hitler believed that Britain would not make peace, because she hoped to bring Russia into the war. From 1940 onwards, there had been increasing friction between Russia and Germany concerning their respective spheres of influence in Eastern Europe. If accounts were to be settled, the sooner the better. Finally, in November 1940 Roosevelt had been re-elected for a fourth term on a platform of all aid short of war for the enemies of Nazi Germany. Hitler remembered the decisive effect of American intervention in 1917. Hence the need for the Third Reich to make herself self-sufficient as quickly as possible became correspondingly more urgent. To be dependent on the Russians for the basic war materials was something which Hitler considered politically unwise. The raw materials had to be seized.

All these factors led to the German invasion of Russia on 22 June 1941, Operation Barbarossa. The invasion of Russia was an expression of the radicalizing momentum of the regime. How close run a thing was it? Two special factors critically influenced the final outcome. Germany had intervened in the Balkans to rescue her Italian allies. This imposed a five-week delay and hence the Russian winter struck the German campaign five weeks earlier than would otherwise have happened. Then the German army was paralysed for three months by a dispute between Hitler and his generals concerning the strategic objectives of the campaign. As a result, in part, of these difficulties the *Blitzkrieg* of 1941 was inconclusive. Hitler sacked his entire military staff and took personal command. He threw all his forces in Russia into a final drive on the south. Hitler's policy was to seize Russian resources, isolate America by means of U-boats, dig in and wait and see. In the autumn of 1942 there were two turning-points. On 7 September Hitler was told that his forces in the Caucasus could advance no further. On 8 November the Americans landed in North Africa, showing the inexorable commitment of the United States to the war in Europe. The one hope with which Hitler was left was to hold out until his enemies quarrelled. This was the traditional Prussian strategy. Hitler was right – the improbable coalition of the Western powers and the Soviet Union would in time fall apart – but his timing was wrong, for their unity was maintained until Germany had been militarily defeated.

Hitler, however, had more important concerns than military victory. The war in the east was the catalyst and harbinger of the anti-Jewish policy. It is well known that six million Jews were exterminated in the implementation of the Final Solution to the Jewish question. Their fate was shared by 3.3 of the 5.7 million Soviet prisoners of war taken by the German army. The measures taken in relation to the Russian prisoners prepared the ground for the systematic execution of the Final Solution.[9]

Between the war in the west and the war in the east there was a wholly different objective and therefore a different strategy. In the west Hitler's aim was containment and neutralization, which he hoped to achieve by military victory, which left the society and economy of his opponents essentially intact. His aim in the east was obliteration to create a *tabula rasa* for the new order which was in process of realization. Hitler ordered that the campaign against the Soviet Union was to be conducted as a war of race annihilation. To this decision, the army leadership – which had long ago forfeited its moral independence – gave its unqualified support.[10] German conservatives threw in their lot with the nihilistic agents of a permanent revolution.

The annihilation policy, escalated by the unresisting participation of the army, became increasingly more radical. The Final Solution of the Jewish problem was conceived according to the model of the annihilation of prisoners of war. The Nazis had improvised in their treatment of the Jews since 1933. In 1942 the decision was taken that the Jews were to be abolished. The gas chambers – the technical means by which the Final Solution was to be implemented – were first tried out on the mentally defective and then on Russian prisoners. Thereafter they were used on an industrial scale in the remote obscurity of eastern Poland, beyond the pale of any human or moral law.

The crimes by which National Socialism was most conspicuously characterized would not have been possible without the collaboration of large sections of the traditional ruling classes, who had betrayed the ethic of responsible service. But to these groups also was attributable the one serious attempt to rid Germany of its disastrous leadership. They decided that the experiment of putting the servants in charge was now to be discontinued. Von Stauffenberg's Bomb Plot of 20 July 1944 came within a fraction of success, but was flawed by an element of bad luck and hesitancy.

THE OCCUPATION PERIOD AND ITS EFFECTS

The unconditional surrender of Germany on 8 May 1945 left a political, economic and military vacuum in the centre of Europe. The wartime allies had agreed in 1944 that after Germany's defeat the country should be divided into British, American and Russian zones of occupation and that Greater Berlin should be similarly divided into sectors. At Yalta in 1945 Stalin acceded to the creation of a French occupation zone and sector, to be carved out of the areas allotted to the British and Americans. Germany as a whole was to be governed by the Control Council consisting of the commanders of the four occupation zones. In Berlin the highest authority was to be the *Kommandatura* made up of the four sector commanders.

The Germany of which the Allies took control was a very

different country from that which had been unable to sustain the democratic constitution of Weimar. The Nazi period marked a decisive caesura in German political development. There had been a number of very significant changes during the period of Nazi rule. The massive mobilization attendant upon the regime was accompanied by a decline in sectional and local attitudes and loyalties. The traditional governing class with deep roots in the landed aristocracy was gradually displaced as the Third Reich consolidated its position. The revolt of 1944 represented, in part, that class's reaction; its failure meant the end of what independence the army and civil service still possessed by then. Several, and more important, changes were associated with the defeat of the Third Reich. Its collapse and the ensuing Allied occupation caused massive transfers of population. This led to a further erosion of sectional loyalties. It also made possible the creation of a biconfessional Christian Democratic Party since the confessions were now equally balanced in the Western zones and there was no longer any need for a political expression of the defence of Catholic minority interests. The CDU was the first conservative party in Germany to espouse democratic principles and win mass popular support. Its emergence was to be a key factor in the establishment of democracy in the Western zones. The Russian victories in the east resulted in the disappearance of the territorial basis of the east Elbian aristocracy and the end of their place on the centre stage of German politics. The defeat of Hitler led to the presence of the occupying powers on German soil and they made a not inconsiderable contribution to the establishment of a liberal democratic regime within Germany.

The internal and external reaction to the experience of the Third Reich had a number of long-term effects. It greatly strengthened the position of the churches as Germans sought expiation and explanation. It effectively killed the mass appeal in Germany of extreme nationalism. The experience of defeat was so traumatic and total, and the revelations of the extermination camps were of such dimensions, that the type of hypernationalism that had sustained the appeal of the NSDAP was henceforth unimaginable on a mass basis.

The preconditions for liberal democracy in 1945 were thus, despite the outward appearance of complete destruction, much stronger than before the advent of the Third Reich. They were only preconditions, however, and much was to turn on the decisions and actions of German and Allied politicians.

As ever, a German national identity was an elusive concept. In 1940 Poland had been partitioned between the Germans and the Russians, in accordance with the secret protocol to the Nazi–Soviet Pact of 25 August 1939. This moved the Russian frontier 100 miles west. Stalin had deported the whole Polish population from these areas, in order to be sure of holding what he had. After the war Stalin did not wish to give up these territorial gains. He therefore decided to compensate the new Polish state with German territory. Russia assumed the government of East Prussia, including the port of Königsberg, to be renamed Kaliningrad. The rest of the German territory east of the Oder and the Lauitzer Neisse was placed under Polish administration. Poland was shifted some hundred miles west. To ensure the permanency of these changes the systematic expulsion of the German inhabitants – over ten million people – was set in hand. These measures departed from the Western Allies' understanding of the wartime agreements. However, there was nothing that could be done to stop the Russian moves. The Potsdam Agreement of August 1945 provided that these areas should be placed under Russian and Polish administration pending a final peace treaty and that Germans living in this territory and in Hungary, Poland and Czechoslovakia should be transferred to Germany in what was called optimistically or cynically 'an orderly and humane manner'.

The initiative in German politics lay wholly with the victors. Germany was too important to be allowed to go its own way. The Russians took the initiative in starting political life in their zone on a new basis. The Russian Zone Commander's Order No. 2 of 10 June 1945 permitted the formation of four political parties: the KPD, SPD, CDU and LDPD (Liberal Democratic Party). Influenced by the Soviet example, the Western powers licensed the same four parties in their zones, the Liberals in the Western zones being known as the FDP (Free Democratic Party).

In the course of the reorganization of public authority in Germany, the occupation powers transferred functions step by step to German administrative authorities. Already in July 1945 the Russians had set up *Land* administrations in their zone. By the end of 1945 the Americans had also divided their zone into *Länder* and established German authorities at *Land* level. In the British and French zones this stage was not reached until 1947. With few exceptions the territories of the new *Länder* in the

Western zones were completely different from those of the Weimar *Länder*. Ever since Bismarck's unification of 1871 the dominant German state had been Prussia. One-third of its former territory lay in the Western zones, one-third in the Russian and the remainder in the Eastern territories effectively annexed by Russia and Poland. The Control Council issued a law of 25 February 1947 declaring that Prussia had ceased to exist. Because of its dissolution the *Länder* established after 1945 were largely new creations. In the west only Bavaria, Bremen and Hamburg represented the historic *Länder*. In any case the huge influx of population from the east erased existing population structures.

The breakdown of German central government, the failure of the Control Council to develop its own administrative organs, the dismemberment of Germany and redistribution of its population, all had the consequence that the individual zones of occupation developed in their own way. The Potsdam Agreement had envisaged an essentially passive occupation policy, reflecting the thinking behind the wartime Morgenthau Plan, which had advocated the deindustrialization and reagrarianization of Germany. In the British zone in particular, the pressure for action was irresistible. The great urban populations lay on the verge of starvation. In the past they had drawn foodstocks from the agricultural areas to the east, but the Russians would not allow any food exports from their zone to the west, until their demands for reparations were satisfied. Problems were compounded by the interminable winter of 1946–7. The British could not pay for food imports, given their chronic shortage of dollars.

By this stage in the occupation period Western goals – especially those of the United States – had changed as they became more definite. The initial Western aims were Allied ones formulated in the context of the wartime alliance against Germany. These aims were very far-reaching and involved the complete transformation of the German social and economic order, since it was argued that a root and branch democratization was a precondition for the establishment of a democratic regime. The collapse of Weimar and the failure of the Germans to overthrow Nazism by themselves made this a powerful argument. According to this view the Allies would have to make up for the failures of German political development by carrying through an 'artificial revolution' in which the old elites were replaced by new political groups firmly committed to liberal democratic principles.

Some parts of this programme, outlined in the Potsdam Agreement, were carried out. Nazi organizations were made illegal and a considerable amount of dismantling of industrial facilities (*Demontage*) took place, often against sharp resistance from factory workers. The centrepiece of the programme – Denazification – was, however, only a very partial success. It proved difficult to find enough people who had not been involved in the Nazi regime to take over the myriad tasks of administration and organization of the shattered economic and social structures.

The concept of the 'artificial revolution' was always unlikely to be realized. It would have needed a long period of occupation and a great deal of determination and resources of skilled manpower on the part of the Allies to carry it through, neither of which was available in this case. The British government had a desperate struggle to secure essential supplies and materials for its own immediate national needs, and found the task of feeding the industrial zone an almost insuperable problem. The Americans quickly yielded to the pressures to 'bring the boys home'.

By late 1946 it was proving very difficult to implement the initial goals in Germany. External pressures also changed Western perceptions. As relations with the Soviet Union deteriorated the Western zones began to be seen as a potential ally against Soviet expansion. This led to a sharp and permanent change in American and British priorities. The accent was now on stabilization and far-reaching attempts at economic and social change were largely abandoned. What the Western Allies now wanted from the Germans was not a complete transformation of all German institutions but the formal acceptance and maintenance of a liberal democratic order. There were a small number of committed democrats who welcomed this opportunity and who emerged into leading positions in the occupation period, much helped by the strict licensing of political parties which created a 'protected party system'. The great majority of Germans in the West were initially fiercely anti-communist but were apathetic democrats.

In his Stuttgart speech of 6 September 1946 US Secretary of State Byrnes announced the historic American decision not to revert from interventionism to isolationism, as had occurred after the First World War. In September 1946 a number of fusion agreements between the British and American zones were signed. On 1 January 1947 the two zones were fused economically as the Bizone. This was equipped with its own political institutions: an elected assembly in Frankfurt, the Economic Council (*Wirtschaftsrat*); an Executive Council consisting of delegates of the *Land* governments; and five German directors of administrations for economics, food and agriculture, finance, transport and post and telephones. With the addition of the small French zone in 1948 the Western zones became the United Economic Region (*vereinigtes Wirtschaftsgebiet*). From 9 February 1948 the Executive Council was renamed the Council of the *Länder* (*Länderrat*) and the five Directors elected by the Economic Council formed a collegiate executive. The region also had its own central bank and supreme court. In this developed institutional form the United Economic Region was the harbinger of the Federal Republic. In the Economic Council the 'Frankfurt Coalition' of the CDU, FDP and DP (*Deutsche Partei*, a small conservative party based around Hannover) gained a majority in 1948, and elected as Director for Economics Ludwig Erhard, father of the 'Economic Miracle' and Chancellor from 1963 to 1966.

THE FOUNDATION OF WEST GERMANY

The decision to turn the Western zones into a new and separate state had not yet been taken. The decision itself resulted in part from changes in the international situation, so that it has been said that 'the Federal Republic was born in 1949 as a twin sister of the Atlantic Alliance'. Germany was too important to be allowed to go its own way. If Germany was to be established on a united basis, the Western powers on the one hand and the Russians on the other, wanted some assurance that such a state could not menace them either independently or in conjunction with the rival power bloc. In 1946 the Russians forced the union of the KDP and the SPD in their zone to form the SED (*Sozialistische Einheitspartei*, Socialist Unity Party). They believed that a popular front party would have a powerful electoral appeal in Western and Eastern zones alike and would keep Germany out of the Western orbit. But the leading figure in the Western SPD – Kurt Schumacher – vehemently and successfully opposed such a marriage there. In the Berlin elections of 20 October 1946 the SED fared disastrously against the SPD. Thereafter Soviet interest in a united Germany diminished and their primary interest lay in delaying the resurgence of the Western zones.

The failure of the Moscow Foreign Ministers' Conference (10 March to 24 April 1947) confirmed the irreconcilable differences between the wartime allies. The Munich Conference of the Minister-Presidents of the German *Länder* from all occupation zones showed that the German leaders themselves were divided in their views about the future of Germany. The London Four Power Conference of December 1947 also ran into sand. Thereafter the Western Allies worked with strengthened resolve towards the unification of their zones. The decision to set up a separate West German state was taken at the London Conference of the three Western powers and the Benelux countries and was embodied in the London Recommendations of 7 June 1948.

On 20 June 1948 the Western powers introduced a new currency – the Deutschmark – in the Western zones and West Berlin. This triggered the revival of the West German economy without which the new state would never have become self-supporting economically or consolidated itself politically. The Russians responded by imposing the Berlin Blockade on 24 June 1948. On 1 July 1948 the three Western commanders authorized the Minister-Presidents of the eleven Western *Länder* to convene a constitutional assembly. Their written directive specified that the assembly should enact 'a democratic constitution which will establish for the participating states a government structure of the federal type and which will protect the rights of participating states, provide adequate central authority and contain guarantees of individual rights and freedoms'. The constitution should also 'provide for an independent judiciary to review federal legislation, to review the exercise of federal executive power, and to adjudicate conflicts between federal and *Land* authorities as well as between *Land* authorities, and to protect civil rights and the freedom of the individual'.

The Minister-Presidents convened first at Koblenz, then at Niederwald, to decide how to respond to the Allies' decision. They did not wish to be accused of betraying the German national cause, but there was no way forward other than accepting the Allies' demands. They accepted the Allied commission subject to three provisos: the assembly would not be called a 'constituent assembly' but 'Parliamentary Council' (*Parlamentarischer Rat*); the Council would not draft a constitution (*Verfassung*) but Basic Law (*Grundgesetz*); and the Basic Law would be ratified not by popular vote at a referendum but by votes in the *Land* Parliaments (the *Landtage*). The classical idea of a constituent assembly submitting a constitution to referendum was thus to be mediated through the *Landtage*. The aim of these modifications was to show that the new political organization would be a provisional arrangement, postponing but not pre-empting a resolution of the larger question of German reunification.

In anticipation of the convening of the Parliamentary Council the Minister-Presidents appointed an Experts Commission of constitutional lawyers to prepare a draft of the Basic Law. Each *Land* sent one representative. They met from 10 to 23 August 1948 at Herrenchiemsee in Bavaria and submitted their report on 25 August. The Herrenchiemsee Draft comprised the text of a complete constitution, equipped with alternative clauses and a reasoned commentary. The final version of the Basic Law clearly shows its ancestry and does not depart from the Herrenchiemsee Draft in essentials. On 16 August 1948 a majority of the Minister-Presidents decided on Bonn as the meeting place for the Parliamentary Council – another decision whose consequences were more far-reaching than was forseeable at the time.

The Parliamentary Council was elected from the *Landtage* in proportion to the population of the eleven *Länder*. Each *Land* was allotted one representative per 750,000 of population with an additional member for each remainder over 200,000. The assembly had sixty-five members. The party composition was: CDU/CSU 27 members (the CDU formed a common party group with the Christian Social Union, an exclusively Bavarian party); SPD 27 members; FDP 5 members; KPD 2 members; Centre Party 2 members; DP 2 members. In addition, five non-voting members from West Berlin were admitted. The work of the Council was divided between six committees. The various committee drafts were edited into an overall text by a highly influential 'Committee of Three'. In addition there was an inter-party liaison committee – 'the Committee of Five'. Party balance was maintained by electing Adenauer (CDU) as Chairman of the Council and Carlo Schmid (SPD) as Chairman of the Principal Committee.

The proceedings of the Council opened in Bonn on 1 September 1948, in the building which subsequently became the home of the Bundestag. While party differences were maintained, the leading feature of the proceedings was the remarkable constitutional consensus. The final draft of the Basic Law was passed by fifty-three votes to twelve on 8 May 1949. On 12 May it was ratified by the Military Governors, subject to certain reservations. After ratification by all the *Landtage* – except the Bavarian – it took effect on 24 May. The first Bundestag was elected on 14 August 1949, and the first West German government led by Konrad Adenauer as Chancellor took office on 7 September 1949. At the same time the institutions of the United Economic Region were dissolved.

Meanwhile the Russians had in their zone set in hand the process whereby, as counterpoise to the founding of the Federal Republic in the West, the German Democratic Republic (*Deutsche Demokratische Republik*, DDR) was established in the East. On 7 October 1949 the Russian occupation authorities formally handed over power to the new East German government.

West Germany was produced by three factors: pressures from political groups within Germany; the policies of the occupying powers; and the demands of the Cold War. The outcome of the Second World War resulted in the political and territorial dismemberment of Germany, and the East–West conflict caused the division of Europe into two power blocs with different values and objectives. Germany was removed from its historical central position and found itself on the outer edge of the two systems. The Federal Republic became the east of the West, while the German Democratic Republic became the west of the East.

Who decided that Germany should be partitioned? Germany had already been divided by the result of the war, which Hitler had launched. The steps taken by the various occupation powers after 1945 largely confirmed an existing situation rather than created a new one. As Ernst Reuter, Chief Bürgermeister of West Berlin, told the Minister-Presidents as they conferred at Niederwald about how to react to the Allied directive of 1 July 1948: 'The division of Germany will not be caused: it has already happened.' Moreover, the question, what is Germany permitted – as in the past – a number of answers by reason of the fluidity of the concept.

Among the West German population fear of Russia and hostility to communism were the dominant sentiments. The

Russians had advanced through Germany with fire, sword and rapine. Three-quarters of the expellees from eastern Europe ended their trek in the Western zones. One-quarter of the population had relations, friends and acquaintances in and from the East. Among conservatives fear of communism took the place of hostility to parliamentary government. West Germans were united by anti-communism. It provided the social cement of the new state, which offered them – within the protection of the West – security against the Soviet Union and a chance to regain self-respect, self-confidence and self-government. Among the Western powers the dominant concerns were first that the Western zones should not be a drain on the debilitated economies of Western Europe; and secondly, that West Germany should not be drawn into the Soviet sphere of influence.

THE CONTRIBUTION OF HISTORY TO GERMAN POLITICS

The dilemma of German politics from the rise of Prussia to the seventeenth century had been the choice between statehood and national expansion, political modernization and authoritarianism, West and East. In his novel *The Magic Mountain* Thomas Mann describes the dichotomy in Germany before 1914. In 1949 this choice was made for West Germany, in a form which has proved more enduring than its founders may have anticipated. Within twenty years West Germany had become not only a model democracy but the third industrial state in the world. With the inception of the European Economic Community in 1958, the Federal Republic took the lead in European unification.

However, even after forty years, West Germany lacked historical self-assurance, and its existence could not be taken for granted in the way that the United States, Britain and France, for example, seem to be permanent features of the international landscape. West Germany was essentially the product of the bipolar division of the world, and a significant modification of that division would weaken the attachment of West Germans to their state and strengthen the attraction of some larger grouping.

'It is characteristic of the Germans that the question "What is Germany?" never dies out among them.' West Germans remained aware of belonging to a wider community, both in space and time, with a common history whose sharp discontinuities have been counterbalanced by a marked institutional continuity. This pattern has not been disturbed by the creation of a new united Germany.

MAIN DATES 1945 ONWARDS

8 May 1945	Unconditional surrender of German Reich
5 June 1947	Marshall Plan
24 June 1948	Berlin Blockade
1 September 1948	Parliamentary Council convened in Bonn
24 May 1949	Basic Law ratified
15 September 1949	Adenauer appointed Chancellor
2 October 1949	Foundation of German Democratic Republic
5 May 1955	Paris Treaties – West Germany becomes sovereign
7 July 1956	Conscription introduced
25 March 1957	Treaty of Rome (EEC Treaty) signed
1 May 1958	EEC founded
15 November 1959	Bad Godesberg Programme of SPD
13 August 1961	Berlin Wall built
1 December 1966	Grand Coalition
3 September 1971	Four Power Agreement on Berlin
21 December 1972	Basic Treaty with East Germany
5 September 1977	Abduction of Hans-Martin Schleyer
1 October 1982	Constructive vote of no confidence in Helmut Schmidt
9 November 1989	Breaching of Berlin Wall
30 June 1990	State Treaty
1 July 1990	Economic and Monetary Union
3 October 1990	German Unity

3 The Constitutional Dimension

Constitutionalism is the theory of limited government – the belief that the powers of government should be controlled in order to safeguard individual freedom. The central problem of constitutional theory and practice is the adjustment of the claims of the individual and the community. In Shelley's words: 'The vessel of state is driven between the Scylla and Charybdis of anarchy and despotism.' In West Germany these two dominant concerns have been reinforced by immediate historical experience. The Weimar Republic is regarded as a paradigm of weak and unstable democracy, the Nazi regime as the epitome of unlimited and uncontrolled power. The Rechtsstaat is the particular German version of constitutionalism. It broadly corresponds to the Anglo-Saxon rule of law, but places a larger emphasis on formal, legal controls of government, as contrasted with informal, political restraints. The Basic Law (*Grundgesetz*) of 1949 is the legal source both of the rights of the individual and of the powers of government. In accordance with its twin concerns it falls into two parts: a basic rights section (Articles 1–19) which confers and guarantees the rights of the individual; and the remainder, dealing with state organization. The Basic Law is a product of German tradition and also embodies a conscious decision about the future form and structure of German society. It is more than a legal text, a mere pattern of political organization, a set of rules binding on the government. It establishes the organizational forms of political life, including the political parties; it defines and directs the aims of the state; and it requires allegiance to certain values.

THE DEVELOPMENT OF THE RECHTSSTAAT

At the opening of the nineteenth century, the Rechtsstaat became the centre point of German liberalism. Its origins lie in the secularization and depersonalization of political authority.

At the end of the eighteenth century government ceased to be regarded as a divine dispensation but was held to be 'a contrivance of human wisdom to provide for human wants' (Burke). The crown ceased to be a right and became an office. States ceased to be the property of rulers but became the expression of the common political identity of the inhabitants. Loyalty to the person of the monarch gave way to allegiance to the abstraction of the state.

The term 'state' (*Staat*) entered general usage in Germany in the second half of the eighteenth century. The Prussian General Code of Law of 1794 replaced the term hitherto used for civil servants 'royal servants' with the term 'state servants'. A watershed was marked by vom Stein's Municipalities Decree of 19 November 1808 which provided that in towns the governmental power was to be exercised 'in the name of the state'.

The dominant feature of the nineteenth century was the confrontation between monarchy and popular sovereignty, to which all other conflicts were related. Liberals sought to replace royal by popular government and find security against the state through a constitution. The idea of the Rechtsstaat was a weapon against the monarchical and aristocratic order. Liberals were inspired by the modern secular system of Natural Law which developed in the seventeenth and eighteenth centuries, and whose central tenet was the idea of inherent and indestructible human rights. It derived the existence of government from the Social Contract, whereby individuals accepted a reduction of their natural rights in return for the secure enjoyment of the remainder. It brought forth the age of written constitutions and codified basic rights.

The term Rechtsstaat was first used by Adam Müller in 1809. Robert von Mohl and Carl Theodor Welcher – writing somewhat later – used the term to indicate a state based on reason, in which law and justice were one.[1]

The Vienna Settlement of 1815, which established the German Federation (*Bund*), also required each member of the Bund to introduce a constitution. The model for the state constitutions was provided by the French Constitutional Charter of 1814. The movement in favour of written constitutions began in the more liberal south German states; Bavaria and Baden introduced constitutions in 1818. The north German states followed later, Prussia bringing up the rear in 1850.

All these constitutions provided for the establishment of a

parliament alongside the existing monarchical executive. The key question was: how should responsibility be divided between government and parliament? The early German constitutional-ism adopted the formula of Freiherr vom Stein that all measures concerning the 'liberty and property' of the citizen required the consent of parliament, i.e. must take statutory form. Everything else lay in the sphere of the executive. Those acts of the executive limited by parliament's powers were said to be 'subject to statutory authorization'. This principle was gradually ex-tended in the nineteenth century but never reached all areas of state activity. The scrupulous delimitation of state powers found no parallel in the conduct of external relations, which formed a permanent exception. The command and disposition of the armed forces and minor domestic acts of government, such as the granting of pardons and honours, were also held to be outside the sphere of statutory authorization.

If the state could only act where it was empowered by statute to do so, the citing of statutory authority became the precondi-tion of all administrative action. The German Rechtsstaat pro-duced a special style of administration, characterized by 'the hunger for legal rules'. The Rechtsstaat implied legal controls of government through parliament, rather than the interaction of parliament and the executive.

The crucial development in the emergence of the Rechsstaat was the establishment of the requirement that all entrants to the higher general administrative service should complete a legal training. This created the 'lawyers' monopoly' (*Juristenmonopol*) of senior civil service posts. This requirement was effectively introduced in 1818 and confirmed in 1846.[2] Alexander von Humboldt gave the universities the double role of providing a general, non-vocational education, and of training entrants for the higher administrative service. A Prussian law of 1879 gave the education of higher civil servants its modern basis: three years' study of law at a German university; the First State Examination; a year's practical training in the government service as a *Referendar*; the passing of the Second State Examina-tion; and a further period of work as an *Assessor*.

The introduction of academic legal qualifications opened the higher grades of the civil service to middle-class entrants, who could compete for places on the same terms as the upper classes, for access to educational opportunity depended upon wealth, not status. The civil service became the preserve of the educated and propertied middle class. This in turn reconciled the middle classes to the state.[3] The integration of state and society favoured a benevolent and expansive concept of the role of the state. The state administration constantly expanded by taking in new social tasks in the field of education, welfare and the public services, on the principle that, as was said in 1826, 'A state which only protects its citizens from murder and theft but which does nothing to promote higher human purposes is rightly and universally regarded as unworthy of the name of state.[4]

The liberal middle classes were thus accorded through the administration an influential though not a decisive position in government. After their defeat in the Prussian constitutional conflict of 1862–6, most liberals reconciled themselves to a situation in which the dynasties and the landed classes were in effective control of government. The liberals' policy was to press for legal and institutional limitations on the conduct of affairs rather than for enhanced parliamentary participation in government. As it finally emerged the Rechtsstaat was defined in terms of the supremacy of law, the subordination of the administration to law, the liability of the state for the unlawful acts of its agents. guarantees against the unfair application of laws through appeal to administrative courts, and a continuous improvement in the system of public law which excluded from it those elements which reflected the capricious influence of political or administrative convenience.

The right to require that the exercise of state power should conform with the law only deserves the name of freedom as long as law itself retains some reliable and credible connection with morality, and the term 'law' is not used in a purely formal, political sense as meaning anything enacted by the legislature. If 'law' is a description of every command issued by a particular body or through a particular procedure, the principle that government must conform to law is pure absolutism.

Such a formal theory of law enabled it to be argued after the Nazi seizure of power either that Hitler came to power legally on 30 January 1933, or that the Weimar Constitution was only legally repealed by the Enabling Act of 6 March 1933, which transferred all the powers of the Reichstag to the Reich government. These arguments are inconsistent with the view that every political system rests on certain constitutional fundamentals: 'A constitution does not consist of the positive individual provisions of the constitution. Every constitution rests on definite values, by which its whole system as well as its individual provisions are borne.' If these constitutional fundamentals alter, as they had been changed by the Nazi seizure of power if not earlier, the constitution has been overthrown, regardless of how far such actions or events can be regarded as authorized by law.[5]

The nineteenth-century cult of positivism, the formalization of the Rechtsstaat ideal, the radical rebellion of National Socialism against tradition, morality and all humanitarian rules of conduct, had promoted the bifurcation of *Recht* into separate compartments of law and justice. In its constitutional order the Bonn Republic has sought to reassert the broad political concept of a constitution and to re-establish the link between law and moral ideas. This emphasis on the transcendent element in the concept of law gives the West German constitution its distinctive character and sets it apart from the less exalted and more empirical notion of the rule of law. As Arnold Brecht wrote in 1945:

It would be advisable . . . for the new German constitutional order to contain certain sacrosanct principles and standards which could not be abolished or suspended by emergency decrees or by any parliamentary or plebiscitary majorities, either directly or indirectly.

THE BASIC RIGHTS

The philosopher of the new constitutional order established in 1949 is Rudolf Smend.[7] Smend developed his theories in the Weimar Republic, an era of disintegration and disorder. His central concern was 'integration': how to unite a political society. He analyses three modes of integration: objective integration through shared values; functional integration through common political institutions; and symbolic integration through collective symbols – flags, anthems, anniversaries and ceremonies. The function of a constitution is – he argued – to promote integration. A constitution is more than a legal text: it is – in his favourite phrase, which the Federal Constitutional Court has made its own – 'an order based on values' (*Wertordnung*). These values are not mere moral exhortations or aspirations. They are given legal force by the constitution. Their legal force is not merely declaratory, an indication of what is approved. They are binding legal rules (norms).

In accordance with this approach, the framers and interpreters of the Basic Law have emphatically and consistently maintained that every part of the constitution has normative effect and so imposes legal rights and obligations. For example, the Federal Constitutional Court holds that the Preamble to the Basic Law, in its *invocatio dei* ('In awareness of its responsibility before God and man . . .') establishes 'the absolute validity of supra-state norms', while the reference to reunification, in conjunction with Article 146, imposes on all organs of government the duty to work to achieve German reunification.

Many of the most important provisions of the Basic Law are not legal rules in the conventional sense, in that they have no definite content. The Basic Rights provisions in particular are simply legislative general clauses, which contain not a rule but a standard of conduct. They go beyond law into ethics. It is inherent in the nature of such provisions that they require specific realization and interpretation by the legislative arm and the courts. The introduction of a binding code of Basic Rights in the Basic Law had led to a great extension of judicial power and influence. This is a further element which distinguishes the modern Rechtsstaat from its predecessors.

In order to achieve a compromise between the freedom of the individual to do as he likes, and the need to ensure orderly and coherent government, the idea of Basic Rights has undergone considerable refinement.

The liberal theory of Basic Rights regards them as rights of non-interference against the state. They are about 'negative' liberty, freedom from the state. This remains their essential core. Some of these freedoms can only be realized in a collective, institutional framework. The right to education is meaningless unless schools and institutions of higher learning are established and maintained. Hence the obligation of the state to respect particular freedoms of the individual may carry with it the concomitant obligation to provide certain institutions, which accordingly are guaranteed by the Basic Rights, along with the individual freedoms which they exist to effectuate. The institutions guaranteed by the Basic Rights include: the Bundestag (Article 38), the legal immunity of Bundestag deputies (Article 46(2)), the freedom of party formation (Article 21), the political parties, (Article 21), the state school system (Article 7), property (Article 14), the universities (Article 5). Arguably local government and the career civil service should be included in this list.

In the case of the political parties, the institutional guarantee now extends to the state financing of the political parties.

The objective element in the Basic Rights can be taken a stage further by arguing that they entail the maintenance and protection not only of certain institutions but also of certain values. The key decision of the Federal Constitutional Court establishing the 'value-theory' of Basic Rights was the Lüth judgment of 1953. This concerned a film director who had been associated with the Nazis. The state of Hamburg took measures to discourage the showing of his films, and the director complained that his freedom of artistic expression had been violated. The court stated:[8]

Undoubtedly the Basic Rights are intended in the first place to secure the individual's sphere of freedom from violation by public authority ... However, it is equally true that the Basic Law has in its Basic Rights section established an objective value order ... The value system must be effective as a fundamental decision of constitutional law for all spheres of law.

Thus the individual's sphere of freedom, as secured by the Basic Rights, finds its limit *inter alia* in the requirement to conform to certain paramount moral values laid down and given legal force by the constitution. When used to sanction official disapproval of the Third Reich, this approach is unlikely to be controversial. However, the claim that the Basic Law enshrines some permanent set of values requires considerable caution and delicacy in its application, otherwise the Court might seek to impose via the Basic Law a homogeneous and unchanging core of belief on a morally pluralistic and evolving society. In 1974 the Court relied upon the 'value-theory' of Basic Rights to declare unconstitutional the Bundestag's first attempt at extending the grounds upon and circumstances in which abortion was permissible. In vetoing these parts of the Fifth Criminal Law Amendment Act the Court declared: 'The state cannot escape its responsibilities by recognizing a "law-free zone" in which it does not express any view but leaves this to the independent responsibility of individual decision'.[9] Such passages indicate the perils and difficulties of eroding the distinction between morality and law.

The 'democratic-functional theory' of Basic Rights also provides a means of limiting individual freedom in the interests of society as a whole. Basic Rights, it is argued, are conferred on the citizen not only in the individual but in the public interest. The democratic political order must be protected against misuse of Basic Rights. The abstract idea of the Rechtsstaat must not be set above the values which it is designed to defend. Unlike the Weimar Republic, the Bonn Republic is prepared to defend itself. It is, in a phrase of Thomas Mann's, a 'militant democracy' (*wehrhafte Demokratie*). Thus in its 1952 decision banning the neo-Nazi Socialist Reich Party and its 1956 decision outlawing the KPD, the Court confirmed that a 'value order' was an element of the 'free democratic basic order' and that parties which denied these values put themselves outside the constitution.[10] In 1976 the Court upheld the administrative practice of excluding radicals from appointment to the public service (the so-called 'vocational ban', *Berufsverbot*) in these terms:[11]

The Constitution is not morally neutral but grounds itself on certain central values, takes them in its protection and gives the state the task of protecting and guaranteeing them. It establishes a militant democracy.

The 'democratic-functional' theory of Basic Rights is based on the view that the freedom of the individual include the freedom to be governed. The 'participation' theory of Basic Rights claims that the freedom of the individual embraces the right to share those social and economic conditions of life which promote the realization of the liberal idea of freedom. This approach has so far had little influence in practice and has attracted some ridicule:

If one wishes to develop the Basic Right to state provision of benefits, that would ultimately lead to free travel on public transport as a constitutional obligation for the realization of the Basic Right of freedom of movement, unless one wishes to go further and deduce from this Basic Right a constitutional guarantee of the right to have a car placed at one's disposal.[12]

STATE ORGANIZATION

While the political institutions established by the Basic Law will be considered separately, certain sections of the Basic Law establish a framework within which these institutions operate.

Article 1(3) states: 'The following Basic Rights shall bind the legislature, the executive and the judiciary as directly enforceable law.' The reference in Article 1(3) to 'Basic Rights' (*Grundrechte*) contrasts with the reference in Article 1(2) to 'human rights' (*Menschenrechte*). Basic Rights are equivalent in substance to human rights but formally are creatures of positive law, deriving solely from the constitution. They are not merely programmatic assertions but have compulsory legal force. The effect of Article 1(3) is to transform moral law (human rights) into positive law (Basic Rights). The political order is bound by values. Hence parliament is not fully sovereign but is subordinate to the constitution and the values enshrined by it. Statutes only exist in the framework of Basic Rights. Exercises of state authority inconsistent with the Basic Rights are void for unconstitutionality. In common with the United States and other continental constitutions, the Basic Law invokes the separation of powers principle, i.e. the theory that the powers of the state should be exercised by a trinity of powers – legislature, executive and judiciary – and that these powers should be distinct both functionally and in terms of personnel. To this principle many exceptions are recognized and it cannot be said to have had a significant influence on constitutional practice.

Article 19(4) states: 'If anyone's rights are violated by public authority, recourse to the courts shall be open to him. If jurisdiction is not otherwise specified, recourse shall be to the ordinary courts.' The introduction of a code of Basic Rights greatly increased the formal legal rights of citizens. Article 19(4) provides that judicial remedies will be available, whenever these rights are infringed. It constitutes accordingly 'the leading formal Basic Right'.

Article 20 provides:

(1) The Federal Republic of Germany is a democratic and social state.
(2) All state authority emanates from the people. It shall be exercised by the people by means of elections and voting and by specific legislative, executive and judicial organs.

Article 20(1) is construed in conjuction with Article 28(1) which states: 'The constitutional order in the Laender must conform with the principles of the republican, democratic and social Rechtsstaat in the sense of this Basic Law.' Article 28(1) is regarded as a gloss on Article 20(1). It is accepted that the

Rechsstaat principle is implied by Article 20. However, the Federal Republic is not only a Rechsstaat but a social Rechtsstaat. This phrase, introduced into the Basic Law by a side-wind, has provided a constitutional peg for an enormous range of communal provision.

While creating and conferring negative liberty in the sense of rights of non-interference against the state, the Basic Law does not protect 'social rights', such as the right to employment, housing, a minimum standard of living. A limited exception is afforded by Article 6(4): Every mother shall be entitled to the protection and care of the community.' Fundamental freedoms in the liberal sense have been criticized as providing bulwarks for the defence of private property against redistributive social justice: 'Classical basic rights . . . have an inherent tendency to preserve the social status quo.'[13] In the Weimar period social democratic theorists sought to combine the heritage of civil rights, legal and political equality with a concern for social welfare and justice. They advocated that liberal freedom rights should be supplemented by social basic rights to produce a 'social Rechtsstaat'.[14]

Both the Christian Democrats, who in 1948 obtained a majority in both the Economic Council and the Parliamentary Council, and the American occupation authorities were hostile to the concept of social rights, because they believed that they were unachievable and incompatible with a free market economy. The members of the Parliamentary Council were in agreement that the Basic Rights must be 'made concrete', that they must be legally binding on all organs of government, and that they must be capable of enforcement through the courts. Only the classical basic rights seemed capable of being rendered specific in this sense. In the harsh and straitened circumstances of post-war Germany, the inclusion of social rights in the Basic Law would have appeared merely declaratory and programmatic.

While the Christian Democrats succeeded in excluding social rights as such from the Basic Law, von Mangoldt (CDU) suggested as a compromise that the 'social state' formula should be adopted in Article 20. By that means a harmless constitutional obligation would be imposed on the state in the areas of health, education and welfare, without conferring enforceable rights on individuals.

From these inauspicious beginnings the social Rechtsstaat formula has – by reason of its very openness – grown to be one of the most important provisions in the Basic Law. The constitution has changed from being a simple defence of the individual against state power to being the groundplan of a social welfare state, in which nevertheless the essential liberal freedoms retain their integrity. It qualifies the Basic Rights as a whole by requiring them to be interpreted in a social context.

Whilst Article 20 does not contain 'any direct delineation and guarantee of a particular economic order', it does prescribe with a much greater specificity what the political order must be. The essentials of the constitutional political order are: respect for Basic Rights, above all the right to life and the free development of personality; the sovereignty of the people; the division of powers; the accountability of government; the subordination of the administration to law; the independence of the judiciary; the multi-party system; and equality of opportunity for political parties with the right of loyal opposition.

There is too a broad assumption that 'democracy' means 'representative democracy'. This appears from the role assigned to the Bundestag, elections and political parties in the constitutional system. What is required is that power should be legitimated rather than exercised by the people. This rejection of referendums may be ascribed, first, to the negative role played by direct democracy in the Weimar Republic, where plebiscite campaigns fuelled protest without achieving anything positive; secondly, to the exploitation of the plebiscite by the Nazis as a way of using the instruments of democracy against democracy.

The provisions for amendment of the Basic Law are in line with its pro-representative, anti-plebiscitarian thrust. Article 79 states:

(1) The Basic Law can be amended only by laws which expressly amend or supplement the text thereof.
(2) Any such law requires the consent of two-thirds of the members of the Bundestag and two-thirds of the votes of the Bundesrat.
(3) An amendment of this Basic Law through which the division of the Federation into Laender, the participation of the Laender in principle in the legislative process or the principles laid down in Articles 1 and 20 are derogated from, is invalid.

Article 79(1) forbids any alteration of the Basic Law except by means of an express alteration of its wording by statute. This is an attempt to prevent political practices being established which

63

substantially depart from the provisions of the constitution, yet become accepted as regular. Such extra-constitutional changes were common in the Weimar period, e.g. the use of the emergency decree provision of the Weimar Constitution (Article 48) to pass ordinary legislation.

Given the West German party system, it has proved relatively easy to pass constitutional amendments under Article 79(2). Up to 31 December 1987 thirty-five laws altering the Basic Law had been passed: sixty-five sections of the Basic Law were amended; five sections removed; and thirty-four additions made. The bulk of these changes, however, were technical alterations, concerned with the allocation of revenues between the Federation and the *Länder*.

Article 79(3) seeks to make the leading principles of the constitution inviolable: hence it is known as the 'eternity guarantee'. This is intended to prevent 'a revolutionary anti-democratic movement from transforming the basic principles of the Rechtsstaat into their opposite'.

THE FORM OF THE STATE

The Basic Law, as amended by the Unification Treaty concluded between West and East Germany on 31 August 1990, now defines in the new Preamble the geographical extent of Germany. Prior to this, Article 23 simply contained an enumeration of the Laender in which the Basic Law took effect. The five East German Laender and the Land Berlin acceded to the Federal Republic on 3 October 1990, under the terms of Article 23. Thereupon Article 23 was repealed (Article 4.1 and 2 of the Unification Treaty).

The original list of Laender in Article 23 never corresponded to reality in that it included 'Greater Berlin'. The wartime allies had distinguished Berlin as a special zone of occupation, divided into four sectors. Berlin was until 3 October 1990 *sui generis*. The Western sectors of Berlin sent five representatives to the Parliamentary Council. The Berlin members were not full members in that they did not have voting powers. This precedent tended to influence later developments. The Parliamentary Council – wishing to assert the survival of the Reich with its capital in Berlin – was anxious to incorporate Berlin into West Germany. Hence its inclusion in Article 23. Because of the special treaty position of Berlin, the Western Allies would not concede this claim. On 12 May 1949 the Western Military Governors ratified the Basic Law, subject to a 'Berlin reservation', which provided that (i) Berlin representatives in the Bundestag and Bundesrat were not to have voting rights; (ii) Berlin could not be directly ruled by the Federal government.

This reservation was not rescinded until October 1990.

While homage continued to be paid to the formal legal separateness of West Berlin, it became ever more integrated into West Germany, as far as its special geographical situation permitted. Federal legislation was adopted in West Berlin by a special resolution of the West Berlin City Parliament. West Berlin courts were integrated into the West German court hierarchy, with the partial exception of the Federal Constitutional Court. Because of its residual international status, West Berlin was specifically excluded from NATO and the West European Union.

Since the French Revolution united statehood with common nationality, the existence of a national group of citizens has been the basis of the state. There are two principles for determining nationality: parentage (jus sanguinis, *Blutsrecht*); and birth-place (jus soli, *Bodenrecht*). German nationality has traditionally been based on the parental principle. After 8 May 1945 German nationality continued to be ascertained by reference to the Reich and State Nationality Law of 1913. No distinct West German nationality has ever been introduced. This meant that East German citizens, being Germans, automatically had West German citizenship.

The state established in 1949 was not fully sovereign. The Basic Law took effect subject to the Occupation Statute, which came into force at the same time. The occupation regime was gradually dismantled, and sovereignty granted by instalments. The Transition Treaty of 23 October 1954 provided that West Germany should become sovereign, enter NATO and accede to the Brussels Pact, which in its enlarged form would be known as the West European Union. This Treaty took effect, and the Occupation Statute was repealed, on 5 May 1955.

At the Casablanca Conference (14–15 January 1943) Great Britain and the United States agreed to continue the war until Germany's unconditional surrender. In an influential article published in 1944 the jurist Kelsen argued that, if Germany surrendered unconditionally, it would cease to exist as a state.[15] Although Germany did so surrender on 8 May 1945, the Allies were not going to allow Germany to escape so easily from the consequences of National Socialism and a lost war. Most Germans clung for the time being to the idea of a united Germany. When it was established, the Federal Republic claimed a direct and uninterrupted succession from the German Reich. This was integral to the contention that West Germany was a mere provisional arrangement pending reunification. This claim also led to the policy of non-recognition of East Germany as a state.

The increasingly implausible constitutional theory of the continued existence of the Reich in the form of West Germany proved an obstacle to the improving of relations between West Germany and Eastern bloc countries. On 21 December 1972 West and East Germany entered into the Basic Treaty (*Grundvertrag*). West Germany recognized the separate existence of East Germany and guaranteed the inviolability of its frontiers. The Bavarian government (CSU) challenged the constitutionality of the treaty in the Federal Constitutional Court. The Court affirmed that West German governments were obliged by the Basic Law to work for reunification but recognized that the constitution also left the government a wide discretion how best to pursue that goal (see chapter 10).[16]

THE FEDERAL CONSTITUTIONAL COURT

In the development of the constitution and the elements of the political system, the Federal Constitutional Court had played a role whose importance can scarcely be exaggerated. The Court was established at Karlsruhe in 1951. Its position is unique and was not foreseen in 1949. The key feature of its powers is that it possesses the 'judicial power of review' (*richterliches Prüfungsrecht*). Judicial review consists in the testing of the ordinary law against the law of constitution. It involves the power to nullify legislative acts on constitutional grounds. The power to determine whether or not statute conforms with the higher law of the constitution represents a notable extension of judicial authority at the expense of parliament. A court, in nullifying a statute passed by parliament, is saying not what law is, but what is law; it is functioning as a negative legislature.

German tradition stresses the absence of political components in the work of the judiciary. The growth of constitutionalism raised the problem of how the limitations imposed on the state were to be enforced. Who was to be 'the guardian of the constitution'?[17] Liberals, looking to the example of the American Supreme Court and unresponsive to the idea of parliamentary sovereignty, came to regard a court as the natural institution to discharge this role. Such an arrangement best corresponded to the philosophy and practice of the Rechtsstaat.

Bismarck had refused to contemplate the possibility of Prussian judges exercising a supervision over political decisions. He was influenced in particular by his experiences of the Prussian constitutional crisis of 1862–6, when a large number of judges had belonged to the Progressive majority in the *Landtag*.[18] The enactment of the Weimar constitution resurrected the question of whether or not the supremacy of the constitution should be vindicated by a court. Hugo Preuss – 'the father of the Weimar Constitution' – had long maintained that the Rechtsstaat was crowned by the judicial power of review of statute. The Weimar National Assembly compromised by creating the Supreme Court for Constitutional Conflicts, which had extensive powers in the field of constitutional review (*Staatsgerichtsbarkeit*). Constitutional review had become well established by the end of the nineteenth century and consisted in the resolution through judicial procedure of disputes between different units of government. Walter Simons, President of the Supreme Court from 1922 to 1929, deplored its inadequate powers and status. A constitutional court, he wrote, 'formed a necessary counterweight to the power of the legislature'. He urged that the Conflicts Court should be able to pronounce on whether or not Reich law conformed with the constitution and that all inferior courts should have power to submit to the Conflicts Court by way of preliminary reference the question of the validity of any state.[19]

The Herrenchiemsee Draft of the Basic Law provided for a constitutional court. An *aide-memoire* of the Military Governors to the Parliamentary Council directed that 'the Constitution should provide for an independent judiciary to review federal legislation, to review the exercise of federal executive power, and to adjudicate conflicts between federal and *Land* authorities as well as between *Land* authorities, and to protect civil rights and freedom of the individual'. The experience of the Nazi Enabling Law of 24 March 1933, by which the Reichstag had transferred its powers to the government, also influenced the Parliamentary Council in favour of establishing a constitutional court. By the Enabling Law, it was argued, the Weimar system had been legally liquidated. A constitutional court could not have prevented dictatorship by annulling the law. It could, however, have made clear the difference between constitutional amendment and political revolution. A revolution like that of Hitler should be denied the possibility of expressing itself through constitutional forms. Men who are determined to enforce change will resort to force when legal means are exhausted or denied. But it is better that their efforts should be plainly revolutionary than that they should be able to pervert the constitution for their purposes. Finally, a constitutional court would in part replace the function of the Weimar President in acting as a counterweight to parliament.

The decision in 1949 to establish a court to enforce and interpret the Constitution was a historical act of revenge on Bismarck. The jurisdiction of the Court is defined by Articles 93 and 100 of the Basic Law, and comprises six areas:

1   Constitutional review (*Verfassungsbeschwerde*): Article 93(1) No. 4a, Article 94(2). Where an individual claims that a Basic Right has been infringed by act of public authority and he has exhausted all other means of legal redress, he can bring an action for constitutional review. This is the one exception to the rule that limits access to the Court to official agencies and bodies.
2   Disputes between branches of Federal government (*Organs-streitigkeiten*): Article 93(1) No. 1. Where there is a dispute between organs of the Federation – i.e. the Federal President, the Bundestag, the Bundesrat, the political parties, the Bundestag party groups or even individual members of the Bundestag – over the interpretation of the Basic Law, the dispute may be referred to the Constitutional Court. The writ is only admissible if the applicant's rights conferred by the Basic Law have been injured (§64 BVerfGG).
3   Abstract norm-control procedure (*abstraktes Normkontrolleverfahren*: Article 93(1) No. 2. When either the Federal Cabinet or one-third of the members of the Bundestag are of the opinion that a statute (*Gesetz*) may conflict with the Basic Law, they may refer the question by motion to the Constitutional Court. The norm-control procedure is 'abstract' in the sense that the question of the law's validity may be purely hypothetical and need not have arisen in the course of or be material to an actual legal dispute.

4   Concrete norm-control procedure (*konkretes Normkontrol-leverfahren*): Article 100(1). Where any court hearing a non-constitutional matter regards it as necessary to enable it to give its judgment to ascertain whether or not a statute conforms with the constitution, it can submit to the Constitutional Court as a preliminary question for decision whether or not the statute is valid.

5   Disputes between the Federation and *Länder* (*Bund–Länder* disputes): Article 93(1) Nos. 3 and 4. Where there is a dispute between the Federation on one hand and a *Land* or number of *Länder* on the other about their respective rights and obligations under the Basic Law, this can be referred to the Constitutional Court to determine.

6   Party bans: Article 21(2). Where the Federal government, the Bundesrat or the Bundestag believes that a political party is anti-constitutional, it can refer the question to the Constitutional Court, which decides whether or not the party should be banned. This procedure has only been activated twice since 1949. The neo-Nazi *Sozialistische Reichspartei* (SRP) was banned in 1952; and the KPD in 1956.

While the Basic Law regulated the jurisdiction of the Court with some precision, it largely left the structure, organization, procedure and remedies of the Court to statute (Article 94). The Law on the Federal Constitutional Court (*Bundesver-fassungsgerichtsgesetz*=BVerfGG) was passed in 1951, has been frequently amended and now applies as re-enacted on 3 February 1971.

The Bundestag was initially unable to reach agreement about the structure and composition of the Court. The CDU wanted a court composed largely of career judges. The SPD wanted to draw on people of broader public and political experience. The real dispute centred on the political affiliations of the members of the Court. In Germany judges – like civil servants – are free to belong to political parties and take part in party politics. The party membership of judges has always been an important factor in judicial appointments and promotions. Both the CDU/CSU and SPD were reluctant to allow a situation to arise where one party might have a majority of nominees in the Court. In 1951 they compromised by agreeing in effect to establish two separate constitutional courts, a First and Second Senate, each with its own judges, jurisdiction and administrative support The

President heads the First Senate, the Vice-President leads the Second Senate. The unspoken assumption behind this accord was that the CDU/CSU nominees should have a majority in the First Senate and that SPD nominees should predominate in the Second.

The Basic Law lays down that the members of the Court are to be selected half by the Bundestag and half by the Bundesrat (Article 94(1)). Each Senate has eight judges, including the President or Vice-President. Three of the judges in each Senate must be chosen from the judges of the Federal high courts. All judges must be qualified for judicial office under the German Judges Law, i.e. have completed civil service training in law up to the Assessor grade. Judges are appointed for a single fixed term which lasts for twelve years, or until they reach the retiring age of sixty-eight, if this date is earlier. The Federal Minister of Justice presents to the Bundestag and Bundesrat a list of eligible Federal judges and of candidates nominated by the political parties. Because the law requires a two-thirds majority for an appointment, government and opposition parties must agree in advance whom to elect. This situation produces intensive bargaining. The Bundestag's electoral functions are discharged by the prestigious Judicial Election Committee, the Bundesrat's by a committee of *Land* Ministers of Justice. These committees regularly appoint their own members to the Court. The Bundestag and Bundesrat each elect half the members of each Senate, and alternate in appointing the President and Vice-President.

The Constitutional Court has three remedies at its disposal. These are:

1　Declaratory judgments, i.e. an authoritative statement of the law (BVergGG §31(1)). The act of public authority which is the subject of the proceedings is invalid if it conflicts with the law as expounded by the Court.
2　Judgments taking effect as statutes in cases of concrete or abstract norm control (BVergGG §31(2)). The Constitutional Court can declare a statute or part of it 'null and void' (*nichtig*) or 'unconstitutional' (*verfassungswidrig*), i.e. not conforming to the constitution but not absolutely void.
3　Injuctions (BVergGG §32). These have been used very sparingly. The best-known example is the injunction of 21 June 1974, which not only suspended the effect of a section of the Fifth Criminal Law Reform Act which

allowed abortion within the first twelve weeks of pregnancy, but substituted an interim provision allowing abortion on specified grounds, which was to apply until the Bundestag had amended the law in accordance with the Court's judgment.

Decisions are reached by a majority. Since 1970 judges have been allowed to publish dissenting opinions – the only German court in which public dissent is allowed. Because of the enormous volume of motions for constitutional review, each Senate has since 1963 had a committee of three judges to sift the applications. These committees, which must give reasons for not allowing a complaint to be taken further, eliminate 97 per cent of the complaints submitted. Between 1951 and 1984, the Court received nearly 60,000 complaints of which only 1.25 per cent were successful. In 1986 financial deterrents were introduced to try to ease the caseload. Any citizen now filing a complaint which is either rejected at the preliminary stage or after a hearing may be required to pay a fee of up to DM 1,000.

In exercising its norm control jurisdiction the Court acts as a restraint on the possibilities of abuse inherent in the legislative process. Between 1951 and 1987 156 laws have been held by the Court to be as a whole or in part contrary to the constitution. However, the Court's role in policy-making has been positive and not merely negative. The Court has not contented itself with saying what is not law. It has regularly gone further and said what is and ought to be law. The Court has thus played an influential role in determining questions affecting the public financing of political parties; the status of political parties; the position of civil servants serving as elected members of political bodies; the guidelines to be followed in relations with East Germany; the rights of university professors in the governance of universities; the implementation of the principle of sexual non-discrimination in relation to income tax and pensions.

The enactment of a code of Basic Rights and Constitution does not resolve political disputes. It converts them into a legal form and forum, leaving the resolution to the members of the Court. In matters falling within its jurisdiction, and questions of the extent of its jurisdiction, the Court cannot be overruled by anyone, including parliament. It truly speaks the last word. Above it is only – as used to be said of the old Reichsgericht – 'the blue sky'.

The Court thus has exclusive competence to determine what is the spirit and letter of the Constitution. It is the custodian of Basic Rights and of party democracy; equalizer of social-economic opportunity; and the umpire of the Federal system and intra-governmental disputes. Despite its limitations, the Court has made a major contribution to fixing the framework of principles within which government in the broad sense must work.

There are two common threads in the jurisprudence of the Court. In the first place, it has consistently concerned itself with justice rather than strict law and sought to bring law in the formal sense into an appropriate connection with morality. The Court has been concerned to bring out the spirit and ethical meaning of the Constitution. This freedom has been open to the Court because in interpreting the provisions of the Constitution the Court is largely concerned with the concretization of general legal principles (*Generalklauseln*) rather than the exposition of casuistically formulated legal rules (*Rechtssätze*).

The second feature of the jurisprudence of the Court is that the Court has, in accordance with the pragmatic and undogmatic character of the Basic Law, eschewed democratic perfectionism. Meticulous observance of constitutional principle is to be tempered by regard for political effectiveness. This stems from a reaction against and wish to avoid the repetition of the weakness and instability of the Weimar Republic. A variant of this principle is the doctrine that West Germany is – unlike the Weimar Republic – a democracy willing to defend itself. The same approach underlies the 'democratic-functional theory' of Basic Rights.

This Weimar fixation was intensified by confrontational attitudes of the Cold War in the 1950s, when there was a domestic climate of fervent anti-communism, which Adenauer's government both reflected and shaped.

When the Court has taken the view that a question affects the fundamentals of the democratic system, it has invoked the 'political effectiveness' principle – or one of its variants – and on occasions proved 'more executive-minded than the executive'. In 1956 it held the KPD to be anti-constitutional and so subject to a party ban because its aims as revealed by its ideology were hostile to the constitutional order. The Court's policy followed from the major articulate premise of the case: that West Germany is a 'fighting democracy' which cannot maintain a posture of neutrality towards parties which reject the principles of liberal democracy. When in 1962 the police entered the offices of the news magazine *Der Spiegel*, seized large quantities of documents and arrested a number of members of the staff, the Federal Minister of the Interior – Hermann Höcherl (CSU) – conceded that the action had been 'somewhat outside legality', but robustly remarked that 'my officials cannot permanently run about with the Basic Law under their arms'. One might have thought that this was the sort of heavy-handed executive action which the Constitutional Court was in business to curb. However, the magazine's motion for constitutional review was rejected, because the police authorities had acted upon reasonable grounds and adopted means commensurate with the threat to the state, which was thought to exist. Four members of the Court refused to sign the judgment.[20] When in the early 1970s civil service authorities began or revived the practice of excluding radicals from the public service, the Constitutional Court again invoked the 'militant democracy' theory to uphold the constitutionality of the policy.[21]

When resolving disputes between institutions, the Court has been careful not to alter the balance of power between them or support the aggrandisement of one organ at the expense of others. When in 1962 Adenauer's government sought to introduce a commercial television service over the heads of the *Länder*, the Court delivered a tremendous philippic against the government's actions. But it concentrated on analysing and exposing the procedural shortcomings in the conduct of the Federal government and the decision, neither in itself nor in its consequences, did not favour or foster a revival or extension of the powers of the *Länder*.

LAW AND POLITICS

The embodiment of rules in a formal constitution policed by the courts has had political as well as legal value, and helped to shape the political culture of the country. The example of the Federal Constitutional Court has refuted the old theory which made a sharp distinction between legal questions and political questions, and declared the latter to be unjusticiable. Constitutional interpretation is continuously influenced by the political issues of the day. Because of the pervasive influence of the Basic

Law and the intensely legalistic political culture, political issues are often formulated in constitutional law terms, so that the authority and legitimacy of law is invoked to justify and under-pin ideological and partisan aims. Policy is discussed not in terms of expediency but in terms of constitutionality. Advocates of greater welfare spending invoke the social state obligation imposed by the Constitution. Advocates of greater defence spending justify this by reference to the 'defence obligation' (*Verteidigungsaüftrag*) which is held to be an implied provision of the Constitution.[23]

With this presentation of political questions in legal terms goes a widespread reliance on judicial means of resolving disputes rather than on the political means of bargaining, negotiation and compromise. Parties in opposition to the Federal govern-ment have regularly sought to overturn in the Federal Constitu-tional Court by means of the abstract norm control procedure measures which they have been unable to defeat in parliament. The SPD challenged the constitutionality of Adenauer's Peters-berg Agreement of 1950 with the Western Allies. The SPD used the instrument of judicial review in an attempt to block rearma-ment. The CSU government of Bavaria requested the Court to pronounce on the constitutionality of the Basic Treaty with East Germany in 1972.

The German political system and political culture embody the widespread conviction not only that public actions should be capable of justification by reference to legal norms but also that the courts are an appropriate instrument to achieve this conformity. There is a very extensive reliance on judicial means of resolving contentious issues. The spectrum of judicial conflict resolution extends from high politics through the field of employment and covers all matters of ordinary administration and social provision. For example, if a child is suspended from school or if a university rejects a thesis submitted for a degree, in either case an appeal to the administrative court may be routine-ly available.

The Basic Law, the rules of administrative justice, and the wide availability of means of legal appeal, both constrain the freedom of action of government and administration and powerfully influence the way in which they are organized and operate. Because of the facility with which all kinds of disputes can be shifted at an early stage to an accepted form of judicial arbitration, the scope for social discord is greatly reduced: 'The constitution seeks to create a core of agreed values and institutions, which can be accepted as settled once and for all. Thereby it exercises a stabilizing and unburdening effect. . .'[24]

These arrangements and the behaviour which they engender have often been criticized on the grounds that they both demonstrate and contribute to a weakness in the democratic process: people prefer to have decisions made for them, rather than make their own decisions through pragmatic bargaining and compromise. These fears may be, but need not be, justified. The Rechtsstaat framework influences the mode in which the political process is carried on but not the content of politics as such. The Basic Law identifies constitutionality with substantive democratic legitimacy. The questions 'Is this democratic?' and 'Is this constitutional?' are, in the German context, not really distinct, because democratic political behaviour involves conformity with accepted rules and standards.

Every political society needs to find a basis of unity for its members. West Germany in 1949 was an invented state. Anticommunism and the constitutional order provided the principal sources of political cohesion in the new political entity. The Basic Law sought to place the fundamentals of a Western type of democracy beyond controversy and outside the range of legitimate change. The essential features of the constitution are 'non-negotiable' (*Nichtabstimmbar*). In the early days of the Bonn Republic members of the higher courts freely invoked a revived Natural Law. As the years have passed, constitutional law has taken on a life of its own so that the Basic Law legitimates itself and does not require some Natural Law justification. Since the 1960s there has been a marked shift from moral absolutism to relativism.

The Basic Law sought to found a pluralistic society and democratic political system upon a relatively narrow consensus, based upon moral absolutes. This was part of the traumatic reaction to the evils of National Socialism. With the shift in the 1960s from a moralistic view of life to more pragmatic, functional and pluralistic attitudes, the simple verities of the Basic Law became more difficult to apply. But this did not diminish their influence and importance. Laws work by virtue of their ability to reflect and influence opinion and behaviour, not because they are commands to which are annexed sanctions in the event of non-compliance. Government does not operate as it does in Germany because of the compulsion of the Basic Law. The

75

Basic Law is rather a prediction of how government is likely to operate.

A theory of basic rights is at bottom a political theory, a theory about the nature and limits of state action. The Basic Law strongly reflects the liberal principles of the limitation of state activity and the autonomy of the economy. The constitution, however, can only provide a set of conditions under which political change can take place; it cannot freeze the status quo or pre-ordain the direction which intellectual and political development should assume. The claim that law should be superior to power has a certain rhetorical force but ultimately rests on the fallacy that personifies law as if it were something self-creating or self-administering. Taken to extremes, this principle would leave society with no government except the will of judges.

In Germany, as in other modern democracies, there is no single dominant source of power, either in theory or in practice. The constitutional system defines but does not usurp the powers and responsibilities of government and parliament. The Basic Law embodies a theory of the state accepted by a majority of Germans, and in particular by the decisive forces in society, and this is the ultimate test of any constitutional theory.

4   The Executive Dimension

THE STATE AS THE EXECUTIVE

In its narrow sense 'the state' means the executive. The executive comprises government (*Regierung*) and administration (*Verwaltung*). The distinction is hierarchical, not constitutional: there is no Chinese wall rigidly dividing politics and administration into separate spheres carried on exclusively by, on the one hand, elected politicians bearing sole responsibility, and, on the other hand, appointed civil servants who are politically neutral and bear no constitutional responsibility. The division between parliament and the civil service is overlaid by that between executive and legislature.

Historically both politics and administration were in the hands of civil servants. Continental bureaucracies were formed and conditioned before the arrival of parliament. The civil service was not an agent of government: it was the government. Germany in the eighteenth and nineteenth centuries was characterized by 'government by the civil service' (*Verwaltungspolitik*). Civil servants necessarily concerned and identified themselves not simply with the means but also with the ends of politics. With the rejection of the theory of monarchical government and in the absence of institutions and doctrines of popular representation or of any theory of parliamentary sovereignty, there was no single source of outside authority which civil servants could invoke to justify their powers. They had an alternative and higher loyalty to that which they owed to particular monarchs, ministers, cabinets or assemblies. Governments came and went: the state endured and its continuity was embodied in the civil service. The took decisions by reference to their concept of the public interest. The traditional bureaucratic ethic stressed the political neutrality of the state, its superiority to social interests and its isolation from organizations embodying them. Seeking an impartial and objective standard to apply, they relied upon law. Traditional administrative law was regarded as furnishing impartial, rational, apolitical, objectively correct solutions to political problems. On this view, administration was not an exercise in pragmatic wisdom but a rational application of law. Administration was oriented not around politics but around law.

The bureaucracy thus occupied *une position déjà prise*. It stood in what the Basic Law calls 'a special relationship of trust and loyalty to the state'. Parliament emerged in the Rechtsstaat as the poor relation of the state, its function restricted to the enactment of general laws and downgraded to sectional representation. With the introduction of parliamentary government in 1918, a layer of elected politicians was superimposed on the existing administrative apparatus. Ministers were not civil servants, but rarely developed a distinct role. The example of state secretary Joël in the Reich Justice Ministry was typical. While fourteen ministers of justice came and went, Joël remained state secretary of the Justice Ministry for virtually the whole of the Weimar period. Twice he was himself acting Minister of Justice. 'The man in the Reich Justice Ministry who actually rules,' wrote one newspaper, 'has always been state secretary Joël.'[1] He was 'in the continual change of the official leadership in the ministry the fixed pole in the flux of phenomena'.[2] In 1932 he was pressed to become Justice Minister in von Papen's 'Cabinet of Barons'. Joël, though not an ardent supporter of the Republic, recognized a shady undertaking when he saw one, and insisted on retirement.

The great boast of the German bureaucracy was encapsulated in Mayer's dictum: 'Constitutional law comes and goes: administrative law stays the same' (*Verfassungsrecht vergeht; Verwaltungsrecht besteht*).[3] After 8 May 1945 it was claimed that the change of state form with the rise and fall of National Socialism had not broken the continuity of the career civil service.

In 1953 the Federal Constitutional Court boldly drew a line under the past by ruling that all civil service law ceased to take effect on 8 May 1945. The civil service had – the Court concluded – been permeated by National Socialist goals and concepts and the relationship of the civil servant to the state transformed into an exclusive devotion to the Führer and party. Article 33(5) only guaranteed the career civil service as an institution in so far as its traditional form accorded with the requirements of the new democratic system.[4] This decision of the Court finally disposed of the claim of the civil service to be above party, to be a state within a state isolated from political forces. It cleared the way for a reappraisal of the civil service's relationship to government and the political parties, following the establishment of the new parliamentary system.

CONSTITUTIONAL PROVISIONS

German dualism had juxtaposed executive and legislature without resolving their relationship by establishing whose will should prevail in a dispute between the two. The executive only gradually became responsible to a representative legislature and there is a continuing acceptance of a degree of separation between legislature and executive. Although the development of coherent parliamentary parties after 1945 radically changed the relationship between government and legislature, the executive remains distinct from the Bundestag.

German liberals had two traditional fears of the subordination of the executive to parliament. In the first place, the traditional party system was associated with a fear of what Max Weber called 'leaderless democracy' (*führerlose Demokratie*). Secondly, there was fear of Caesaristic or oligarchic exploitation of parliamentary sovereignty: that some individual or party could gain control of the legislature and make their will law. While the Weimar experience compounded the former anxiety, the Nazi dictatorship compounded the latter. The doctrine of parliamentary sovereignty was inconsistent with the idea of the Rechtsstaat, which rejected the theory of sovereignty – that there should be some ultimate focus of authority in the system – in favour of an interlocking system of institutional counterweights established and regulated by public law. As Schmitt puts it:

It is a criterion of the Rechtsstaat that it delimits all state functions into particular areas of responsibility and regulates the state omnipotence into a system of competences, so that nowhere at any point can the abundance of state power appear without restriction in direct concentration.[5]

These traditional apprehensions and concepts were shared by members of the Parliamentary Council and are still current in Germany. In a dispute between the government and the Federal Constitutional Court in 1953, over the question of the Court's review of the constitutionality of the European Defence Community treaty, Judge Friesenhahn declared: 'We have two alternatives: either we shall be governed by a state based on law or we shall be ruled by the sovereign dictatorship of parliament.'[6]

The members of the Parliamentary Council were in part animated by needless anxieties and proceeded from false assumptions. They anticipated a perpetuation of the party system of the Weimar Republic, whereas the most striking feature of the West German party system since 1949 has been the consolidation and simplification of the party system, which has achieved a stability which at least until the emergence of the Greens in the 1983 Bundestag election verged on stagnation. Nevertheless, these expectations, if not borne out by events, have not invalidated the constitutional arrangements settled by the Parliamentary Council.

Constitutional arrangements cannot determine the substance of a political system: at most they can act – in Smend's phrase – as a 'stimulus and restraint'. What can be said is that the Basic Law has not hindered but has indeed fostered the development of political practice. Hence in this field that has been a high degree of congruence between constitutional law (*Verfassungsrecht*) and constitutional reality (*Verfassungswirklichkeit*).

The Basic Law marked what C. J. Friedrich called a 'negative revolution'. The Basic Rights section constituted a rejection of National Socialism. The state organization section attempted to make good the shortcomings of the Weimar Constitution. As a whole it reaffirmed liberal individualism, pluralism and parliamentary democracy. It marked a recovery of lost ground rather than any significant advance to new territory. Luminaries as diverse as Otto Braun, former Minister-President of Prussia, and Molotov, Soviet Foreign Minister, even contemplated a return to the Weimar Constitution.[7]

The Weimar Constitution, it was generally agreed, had suffered from two principal defects. In the first place, it was relativist; it proclaimed no value system as its basis; it lacked normative quality. Secondly, it failed to protect 'the vital interests of the state'. The dilemma which the members of the Parliamentary Council faced is well expressed by Fromme:[8]

The experience of National Socialist rule produced fear *of* the state, the experience of the Weimar Republic produced fear *for* the state. The former had an anti-state, the latter a pro-state tendency. The Parliamentary Council feared a democratic state incapable of functioning as much as a dictatorship too capable of functioning.

The Basic Law establishes a modified parliamentary system, in which the powers of parliament over the executive are restricted in the interests of promoting executive stability, and the powers of the executive over parliament are curtailed to prevent authoritarian government. The resultant system of executive government has been called 'Chancellor democracy'.[9]

In its provisions dealing with the Chancellor, the Basic Law differs markedly and consciously from its Weimar predecessor. The President is reduced to a formal and representative role, the powers and role of the Weimar President being redistributed principally to the Chancellor and Bundestag. The Bundestag is elected for a fixed term and can only in special cases be dissolved before the expiry of its term. The Federal Chancellor is given all the powers of the Bismarckian Chancellor. Finally, the traditional notion of an equilibrium between executive and parliament, which the Weimar Constitution perpetuated by seeking to balance the President against the Reichstag, is replaced by a general system of checks and balances.

The Weimar Constitution established a double executive of President and Chancellor. In Carl Schmitt's words: 'The state president is the republicanised monarch of the parliamentary monarchy.'[10] The President was an Ersatz Kaiser. The President was elected for seven years. The institution of the presidency was intended to serve two purposes: first, to guard against the dangers of leaderless democracy; secondly, to prevent the danger of parliamentary dictatorship by providing an emphatic counterweight to the Reichstag. The President was invested with three principal powers. He had power to form the government, being able to appoint and dismiss the Chancellor independently of the Reichstag. Under Article 48 of the Constitution he could legislate by emergency decree in place of the Reichstag, subject to ministerial countersignature and provided that the Reichstag did not exercise its power to annul such decrees. He could dissolve the Reichstag at will, subject to certain insignificant restrictions. Because of the paralysis of Weimar Reichstags, presidential decrees were rarely in danger of repeal. Article 48 decrees became a substitute for parliamentary legislation. The President was accordingly able to install a Chancellor without regard to the appointee's support in the Reichstag, because the government could by emergency decree legislate independently of parliament. The requirement of ministerial countersignature of presidential decrees became a mere matter of form. President and Chancellor could trump any action of the Reichstag by using the power of dissolution. Between 7 June 1920 and 7 February 1933 seven Reichstags were dissolved prematurely. The existence of the presidential powers was a permanent invitation to the Reichstag parties to ignore political responsibility and cling to ideological positions rather than to work together to solve common problems.

While the presidential powers were not used in the Weimar period to establish a presidential system of government, they were used to undermine the parliamentary system, and ultimately to install Hitler in office and abolish opposition to the Nazi regime.[11]

The Parliamentary Council was unanimous that the President should not be directly elected, that he should be stripped of his powers and as far as possible reduced to a representative and formal role. The Parliamentary Council killed the Kaiser. While retaining the concepts of counterweights to parliament, the Parliamentary Council recognized that the notion of an equilibrium between parliament and some other state organ was a dangerous illusion.

The President under the Basic Law is elected by the Federal Assembly for a period of five years. The Federal Assembly consists of the members of the Bundestag (usually 656 representatives) and an equal number of *Länder* representatives, selected by the *Landtage* (Article 54). Presidential acts require ministerial countersignature (Article 58), except in the small number of instances where he retains a discretion. His duties are largely formal and representative. The substantive powers of the Weimar President have been recast and redistributed.

The Chancellor is elected by the Bundestag on the nomination of the President (Article 63(1)). If the candidate obtains an absolute majority, he is appointed Chancellor by the Federal President. If within fourteen days of the first election, neither the President's nominee nor any other candidate has obtained an absolute majority, the President has a choice between appointing the candidate who obtains a relative majority or dissolving the Bundestag.

While Article 63 gives the essential power of choosing the Chancellor to the Bundestag, in practice the choice is made by the electorate, except when a Chancellor leaves office between elections. From at least the second Bundestag election of 1953, general elections have become a Chancellor-election, in which the electorate votes for one of two Chancellor-candidates, and the party or coalition which they head. The Bundestag then endorses the decision of the electors. When a Chancellor resigns between elections, the government political parties decide who shall be his successor. In all the elections of Chancellors in the Bundestag since 1949, the candidate nominated by the President has obtained an absolute majority on the first ballot.

Only in two circumstances does the President have any discretion in the matter. First, if the political parties cannot reach agreement among themselves, the President must become involved in the negotiations. This happened in 1961. Secondly, if a candidate only obtains a relative majority in the Bundestag, the President can decide what step to take next. This has not so far occurred, though there were fears that it might occur after the 1983 election.

The Federal Chancellor embodies the Federal government, which is an organ of the state endowed with autonomous powers and responsibilities. In the Weimar Republic the government could be dismissed by a negative parliamentary majority, i.e. a majority which could agree to dismiss the Chancellor but not on his replacement. On 23 November 1923 Stresemann was refused a vote of confidence. On 12 May 1926 the second government of Luther and on 16 December the third government of Marx were removed from office by votes of no confidence.

The Basic Law provides that, once elected, the period of office of the Chancellor and Ministers shall only terminate when a newly elected Bundestag assembles (Article 69(2)). To this rule there are two exceptions: first, if the Chancellor resigns; secondly, if the Bundestag passes a 'constructive vote of no confidence' under Article 67(1), which states: 'The Bundestag can only pass a vote of no confidence in the Federal Chancellor by the election with an absolute majority of his successor.' Thus the Bundestag can only dismiss a Chancellor by simultaneously electing a new one. The constructive vote of no confidence has only been used on two occasions since its introduction. On 24 April 1972 247 out of 496 members of the Bundestag voted in favour of the motion of no confidence in Chancellor Brandt. The motion failed to obtain an absolute majority of 249 but it was a close-run thing. On 1 October 1982, because the FDP switched support from the SPD to the CDU/CSU an absolute majority was achieved in a vote of no confidence, 256 members voting for the replacement of Chancellor Schmidt by Helmut Kohl.[12]

After the experience of the use of Article 48 in the Weimar Republic, the Parliamentary Council was extremely reluctant to provide the executive with emergency powers. The solution eventually adopted was contained in Article 81, which enables 'legislative emergency' to be declared if the Bundestag is deadlocked.

If the Chancellor seeks but fails to obtain a vote of confidence, he can request the President to dissolve the Bundestag (Article 68(1)). If the President refuses a dissolution and the Bundestag thereafter rejects a bill which the Chancellor designates as 'urgent', the President can, on the motion of the Federal government with the consent of the Bundesrat, declare the bill to be law under the legislative emergency procedure, without the consent of the Bundestag (Article 81(1)). The state of legislative emergency is limited to six months.

The Weimar Reichstag's loss of power was also self-inflicted. By Enabling Laws the Reichstag empowered the government to legislate in the name of the Reichstag. The culmination of this practice was Hitler's Enabling Law of 24 March 1933, which liquidated the remains of the Weimar Constitution. The members of the Parliamentary Council wished to prohibit Enabling Laws altogether. In the end, they contented themselves under Article 80 by seeking to prohibit general and indefinite enabling measures.

On the ratification of the Basic Law and under the Transition Treaty of 1954, the Western Allies reserved to themselves certain rights of intervention in West Germany in the interest of the protection of their forces stationed there, until the German parliament should confer adequate emergency powers on the German government. Because of the requirement for a two-thirds majority in both Bundestag and Bundesrat for constitutional amendment, the enactment of such provisions was delayed until the formation of the Grand Coalition of CDU/CSU and SPD in 1966, which gave the government a comfortable two-thirds majority.

The time chosen for this exercise in bureaucratic tidying-up was singularly unfortunate. The neglect of internal reform in the Adenauer years and the changing domestic and international climate, caused above all by the outbreak of the Vietnam War, had built up forces of discontent in West Germany which were stimulated by the virtual elimination of parliamentary opposition as a result of the formation of the Grand Coalition. The facility with which CDU/CSU and SPD had reached agreement appeared to indicate that no differences of principle divided them, and that they were simply different instruments of the same power elite. The enactment of the Emergency Powers Act 1968 provided both the catalyst and occasion for the emergence of an extra-parliamentary protest movement (*ausserparlamentarische Opposition*, APO). This movement in turn spawned vehemently radical fringe groups, whose existence has remained an endemic and occasionally epidemic factor in German politics, and constituted a dissonant element in the prevailing consensus.[13]

The actual legislation whose birth was attended by these convulsions has not been tested in practice. A distinction is made between external emergency and internal emergency. The provisions relating to internal emergency (natural disaster or breakdown of order) are modest, enabling one *Land* to require the assistance of the emergency services of other *Länder*. External emergency comprises a state of tension and state of war. A state of tension is established by a two-thirds majority in the Bundestag, and results in the Federal government's being invested with additional powers in the fields of conscription and restriction of freedom of movement (Article 80a(1)). A state of war is also declared in principle by a resolution of the Bundestag or by the fact of an armed attack on the Federal Republic (Article 115a). Once a state of war exists, command of the armed forces passes from the Minister of Defence to the Federal Chancellor. If the Bundestag is unable to convene, legislative power goes to a joint committee of the Bundestag and Bundesrat. The Federal government obtains extensive powers to issue emergency decrees. Either the Bundestag or Bundesrat can at any time declare the emergency to be at an end.

The Bundestag is elected for a fixed term of four years. Its term of office ends when a new Bundestag assembles (Article 39(1)). Before the automatic expiry of its term of office, the Bundestag can neither dissolve itself nor in general be dissolved. The absence of a parliamentary power of self-dissolution distinguishes the Basic Law from the *Land* constitutions.[14] The inability of the Bundestag to end its own term of office is the logical corollary of the constructive vote of no confidence procedure. Article 67 is intended to give governments a degree of independence from fluctuating majorities in the Bundestag.

This intention would be frustrated if the Bundestag could dissolve itself. The inability of the Chancellor to decide whether and when to end a parliament is a restriction on the power of the executive. The President can only dissolve the Bundestag before the normal end of its term of office in two cases. If a candidate for the office of Chancellor can only obtain a relative majority of votes in the Bundestag, the President can either appoint him Chancellor or dissolve the Bundestag (Article 63(4)). If the Federal Chancellor introduces a motion of confidence which fails to obtain an absolute majority of members of the Bundestag, the Chancellor can ask the President to dissolve the Bundestag under Article (68(1) which states:

If a motion of confidence proposed by the Federal Chancellor does not receive the support of the majority of members of the Bundestag, the President can, on the request of the Federal Chancellor, dissolve the Bundestag within twenty-one days. The right of dissolution is extinguished, as soon as the Bundestag elects another Federal Chancellor by a majority of members.

This provision is – according to the Federal Constitutional Court – 'an open constitutional norm, which is susceptible of and requires concretization'.

Not a single Weimar Reichstag served its full term. Only two Bundestags have been terminated prematurely since 1949: the Sixth Bundestag elected in 1969 was dissolved in 1972; and the Ninth Bundestag elected in 1980 was dissolved in 1983. In both cases this result was achieved by means of Article 68(1).

On 27 April 1972 a constructive vote of no confidence proposed by the CDU/CSU against Chancellor Brandt (SPD) failed to attain the requisite majority by two votes. On 28 April the budget failed to achieve a majority in the Bundestag, the vote being 247 for, 247 against. On September 1972 Brandt sought a vote of confidence. After the 48-hour gap required by Article 68(2), he was refused a vote of confidence, 233 voting for it, and 248 against. However, seventeen out of eighteen ministers deliberately failed to vote for their own motion, in order to secure its rejection and open the way to fresh elections. The Chancellor proposed a dissolution, which the President – after some hesitation and discussions with the leaders of the parties – granted. Thus the Chancellor sought a vote of confidence in order to engineer a dissolution. However, the budget vote showed that the government had genuinely lost its majority in the Bundestag, even if the mechanism for securing a dissolution involved a manipulation of the constitution.

The events of 1982–3 imposed a much greater strain on the Constitution. In the Bundestag election of 1980 the social–liberal coalition of SPD–FDP had been returned to office with an increased majority. By the autumn of 1982 a serious rift had developed between the SPD and the FDP parliamentary party. The FDP leadership resolved to switch their support from the SPD to the CDU/CSU. This would give a clear majority in the Bundestag for a conservative–liberal coalition government (CDU/CSU–FDP).[15] On 20 September 1982 the Chairman of the CDU, Helmut Kohl, and the Chairman of the FDP, Hans-Dietrich Genscher, agreed that their parties would replace Chancellor Schmidt (SPD) by Kohl by means of a constructive vote of no confidence, and then obtain a dissolution of the Bundestag and hold fresh elections on 6 March 1983. The only method of achieving an early dissolution was under Article 68(1), following the 1972 precedent. The two party leaders assumed that, once a vote of confidence had failed and the Chancellor thereupon advised dissolution, the President had no discretion in the matter. Where Article 68(1) said that 'the President *can* . . . dissolve the Bundestag', they took it that 'can' in fact meant 'must'.

On 1 October 1982 the Bundestag passed a constructive vote of no confidence in Chancellor Schmidt by appointing Kohl Federal Chancellor, the CDU/CSU and FDP voting for the motion (256 votes), the SPD and a few dissentient FDP members against (235 votes). Although he had a clear Bundestag majority, Chancellor Kohl on 15 December 1982 introduced a motion of confidence in the certainty that it would be defeated. When the vote was held on 17 December 1982, the members of the government parties abstained, with the result that it failed by 218 to 8 votes, with 248 abstentions. The Chancellor immediately advised President Carstens to dissolve the Bundestag.

The President acceded to the Chancellor's request for two reasons, both of which were open to question. First, he said, one could not go behind the rejection of the vote of confidence to distinguish a genuine from an artificial rejection: 'It is not possible for the Federal President to ascertain for what reasons an individual deputy may have refused the Federal Chancellor his support.' Second, the FDP had only agreed to support the

CDU/CSU for a time, conditional on there being fresh elections, so the government did not have a true majority; Kohl had only been elected Chancellor subject to a proviso. The reasoning seemed inconsistent: one was not allowed to go behind the vote of confidence but one could go behind the constructive vote of no confidence. Moreover, a Chancellor 'subject to a proviso' is a creature unknown to the Basic Law which – consistently with its policy of strengthening the Chancellor – holds that there are only two possibilities: either a person is or is not Chancellor.

Every Bundestag member can in appropriate circumstances claim the right of an institution of the Federation to bring a case in the Federal Constitutional Court if his constitutional rights as a parliamentarian are violated (Article 93(1) No. 1, see p. 62). Four members of the Bundestag brought such a case on the grounds that the premature dissolution of the Bundestag affected their rights as members of parliament. This faced the Constitutional Court with the question whether or not a fictitious rejection of a vote of confidence fulfilled the constitutional prerequisite for a dissolution of the Bundestag.

The clear intention of the Basic Law was to protect the Bundestag from dissolution before the expiry of its full legislative term except in very special circumstances. The government parties appeared to be seeking to circumvent the clear intention of the constitution by an artificial and collusive rejection of a vote of confidence. The rule of the constitution appeared to have been broken in spirit, if not in letter.

The Federal Constitutional Court, however, has always drawn back from a direct confrontation with the predominant weight of political opinion. In its judgement of 16 February 1983 it held that this dissolution – on its particular facts – was valid but a future dissolution in similar circumstances would be likely to be unconstitutional.[16] The Court thus refrained from overruling the decision of the President or censuring the conduct of the political parties. Nor did the Court cause political turmoil by invalidating an election just before it was due to take place. However, it signalled unmistakably that any future use of a fictitious defeat on a vote of confidence to secure a premature dissolution would be void. This interpretation of Article 68(1) has established that the President does not have an unregulated discretion in deciding whether or not to dissolve the Bundestag: his task is limited to deciding whether or not the factual prerequisites for a dissolution are satisfied. Article 68(1) cannot be used to give parliament a power of self-dissolution not contained in the Basic Law. There remains no way of terminating a parliament before the automatic expiry of its term, except where the Chancellor only has minority support. This situation can only be changed by constitutional amendment.

THE PRESIDENCY SINCE 1949

There have been six presidents since 1949:

Theodor Heuss	Elected 12.9.1949
Heinrich Lübke	Elected 1.7.1959
Gustav Heinemann	Elected 5.3. 1969
Walter Scheel	Elected 15.5.1974
Karl Carstens	Elected 23.5.1979
Richard von Weizsäcker	Elected 23.5.1984.

All have been party appointments, in the sense that all were immediately before their election active politicians and votes at the Federal Assembly were divided along party lines. The election of Heinemann (SPD) in 1969 by the votes of the SPD and the FDP – at a time when the SPD nationally was in coalition with the CDU/CSU – presaged the formation of the social–liberal coalition. Because the powers of the President are so restricted, it is immaterial that they are political appointees. Presidents have sought to develop what powers they have. Adenauer even contemplated taking the presidency in 1959 in the belief that he could thereby block the election of Erhard as Chancellor by nominating some other candidate to the Bundestag. A weekend's study of Article 63 disabused him of this illusion and led to the withdrawal of his candidacy on 5 June 1959, to the considerable if temporary devaluation of the office.[17]

In the appointment of ministers the President is obliged to follow the proposal of the Federal Chancellor. He can and does express opinions but has no veto. In 1963 Lübke unsuccessfully resisted the appointment of Gerhard Schröder as Foreign Minister.

The President takes the first formal move in the nomination of the Chancellor. When in 1961 the FDP initially refused to serve under Adenauer, Lübke intervened to seek to persuade them to renew their coalition with the CDU/CSU. In 1965, as

Erhard's Chancellorship floundered, Lübke pressed for the formation of a Grand Coalition.

The Basic Law thus strengthened the position of the Chancellor against the Bundestag and eliminated the President as a rival source of executive power. In this transformed constitutional context it endowed the Chancellor with the powers of the Bismarckian Chancellor. The traditional symbol of the Chancellor's role and pre-eminence is the 'guidelines competence' (*Richtlinienkompetenz*). This is conferred on him by Article 65 of the Basic Law, which states:

The Chancellor determines and bears responsibility for the guidelines of policy. Within these guidelines each Federal Minister conducts his department independently and under his own responsibility. The Federal Cabinet decides on differences of opinion between ministers. The Chancellor conducts the business of government in accordance with the rules of procedure adopted by it and approved by the Federal President.

This article – which comes verbatim from Articles 55 and 56 of the Weimar Constitution – is generally held to establish three principles:

1 The Chancellor principle (*Kanzlerprinzip*).
2 The departmental principle (*Ressortprinzip*).
3 The cabinet principle (*Kabinettsprinzip*).

The 'guidelines competence' was the hallmark of the office of Chancellor as established by Bismarck. The guidelines competence is the formal and general authority of the Chancellor to determine government policy, in order to coordinate the work of the various departments. The need for this faculty arose from the deliberate omission of a Reich Cabinet from Bismarck's system: Bismarck was the only Reich minister. One by one, policy-making and administrative functions were hived off to and vested in Reich Offices for such matters as Interior, Justice, Finance, Admiralty, Posts and Railways. The head of each office was a civil servant of State Secretary rank. He was accountable to the Chancellor, who was the State Secretary's service superior and could intervene in the affairs of the office. Each office worked independently of the others. In 1878 the Reich Chancellery (*Reichskanzlei*) was established under Rudolf von Delbrück to act as a secretariat to the Chancellor.[18]

To coordinate the executive four means were employed. First, there was the Chancellor's guidelines competence. Secondly, there was the Reich Chancellery to mediate the Chancellor's influence. Thirdly, the Reich Chancellor simultaneously held the offices of Prussian Prime Minister and Prussian Foreign Minister. Fourthly, the Reich State Secretaries were also appointed ministers without portfolio in the Prussian cabinet.

Once Bismarck had gone, there was a great fragmentation of power and responsibility. The best comment on German government before the First World War was that of the Austro-Hungarian Foreign Minister Berchthold, when he received contradictory instructions from the Chancellor and the Chief of the General Staff respectively: 'This is absurd – who is in charge, Bethmann or Moltke?'[19]

The Weimar Constitution both established a Reich Cabinet answerable to parliament through the Chancellor and retained the Chancellor's guidelines competence. Weimar Cabinets consisted of multi-party coalitions. The dependence of the Reich Chancellor on coalition support sharply restricted his prerogatives. The ministers were in effect delegates of their parties, the Cabinet a congress of ambassadors. The guidelines competence was transferred to a Coalition Committee, a committee of representatives of the parties supporting the government. This body decided the parameters of government policy.

The Federal government is embodied in the Chancellor. The ministers are appointed by the Federal President on his nomination. The principal link between the executive and the legislature is through the Chancellor. The Chancellor's prerogatives include 'the power of organization'. This means that the Chancellor can determine the number and responsibilities of ministers. This is a considerable power, which can be used to satisfy the claims of coalition partners and to promote and relegate individual ministers and ministries.

The three principles of Article 65 have produced a combination of the collegiate system and individual leadership. 'The meaning and purpose of the guidelines competence,' writes Eschenburg, 'is that the Chancellor can operate as a counter-weight to the centrifugal tendencies of party allegiance and

departmental interests.'[20] The guidelines competence raises
expectations of the office of Chancellor which individual Chancellors, given the prevalence of coalitions, the dual nature of the
legislature and the ubiquity of established interests, find difficulty in satisfying.

THE FEDERAL CHANCELLORS SINCE 1949

In the fourteen years of the Weimar Republic there were twenty
Chancellors. Since 1949 there have been six Chancellors and
Adenauer's period of office alone outlasted the whole of the
Weimar period. The Chancellors of West Germany have been:

Konrad Adenauer (CDU)	20.9.1949	– 15.10.1963
Ludwig Erhard (CDU)	17.10.1963	– 1.12.1966
Kurt Kiesinger (CDU)	1.12.1966	– 20.10.1969
Willy Brandt (SPD)	21.10.1969	– 6. 5.1974
Helmut Schmidt (SPD)	16.5.1974	– 1.10.1982
Helmut Kohl (CDU)	1.10.1982	–

Edinger has suggested two models of the Chancellor: a
dominant Chancellor using political party as an instrument, and
a constitutional Chancellor who leads a team of equal party
leaders.[21] This classification does not take one very far, however,
as only Adenauer clearly belongs to the first category. After
1961, moreover, he was dependent on the FDP for his governmental majority and his personal ascendency was on the
decline.

Adenauer was not interested in collegiate government. He
subordinated his ministers to the great interest groups, with
whom he often dealt directly over the heads of ministers.
Otherwise he concentrated on a few vital issues and left his
ministers relatively free to run their departments. His preference was for a tactic of taking small steps which derived from
and were related to the immediate situation and task. But there
stood behind them a clear overall conception, whose origins
were to be found already present in the period before his
election to the post of Chancellor. He subordinated all other
political questions to what he saw as the world-wide confrontation between freedom and communism. This provided the
framework for all his other policies: integration in the West;
restoration of capitalism and the Rechtsstaat; acceptance of the
de facto division of Germany; the stabilization of the 'provisor-

ium' of West Germany; the acceleration of progress from Occupation Statute to sovereignty; German rearmament. When a separate Foreign Ministry was established in 1952, he became his own foreign minister. The central section was staffed by trusted personnel transferred from the Federal Chancellor's Office: Hallstein, Blankenhorn and Grewe. Adenauer always staunchly resisted any pretensions of the Foreign Ministry to develop its own policy. 'Adenauer,' it was said, 'hates only three things: the Russians, the British and the Foreign Office.'[22]

While Adenauer's style verged on the authoritarian–plebiscitary, he appreciated and demonstrated the Chancellor's dependence on party. A Chancellor's control over party, especially in a federal system, is crucial. Tenure of the party chairmanship and close relations with the chairman of the parliamentary group (*Bundestagsfraktion*) are essential, especially as the latter has much greater independence than in Britain. When a national CDU organization was established in 1950, Adenauer became chairman of the party, a post which he retained after his resignation as Chancellor.

Adenauer had strenuously but unsuccessfully opposed the appointment of Erhard as his successor. From his position as Chairman of the CDU, Adenauer continued to denigrate Erhard, even after the latter's election as Chancellor. Erhard, unable to use the CDU as his instrument, tried instead to be a plebiscitary *Volkskanzler*, appealing to the people over the heads of the party. This worked for the 1965 Bundestag election but did not survive the North Rhine–Westphalia *Landtag* election of 1966, when the national popularity of the Chancellor could not save the CDU *Land* party from a severe electoral setback. Isolated from his party and unable to persuade the FDP to continue in the government coalition, Erhard was obliged to resign on 30 November 1966. Under Erhard power shifted from the Chancellor to the parliamentary and *Land* parties.

This trend was reinforced under Kiesinger. Kiesinger was chairman of the Grand Coalition, which lost in homogeneity what it gained in size. He was referred to as being 'a mobile arbitration committee'. The spectre of the Weimar Coalition Committee revived in the shape of the Kressbronner Kreis, an informal committee of ministers, leading officials and parliamentarians, who in effect decided upon the guidelines of policy in place of the Chancellor. In this group the central terms of the party agreement were semi-institutionalized.

The SDP–FDP coalition of 1969–82 achieved its political coherence by virtue of the self-effacement of the SPD, which allowed the FDP a policy veto. The principal policy achievement of the Brandt era – the Eastern treaties – also gave prominence to Walter Scheel, Foreign Minister, Vice-Chancellor and leader of the FDP, alongside Chancellor Brandt. Brandt sensationally resigned as Chancellor in 1974, when his personal assistant was found to be an East German agent. The circumstances of his resignation precluded a return to government office, and this rendered him less dangerous to his successor as Chancellor, Helmut Schmidt, than might otherwise have been the case. Brandt retained the party chairmanship but – unlike Adenauer – used this post with the aim of supporting rather than undermining the government, notwithstanding that his successor had a notably more pragmatic and less visionary approach to politics than his own.

The perception of the Chancellorship formed by Adenauer in the fluid conditions of the early years of the Republic was given a second lease of life by Schmidt. He was the only Chancellor capable of mastering all the policy areas with which a head of government must be familiar. He was always Chancellor of the coalition rather than of the SPD. In the SPD the voices of those who preferred ideological purity in opposition to the impure realization of ideas in government, increased in influence. It was an echo of the fatal siren call of the SPD left in the Weimar Republic: 'The SPD has become great in opposition' (*In der Opposition ist die Sozialdemokratie gross geworden*).[23] Schmidt's loss of support in the SPD made him more dependent on the FDP. The FDP leaders concluded that the electoral appeal of Schmidt as Chancellor was insufficient to counterbalance the decline in support for the SPD. Aware that the FDP had to be part of the Federal government in order to survive as a national party, they decided to change sides to the CDU/CSU in 1982. They regarded the ditching of a widely respected Chancellor, in somewhat undignified circumstances, as the lesser of two evils.

When Helmut Kohl became Chancellor, he had the advantage of a solid base in his own party, having been CDU Party Chairman since 1973. By allowing Strauss's unsuccessful Chancellor candidacy in 1980, he had effectively seen off the threat from the CSU and CDU right. His student ambition to become Chancellor was finally fulfilled. In office he has proved to be a moderate, cautious, somewhat hesitant figure. He emerged as a more substantial and accomplished leader than some had feared, and others had hoped. His difficulties have lain less in the gaining of a political profile, than in the control of administration. He has been much criticized for failing to master policy detail and for the weakness of the coordination function under his Chancellorship. West German policy-making under Kohl, it has been suggested, is characterized by sectorization and loose coordination, justified in the name of consensus. This has resulted in a reassertion of the departmental principle, apparently unrestrained by chancellorial leadership. The death of Franz Josef Strauss in October 1988 removed from the scene the most powerful right-wing critic of Kohl, and made it easier for Kohl to vindicate the prerogatives of his office.

THE OFFICE OF THE FEDERAL CHANCELLOR

The Chancellor not only presides over the Cabinet but has his own department – the Office of the Federal Chancellor (*Bundeskanzleramt*) – which both acts as cabinet secretariat and transmits the Chancellor's influence through the whole government machine.

The Federal Chancellor's Office is the largest Federal ministry in terms of senior posts. It is the linear successor to Bismarck's Reich Chancellery. Bismarck's Chancellery was a super-ministry, to which the various functional Reich Offices were subordinated. In the Weimar Republic it declined in importance because the offices were upgraded to ministries, which were no longer formally subordinate to the Chancellery. The last Weimar head of the Reich Chancellery was Hermann Pünder, who re-emerged in 1948 as Director of the Executive Council of the United Economic Region and became first head of the re-established Federal Chancellery (*Bundeskanzlei*) in 1949. This was renamed the Federal Chancellor's Office in 1952.

The Federal Chancellor's Office is unknown to the Basic Law and represents one of the most significant departures of political reality from the constitution. It has once again become a leading instrument of government, with responsibility for coordination, planning and implementation and conduct of policy. Its augmented importance partly stems from the greatly strengthened position of the Chancellor under the Basic Law, and also from the circumstance that the Bonn system is more decentralized than the Weimar system and hence several Federal ministries are distinctly lightweight in administrative and political terms. It is organized in six sections, three of which shadow the work of Federal departments and so are 'mirror image sections'. The Rules of Procedure of the Federal Government state that Federal ministries must inform the Chancellor of 'matters significant for the determination of the guidelines of policy and the conduct of the business of the Federal government'. Ministries send in monthly reports which are annotated and submitted to the Chancellor via the state secretaries. It is also responsible for monitoring the progress of legislation in the Bundestag and for negotiating with parties and parliamentary committees to overcome obstacles to the passage of bills. It prepares and executes the decisions of the Cabinet, and coordinates the ministries in the exercise of the Chancellor's guidelines competence. In foreign and defence policy its role is of especial importance. Access to the Chancellor is controlled by this Office. The head of the Office presides over the informal cabinet of state secretaries – the *Ministerialbürokratie* – which meets on Monday mornings. Like other Federal ministries, it has a number of 'subordinate offices' attached to it, including the intelligence services and the Federal Press and Information Office. The latter is an enormous publicity apparatus at the disposal of the Chancellor and its head – the Government. Spokesman – is a leading figure in government.

In its modern form the Federal Chancellor's Office has become the place where – in theory – all the threads of government run together. Its role is to serve as a centripetal force against the centrifugal tendencies of the ministries. Its effectiveness varies greatly with the style of government of a particular Chancellor. Under Adenauer and Schmidt it realized its full potential. Under Kohl the departments have been left a much looser rein to go their own way, and the influence of the Chancellor's Office has been muted.

The veritable organizer of Chancellor democracy and creator of the Office in its modern form was Hans Globke, State Secretary of the Office from 1953 to 1963. As an administrator in the Interior Ministry in the Third Reich, he had played a controversial role. Accordingly, he was wholly dependent upon Adenauer for his position, and could present no political threat. This in turn enabled Adenauer to have complete trust in him. Globke introduced the *Referentensystem*, whereby an official was made responsible for one or two ministries in order, through permanent contact with the particular ministers and officials, to create the prerequisites for observation, activation and coordination of the departments. An appointment to the Federal Chancellor's Office gained in government circles the significance which once attached to an appointment to the Prussian general staff. An official who proved himself under Globke's demanding regime was thereafter marked out for promotion to a ministry, where he would remain the contact man for the Chancellor's Office. Globke was the closest confidant and adviser of Adenauer, who could stand in for the Chancellor.

Under Erhard (when Westrick headed the Office), Brandt (Ehmke) and Kohl (Schäuble) head of the Federal Chancellor's Office was given the rank and title of a Federal minister. Ehmke sought to build an extensive planning function into the Office, but any overall scheme unduly restricts the initiative of departments to develop policy, and in any case rests, as has been observed, 'on an erroneously rationalistic perception of the nature of political leadership'.[24]

THE DEPARTMENTAL PRINCIPLE

Within the Chancellor's guidelines, policy formulation is carried on by the Federal departments. In 1989 the Federal government comprised the following ministries: Federal Chancellor's Office; Foreign Office; Interior; Finance; Economics; Defence; Justice; Food, Agriculture and Forestry; Labour and Social Affairs; Posts and Telecommunications; Transport; Inner-German Relations; Youth, Family Affairs and Health; Regional Planning; Research and Technology; Education and Science; Economic Cooperation; Environment and Reactor Safety. The function of several of these ministries – particularly of those later on in the list – is of limited significance. Only the Foreign Office, Defence, Finance, Transport, and Posts have their own executive apparatus. The remainder of the ministries are basically a planning staff, concerned with the drafting of legislation, the building of consensus, the allocation of finance, and coordination and supervision of *Land* ministries and semi-autonomous agencies. Most Federal ministries should be regarded as planning staffs rather than administrative line organizations. This characteristic is reinforced by the existence of departments within departments.

To relieve ministries of administrative duties numerous 'Federal higher authorities' (*Bundesoberbehörden*) exist (Basic Law, Article 87(3)). Federal higher authorities are subordinated to a parent ministry and are responsible on a nation-wide basis for a specific function whose discharge requires special technical knowledge and which can be carried out largely independently of and without impinging on other policy areas. Many Federal higher authorities are larger and more important than the ministries to which they are formally subordinate. The Federal Administrative Office deals with all questions of citizenship. The Federal Insurance Office in West Berlin supervises on behalf of the Ministry of Labour and Social Affairs the two thousand or so Insurance Funds (*Krankenkassen*) which administer the welfare state. The Transport Ministry is formally responsible for weather forecasting, but this work is actually performed by the German Meteorological Office in Offenbach. A very approximate equivalent of a Federal higher authority in British government is the collection and management of inland revenue by the Commissioners of Inland Revenue, under the authority, direction and control of the Treasury (Inland Revenue Regulation Act, 1890).

Where administrative functions are not discharged by autonomous agencies, they are largely devolved to the *Länder*. In areas where the *Länder* have responsibility for policy as well as administration – above all education – the functions of the Federal ministry suffer further attenuation. The Minister of the Interior lacks the classic feature of this post on the continent – command of the police – because this belongs to *Land* Interior Ministers. Federal ministries, in general, are all chiefs and no indians.

The Ministry of Finance is concerned with budgetary policy and taxation, while the Ministry of Economics deals with commercial and economic policy. The merger of these two departments in the past to form a super-ministry has not proved a success. The Finance Ministry's powers over the national budget are anchored in the Basic Law, and ensure it a central role in government, reinforcing the coordinating function of the Chancellor. Under Article 112 the Finance Minister must approve all supplementary expenditure.

In the 1960s financial control of public expenditure through annual budgets fell out of favour in West Germany, though not as much as elsewhere. It was criticized for concentrating on candle-ends and ignoring macroeconomic factors. To supplement traditional budgetary methods, medium-term financial planning based on estimates of economic growth was advocated. In 1966 the Finance Ministry was given responsibility for drawing up a five-year plan, containing budgetary projections of revenue and expenditure in the light of macroeconomic assumptions and targets. A Cabinet committee was established, known as the Finance Cabinet. A consultative Financial Planning Council was set up consisting of the Federal and *Land* finance ministers, four local authority representatives and a member of the Federal Bank.

Ministers tend to confine their career to a single ministry, rather than to progress up a hierarchy of offices. Erhard was Economics Minister from 1949 to 1963. Josef Ertl was Minister of Agriculture from 1969 to 1983. Hans-Dietrich Genscher has been Foreign Minister since 1974. As a result, ministers are associated by the public with a particular function rather than a general political role. Ministers develop a departmental rather than a governmental point of view, primarily concerned with the affairs of their ministry rather than with the integration of departmental policies into a wider government programme. Rather than a unified central administration, there is a loose confederation of ministries. Adenauer's ministers in particular had the appearance of Imperial state secretaries.

The parliamentary responsibility of ministers is secured in a number of ways. Ministers are conventionally required to be members of the Bundestag. While there is no premium on parliamentary performance as such, they speak on behalf of their departments in parliament and may answer parliamentary questions. Although they cannot be dismissed by the Bundestag, because the individual ministers stand and fall with the Chancellor, loss of support for a minister in his parliamentary group usually causes his resignation. The number of government posts for parliamentarians has been increased by the creation of the posts of state minister and parliamentary state secretary. Nevertheless the ratio of government posts to membership of the Bundestag is low: while some 17 per cent of the British House of Commons hold a post in government, in the Bundestag the rate is 8 per cent.

State ministers are a type of deputy minister in the Federal

Chancellor's Office and Foreign Ministry. Parliamentary state secretaries were introduced in 1967 when, with the formation of the Grand Coalition, there were too few existing posts to go round. Each minister has a parliamentary state secretary to assist him in his work. Parliamentary state secretaries must be members of the Bundestag and are appointed by the President on the nomination of the Federal Chancellor, after he has consulted the minister concerned. The function of the parliamentary state secretaries has not yet been clearly established. He has a limited supervisory role in his ministry; he answers questions in the Bundestag on behalf of his minister; he cannot deputize for his minister in Cabinet or the department. In September 1982 the CDU advocated the abolition of the post of parliamentary state secretary. However, after returning to Federal government on 1 October 1982 the CDU retained the position and has shown no sign of wishing to dispense with it.

The senior civil service rank is that of state secretary; the larger ministries (Chancellor's Office, Foreign Office, Interior, Finance, Economics, Defence), have two while the remainder have one. They constitute the 'ministerial bureaucracy', are political appointees of the ruling parties and are effectively part of the government, not its agents, policy-makers not advisers.

THE CABINET PRINCIPLE

In constitutional theory the Federal government is the Cabinet. The only ministers not belonging to the Cabinet are the parliamentary state secretaries. The Cabinet suffers erosion from the Chancellor's right to formulate general policy, and the ministers' right to establish departmental policy. The size of Cabinets since 1949 has varied from thirty (Adenauer's last cabinet) to seventeen (Adenauer's first, Schmidt's first and Kohl's cabinet). Such figures may be misleading because, at least in recent years, the smaller the size of the Cabinet, the larger the number of positions outside the Cabinet. The Cabinet is indeed not a precisely defined entity, because a wide range of individuals not themselves being Cabinet ministers take part in its meetings. These include: the official head of the Federal Chancellor's Office; the head of the President's Office; the Government Spokesman; the Chancellor's private secretary; official state secretaries representing their minister; the parliamentary leaders of the government parties. The President of the Federal Bank and the armed forces chiefs may likewise attend. This extended membership and the participation of civil servants in policy-making side by side with politicians dilute the corporate character of the Cabinet.

The Cabinet holds weekly meetings. It does not have a developed committee system. Reliance is placed rather on ad hoc meetings of ministers, civil servants and specialists, arranged and coordinated by the Federal Chancellor's Office. Such cabinet committees as do exist – on economics, defence, foreign affairs, education and the environment – also take in outsiders. The main function of civil service participation in the work of the Cabinet and its committees is to work out interdepartmental compromises. The Cabinet executes a good deal of its business by written procedures, involving no discussion or exchange of views. The rules of procedure provide that a draft decision may be circulated to ministers; if within certain time-limits no one requests that the matter be put on the agenda, the decision is automatically approved.

The Cabinet is primarily an assembly of heads of departments which must formally ratify important policy proposals originating from within the departments. Indeed, its members have little interest in enhancing the policy-making and policy-controlling capacities of the Cabinet, because to do so would weaken their ministerial autonomy. The Cabinet as an institution does not have an adequate bureaucratic infrastructure to enable it to perform a coordinating role. The Federal Chancellor's Office has never become fully effective as a Cabinet secretariat, as an instrument of the Cabinet in its collective capacity.

Under the Basic Law the Cabinet is assigned a number of important prerogatives: it has the right to introduce legislation (Article 76(1)); it can be given power to issue delegated legislation (Article 80(1)); it can veto laws increasing expenditure or decreasing income (Article 113(1)).

Cabinets have since 1949 invariably been coalition-based. In 1961 a Coalition Committee was formed to supervise the work of the government. The same body operated more informally in the Grand Coalition period (1966–9). The Chancellor must retain the support both of his Cabinet colleagues and of the coalition parties, above all the FDP, which normally holds the balance of power.

THE ADMINISTRATION

The administration showed much more marked continuity after 1945 than the political executive, both in institutional and personnel terms. Ellwein writes of 'the astonishing continuity of German administrative history'.[25] While the geographical and political form of Germany has been repeatedly transformed, West Germany retains an administrative system which has developed in a seamless line from the system established by the Prussians in the early nineteenth century.

The modern professional civil service was the creation of the Prussian reforms of 1807–11. The Prussian Reformers made civil service status dependent on educational qualifications and dovetailed the civil service and educational hierarchies. One of the leading features of German public administration is the enormous breadth of the civil service concept. The civil service is not only everyone who wields state authority but also every judge, school teacher, university professor, postman, train driver and municipal grave-digger.

The Prussian system divided the personnel of the public service into three classes: officials (*Beamter*); public employees (*Angestellten*); and workers (*Arbeiter*). This class system has long been regarded as functionally otiose. The Allied Military Governors sought to reform the public service in two directions: first, they wanted to abolish the class system; secondly, they sought to deprive civil servants of the freedom to be candidates in elections (passive electoral right) and make the holding of elected office incompatible with the retention of civil service status.[26] Resistance to these changes was overwhelming. The Parliamentary Council – dominated by officials – enacted Articles 33(4), (5) of the Basic Law, which state:

Article 33(4)   The exercise of sovereign power is as a rule to be entrusted as their permanent responsibility to members of the public service, who stand in a special relationship of trust and loyalty to the state.

Article 33(5)   The law of the public service is to be regulated taking into account the traditional principles of the career civil service.

The Civil Service Law of 1937 – which although enacted by the Nazis was drafted in the Weimar Republic – was re-enacted in June 1950 without substantial modifications (*Bundesbeamtengesetz*).

All persons engaged in public administration serve in a special legal relationship whereby the public law institution is the employer. In German law the term 'workers' means persons whose legal relationship to their employer (*Arbeitgeber*) is governed by private law. The legal relationship of officials to their employer, being a body governed by public law (*Dienstherr*), is accordingly subject to public law. The essence of a private law employment relationship is a mutual obligation to engage in an economic exchange of labour in return for remuneration. On the other hand, civil service status has not only economic but primarily political significance and is characterized above all by a wider obligation of loyalty. In German law appointment as a civil servant is permissible only for the purpose of discharging public functions which, for reasons connected with state security or with public life, may not be exclusively carried out by persons whose relationship to their employer is governed by private law. The civil servant exercises authority in the name of the state (or public body), as a rule as the holder of a public office. Civil servants can be appointed for life, for a limited period or on probation. One of the main duties of the civil servant to his public employer is loyalty, which includes adherence to the republican and democratic constitution of the Federal Republic. A substantial part of the tasks of government, and in particular the operation of public law corporations, is discharged by public employees as opposed to officials. Of the total public service (excluding the armed forces) 42 per cent are officials, 34 per cent employees and 24 per cent workers. Officials cannot legally strike. Disputes relating to the employment and remuneration of officials are decided by the Administrative Courts, not the Labour Courts. The legal rights and duties of federal officials are set out in detail in the Federal Civil Service Law; those of *Land* and local authority officials are prescribed in the Federal Civil Service Framework Law and corresponding *Land* legislation. Public employees and workers are engaged by way of private law service contracts, although their employment still remains a public law relationship with special duties, including that of loyalty.

The tripartite division of the public service has little practical justification and its abolition is regularly advocated in projects of civil service reform.[27] This structure is mirrored *inter alia* by trade union organization. Officials belong to the *Deutscher Beam-tenbund* (DBB), employees to the *Deutsche Angestellten-Gewerkschaft* (DAG) and workers to the industrial trade union *Öffentlicher Dienst, Transport und Verkehr* (ÖTV).

The unity of the public service is most strikingly realized in the grading of all posts in state administration – including the railways, post office and armed forces – according to a uniform scale of ranks and salaries first introduced in 1927. Posts are divided into those with incremental salaries ('A' posts) and those with fixed salaries ('B' posts), graded from A1 up to A16 and B1 up to B11 respectively. There is a horizontal class structure, based on educational levels on entry and divided into four 'career groups' (*Laufbahngruppen*). Each career group is in turn divided into four ranks, which constitute a self-contained career ladder. The career groups according to the Decree on Federal Career Goups (*Bundeslaufbahnverordnung*) of 1970 are set out in table 4.1.

Table 4.1 Career groups within the public service

Career group	Grades	Entry qualification
Higher Service (*höherer Dienst*)	A13–B11	3 years at university, with state examination
Executive Service (*gehobener Dienst*)	A9–A12	Grammar School Certificate (*Abitur*)
Clerical Service (*mittlerer Dienst*)	A5–A8	Secondary School Certificate (*mittlere Reife*)
Basic Service (*einfacher Dienst*)	A1–A4	Intermediate School Certificate (*Hauptschulabschluss*)

The Higher Service consists entirely of officials. In the Executive Service officials and public employees are roughly equal in numbers. In the Clerical and Basic Service public employees predominate. Workers (*Arbeiter*) are only found in the Basic Service. The bulk of workers are found in the Post Office and Railways. Outside these organizations and the armed forces, workers only constitute 5 per cent of those employed in public administration. The key division is between A8 and A9. All entrants to A9 posts upwards must have been awarded the *Abitur*, the certificate of fitness for university established in

Prussia in 1788, which only the Gymnasium can bestow. Commissioned ranks in the armed services begin at A9. An official can only be promoted from one career group to another if the educational qualifications of the higher group are satisfied.

The administrative hierarchy of the Higher Civil Service roughly corresponds to the Open Structure of the non-industrial Home Civil Service in Britain, which took effect from 1 January 1986, down to and including the Principal grade, as follows:

British Grade	German Grade
Grade 1 (Permanent Secretary)	B11 (*Staatssekretär*)
Grade 1A (Second Permanent Secretary)	
Grade 2 (Deputy Secretary)	B9–B10 (*Ministerialdirektor*)
Grade 3 (Under Secretary)	B5–B7 (*Ministerialdirigent*)
Grade 4 (Executive Directing Bands and corresponding Professional and Scientific grades)	
Grade 5 (Assistant Secretary; corresponding Professional and Scientific grades)	B3–B4 (*Leitender Ministerialrat*)
Grade 6 (Senior Principal; corresponding Professional and Scientific grades)	A16–B2 (*Ministerialrat*)
Grade 7 (Principal; corresponding Professional and Scientific grades)	A15 (*Vortragender Rat*)
Administration Trainee	A13 (*Assessor*)

The State Examination, which is organized not by universities but by state examining boards, need not be in the subject of law. To that extent the 'monopoly of the lawyers' has been dismantled. However, the bulk of successful applicants for administrative posts in the Higher Service in practice have undergone an academic and practical training in law, which remains the civil service training par excellence.

Although the great bulk of civil servants are in the employ of the *Länder* and local authorities, the organization, structure and remuneration of the civil service are unified by Federal legislation, principally the Federal Civil Service Law. The Bundestag is empowered to issue framework legislation to regulate 'the legal relationship of the persons employed in the public service of the *Länder*, municipalities and other corporations of public law' (Article 75(1)). Notwithstanding this common legal structure, the civil service is not a unified body. It has no officer corps and has never developed a uniform central system of recruitment and management. The scale of public sector employment is very considerable. In 1987 the percentage of the working population employed in the public sector (including the Post Office and Railways but excluding the armed forces) was 14 per cent (3.8 out of 26 millions).

THE CIVIL SERVICE AND POLITICS

Because the civil service was engaged in politics in the sense of state leadership before the introduction of representative in-stitutions, the growth of parliament and political parties in the nineteenth century simply provided a new forum for the politic-al activities of civil servants. There has never been in Germany a sharp division between politics and administration, between policy-making by politicians and policy advice by civil servants.

The principle of irremovability was never extended to the higher ranks of the civil service, because of the degree and significance of their political responsibilities. In 1848 a special category of 'political' official was introduced, who could be removed from office at will and placed in temporary retirement. From B7 upwards all official posts are 'political', i.e. the Federal President can at any time place the officials in temporary retirement (§36 Federal Civil Service Law). This power is essential if the government is to secure a responsive administra-tion, in a context where civil servants are required to formulate policies politically acceptable to ministers, not to give ministers a choice between alternatives. More frequent than outright re-moval is redeployment to a post of peripheral importance.

While officials have often preferred to remain outside party politics, since 1847 parallel careers in the bureaucracy and parliament have been common.[28] The foundation of the Weimar Republic changed the attitude of civil servants to the state: the profession of indifference to party politics often became simply a veil for hostility to the Republic. Neutrality was a mask for passivity and obstruction. The Nazis overrode the old administrative structure by subjecting it to party control and establishing their own party administration alongside the traditional apparatus of government. The leading cadres of the civil service were thoroughly Nazified, while pressure was exerted on all officials to join the Nazi party and its organizations.

In reaction to the Nazi period, the traditions of the career civil service were revived after 1945. In the changed post-war conditions there was a great influx of civil servants into the political parties. This fostered the practice of appointing party members to political and non-political posts alike. It has been argued that the political parties have taken over the state apparatus, cartellized it amongst themselves and used it to disseminate their influence in society. The result is a 'party-state' (*Parteienstaat*), characterized by a 'partybook adminstration' and the enmeshing (*Verfilzung*) of career patterns and styles of behaviour which has served to blend parties and the bureaucracy.[29]

This view rests essentially on an exaggerated and artificial division between politics and the civil service, which derives from the classic British model but has never been part of the German system.

The great change after 1945 has been the establishment of a political consensus. There is no longer an antimony between serving the state and serving a political party. Civil servants in Germany have always been political. The difference is now that rule by civil servants (*Verwaltungspolitik*) reinforces rather than militates against the party democracy. It is not something apart from and claiming to be superior to rule by the parties. While there has been an extension of the political parties' patronage over office, West Germany has not developed the spoils system. Political patronage is beset by the law of diminishing returns. The greater the number of civil servants belonging to political parties, the more difficult it is to distribute the fruits of office according to party allegiance. The flexible relationship between politicians and civil servants has promoted continuity, consensus and political control of the administration. In Britain the discontinuity of the political system is counter-balanced by the continuity of the administration. In Germany by contrast the political executive and the administration reflect and are affected in like degree by the same broad political trends.

INDIRECT STATE ADMINISTRATION

All civil servants are employed by various public law entities. A public law corporation (*öffentlichrechtliche Körperschaft*) is the organized combination of persons which is a legal entity independent of the change of the individuals belonging to it and which has been created in accordance with public law for the purpose of serving the public interest. The Federation and the *Länder* are such public law corporations. By virtue of the circumstance that each of them comprises a defined territory in which persons are resident, they constitute a special type of public law corporation known as 'area authorities'.

The fact that individuals constitute an essential element of this type distinguishes the area authority from other legal entities in the sphere of public law, especially from the public law institution (*Anstalt*). Examples of public law institutions are the Federal Bank, many *Land* banks, public savings banks (*Sparkassen*), the television and radio corporations and the universities. Public law institutions are not part of the state administration properly so called (*Staatsverwaltung*) but a type of indirect or mediate state administration (*Selbstverwaltung*). While they exist to serve public purposes, they are self-governing and only subject to a limited state control. This includes in some cases the appointment by the state of senior officers, or their appointment subject to state approval. Public law institutions are all organizations created or sanctioned by the state as forms of self-government by which tasks of state government are carried out by the mediate state administration.

THE 'VOCATIONAL BAN'

The 'special relationship of trust and loyalty to the state' – which is as old as the career civil service itself – requires a fundamental loyalty to the state on the part of the official. The West German state established in 1949 was particularly sensitive to this need, first because in the Weimar Republic the civil service was widely regarded as having been deficient in this fundamental loyalty; second, because West Germany was particularly exposed to infiltration from the east. Against this background, §52(2) of the

Federal Civil Service Law contained the 'democratic order clause' which states: 'any candidate for appointment to the public service must be able to guarantee that he will at any time defend the free democratic basic order in the spirit of the Basic Law'. This derived from §71 of the 1937 Civil Service Law.

In the late 1960s, with the changed political climate, applicants of radical persuasion came forward for civil service posts e.g. as teachers. To conservatives and public opinion at large this appeared to be part of a larger scheme of subversion from the left, the oft proclaimed 'long march through the institutions'.[30]

In view of both public reactions and what was perceived as a real threat to the integrity of the public service, the Federal and *Land* governments issued the 'Radicals' Decree' of 1972 (a misnomer: it was not an administrative regulation but a circular, agreed by the Chancellor and the Federal and *Land* Ministers of the Interior, reminding public authorities of the democratic order clause in the civil service laws). As a result government offices began to investigate candidates for the civil service in order to exclude those whose fundamental loyalty to the state was suspect. This practice was widely challenged before the administrative courts but was ultimately upheld by the Federal Constitutional Court in 1975, which held that it followed from the special duty of loyalty to the state of the official that he must unambiguously distance himself from groups which opposed the existing constitutional order.

This overt political scrutiny of applicants to the civil service was named by its critics the 'vocational ban' (*Berufsverbot*). In proportion to the number employed, the number adversely affected by the ban has been very modest – about a thousand people have either been dismissed or denied appointments. Against this figure must be set the very large number of cases investigated by the Office for the Protection of the Constitution – over 700,000. Besides raising important matters of principle, the ban proved unwieldy in operation because of the great breadth of the civil service. Moreover, defending the constitution is not the same as defending the status quo. The constitution is a framework within which constructive change, which involves constructive dissent, is possible. With the conservative shift in political attitudes which set in at the end of the 1970s, the problem largely solved itself in practice without having been resolved in principle, and most authorities here discontinued this form of enquiry into applicants' backgrounds.

CONCLUSION

Because of the measure of decentralization achieved by the federal system, central government in West Germany remains relatively modest in terms of its size, resources and influence. The Basic Law inaugurated a system of parliamentary government, in which the prime division is between government and opposition. This was combined with an administration which showed a remarkable continuity, notwithstanding its transformation by a totalitarian dictatorship. The old fiction that the state is above the parties has lost its significance. It is accepted that the government must accord with the popular will as expressed in parliament. This has blended with established civil service practices. The Thatcher revolution in British government has brought two changes for the civil service. Ministers expect to be assisted by civil servants sympathetic with both their goals and approach. Civil servants are no longer required to offer ministers a choice between various alternatives, but rather to provide means of achieving predetermined aims, in a politically sensitive manner. Secondly, the civil service has lost the policy veto which it formerly, up to a point, enjoyed.[31] In Germany civil servants had long been closely associated with the political parties, and the consolidation of government and party in West Germany since 1949 has been accomplished within established moulds. The civil service has not – since 1949 – claimed or enjoyed, as against the government of the day, the sort of autonomy which the British civil service regarded as part of its birthright.

In Germany an impoverished and exhausted country has been rebuilt into a new state by the merging of the inheritance of the past with a parliamentary democracy containing indigenous, West European and American elements. That the Federal Republic consolidated itself so successfully, and in such an unexpectedly short time, and has displayed an unusual degree of stability and effectiveness subsequently, is ascribable in some measure to the quality of Federal executive leadership and administration which the state has enjoyed.

5   The Legislative Dimension

The definition of the legislature in Germany is superficially simple. The German word *Parlament* means the Bundestag.[1] The Bundestag is democratically legitimated by election and is – according to the Basic Law – the one and only legislature. The normative principle is laid down by Article 77(1) which states: 'Federal laws are enacted by the Bundestag. After their enactment they shall without delay be transmitted to the Bundesrat by the President of the Bundestag.' In constitutional theory the legislature is unicameral, the Bundestag alone making law. In practice, other constitutional organs, principally the Bundesrat, have considerable influence in determining the content of legislation. The Bundestag must take account of the constraints within which it works and the attitude of the other bodies entitled to intervene in the legislative process. The Bundesrat is an appointed assembly, consisting of delegates of the *Land* governments. In constitutional theory it is not and cannot be the second chamber of a bicameral legislature, because it is neither constitutionally empowered nor democratically legitimated to exercise such powers.

The legislative process is broadly as follows:

1   The Basic Law established a distinction between (i) constitutional amendments, (ii) 'simple laws' (*einfache Gesetze* or *Einspruchsgesetze*), and (iii) 'consent laws' (*Zustimmungsgesetze*). Constitutional amendments require a two-thirds majority in both Bundestag and Bundesrat. All other laws are either simple or consent laws. A simple law is resolved by the Bundestag subject to the suspensory veto (*Einspruch*) of the Bundesrat. A consent law is a law resolved by the Bundestag but requiring the consent of the Bundesrat, i.e. subject to an absolute veto.

2   The right to introduce bills in the Bundestag belongs to (i) the Federal government, (ii) the Bundesrat, and (iii) subject to its Rules of Procedure, the Bundestag itself. The bulk of legislation (60 per cent) stems from the government, and some 77 per cent

of government bills become law. Of the 34 per cent of bills introduced by the Bundestag, some 18.3 per cent become law.[2] These are usually bills of less importance. A significant minority of Bundestag bills derive from the Opposition, this being an aspect of the constructive role which is ascribed to them in the legislative process. Government bills are drafted in ministries, which produce an 'Experts' Draft' (*Referentenentwurf*). There is no equivalent of Parliamentary Counsel, who drafts all government legislation, on the instructions of departments. The Ministry of Justice is the central provider of legal advice and services in connection with the drafting of bills. The Experts' Draft must be discussed and voted on by the Cabinet before proceeding further.

3 Government bills are submitted first to the Bundesrat ('first' or 'political passage'). The Experts' Draft is then transmitted to the Bundestag, together with the Bundesrat's Opinion (*Stellungnahme*). The Bundesrat's Opinion indicates both to the Federal government and to the Bundestag what position the Bundesrat is likely to adopt when the legislation returns there.

4 Bundesrat bills go first to the Federal government which transmits them to the Bundestag, together with their Opinion.

5 The next stage is the passage of a law by the Bundestag (*Gesetzesbeschluss*). Conventionally there are three readings in the Bundestag. The first reading consists of the President's referring the bill to a legislative committee for examination (§§60, 77, 78 Rules of Procedure). Only exceptionally does a debate take place on the principle of a bill before it is handed over to a committee. After detailed examination, the committee reports back to the plenum. It is possible for the bill to go back to committee before being voted on by the plenum at the third reading. In practice the second and third reading stages are usually fused and the Committee's report accepted unanimously (§§80, 85 Rules of Procedure). The passage of the law effectively is accomplished by the legislative committee.

6 The 'taking effect' (*Zustandekommen*) of the law takes place next in the Bundesrat. If the Bundesrat disagrees with a law, the law may be referred to the Mediation Committee (*Vermittlungsausschuss*). Every law can be referred to the Mediation Committee. In the case of a simple law, only the Bundesrat can convene the Mediation Committee. In the case of a consent law, either the Bundesrat or the Bundestag or the Federal government can make use of this facility. The Mediation Committee consists of

twenty-two members, eleven drawn from the Bundesrat, eleven from the Bundestag. It is not part of either assembly, being an autonomous constitutional organ with its own Rules of Procedure. The purpose of the Mediation Committee is to agree a version of an act acceptable to both assemblies so that it is unnecessary for the Bundesrat to use its veto powers (Article 77(2) Basic Law).

7 If the Mediation Committee proposes amendments to the act, the Bundestag must vote again on it.

8 The invocation of the Mediation Committee does not preclude the Bundesrat from exercising its normal veto powers. In the case of a simple law, the Bundesrat can impose a suspensory veto but an absolute majority of the Bundestag can overcome the Bundesrat's *Einspruch*. In the case of a consent law, if the Bundesrat does not pass the law it does not take effect.

9 If the Bundesrat agrees to a law, or does not convene the Mediation Committee, or does not impose a suspensory veto, or if the suspensory veto is rejected by the Bundestag, the law 'takes effect', i.e. it cannot be subsequently altered except by a new law (Article 78).

10 At the next stage the law comes into force by being signed by the Federal President and promulgated in the Federal Statutes (*Bundesgesetzblatt*) (Article 82(1)). The Federal President has the right and duty to review the formal constitutionality of the law, i.e. whether it has been enacted in accordance with the provisions of the Constitution. If the President forms the opinion that the law is a consent law and the Bundesrat has not in fact consented to it, he can and should refuse to let the law come into force.

11 Once a law has come into force the Federal Constitutional Court must, on the motion of a party entitled to bring such proceedings, review the material constitutionality of the law under the abstract norm control procedure.

Thus the Bundestag alone makes law in a strict and technical sense but it does not have the last word.

FUNCTIONS AND ORGANIZATION OF THE BUNDESTAG

The electoral system is explained on pp. 181–4. The end result of the German electoral system is a pure party list system of proportional representation in which, in principle, a party that wins 40 per cent of second votes wins 40 per cent of seats in the Bundestag, made up of constituency members and members drawn from the party's *Land* lists of candidates. Plurality – as opposed to proportional – electoral systems notoriously magnify the total of seats gained by the party most successful in the constituencies. In West Germany, by contrast, only once since 1949 has a single party succeeded in winning more than 50 per cent of second votes – the CDU/CSU in 1957, which obtained 50.2 per cent of second votes. This is not a true example, as the CDU and CSU are not a unified single party. Hence in order to obtain a majority in the Bundestag governments are necessarily coalition-based. This in turn affects the work of the Bundestag, its organization and its relation to government.

The general function of the Bundestag is to participate directly and indirectly in the general leadership of the state. Apart from its legislative prerogatives, the Bundestag has only powers of surveillance and control and cannot constitutionally assume executive or administrative functions which are reserved to the Cabinet and the agencies under its authority. On the other hand the role of the legislature in the enactment of statutes is – according to the Federal Constitutional Court – an inalienable prerogative which must not be abridged.

The individual functions of the Bundestag may be analysed as:

1 The passage of legislation, taking it up to the stage when it is ready for submission to the Bundesrat.
2 The appointment and dismissal of the Federal government.
3 The recruitment and training of executive personnel.
4 The control of the executive.
5 Interest group representation.
6 The compromise of party differences.
7 The representation of the people.
8 The legitimation of power.

In order to regulate its organization and conduct of business, the Bundestag gives itself Rules of Procedure (Article 40 of the Basic Law). The current rules derive closely from those of the Weimar Reichstag. The mode of organization differs, however, from previous German parliaments. The fundamental unit in the organization of the Bundestag is not the individual member but the parliamentary group (*Fraktion*). The parliamentary group derives from §10 of the Rules of Procedure. According to §10, as amended in 1969, a group is an association of at least 5 per cent of the members of the Bundestag (twenty-six members) who either belong to the same party or belong to parties which do not compete with each other in any *Land*. If deputies not satisfying either of these criteria wish to be treated as a party group, this can only be done with the consent of the Bundestag. The second limb of the definition is inserted for the benefit of the CDU/CSU, who outside the Bundestag are two separate and distinct parties but in the Bundestag have ever since 1949 formed a single party group (*Fraktionsgemeinschaft*). They do not compete against each other in any *Land*, the CSU only existing in Bavaria where there is no CDU organization. There is a marked differentiation of function between the *Fraktionen* of the ruling parties and the government.[3]

There is a close link between national party and parliamentary group, because a high percentage of leading politicians belong to the Bundestag. However, by no means all national politicians belong to parliament. Both the Federal government and the Bundestag are weakened by the co-existence of executive posts in the *Länder* equal in status and attraction to office in national government or the Bundestag. In 1957 Willy Brandt relinquished his Bundestag seat to become Governing Mayor of West Berlin, a position which he held until 1966. In the Bundestag elections of 1961 and 1965 he was the Chancellor-candidate of the SPD. After the SPD's defeat in these two elections he returned to his post in Berlin rather than take a seat in the Bundestag. After the 1980 Bundestag election Strauss relinquished his Bundestag seat in order to become Minister-President of Bavaria. In February 1986 Walter Wallmann resigned his post as Environment Minister to become Minister-President of Hessen.

As a result of the consolidation of the party system, parliamentary groups have become larger but more heterogeneous. In order to promote agreement within the party group, differences have to be compromised. In most cases the individual deputy will conform to majority decisions of his group. Each parliamentary group has its own Rules of Procedure to regulate its internal organization and conduct. The groups are not uniform in their rules. In principle they have a chairman, executive and working parties (*Arbeitskreise*). Each working party in turn forms subcommittees (*Arbeitsgruppen*). The role of the working party is to develop party policy in particular fields. The highest authority in the parliamentary group is the general meeting, which is held at weekly intervals in parliamentary sessions. The groups are entitled to offices, administrative facilities and public funds. The major parties receive an annual grant to maintain party foundations (*Stiftungen*), which serve as research and educational organizations. The CDU maintains the Konrad Adenauer Foundation; the SPD has the Friedrich Ebert Foundation; the CSU operates the Hans Seidel Foundation; and the FDP have the Friedrich Naumann Foundation. The Federal Constitutional Court ruled in 1986 that public money should also be available for the Greens to have their own foundation. The Greens have accepted this idea in principle but, unable to agree amongst themselves what form the party institute should take, propose to set up a 'Rainbow Foundation' as a loose grouping of a number of party institutes.

It is only possible to belong to a Bundestag committee through membership of a parliamentary group, because under the Rules of Procedure each group is entitled to a share of committee chairmen and members proportionate to its representation in the Bundestag (§68(2)). The whole procedure of the Bundestag assumes the existence of and is geared to parliamentary groups. For example, the number of members needed to present an interpellation (*Grosse Anfrage*) to the government or introduce a bill is the same as the number needed to constitute a party group.

The larger groups have become mini-parliaments. Originally intended to serve organizational purposes they have become a forum for debating legislation and party policy. The individual deputy can only operate subject to the approval and supervision of the parliamentary group. Any initiative by a deputy – such as a parliamentary question – must be submitted to and approved by the executive. Members of the party group on a committee are required to meet together before committee meetings to agree the course which the party should follow. They are required to seek the permission of the group before deviating from that line. Speakers in debates in the plenum are chosen by the party group and allotted a certain time in advance of the debate. The influence of the group is thus very extensive and is enshrined in and encouraged by the Rules of Procedure. In theory the individual deputy is required to adhere to predetermined positions both in plenary sessions and in committee operating as the delegate of the group. To bind members of parliament by party instructions can make compromise impossible and stultify parliamentary life. In practice, the party groups are subject to countervailing pressures which limit the effect of party discipline. These pressures include the strongly consensus-oriented nature of the established parties.

The first task of a new Bundestag is the election of a speaker. By custom the speaker belongs to the largest parliamentary group. In contrast to the British Speaker of the House of Commons the Bundestag President is not neutral in party political terms and can take part in votes. The influence of the speaker is largely mediated through the Steering Committee (*Ältestenrat*) over which he presides. This consists of the speaker, deputy speaker and twenty-three members nominated by the *Fraktionen*. The chairmen of each parliamentary group invariably belong to this committee, which plays an organizational role of immense importance. There is no government post corresponding to that of Leader of the British House of Commons. The Federal government has no direct influence over the conduct and organization of parliamentary business. It is represented in the Committee by the official Secretary of State in the Office of the Federal Chancellor and by the chairmen of the government parliamentary groups. Amongst its functions the Steering Committee decides – in cases of doubt – to which committee a bill should be referred.

Parliamentary groups of the coalition parties do not accept uncritically government proposals, particularly when such proposals derive from ministries held by another party to the coalition. In the Grand Coalition period in particular (1966–9), all major policy initiatives had to pass through elaborate procedures of scrutiny and bargaining before their adoption could be assured. The positions of the parliamentary chairmen of both major groups – Barzel (CDU/CSU) and Helmut Schmidt (SPD) – developed into centres of power almost on a level with the Chancellorship. At all times the chairmen of government parliamentary parties play a leading role in the political process and

117

are for practical purposes members of the Cabinet.

The outstanding feature of the development of the Bundestag has been the eclipse of the plenum by the parliamentary group and committees. The plenum registers decisions taken else-where. The most important task of the plenum is to elect or replace the Federal Chancellor. This is a matter decided by the leadership of the parliamentary groups and the electorate. Except by the 'constructive vote of no confidence' procedure, the Bundestag cannot dismiss the government. Even the loss of the budget in 1972 was not immediately a resigning matter, though it did lead the government to engineer a dissolution.

Except when exercising its elective function, the Bundestag debates rather than decides matters. Through the medium of their majority on the Steering Committee, the government parties are able to control debates, and the parliamentary groups organize the conduct of debates in advance.

The principal occasion for a debate is an interpellation (*Grosse Anfrage*, §105 Rules of Procedure). An interpellation is a written question presented by a parliamentary group, followed usually by a debate. In practice, interpellations are brought either by the government or by the opposition in order to provide an occasion for a public debate on a policy issue. Until the Tenth Bundestag (1983–7) the use of interpellations had consistently declined, from 160 (1949–53) to thirty-two (1980–3). In 1983–7 the number rose sharply to 175. This was attributable partly to the arrival of the Greens, partly to a conscious decision to revive the institution.

The principal annual debate is that on the Federal Budget. The financial year is the same as the calendar year, and according to the Basic Law the Bundestag must pass the budget for the next financial year before the end of the current financial year (Article 110(2)). In fact, the Budget has never once since 1949 been passed on time. In this situation the transitional arrangements provided for by Article 111 take effect. Until the Budget is passed the government may continue to make pay-ments and borrow money necessary to maintain the status quo. Article 111 says nothing about income. Taxes are voted on a continuing, not an annual basis. The fact that the Budget is not passed on time does not mean that there is a failure of supply. All that happens is that the tax changes proposed in the Budget are delayed. The constitutional exception of Article 111 has become the norm. The Budget in West Germany has nothing like the constitutional and political importance which the annual Finance Act enjoys in the British political process.

Every plenary session begins with one hour's question time (*Fragestunde*).[4] This was introduced in 1912 in imitation of the procedure in the House of Commons, and was revived in 1952. Though modelled on the British institution its substance is quite different. In the first place, a member needs the permission of his party group to submit a question to a minister for oral answer. Secondly, the minister need not answer the question personally, but can and usually does have the question answered by his parliamentary or official state secretary. Above all, the institution does not have the function of providing a testing ground for ministers and future ministers, because parliamentary ability is not as such a prerequisite for appointment to Cabinet office.

Whilst the plenary sessions have a vital public and constitutional function, they are not – unlike the British House of Commons – theatre. Government and opposition are only occasionally, not regularly, formed up to do battle along adversarial lines. Everybody knows in advance who is going to say what and for how long. There is no premium attached to parliamentary performance as such, unrelated to substantial political or administrative skills, and little opportunity to display it.

THE COMMITTEE SYSTEM

Some individual committees – such as those for Defence, Foreign Affairs and Finance – are expressly mentioned in the Basic Law. Otherwise the Bundestag determines through its Rules of Procedure the number and responsibilities of the various committees. The committee system constitutes a major departure from the past. The direct forerunner of the Bundestag was not the Weimar Reichstag but the Economic Council of the United Economic Region. The Weimar Reichstag was a political assembly, rendered unworkable by profound ideological cleavages. Its members were often too sharply divided on fundamentals to be able to work together constructively. Its legislative committees were few in number and generalist. The Economic Council was essentially an administrative assembly, the bulk of political decisions being reserved to the Western Allies. Its members were perforce concerned largely with matters of detail and technical questions of drafting. Instead of a small number of generalist committees, it acquired a large number of specialist committees. The political powers of the Bundestag – as successor to the Economic Council – were restricted by the Occupation Statute, because the new state had only limited sovereignty. The Bundestag was regarded as merely an organ of a provisional regime, pending reunification. With the elimination of the anti-parliamentary extremes of right and left, there existed a secure consensus in favour of parliamentary government. In these circumstances domestic legislation appeared to be principally an administrative matter, a question of means rather than ends. In 1949 the Bundestag adopted the specialist committee system, instituting thirty-six such committees. In 1989, in the Eleventh Bundestag, there were twenty such committees, with membership ranging from seventeen to thirty-three. In principle, one committee corresponds to each Federal ministry, though in the sphere of Finance there are two Bundestag committees. While the committees shadow the ministries, they are in turn shadowed by the working parties of the parliamentary groups.

Plenary sessions are infrequent, numbering only about sixty a year, and the deputy spends the bulk of his time in party and committee meetings. When bills arrive in the Bundestag, they are usually referred automatically to a committee. The Speaker simply announces that the Steering Committee recommends that a bill be considered by a particular committee.

The outstanding feature of the work of the committees is the participation of civil servants in their proceedings. In the days of Bismarck the enduring practice was established that the government – as promoters of a bill – should put its case to the Reichstag and be represented in committee, in the absence of Reich ministers, by civil servants, who were responsible not only for explaining the scope and intendment of a bill, but also for assisting in the passage of the bill into law. This practice followed naturally from the holding of 'political' posts by civil servants. Ministers also take part regularly in committee proceedings. Thus the real meeting ground of ministers, civil servants and members of parliament is in the committees. Civil servants are also regularly invited to attend meetings of the working circles of parties, where the party policy to be adopted in committee is resolved.

Ministers and civil servants normally stay in one department with the aim of developing a high degree of specialization in its business. The committees mirror this characteristic of the executive. The broadly representative character to the political parties as *Volksparteien* renders them amenable to the recruitment of a spectrum of interest group spokesmen. The electoral system enables interest groups to nominate their representatives through the political parties directly on to the relevant committees of the Bundestag. Pressure groups thus strengthen the party oligarchy. The Economics Committee of the Bundestag is dominated by the Federation of German Industry, the Agriculture Committee by the German Farmers' Union and the Home Affairs Committee by the German Federation of Officials. The committees provide a focal point for consultation between interest groups and government departments.

While the *Bundestagsfraktion* chooses its representatives for each committee, it does not have an unrestricted choice. It may be bound by an agreement with an interest group to appoint to a particular committee a deputy who has been elected to parliament principally to be so appointed. Specialist knowledge and interest is normally considered a prerequisite for a committee post.

The party members on a committee appoint a reporter (*Berichterstatter*) to keep the parliamentary group informed of the work of the committee. There is a high degree of continuity in the membership of committees. The more often a deputy is reappointed, the greater his independence from party. Members of committees begin to see matters from a committee rather than a party point of view. Committees develop their own sense of identity and comradeship, which transcends party divisions and weakens party ties. It is a matter not of the 'state above the parties' but 'the committee above the parties'. In committees 'a spirit of cooperation' is the rule.[5]

Because of the dilution of party loyalty in committees, government control of committees through its parliamentary majority is weakened. As a result, the committees are effective forums in which to integrate conflicting demands, give expression to interest group claims and promote consensus. Parliamentary groups have two means of calling committees to account: they can replace their members on the committee and vote against a bill when the committee reports back to the Bundestag. Only limited use can be made of these powers. Simply by virtue of his membership of a committee over a number of years, a committee member attains a certain indispensability. Also, members of a parliamentary group will themselves also be members of legislative committees, and will recognize that they all have a vested interest in preserving the relative autonomy of committee work. To reject a committee's bill is rarely a practical possibility. The system of delegating responsibilities to committees presupposes that one will normally accept the delegated determination – that is what the committee is there for – and any general rejection of committees' decisions would lead to the breakdown of the system. The committees, although their members are appointed by the parliamentary groups, are within limits able to dictate to the groups through the medium of the reporter. Thus the committees are autonomous sources of influence in the Bundestag, and their position has to be respected by the government and parliamentary groups. Bills may be amended and altered in substance and intention, and a new bill substituted for that submitted, though this will normally be the result of party objections rather than committee solidarity. The committees take legislative decisions and play a creative role. As Tony Burkett puts it: 'One thing is certain: the committee system has been an effective and efficient method of exercising control over the bureaucracy as well as over government, but it has also increased the power of pressure groups, especially over legislation.'[6]

When the committee reports back to the plenum of the Bundestag, their written report is generally accepted without debate. Legislation is normally passed by all the parties, not by the government against the votes of the opposition. The exact figures cannot be stated, because the voting figures on third readings are not usually recorded. The official report of proceedings simply states that a law was passed 'by a majority' or 'unanimously'. Between 1972 and 1983 it would appear that some 65 per cent of legislation was passed by the Bundestag either unanimously or with only a few dissentient votes. In 1983–7 this figure declined sharply to 15 per cent, because of the entry of the Greens into parliament, who were inclined to vote against most legislation. In most respects, however, the

Greens have been obliged by the logic of their position, if not by their convictions, to conform to the established pattern of parliamentary behaviour.

Thus, even in periods of relatively intense political polarization, legislation is not the outcome of a stylized duel between government and opposition, which the government always wins. It is a process which crosses party divisions. 'This procedure,' Hennis has complained, 'makes a farce of the democratic legislative process.'[7] This may be, but need not be, a justified criticism. The fact that the great majority of statutes are passed by majorities far exceeding the voting strength of the government parties presupposes substantial opportunities for the opposition to participate in policy-making and to influence the content of legislation. In every Bundestag the opposition advances concrete legislative proposals both in the form of amendments to government bills and by means of their own draft bills. Nor have the Greens been behindhand in the matter of constructive opposition. This opportunity is offered through the committee system where, in the absence of publicity and without the pressures of nimious and factitious animosity, administrators and legislators collaborate in both the technical and the substantive business of legislation.

An elaborate committee structure, with most influential parliamentarians of all parties acting as chairmen of the important committees, assures to the Bundestag a degree of autonomous influence in policy-making which is not found in the classical parliamentary system based on the Westminster model. It also contributes to the ambiguous style of national politics, in which ideological confrontation between the government and the opposition is combined with pragmatic bargaining and compromise across party divisions.

MEMBERS

'German parliamentarians do not reflect the social profile of the population, but rather the profile of the politically relevant interest groups.'[8] Currently the proportion of Bundestag deputies who are civil servants is put at 37 per cent. The link between the civil service and parliamentary membership is traditional. The passive electoral right of civil servants was – as has been observed – one of the 'traditional principles of the career civil service'. The peculiarity of the position of the civil servant was that after he had been elected as a deputy he continued to be paid as a civil servant. There is a rule of incompatibility but it takes a peculiar form. On election to a parliamentary assembly the civil servant is automatically placed in temporary retirement (*vorläufige Ruhestand*), in which capacity he formerly continued to receive two-thirds of his civil service salary and was able to return to his post as soon as his parliamentary mandate ended. Thus it has always been easier in purely material terms for civil servants to become deputies than members of other occupational groups. This factor encouraged the inflow of civil servants into parliament in the nineteenth century before a limited form of payments for members of the Reichstag was introduced in 1906, but it has not lost force in the twentieth century. In the Bonn Republic, Bundestag members are now highly paid and the continued receipt by civil servants amongst their number of two-thirds of their civil service emoluments became something of a scandal. The Bundestag was described as 'an officials' self-service store' (Peter Conradi).[9] As the salaries of Bundestag members are geared to civil service rates, the civil servant in parliament regularly had the agreeable task of voting himself a double set of salary and pension increases. The Bundestag did nothing to remedy this situation, because it would have been too much like an attack on a vested interest. In 1975, however, the Federal Constitutional Court held that a civil servant elected to a salaried representative office could not be paid both as a parliamentarian and as a civil servant. The Deputies Law of 1976 has now given statutory authority to this proposition.[10] In other respects, the parliamentary civil servant still continues to be in temporary retirement while his mandate lasts, and can reclaim his post in the active civil service at any time.

GOVERNMENT AND OPPOSITION

A legislative may be regarded as having the primary function of controlling the government. In that case, all the parties in parliament are, in a sense, in opposition and the political system is characterized by the division of government and parliament. This was the theory of the function of parliament which underlay German constitutionalism in the nineteenth century, and continued to be influential in the Weimar period. Alternatively, a legislature may have the primary role of supporting the government, in the sense of giving it a parliamentary majority. In that case, parliament is split into the government majority, which merges with the political executive, and the opposition. This is the classic Westminster model, which is structured round the division between government and opposition.

The control function of parliament over government loses its effectiveness in the degree in which their mutual independence disappears. The decline of the parliamentary control function in West Germany is the consequence of the change from a constitutional to a parliamentary system and the corresponding weakening of the contrast between government and parliament.

Where parliament is separate from government, there is no single overriding factor dividing the members. Parliament then consists not of two but of a number of groups. Its degree of independence gives it autonomous powers, by virtue of which it is able to influence the content of legislation. It performs this work in specialist legislative committees and is sometimes described as a 'work parliament'.

Where the government and its parliamentary majority are one, all divisions between members are subordinated to the government/opposition dichotomy. Parliament cannot modify the substance of legislation against the wishes of the government. Its committees are generalist, because they have no need of specialism. The centre of parliamentary life is the plenary session, where the government/opposition clash receives its most intense expression. Such parliaments are sometimes called 'speech parliaments'.

Since 1949 there has been a steady convergence of government and parliamentary majority in West Germany. The Bundestag superficially resembles the adversary system of politics. However, this similarity is partial and incomplete. The struggle for power is carried on in a different way from that which prevails in the British House of Commons, and the Bundestag has elements both of a 'speech' and of a 'work' parliament.

The Bundestag has retained the traditional seating arrangements of continental legislatures, whereby the members are arranged in a crescent facing the speaker president, behind whom confronting the members are the benches for the government and civil servants on a podium to the right of the speaker president. This arrangement expresses the government/ parliament rather than the government/opposition division.

The Bundestag's limited powers over supply have already been noted. The right of the legislature to scrutinize public expenditure has also since the Weimar period been substantially transferred to outside bodies. The Auditor-General for the Federal Republic (*Bundesrechnungshof*) is responsible for auditing the expenditure of Federal ministries (Article 114). It is the linear successor of the Prussian Audit Commission (*Oberrechnungskammer*). Similar bodies scrutinize the expenditure of *Land* governments. The Auditor-General is an administrative body, independent of both Cabinet and Parliament, whose members are nominated by the Minister of Finance and to which no member of parliament can belong. It reports annually to the Bundestag and the Bundesrat. When the Bundestag and Bundesrat have both approved the report, they grant the Federal Finance Minister a discharge (*Entlastung*). In practice this has become a formality.

Parliament does exercise a novel form of control over the armed forces. From the days of the *Septennat*, when the Reichstag voted military expenditure for seven-year periods, and the Weimar Reichswehr which formed 'a state within a state', there had been a tradition of excluding parliament from the affairs of the armed forces. This tradition was reversed after the reintroduction of conscription in 1955. In 1959 the office of Armed Forces' Ombudsman (*Wehrbeauftragter*) was established. Members of the services may complain directly to the Ombudsman, who also investigated matters on the direction of the Bundestag or its Defence Committee. The Ombudsman is appointed by the Bundestag for a period of five years and he makes an annual report to parliament. The work of the Armed Forces' Ombudsman has been important in reinforcing the principle that the serviceman does not belong to a separate caste but is a 'civilian in uniform'.

The paucity of direct controls over the administration is partly attributable to parliament's preoccupation with legislation. In this sphere the government opposition dichotomy is supplemented and in part supplanted by an executive/legislature division. The government has only a limited control of legislative outcomes. It cannot bludgeon through every measure through its command of party but is obliged to make concessions and seek consensus in order to achieve results.

Six factors provide the setting for government/opposition interaction in parliament:

1 The multi-stage legislative process.
2 The federal system.
3 The need for constitutional amendments.
4 The partial separation of government from parliament.
5 The lack of an institutionalized opposition.
6 The central pull of coalition politics.

Even if the government could successfully rely on its majority at every stage of Bundestag procedure, forcing every clause of every measure through by dint of superior voting power, the government would still have to contend with further obstacles in the legislative process. The greater the pressure which the government had exerted in the Bundestag, the stronger would be the countervailing force at a later stage. The existence of the Bundesrat encourages the government to make concessions at an early stage. To make law through an act of will is a last resort rather than a routine exercise.

The Federal government must perforce cooperate with the *Land* governments, not only because they are parties to the legislative process through the Bundesrat but also because they are leading elements in the administrative process. The opposition in Bonn will invariably be the government in some of the *Länder*. Even the Greens have taken part in *Land* government in Hessen and Berlin. With the qualified exception of the Greens, all the parties will always be in power somewhere. Account has to be taken of the views of the opposition parties. This both encourages 'constructive' opposition and diminishes antagonism between federal and state governments.

Because the Basic Law contains much detailed regulation the government needs to be able to amend it, especially the sections dealing with the federal system. This requires a two-thirds majority in Bundestag and Bundesrat, which can only be secured if government and opposition vote together (except in circumstances such as in 1966–9, when the CDU/CSU and SPD formed a Grand Coalition).

The government itself is thinly represented in terms of office-holders in the Bundestag. Junior ministerial posts are held by political civil servants. Moreover, the government posts are distributed between at least two parliamentary groups because of the need for coalitions, so the government's presence is diffused as well as being numerically weak. Within the FDP the pressure for conformity with the parliamentary group is stronger and the ratio of office-holders to backbenchers is higher than is the case with the other parties. The FDP has been in the Federal government since 1949, except for the interludes of 1956–61 and 1966–9. It was the compactness and unity of the FDP parliamentary group which enabled the leadership to carry through the change of sides in 1982, notwithstanding the presence of considerable opposition to this move in the party outside parliament.

The parliamentary leadership of a party constitutes only one of a number of competing power centres. In 1978–80 Helmut Kohl was national CDU chairman and chairman of the CDU/CSU parliamentary group in the Bundestag. Franz Josef Strauss was chairman of the CSU, Minister-President of Bavaria and CDU/CSU Chancellor-candidate in 1980. In 1986 Johannes Rau was Minister-President of North Rhine–Westphalia and Chancellor-candidate of the SPD; Willy Brandt was national chairman of the SPD; and Hans-Jochen Vogel was chairman of the SPD Bundestag parliamentary group. While at any time it is possible to say who is leader of the government, it is not always easy to say who is leader of the opposition. The division of authority institutionally and politically precludes the existence of such a post on a national basis. Moreover, the same factors that induce the government to work with the opposition parties also work in the opposite direction. Thus while there is real polarization in German politics, there are also factors promoting consensus, and a rough equipoise is maintained between the two.

To gain Federal power the major parties have to find a coalition partner, namely the FDP. But the FDP will normally already be in government. The opposition has to oppose the government, but not the FDP. Hence the search for a coalition partner mutes the opposition function, and encourages realism and responsibility. The arrival of the Greens in the Bundestag has not altered this picture. Having taken the step of participation in parliamentary elections, the Greens have been unable to resist the logic of parliamentarization, once successful in elections. Being interested in a specific policy area rather than in the pursuit of power as such, the opportunities for constructive opposition which the Bundestag offers have proved an apt vehicle for the promotion of the Greens' aims.

The Federal government does not have or want a monopoly

of power but rather a preponderance of influence. The consequences of the relative weakness of the government in parliament is the shifting of legislative decisions from the Cabinet and ministries to the committees of the Bundestag. With the Cabinet's decision to agree the Experts' Draft and introduce it in the Bundesrat, direct control of the matter passes to the Bundestag and Bundesrat. Parliamentary government in Germany consists in the rule of parties, not rule by a party.

THE *LANDTAGE*

In theory, substantial legislative powers are vested in the *Landtage*. The Basic Law creates in the Bundestag and *Landtage* sovereign legislatures which are – within the limits imposed by the constitution – invested with plenary powers. When the British parliament has created sovereign legislatures, it has commonly conferred on them the widest power to deal with every kind of subject matter by giving the parliament in question 'power to make laws for the Peace, Order and good Government' of a particular territory (e.g. section 91 British North America Act 1867; section 4 Government of Ireland Act 1920). The Basic Law adopts a different method, preferring to enumerate in detail the subjects on which the Federation and *Länder* may legislate.

The Basic Law distinguishes between the following legislative categories:

1 Exclusive legislation.
2 Concurrent legislation.
3 Framework legislation.
4 Reserved legislation.

A list of subjects is enumerated on which the Bundestag alone can legislate: 'Exclusive legislation' (*ausschliessliche Gesetzgebung*, Article 73). A second list of subjects is enumerated on which either the Federation of the *Länder* may legislate: 'concurrent legislation' (*konkurrierende Gesetzgebung*, Article 74). This extensive catalogue comprises the bulk of matters for legislation. A third list of subjects is enumerated on which the Bundestag can issue 'framework legislation' (*Rahmenvorschriften*, Article 75). If a subject does not fall within any of these lists it belongs to the *Länder*, which have residual legislative competence: 'The legislative power belongs to the *Länder* except in so far as this Basic Law confers legislative competence on the Federation' (Article 70(1)). This constitutes the sphere of 'reserved legislation', which is to be implied from the subjects not mentioned in the Articles setting out the other spheres of legislation.

Where the Bundestag legislates in the concurrent or framework spheres, the general principle applies that 'Federal law overrides *Land* law' (Article 31), so the authority of the *Landtage* in these areas is displaced by that of the Bundestag. The key question is therefore, when can the Bundestag legislate in the concurrent and framework spheres so as to oust the powers of the *Länder*? The answer is supplied by Article 72, which gives the Federation the right to legislate in these areas where there is a 'need' for national legislation in order – *inter alia* – 'to ensure legal or economic unity, in particular the unification of circumstances of life beyond the area of a *Land*' (Article 72(2) No. 3). This criterion is very loosely framed. At an early stage the Federal Constitutional Court held that the test of whether or not Federal action was required was essentially subjective, i.e. it lay within the unreviewable discretion of the Bundestag.[11] The Federation has made full use of its rights under Article 72 to legislate on all substantial matters in the concurrent sphere, so that the powers of the *Länder* have largely been ousted by those of the Bundestag and the distinction between the exclusive and concurrent spheres of legislation abolished. Thus Article 72, originally conceived as a limitation on the power of the Federal legislature, 'has on the contrary been transformed into the actual vehicle of legislative centralisation'.[12] Article 72(3) 'has had practically no influence on the federal system'.[13] Framework legislation is – properly considered – simply a particular variety of concurrent legislation, which adds subjects otherwise not included in the exclusive and concurrent spheres. These include 'the legal conditions of public service personnel' and the 'general principles of higher education'. When the subjects enumerated in the exclusive, concurrent and framework spheres have been totalled up, all that remains on which the general principle of Article 70(1) can bite are a few 'peripheral and residual matters'.[14] The reserved sphere comprises the trinity of the police, local government and education, except in so far as the Federation issues framework legislation concerning the universities. In view of the dominating role of the Bundestag in legislation, Article 70(1) – which says that in principle the *Landtage* constitute the legislature – 'has in practice been made the exception and not the rule'.[15]

THE BUNDESRAT

The expansion of the Bundesrat at the expense of the *Land* parliaments has had an important impact on the role of the Bundesrat in the legislative process. In the Parliamentary Council the question of the composition and powers of the Bundesrat was the single most controversial issue.[16] The Parliamentary Council eventually agreed its composition but not its powers. At the legendary 'breakfast compromise' between Menzel (SPD) and Erhard (CSU), the SPD agreed that the Bundesrat should be composed of delegates of *Land* governments, while the CSU conceded that the Bundesrat should only have restricted powers of veto.

The members of the Bundesrat must be members of *Land* governments. In plenary sessions they are legally obliged to vote as a group in accordance with their government's instructions. Every *Land* has at least three votes; *Länder* with a population of more than two but less than six million have four votes; *Länder* with a population of over six million have five votes (Article 51(2), (3)). This gave the following composition of the Bundesrat prior to unification (see p. 11):

Schleswig–Holstein	4 votes
Hamburg	3
Lower Saxony	5
Bremen	3
North Rhine–Westphalia	5
Hessen	4
Rhineland–Palatinate	4
Baden–Württemberg	5
Bavaria	5
Saarland	3
	41

In addition, there were four West Berlin delegates.

The *Land* heads of government fill the presidency of the Bundesrat in rotation for periods of a year. The members of the Bundesrat can all be represented by civil servants, and most of the administrative committees of the Bundesrat are formed of these proxies.

This system of voting over-represents the smaller at the expense of the larger *Länder*. The four largest *Länder* (Lower Saxony, North Rhine–Westphalia, Baden–Württemberg and Bavaria) contain 57 per cent of the population but only control 35 per cent of the votes in the Bundesrat. It also favours the CDU/CSU at the expense of the SPD, in that it is easier for the CDU/CSU to achieve a majority in the Bundesrat than the SPD.

The role of the Bundesrat is to collaborate with the Federal government in the legislative and administrative process. The Parliamentary Council agreed that the Bundesrat should in general only have a suspensory veto, leaving the Bundestag the right to overrule the Bundesrat's veto. However, in order to safeguard the federal system it was held that the Bundesrat – as corporate representative of the *Länder* – should have an extended power of veto in two circumstances:

1　If a law touches on the administrative organization and powers of the *Länder*, either directly by Federal regulation or indirectly by the extension of Federal administration.
2　If Federal laws affect the division of taxes between Federation and *Länder*.

In these cases the Bundesrat must 'consent' to the laws, i.e. it has a power of veto over measures passed by the Bundestag. In a system which prides itself on precision, the central concept of a 'consent law' is remarkably vague.[17]

The Basic Law, rather than putting forward a general principle to establish when laws are to require the consent of the Bundesrat, adopts an enumeration method, and specifies forty-two categories of laws which require the consent of the Bundesrat. In any given case it is a question of interpretation whether or not a law is a simple or consent law, which must be referred – in the last resort – to the Federal Constitutional Court. According to the original concept of the Constitution, simple laws are the rule, consent laws the exception. It was not intended that the Bundesrat's veto should extend over many areas of legislation, since it was assumed that the *Länder* themselves would – in exercise of their power of legislation in the current sphere – be responsible for the bulk of routine legislation. This expectation proved misplaced, however, because the Bundestag took over most of the powers of the *Landtage*.

While legislative power may have shifted to the Bundestag, the *Länder* retain their administrative responsibilities. Most

Federal legislation contains administrative regulations and organizational details concerning the implementation of the law. In that case the law requires the consent of the Bundesrat under Article 84(1) of the Basic Law, because it intrudes into the sphere of the competence of the *Länder*. The extension of Federal legislation under Article 72 has thus inexorably led to the expansion of consent laws under Article 84(1), which has proved 'the great entrance door' for the inflow of consent laws. Of 3,535 laws resolved between 1949 and 1980, 1,789 (50.6 per cent) were indisputably regarded as consent laws. This included the bulk of significant legislation. In 1983–7 the percentage of consent laws rose further to 60.6 per cent.

The Bundesrat must initially decide whether or not to treat a law as a consent or simple law. In practice, it sidesteps the issue when it arises by referring the law to the Mediation Committee. The Mediation Committee consists – as stated – of an equal number of members of the Bundestag and Bundesrat. The Bundesrat members are not bound by instructions and vote individually. They usually consist of *Land* civil servants, who will be more influenced by administrative considerations than by party differences. These features facilitate the achievement of compromise. In the negotiating process the Bundesrat members enjoy a built-in advantage because if negotiation fails it is always open to the Bundesrat to fall back on its veto powers and treat the law as a consent law. The Bundestag can only reply by asking the Federal Constitutional Court to decide, whether or not it is constitutionally appropriate to regard the law as a consent measure. Between 1949 and 1987 the Mediation Committee was convened 507 times in connection with 480 laws. Of the laws subjected to this process, 428 took effect in the form agreed by the Committee; in thirty-nine cases the Committee failed to reach agreement; in ten cases the Committee was unable to complete its work before the dissolution of the Bundestag; in two instances the Bundestag rejected the version of the law agreed by the Committee; in one case the Federal President declined to promulgate the legislation.

Secondary legislation (statutory instruments and administrative regulations made in pursuance of Federal laws) requires the consent of the Bundesrat but not of the Bundestag (Articles 80(2), 84(2)).

The federal nature of Germany gives rise to three horizontal divisions: at the top level, there is the Bundestag and the Federal government; then the *Landtage* and *Land* governments; and finally the local authorities. Political parties extend through all three levels, so the horizontal divisions of the federal system are transacted by the vertical links of the party system. The parties integrate the federal units. Depending upon the degree of unity between a party at national level and its governments at *Land* level, *Land* governments may find themselves in a dilemma how to use their votes in the Bundesrat. It is a question of priorities: whether they should only represent the *Land* interest, as the principles of federalism suggest should be their primary concern, even if that means a breach of national party unity; or whether they should follow the wishes of the national party leadership, even if this happens to be against the interest of the *Länder*.

Just as national party affiliations soon dominated voting in the *Landtage* elections, so the same factor of common party allegiance soon transcended the institutional divisions between *Land* delegations. From 1949 to 1969 and between 1982 and 1989 the government enjoyed a dual majority in both Bundestag and Bundesrat. The consolidation of the Federal Republic and the emergence of something approaching a two-party system in the 1950s worked in the direction of 'nationalizing' *Land* politics, transforming *Land* elections into contests for the control of blocks of votes in the Bundesrat and opportunities for the electorate to demonstrate their attitude to the ruling coalition in Bonn. Paradoxically, the existence of parallel partisan CDU/CSU–FDP majorities in both Bundestag and Bundesrat enabled the Bundesrat to develop for itself a relatively apolitical, bureaucratic role. After 1969, when the SDP–FDP coalition held a clear majority in the Bundestag but the CDU/CSU had a majority in the Bundesrat, the Bundesrat assumed the role of a potential adversary of the Federal government. As a result of this political divergence between two assemblies, there was after 1972 a sharp increase in the number of occasions when the Mediation Committee was convened. In 1969–72 the Committee was set in motion on thirty-three occasions; in 1972–6 this figure rose to 104; in 1976–80 the Committee was convened on seventy-seven occasions; in 1980–3 the number of times the Committee was utilized was twenty; in 1983–7 this number had fallen back to six, with parallel majorities once more in place.

However, in the period 1969–82 the Bundesrat did not forget its role as the upholder of federalism. In important respects the

Bundesrat is not an appropriate substitute – *Ersatzorgan* – for the execution of the policy of the parliamentary opposition. Moreover, if the *Land* governments were to compromise their strong position in the federal structure for the greater benefit of national parties, they would undermine the spirit and possibly also the letter of the Basic Law. After 1969 the Bundesrat did not engage in systematic obstruction of the government. Nor in the 1950s, 1960s and after 1982 when the government had a dual majority in the Bundesrat and Bundestag, did the Bundesrat abdicate its role and influence as guardian of *Land* interests and become the Federal government's poodle. Precisely because the Bundesrat occupies such an important position in the legislative process, it can afford to take an independent line on those issues which seriously affect the interests of the *Länder* and on which the national party leaders know that they cannot dictate to the ruling politicians in the provincial capitals. It cannot be assumed that the attitude of the Bundesrat will faithfully reflect national party policies. On most issues party allegiances are the dominating factor, but in matters in which the interests of the *Länder* are at stake the Bundesrat can wield decisive influence, regardless of party ties. An outstanding example of this occurred in 1988 when Ernst Albrecht, CDU Minister-President of Lower Saxony, took the view that the CDU/CSU–FDP government's tax reform programme unfairly disadvantaged the poorer northern *Länder*. By the threat of imposing the Bundesrat's veto, he forced significant concessions from the Federal government.

The Bundesrat has shown restraint in exercising its powers. The existence of these powers has a profound influence on the legislative process, so their actual exercise is usually unnecessary. Even so, the Bundesrat remains primarily a veto power in the policy-making process, not an independent centre of active political initiative. The impact of the Bundesrat's veto is apparent from table 5.1. The real question is, however, not whether the Bundesrat has used its powers wisely, but whether those powers should exist at all.

The constitutional foundation for the Bundesrat's role in the legislative process consists in the distinction drawn between simple and consent laws and Article 50(1) which states: 'Through the Bundesrat the *Länder* participate in the legislation and administration of the Federation.'

Hence the Bundesrat's powers are restricted to the exercise of

Table 5.1 Exercise of Bundesrat's veto, 1949–1987

	1949–53	1953–7	1957–61	1961–5	1965–9	1969–72	1972–6	1976–80	1980–3	1983–7
1 Consent laws										
Consent refused	12	11	4	7	10	3	19	15	4	0
Consent given after convening of Mediation Committee	3	5	4	4	8	2	11	6	2	0
Vetoed	8	4	2	3	2	1	8	9	2	0
2 Simple laws										
Suspensory veto by Bundesrat	1	1	3	0	0	1	5	7	7	0
Veto overridden by Bundestag	0	1	1	0	0	1	4	5	6	0
Vetoed	1	0	2	0	0	0	1	2	1	0
3 Total of laws vetoed by Bundesrat	9	6	2	3	2	1	9	11	3	0
Laws passed by Bundesrat	545	507	424	427	453	335	516	354	139	320

its veto: only in the Mediation Committee does it have a formative role in legislation. The Federal Constitutional Court has reiterated the orthodox theory that the Bundesrat is not a second chamber of the legislature and that consent laws are the exception, only being required in 'cases where the sphere of the interest of the *Länder* is especially strongly affected'.[18]

This theory of the constitution is, however, in conflict with the facts of political life. Whatever the constitution may say, the Bundesrat has full power to initiate, amend or reject most federal laws.

The legislative influence of the Bundesrat thus derives from the fact that, because of the unexpectedly wide range of application of Article 84(1), more than half of all laws are consent laws; because all laws can be subjected to a Mediation Committee where the Bundesrat has the upper hand; and because political parties can use the Bundesrat for their national party goals.

Four theories have been put forward to justify the legislative role of the Bundesrat:

1   The participation theory (*Mitwirkung*): the Bundesrat merely 'participates' in the legislative process. The Bundesrat's powers clearly go beyond mere participation.
2   Brake theory: the Bundesrat acts as a restraint on the Bundestag. The Bundesrat's powers to initiate legislation, communicate its opinion to the Bundestag and its influence in the Mediation Committee show the Bundesrat to be exercising a formative not merely a restraining role.
3   Co-responsibility theory (*Mitverantwortung*): the Bundesrat shares responsibility for legislation with the Bundestag. This is to put the appointed Bundesrat on a par with the elected Bundestag and would be a radical breach of the constitution.
4   Compensation theory. The increase in the powers of the Bundesrat compensates for and serves as a counterweight to the contraction of the powers of the *Landtage*, thus preserving the balance of the constitutional system.

This fourth theory really affords a political rather than a constitutional justification. As Ossenbühl puts it:

If one regards the compensation theory simply from the point of view of the constitution, then it is simply a question, whether the Basic Law does or does not allow the compensation idea by way of a tacit constitutional amendment by means of a broad interpretation. The compensation theory leads to a transformation of quantity into quality, i.e. to a fundamental alteration of the system of functions prescribed by the Basic Law. The consequences signify a fundamental alteration of the system, which cannot be legitimately brought about either by constitutional practice or by a broad interpretation by way of a tacit constitutional amendment.[19]

The Bundesrat lacks any material, nationwide, democratic mandate, which is the precondition and foundation of democratic responsibility. This discrepancy between constitutional theory and political practice represents the most significant breakdown in the Basic Law's claim to govern political reality. The result is that the Bundestag is not performing its constitutional function, while the Bundesrat is discharging a function which it does not constitutionally possess and for which it lacks democratic legitimacy.

EUROPEAN LEGISLATION

West Germany was one of the founding members of the European Economic Community. Membership of the Community has entailed a partial transfer of legislative responsibility from the Bundestag to Community organs, principally the Council of Ministers and the Commission. Article 24(1) of the Basic Law gives the Federation, i.e. the Bundestag, power to transfer sovereign powers of the state to international bodies. It is a token of 'open statehood'. Under this provision significant responsibilities have been assigned to Community institutions.

The ability of the Bundestag to transfer law-making powers to international bodies is a further demonstration that the legislative powers of the *Länder* are largely at the disposition of the Bundestag. In the three policy areas of trade, tariffs and agriculture European integration is far advanced and the powers of national parliaments to enact new legislation in these fields are severely curtailed.

Article 2 of the law ratifying the Treaties of Rome imposed upon the Federal government the obligation to notify the Bundestag and Bundesrat of (i) legislative proposals under Article 189 of the Treaty of Rome and (ii) any directives requiring implementation in domestic law.

The Bundestag and Bundesrat have modified their existing procedures, rather than developed new ones, in order to examine proposed Community legislation. The Bundesrat scrutiny is initially conducted by officials, whose views are then considered by the Committee on European Community Affairs. The Bundestag refers the matter to the relevant subject committee, the principal committees concerned being Food, Agriculture and Forestry, Economics, Transport, and Employment, Social Affairs and Health. In 1983 the Bundestag established a consultative Europa-Kommission, consisting of eleven members of the Bundestag and eleven members of the European Parliament. This committee was not re-established after the 1987 Federal election and its responsibility for looking at broad European Community developments was taken over by a new Sub-Committee (Europe) of the Foreign Affairs Committee.

Difficult questions have arisen as to the extent of the transfer of powers which Article 24(1) authorizes. The European Economic Community is, in the view of the European Court of Justice, based on the principle of the supremacy of Community law over national law. The question then arises: does this mean supremacy over ordinary law only; or does it extend to supremacy over national constitutions? What happens to provisions of national constitutions declared to be immutable, as by the 'eternity guarantee' of Article 79(3)? If the Bundestag transfers law-making powers to the European Community, could the Community use those powers in a manner which would, when the Community measures took effect in West Germany, contravene the Basic Law, and in particular its entrenched provisions?

The Federal Constitutional Court has ruled that in any conflict between the entrenched sections of the Basic Law and Community legislation, the former must prevail. The European Court of Justice has held that the general principles of Community law contain fundamental rights provisions, which are inspired by the constitutional traditions common to the member states and offer guarantees equivalent to those conferred by national constitutions. Hence a Community measure which conflicted with fundamental rights as expressed in the constitutions of member states would be invalid because it derogated from the general principles of Community law.[20]

SUMMARY

The legislative process in West Germany has escaped both the incoherence of the American system and the partisanship of the British parliament. Policy switches are rare; change is recognized as incremental; executive and legislature are overlapping but distinct branches in the system of government, with the executive enjoying relative freedom from parliament once appointed, but not able to direct and control the legislative process at every stage. While the legislative process has many components, the principal weight rests with the Bundestag and to that extent it is correct to regard West Germany as having a unicameral system. The formal predominance of the Bundestag may be apparent from these figures. Between 1949 and January 1987 the Bundestag resolved 4,020 laws. Of these, 3,947 were published in the Federal Statutes (*Bundesgesetzblatt*) and took effect. Of the sixty-three that failed thirty-nine were consent laws, which the Bundesrat vetoed; seven were subject to the suspensory veto of the Bundesrat, which the Bundestag failed to override; the Federal President declined to sign five; six were repealed by the Bundestag, after the Mediation Committee had been interposed; one failed to obtain the consent of the Federal government under Article 113; and five lapsed because of the expiry of the Bundestag's legislative term.

The uneasy ghost which haunts the legislative process is represented by the width and uncertainty of the powers of the Bundesrat, whose actual political role is warranted neither by constitutional nor by democratic theory. Its justification lies in terms of the federal system.

6   The Federal Dimension

DECENTRALIZATION AND FEDERALISM

Historically, the problems connected with the attainment of national unity had three aspects: external boundaries; domestic political change; and internal structure. The problems of internal structure were considered in the light of three possible models: a league of states (*Staatenbund*), a Federation (*Bundesstaat*) and a unitary state (*Einheitsstaat*). A state is a bearer of sovereignty. In a federation sovereignty is shared by the national and the constituent states. In a unitary state there is only one bearer of sovereignty, the political unit as a whole. In German terminology both the nation and the federal units are 'states'. The Weimar Constitution used the term *Land* (plural *Länder*) to designate the federal states and this terminology has been retained by the Basic Law, which distinguishes between the Federation (*Bund*) and the *Länder*. The essence of federalism is that the states have a constitutionally entrenched position, as bearers of a limited form of sovereignty.

Where the political subdivisions of a country represent administrative structures that do not possess sovereignty in any form, this constitutes a decentralized rather than a federal mode of organization. While federalism in Germany dates from 1871, decentralization – the authorization of dependent agencies to make decisions of a regional and local character – has an older history. The Prussian reformers of 1807–11 established a system of administration combining functional and regional specialization, which was extended by the development of local self-government (*Selbstverwaltung*) in the course of the nineteenth century. Five classic central departments were established in Berlin – Interior, Finance, Justice, Foreign Affairs and War – and constituted 'upper tier' authorities. With the exception of tax offices there were in principle no specialist adminstrations below the upper tier: instead, the central departments worked through generalist officers in middle and lower tiers.

Prussia provided for the regional coordination of state activities: the state was divided into provinces headed by a governor

(*Oberpräsident*), and each province was in turn divided into government districts (*Regierungsbezirk*) headed by a district president (*Regierungspräsident*). The provincial governor and district president had distinct responsibilities: the district president was not the subordinate of the governor. Both were multi-purpose agencies, with the function of coordinating the work of various ministries in their area.

Beneath these two regional authorities, Prussia was divided into subdistricts (*Kreise*) of which there were two kinds, rural and urban. The rural subdistrict (*Landkreis*) was a unit of state administration, headed by the county director (*Landrat*), an official subordinate to the district president. The *Landkreis* was further subdivided into municipalities (*Gemeinden*), autonomous local authorities headed by a Bürgermeister. The urban *Kreis* (county borough) was known as a *Stadtkreis* or *kreisfreie Stadt*.

This hierarchical system of administration divided all the territory of the state into geographical units and established a tradition of unified decentralization which gave sovereignty to the central power but devolved administrative functions to intermediate (*Mittelstufe*) and lower (*Unterstufe*) levels of authority.

Bismarck's federal system was essentially superimposed on the existing collection of states – principally Prussia. Whilst the Reich had twenty-five federal states, Prussia constituted two-thirds of the area and three-quarters of the population. Although the preponderance of one state made the federal system unbalanced, Bismarck deliberately preserved the numerous petty governments. He took the view that if one wished to preserve the conservative–monarchical landed primacy, one could not get rid of the other state governments without the risk of democratizing and radicalizing the Reich. If one further weakened the standing and prestige of the non-Prussian governments, this would benefit not Prussia but the Reich, an altogether newer and more uncertain entity, rooted in ideas of popular sovereignty. The peculiar institution of Bismarckian federalism was the Bundesrat, with its dual role as an assembly of delegates of the different state governments and as the upper house of the legislature. Bismarck's Bundesrat laid down a heritage of representation of the states in Germany by means of their governments, not their populations. Both Reichstag and Bundesrat could veto each other's resolutions. The essence of the formal structure of federalism was legal unification, enshrined in the principle 'Reich law prevails over state law'. This was laid down by Article 2 of the 1871 Constitution and has now become – in the form of 'Federal law prevails over state law' – Article 31 of the Basic Law.

While the principle of the primacy of Reich law restricted the states' legislative competence, it left their other governmental functions intact. In a classic formulation, Arnold Brecht described German federalism as horizontal rather than vertical:[1]

The line of demarcation that in the United States separates governmental powers of the nation from those of the states has always been vertical. When power to deal with some subject matter was given to the federal government, it was as a rule full governmental power, including administration and adjudication as well as legislation. This was not so in Germany. The imperial constitution of 1871, while liberally granting the federal government the power to legislate in most fields of general significance, left administrative and judicial functions in almost all matters to the states . . . In other words, the original line of demarcation between powers was horizontal rather than vertical.

It suited Bismarck to leave administration in the hands of the states, because this was the easiest method of bypassing the Reichstag. Peter Merkl uses the convenient terms 'executive–legislative federalism' to refer to a horizontal division of powers and 'mutual independence' to refer to a vertical division of powers.[2] Even in the Imperial period from 1871 to 1918 the horizontal system was powerfully modified by the addition of elements of a vertical division. In a number of fields Reich administration expanded rapidly and established its own agencies with full administrative responsibility for particular tasks.

The federal states survived the collapse of Imperial Germany in 1918 because they represented policy differences with the Reich government. The overthrow of the dynasties strengthened rather than weakened particularism, because the *Länder* thereby obtained a democratic legitimation. The political parties in the *Länder* became pseudo-dynasties. The federal element in the political organization of Germany was, however, greatly diminished. The assembly of the *Land* governments – renamed the Reichsrat – lost its absolute power of veto, being given only a suspensory veto (*Einspruch*). Constitutionally it ceased to be the upper house of a bicameral legislature. Above all, through Erzberger's reforms of 1920 the *Länder* lost their financial autonomy. Instead, the Federation fixed the levels of and collected the major taxes throughout the Reich through the Reich Finance Ministry, which controlled tax assessment and collection throughout Germany. The Federation then distributed a portion of tax revenues to the *Länder*.

The Nazis suppressed but did not destroy regional and municipal autonomy. The Reich Reconstruction Law of 30 January 1934 transferred to the Reich all sovereign powers still held by the *Länder*. All Prussian ministries were merged with their Reich counterparts. Otherwise the state cabinets remained in existence but they became the agents and appointees of the Reich government. Both the state legislatures and elected local authorities were dissolved permanently. A Reich Governor (*Reichsstatthalter*) was appointed to supervise each state government, who in almost all cases was a *Gauleiter* (see below). All Prussian civil servants were transferred to Reich authorities. All the seventeen states existing in 1933 were retained as administrative units, except for Lübeck, which was deprived of its *Land* status in 1937, reputedly because it was the only *Land* in which Hitler had never been allowed to speak in the Weimar period. Quite distinct from the federal states, the Nazis established thirty-two party districts (*Gaue*), each headed by a *Gauleiter*. The Reichsrat was abolished. As Reich Interior Minister Frick grandiosely proclaimed in a broadcast on 31 January 1934: 'The dream of centuries is fulfilled: Germany is no longer a weak federation (*Bundesstaat*) but a strong national unitary state (*Einheitsstaat*).'

After 1945 the occupation powers resurrected familiar German institutions, both restoring old and creating new *Länder*. In all four zones German administration was built up from the bottom, but owing first to the French veto and then to the gulf between the Western powers and the Russians, the administrative structure remained incomplete, no national German authorities being established to crown the edifice. Hence the *Land* governments were unexpectedly strengthened, and became the focus and instruments of post-war developments.

Arnold Brecht's first recommendation for the territorial reorganization of Germany after the war embodied the conclusion of the constitutional reform commission in the Weimar period: 'Prussia ought to be eliminated as a single unit within Germany ... The mere existence of a state of her size within a democratically governed nation made it inevitable that differently composed cabinets in the Reich and in Prussia could pursue conflicting policies on almost an equal scale within the greater part of Germany.'[3] The outcome of the war in fact dismembered Prussia, so that its abolition by the Allied Control Council in February 1946 was a formality: one-third had been annexed by Russia and the new westwards-shifted Polish state; one-third was the Russian zone of occupation: the remainder was left in the British zone, and was divided in 1947 between the new *Länder* of North Rhine–Westphalia and Lower Saxony.

In 1945–7 the Western zones were divided into eleven *Länder*. With the exception of Bavaria, Hessen, Bremen and Hamburg, these were new and artificial entities, with neither cultural identity nor historical tradition. The influx of 14 million refugees from the east further eroded regional differences. Nevertheless, the *Länder* established in this period – like the 'licence' political parties and the resurrected civil service – have proved to have great powers of endurance.

The United States believed in Germany's 'democratic salvation through federalism'.[4] Allied security policy – above all as represented at the time by the French – sought to prevent the emergence of a strong central government. Accordingly the Frankfurt Documents specified that the new constitution to be drafted for West Germany should be a 'democratic constitution ... for a governmental form of a federal type which ... protects the rights of the participating *Länder* and creates an appropriate central authority'. The device of federalism by administrative decentralization was to function as a support for the dispersal of power.

These external influences coincided with and reinforced the views of the majority of members of the Parliamentary Council, which enacted the Basic Law. The Nazis' suppression of federalism produced a reaction in its favour. The *Land* bureaucracies had been the historical pillar of German federalism. The Parliamentary Council was made up of *Land* politicians and civil servants, who were not going to legislate themselves out of existence or forgo their own instrument of power in the form of a federalistic Bundesrat. Bavaria had retained its political and cultural identity and its representatives had consistently pressed for greater autonomy from the central government a pressure increased by the licensing of the Bavarian Party in 1948. Catholic social and political teaching was influential in the CDU/CSU and this favoured a decentralized state. The countervailing pressure came from the SPD, who wanted a solution 'as centralistic as possible, as federalistic as necessary'. However, this general principle gave no specific guidance, where the line was to be drawn. The SPD had its own strong regional bases in the north and wanted these to retain an influential role, regardless of the composition of the federal government. On the federal question, Allied and German wishes were largely identical. As Carlo Schmid observes: 'Apart from a few provisions in no way of central importance, the Basic Law would not have turned out very differently than was the case, even if the Allies had been less forthcoming with suggestions.'[5]

Besides the *Länder*, the basic institutions of the Federal Republic were also in place before 1949, in the form of the inter-zonal bodies established in 1947–8. The Economic Council (*Wirtschaftsrat*) became the Bundestag; the Executive Council (*Verwaltungsrat*) became the Federal Government; and the *Länder* Council (*Länderrat*) became the Bundesrat. In 1949, as in 1871, a new federal entity was superimposed upon an existing set of states and institutions.

THE *LÄNDER*

Except for the city-states, Thuringia, Saxony and Bavaria, all the *Länder* are based on new administrative areas created in 1945–7. Population is concentrated particularly in North Rhine–Westphalia, with 16.7 million (21.4 per cent) out of the total population of 61.1 million. Only three cities have more than a million inhabitants, Hamburg (1.8 m), Munich (1.3 m) and West Berlin (3.3 m). West Berlin was not, as has been stated, a constituent *Land* of West Germany.

Until the late 1950s the post-war recovery was based on the traditional heavy industries and industrial regions and centres of pre-war Germany, principally the Rhine–Ruhr. The advent of cheaper hydro-carbon fuels, the range of associated technological advances in the chemical and electronic industries, together with the labour shortages which existed in many of the industrial regions, brought about a diffusion of industrial growth throughout the country, but especially in the south. The 1960s saw an overall drift of people away from the industrial heartlands of North Rhine–Westphalia to the southern *Länder*, above all Baden–Württemberg and more recently Bavaria. In recent years this trend has augmented in intensity. This has produced an economic polarization between north and south, which has put the formal apparatus of federalism under increasing strain, as will the new division between West and East.

The *Länder* differ markedly in size, population and resources. The Basic Law provided an elaborate procedure for the reorganization of *Länder* (Article 29) and a simplified procedure for the amalgamation of the three small contiguous *Länder* in the south-west – Baden, Württemberg–Baden and Württemberg–Hohenzollern (Article 118). After an arduous and protracted campaign, the southwestern states were united to form Baden–Württemberg in 1952. In 1957 the Saarland, which had been under French administration, returned to West Germany to form the tenth *Land*. There have been no subsequent changes, notwithstanding a multitude of proposals for recasting the number of *Länder* and their boundaries.

Each *Land* has a constitution which must conform to the principles of the Basic Law (Article 28(1)). Constitutionally and organizationally a distinction exists between the area-states (*Flächenstaaten*) and city states (*Stadtstaaten*). In the area-states the *Land* government has below it separate local and – in the case of the larger states – district authorities. In the city states the *Land* government is also largely responsible for local government. The constitution of Bremen – the smallest of the *Länder* – is esoteric. There is a *Landtag* which deals with the affairs of the *Land*. The *Land* comprises the city of Bremerhaven and the city of Bremen. Bremerhaven has its own constitution. The *Land* constitution expressly provides that the city of Bremen has the right to devise a constitution for itself, but this has not been done. Instead, the *Landtag* doubles up as the city council. The assembly when sitting as an institution of the *Land* is called 'Landtag'. When sitting as Bremen city council it is called 'Stadtbürgerschaft'.

THE POWERS OF THE FEDERATION AND THE *LÄNDER*

Arnold Brecht points out: 'Federalism is based upon state rights. Delegations of powers that can be withdrawn at any time at the discretion of the delegating authority, or the use of which can be directed by the delegate authority in every detail, does not establish federalism.'[6] The *Länder* undoubtedly enjoy a constitutionally protected position – as the eternity guarantee of Article

79(3) testifies. The Basic Law also establishes a constitutional presumption of *Land* competence. This is contained in Articles 30, 70(1) and 83:

Article 30	The exercise of state powers and the fulfilment of state tasks is the concern of the *Länder*, in so far as the Basic Law does not otherwise prescribe or permit.
Article 70(1)	The *Länder* shall have the right to legislate, in so far as this Basic Law does not confer legislative power on the Federation.
Article 83	The *Länder* shall execute federal law autonomously, in so far as this Basic Law does not otherwise prescribe or permit.

As the recurring formula 'in so far as this Basic Law does not otherwise prescribe or permit' suggests, *Land* competence proves the exception, rather than the rule. Nevertheless, the states retain substantial powers.

The hallmark of vertical federalism is that states have in certain fields independent powers of legislation, coordinate with those of the national parliament. This type of federalism has been sparingly represented in Germany since 1871. There is a long tradition of 'hollowing out' the states' legislative prerogatives. A stable definition of the irreducible minimum of *Land* competences was achieved by §42 of the Third Emergency Tax Decree of 14 February 1924, which contained a pledge that the administrative functions of the police, education and measures of public assistance would be left with the *Länder* and local authorities. Although the Basic Law made extensive provision for the possibility of *Land* legislation by assigning most of the substantial areas of legislation to the 'concurrent sphere' where both Federation and *Landtage* can pass laws, the Federation has – as described in chapter 5 – ousted *Land* legislation in the whole concurrent sphere, leaving the *Länder* supremacy only in the sphere of education, which forms 'the cornerstone of their autonomy'.[7]

The development of what Hesse calls 'the unitary federal state' has not occurred in opposition to the constitution but results from the fact that the Basic Law has itself in the delimitation of legislative competences given the Federation a dominating role.[8] Moreover, the Parliamentary Council specifically contemplated this process by extending the range of consent laws. As Golay explains: 'By additions to the list of *Zustimmungsgesetze*, the federalists were reconciled to grants of powers to the Federation desired by the centralists.'[9] The growth of a more homogeneous society, itself accelerated by the post-war shifts of population, has diminished both the need and justification for regional variations in legislation. There exists in consequence a high degree of federal legislative uniformity. In German federalism it is the function of the national government to make law.

The term 'executive–legislative federalism' only superficially fits the West German system, however, as the *Länder* through the Bundesrat have a substantial role in the federal legislative process, whilst the Federation plays a considerable role in administration.

FEDERAL — *LAND* ADMINISTRATION

It is not the function of the *Länder* to generate and administer distinctive policies through autonomous legal and executive action at regional level. Whilst it is the administrative compe-tence of the *Länder* which gives German federalism its strength, the framework of *Land* administration is closely defined.

In general the Federal government works without its own administrative sub-structure and employs the administrative apparatus of the *Länder* and local authorities. Only the Foreign Office, Defence Ministry and Labour Ministry have their own agencies. In consequence of the division of executive responsibi-lities between the Federal government, *Länder* and local author-ities, the bulk of civil servants are *Land* and local officials, 11 per cent being employed by the Federation, 54 per cent by the *Länder* and 35 per cent by the municipalities.

The threefold horizontal division of German administration broadly corresponds to a functional division. From the point of view of personnel, in the sectors of the central direction of policy, foreign affairs, defence, finance and tax administra-tion, the centre of gravity lies with the Federation; in the sectors of law and order, the administration of justice, and education, responsibility lies with the *Länder*; the municipalities have the predominant role in local government, social and welfare ser-vices, transport and public utilities.

In 1987 some 2,854,066 people were employed in the service of the Federation (313,066) *Länder* (1,549,000) and local authorities (992,000). Of these roughly one-third were in the governmental administration (*Ordnungsverwaltung*, i.e. administration, police, judiciary), and the remaining two-thirds employed in the services administration (*Leistungsverwaltung*, i.e. education, transport, social and health services).

DELEGATED AND AUTONOMOUS ADMINISTRATION

In the execution of laws there is a fundamental distinction between 'delegated administration' (*Auftragsverwaltung*) and 'autonomous administration' (*Verwaltung als eigene Angelegenheit*). This distinction – like much else – has its origins in the practice of Prussian administration.

Elected local authorities were established in Prussia in the nineteenth century. They could not be incorporated in the existing direct state administration because their elected status set them apart from it. They therefore came to constitute institutions of mediate state administration (*Selbstverwaltung*). The power of supervision, control and direction rested in the direct state administration. However, the mode of control exercised by the direct state administration over the indirect state administration differed in kind and degree from the control exercised by a superior authority of direct state administration over an inferior. In the sphere of direct state administration the control exercised by the superior over the inferior body was concerned with the ends of administration: it was a 'political control' (*Zweckmässigkeitskontrolle*). The superior authority can issue directives (*Weisungen*) and administrative regulations (*Verwaltungsvorschriften*) to the inferior authority. In supervising a local authority an organ of direct state administration was concerned only with the form of administration: it was a 'legal control' (*Rechtsmässigkeitskontrolle*). As long as the local authority did not go wrong in law, it was immune from direction from above. In particular it determined who was to administer a law and the administrative procedure to be adopted.

Local authorities were not all-purpose but had statutorily prescribed responsibilities. For certain purposes of direct state administration it was convenient to use local authorities, rather than establish field offices at local level and so multiply administrative bodies. Hence the local authorities were for certain tasks made agents of the direct state administration and effectively incorporated into the hierarchy of the direct state administration. Thus arose the characteristic 'double role' of local authorities. For example, in the case of the urban subdistrict, in the exercise of the police function the *Stadtkreis* (county borough) became a unit of state administration and in performing this task the Oberbürgermeister was the agent of the state acting under direction from his administrative superior. In performing the task which had been allotted to local government, however, he remained the chief executive of the autonomous town council, subject only to legal control. Hence arose the distinction between 'delegated administration' and 'autonomous administration'. Where a body with its own constitution executes a law subject only to legal control, it is said to administer the law autonomously. Where such a body executes a law subject to political control, it is said to execute the law as the agent of the supervising authority, which has delegated the task.

Before 1933 delegated administration from *Land* government to local authority was common. As mentioned, the Oberbürgermeister in the *Stadtkreis*, the Bürgermeister in the municipality had control of the police but in this function they were the agents of the *Land* government acting under its orders. Delegated administration from Reich government to *Land* government was, however, rare. The principal factor inhibiting the growth of delegated administration at state level after 1918 was the inability of the Reich government effectively to supervise state government. The Oberbürgermeister and Bürgermeister were *Land* officials, who could be dismissed if they failed to obey orders when carrying out delegated administration. No such controls or power existed when the Reich government delegated powers to a state government. If the *Land* minister refused to exercise his powers in conformity with federal directives, all the federal minister could do was to write letters and resort to the Court for Constitutional Conflicts. The disputes between the Reich and Thuringian Ministers of the Interior over Frick's attempts to Nazify the state police in Thuringia in 1930 illustrated the impotence of the Reich minister in such circumstances.[10] Hence the Reich government was faced with the choice of establishing a new set of Reich administrative authorities for each fresh function it assumed, or entrusting the implementation of legislation to *Land* governments, which might be politically hostile and over which the Reich had in law and in practice very limited powers of direction and control.

The Nazis' installation of Reich governors for each *Land* with summary powers over state ministers and the establishment of a one-party state enabled the Reich to dominate the *Land* and local authorities. Thereafter extensive use was made of the device of delegated administration of Reich legislation to state ministries, and this largely removed the problems of duplication of authority and divergence of administrative practice which had been the cause of so much political and administrative friction in the Weimar period.

The Basic Law consciously revived federalism in reaction against the despotic centralism of the Nazi period. It also reverted to pre-1933 patterns, by making autonomous *Land* administration of Federal legislation the rule, with delegated *Land* administration only permitted in certain enumerated cases by way of exception.

Federal execution is the only mode provided for the foreign service, the Post Office, the armed forces (*Budeswehr*), the Federal Railways, (*Bundesbahn*) and federal fiscal administration (Article 87). The Basic Law assumes in cases of federal execution a three-tier administrative structure consisting of federal, regional (*Mittelstufe*) and local (*Unterstufe*) levels. However, the Federation only exceptionally has field units at regional and local level. These are normally provided by *Land* ministries, which do not thereby lose their status as *Land* institutions. In certain fields, Federal administration is prescribed, but the Federation may delegate the tasks to the *Länder* as its agent. These fields are: atomic energy (Article 87c); inland waterways (Article 89(2)); civil defence (Article 87b(2)); and the collection of certain federal taxes (Article 108(4)). Delegated *Land* administration is prescribed in the case of federal autobahns (Article 90(2)). Whenever Federal law confers subsidies and the law is administered by the *Länder*, if the Federation provides 50 per cent or more of the cost of the programme, the *Länder* implement the law as agents (Article 104a(3)).

In all other cases the norm of autonomous *Land* administration of Federal law prevails, except in so far as Federal legislation otherwise prescribes. Such a law will prescribe how the law is to be implemented by providing for the regulation of administrative procedures, and the establishment of administrative agencies. This will have the effect of switching administration from the autonomous to the delegated sphere. Such legislation requires the consent of the Bundesrat (Article 84(1)). In practice, the Bundesrat has freely agreed to the enactment of such laws, with the result that the constitutional norm of autonomous administration has become in practice the exception. Delegated administration has ousted autonomous administration, just as Federal legislation has ousted *Land* legislation.

There are several, connected reasons for this process. The Western occupation powers, who particularly insisted on the inclusion of Article 72(2), hoped that it would provide a substantial limitation on the ability of the Bundestag to arrogate to itself legislation lying in the concurrent sphere shared with the *Landtage*. The host of urgent problems confronting West Germany in 1949 required uniform, national solutions, not separate, regional ones. The *Länder* could not be left to go their own way, even if they had had the capacity to formulate and implement individual policies. The transformed party system also favoured the centralization of legislation. Article 72(2) as drafted contained a 'needs' formula which, as interpreted by the Federal Constitutional Court, was held not to raise justiciable criteria and so did not act as a restriction on Federal legislation. Whether or not a need for Federal regulation exists, the Court stated, 'is a question which lies in the reasonable discretion of the Federal legislator, which in its nature is not justiciable and is therefore in principle not open to review by the Federal Constitutional Court'.[11] (See p. 130.)

Thus the volume and significance of Federal legislation as compared with legislation by the *Landtage* greatly exceeded what was contemplated in the ground plan of the Basic Law. In consequence, the Federation has also been required to play a correspondingly larger role in the administrative process. The *Länder* have had little incentive to resist this process. Where the *Länder* administer a programme autonomously, they bear the costs; when they act as agents of the Federation, the Federation pays for the programme (Article 104a(2)). The transfer of programmes from autononous to delegated administration in turn produces greater centralization of finances. The federation has only limited formal powers of supervision, whichever mode of administration is employed, and these have never been tested in practice (Article 84(3)–(5); Article 85(3)–(4)). The *Länder* do not compromise their independent position by yielding up administrative powers. The substitution of delegated for autonomous administration switches a law from the category of simple to consent legislation and so expands the power of the Bundesrat. *Land* governments thus receive a compensation for the erosion both of their own powers and those of the *Landtage*. In the development of the federal system three changes have been dependent on each other: the growth of federal law at the expense of *Land* law in the concurrent sphere; the growth of delegated administration at the expense of autonomous administration; and the increase of consent laws at the expense of simple laws. The *Land* ministries are left with two sets of functions: those in which they exercise their autonomous role; and those which devolve upon them in their derivative role as regional and local agencies of the Federal government. Their administrative experience is fed back into the legislative process via the Bundesrat.

THE FINANCIAL SYSTEM OF FEDERALISM

Max Weber recognized that the key element of every federal government was not the method of decision-making or division of functions but the question of federal finances: 'The financial relationships are what most decisively determine the real structure in a federal government.'[12]

It is fundamental to the principle of *Land* autonomy that the greater part of the financial costs of services are met out of the general allocation of funds to the *Länder* rather than by specifically appropriated grants from the centre. An entire section of the Basic Law is devoted to the financial system of federalism. These provisions have been much amended and revised, together with the legislation which implements them. The system adopted by the Bonn Republic represents a compromise between the two previous methods of public finance. In Imperial Germany the bulk of taxes were paid to the states, which paid 'matriculatory contributions' to the Reich. In the Weimar Republic all taxes were collected by the Reich, which made grants-in-aid to the *Länder*. While the *Länder* were under close financial control by the Reich, the local authorities had remarkable financial autonomy, and in the second half of the 1920s indulged in compulsive overspending which ran directly contrary to the deflationary policy of the Reich government. The Basic Law seeks to reconcile the budgetary and fiscal autonomy of the *Länder* and local authorities with sound finance and an equal level of resources and social provision throughout Germany.

These goals are achieved, first, by dividing up tax revenues between the different levels of government according to a fixed formula (vertical financial equalization); secondly, by redistributing the amounts accruing to the Federation and *Länder*, in order to equalize the relative resources of the *Länder* (horizontal financial equalization). The constitutional and statutory basis of vertical financial equalization rests in Article 106 and the Apportionment Law of 25 February 1971; horizontal equalization is based upon Article 107 and the Finance Equalization Law of 28 August 1969, as amended in 1987.

Vertical financial equalization is the primary distribution of taxes. Central to this process is the distinction between community and undivided taxes. Community taxes (*Gemeinschaftssteuern*, Article 106(3)) are taxes which are shared between different levels of government. Undivided taxes flow exclusively to one tier of government only. The community taxes comprehend the principal taxes in revenue terms: income tax, corporation tax and value added tax (VAT). These provide also 70 per cent of gross tax yields. The remaining taxes are undivided.

In regard to the community taxes the Federation has concurrent legislative power (Article 105(2)). From 1 January 1980 the Federation and *Länder* each receive 42.5 per cent of the yield of income tax, the balance (15 per cent) going to the local authorities. Corporation tax is divided equally between the Federation and *Länder*. According to the local yield principle, income and corporation tax yields accrue to the *Land* where the taxable person resides, as that term is understood in law, although in the case of corporation tax two or more *Länder* may share the tax paid by a company on its profits. Value added tax yields are the subject of a two-way split determined by consent law: from 1987 65 per cent goes to the Federation and 35 per cent to the *Länder*. From the federal share of VAT 1.4 per cent is deducted and paid to the EEC.

Of the undivided taxes, customs duties go to the Federation; capital taxes (wealth and inheritance taxes) accrue to the *Länder*; the business tax (*Gewerbesteuer*) and local taxes on consumption are receipts of the local authorities. The local authorities in turn give 20 per cent of their income from business tax to the Federation and a further 20 per cent to the *Länder*, as quid pro quo for the local authorities' share of income tax.

The approximation of the financial resources of the *Länder* takes place horizontally, i.e. between the *Länder*, in three stages.

1 The *Länder* share of VAT is distributed among the *Länder* not according to the 'local yield principle' but according to the size of population. The local yield principle applies to other taxes and means (roughly speaking) that tax is paid to the *Land* or local authority in which a taxpayer resides. If the taxpayer is the headquarters of a large company, this circumstance will give a revenue boost to the *Land* or local authority which may be disproportionate to the population of the unit in question. Additionally, up to one-quarter of the *Länder* share of VAT is given directly to the 'financially weaker' *Länder*, i.e. a *Land* whose tax income falls below a defined average.

2 By equalization payments. These are worked out in a manner prescribed by the finance Equalization Law. The *Länder* share of corporation and income tax is distributed according to the local yield principle. A 'tax quota' is then established for each *Land*. This is the tax yield per head of population. Next the 'equalization quota' is ascertained. This is the tax yield required to enable the *Land* to provide a level of public services which conforms with the national average. If a *Land*'s tax quota exceeds it equalization quota, it is classified as 'financially stronger' and is obliged to make equalization payments. If a *Land*'s tax quota is less than its equalization quota, it is classified as 'financially weaker' and is entitled to receive equalization payments.

Since 1983 three *Länder* have contributed to the equalization process (Baden–Württemberg, Hamburg and Hessen), while six *Länder* have received these subventions (Bavaria, Lower Saxony, Rhineland–Palatinate, Bremen, Schleswig–Holstein and Saarland). North Rhine–Westphalia – by far the largest of the *Länder* – has neither received nor made payments. Bavaria is teetering on the brink of moving from recipient to contributor status. The great bulk of equalization funds are provided by Baden–Württemberg (70 per cent), while the highest per capita burden falls on Hamburg.

3 In addition, financially weaker *Länder* receive grants-in-aid from the Federation. From 1974 federal grants were fixed annually at 1.5 per cent of VAT. As a result of the Federal Equalization Law, the federal contribution was set at a maximum of DM 1.775 billion a year. All the poorer *Länder* except

Bremen have benefited from these supplementary payments. The reason for the exclusion of Bremen is that the Basic Law in general does not allow direct financial links between the Federation and local authorities. Because it is a city-state, the *Land* government also functions as a local authority and this raises a constitutional obstacle to the direct receipt of federal funds.

The effect of these measures in equalizing the resources of *Länder* may be gauged by the figures given in table 6.1.

Table 6.1 Financial equalization, 1984

	Land	Tax quota (average=100)	
	Before equalization	After equalization	After federal grants
Baden–Württemberg	110.6	104.8	
Bremen	82.4	95.0	
Saarland	83.5	95.0	100.5

The business tax forms the only significant element in the income of local authorities which they are able to vary. All non-agricultural undertakings which carry on a trade are assessed for business tax on their profits and capital value. The rate is set by the local authority. There is an element of chance, however, in the location of business undertakings in particular council areas. Some small local authorities in southern Germany have an income from business tax out of all proportion to their spending requirements because some large international company has chosen to locate its headquarters in their area. The low level of tax which results from the high yield encourages further business activity. By contrast local authorities in Saarland and North Rhine–Westphalia have found that their income from business tax has sharply declined, because of the demise of the older industries in their areas. This restructuring has in turn increased their expenditure on social services and pushed up rates of tax, with the consequence of deterring new investment. As stated earlier, the Federation and *Länder* are each entitled to some 15 per cent of the yield of business tax.

Part of the tax revenues also go to the churches. Members of churches which are public corporations are obliged to pay church tax. This is a supplement to income tax, which is levied and collected by tax offices and paid over to the churches.

West Berlin stood outside the general system of Federal–*Land* finance. The matter is regulated by the law of 1952 on the financial position of Berlin in relation to the Federation. West Berlin enjoyed both extensive exemptions and reliefs from ordinary taxation and direct subsidies from the Federation. These have grown from 36 per cent of the city's budget in 1952 to 52 per cent (DM 11.6 billion). In 1987 Federal subsidies totalled DM 11.950 billion, plus indirect help amounting to DM 940 million.

Taxes which accrue solely to the Federation are assessed and collected by Federal authorities (Article 87 of the Basic Law). All other taxes are administered by the *Länder*, but in the case of the community taxes – which are shared by Federation and *Länder* – the *Länder* act as agents of the Federation. Hence, while there is no central finance ministry along the lines of Erzberger's model, the main tax authorities are effectively joint Federal–*Land* agencies. The *Länder* in turn delegate the collection of local taxes to the local authorities (see table 6.2).

Table 6.2 Distribution of tax revenues (%)

Tax	Federation	Länder	Local authorities
Income	42.5	42.5	15.0
Corporation	50.0	50.0	
VAT	65.0	35.0	
Business	15.0	15.0	60.0
Customs and excise (except beer)	100.0		
Beer		100.0	
Inheritance and gift		100.0	
Local			100.0

The financial system of German federalism has to meet a number of criteria. There must be some overall plan; there must be sufficient flexibility for the *Länder* and local authorities to have a genuine measure of autonomy; the rules must be drawn up by the Federation and *Länder* together; the rules must be capable of adapting to changing circumstances. The system as a whole is designed to work in an apolitical manner; to limit the role of political bargaining and governmental discretion; to take the allocation of revenues outside the range of ordinary political debate; to run as far as possible on automatic pilot. By this means the principle of the financial autonomy of the *Länder* and local authorities can be preserved, while ensuring a uniform level of social provision throughout Germany. The financial arrangements of federalism afford another example of the attempt to 'unburden' the political system through institutional arrangements.

The truth is that the allocation of finance is too intensely political to be removed from politics and that there cannot be apolitical solutions to political problems. However, the political disputes which the system engenders cross party divisions. The Federal Constitutional Court subjected the Financial Equalization Law to an extensive review in 1986. The essential dilemma running through the judgement is: how far can political questions be depoliticized by reliance upon legal means of resolving disputes. The Court observed:

These limitations and restrictions exclude neither political negotiations between all those concerned nor the seeking of compromise and mutual understanding; on the contrary both lie within the meaning of the federal principle. The Federation may in these negotiations act as an 'honest broker'. In the last resort, however, the Federal legislator is subject to the duty imposed by the constitution, to frame the legal settlement in a way that satisfies the normative requirements of the Basic Law. It cannot restrict itself to the authentication of political decisions of a majority of the *Länder* without regard to their content . . . the constitution imposes certain substantive legal restrictions on political compromise.[13]

This passage underlines the extent to which government takes place in a legal framework which is only partly at the disposition of government itself. The influence of the *Länder* in the financial equalization process takes three forms: (i) through the Bundesrat their consent is required to legislation implementing the system; (ii) through the national political parties they can form decisions at federal level; (iii) in the last resort they can take the path to the Federal Constitutional Court in Karlsruhe. While the system guarantees them sources of finance in the interests of *Land* autonomy, it also fixes the amount of their resources in the interests of social solidarity. The result is a broadly uniform level of taxation throughout Germany, and a correspondingly high degree of centralization of finances, notwithstanding the federal structure. At the centre of the web stands the Federal government, which, while it does not make the rules, must operate them. It fixes the rate of the community taxes, which produce the bulk of revenue. It also has significant discretionary powers. By making the execution of Federal laws delegated rather than autonomous, the Federation assumes responsibility for the costs of implementation.

Proposals for reforming the system seek a more rational distribution of resources. The overall plan of finances can, however, only be strengthened at the expense of regional and local autonomy. At present, with the shift of economic strength from north to south, the northern *Länder* and local authorities find their resources increasingly inadequate for their needs, while an undue share of equalization payments falls on Baden–Württemberg. When Bavaria moves from recipient to contributor status, and North Rhine–Westphalia moves from a neutral to a recipient status, these imbalances, and the complaints of the southern *Länder*, will be reinforced. Hamburg also complains that its share of equalization payments is greater per capita than that of Baden–Württemberg.

A further source of current difficulties is the Federal government's tax reform programme. The two main thrusts of the reform are to bring about a permanent reduction in the tax burden, and to make lasting improvements. The sharp reductions in the yield of income and corporation taxes, both implemented and projected, will correspondingly diminish the resources of both *Länder* and local authorities, whose primary source of revenue is a fixed share of the amount raised by these taxes. This will in turn reduce the freedom of *Länder* and local authorities to pursue policies of their own.

There is a German proverb: 'In money matters good-feeling ceases.' Disputes over Federal financing cross party divisions. The equalization arrangements line up contributors against recipients without regard to party allegiance; the Federal government's tax reform programme affects the interests of the *Länder* collectively. In matters affecting the financial system of the Federation, the Bundesrat does not make decisions along strictly party political lines.

The accession of the poorer East German *Länder* to the Federation has increased existing strains, and by the end of the transition period a substantial revision of the financial system will be unavoidable (see p. 12).

ADMINSTRATIVE STRUCTURE WITHIN THE *LÄNDER*

While there is a significant degree of devolution of functions from Federal to *Land* government, government within the *Länder* is relatively centralized. For example, in North Rhine–Westphalia the appointment of teachers throughout the whole *Land* is decided by one central office in Dusseldorf.

The area-states each have a Cabinet headed by a Minister-President and consisting of ministers supported by State Secretaries. The three city-states of Hamburg, Bremen and West Berlin have, instead, a Senate and senators, led in Hamburg and Berlin by a Chief Bürgermeister, in Bremen by a Senate President. Their civil service heads of departments are known as State Councillors.

All *Länder* have ministries of the Interior, Finance, Economy, Transport, Labour and Social Security, and Education. The key minister is the Minister of the Interior, who in the Prussian tradition is head of the general internal administration, has command of the police and is responsible for all matters for which no specific ministry is named. *Land* ministries also have a number of autonomous operational units attached to them. In the city-states the *Land* government doubles as the major local authority, but elsewhere there are a number of political and administrative units below *Land* level.

The province and the office of provincial governor have been abolished. The government district has been retained as a unit of decentralized administration in the six larger *Länder* (North Rhine–Westphalia, Baden–Württemberg, Lower Saxony, Hessen, Bavaria and Rhineland–Palatinate). The District President is a senior 'political' official appointed by the Minister-President and under the control of the Minister of the Interior. He serves as the agent of the *Land* government in matters delegated to him and is the principal executive institution with the *Land*, bringing the threads of government in a district under a single roof. The District President controls the police in his area. He supervises for legality the activities of local authorities and public undertakings. The schools inspectorate and audit office report to him. His office administers *Land* funds for education, roads and housing, whether directly expended or paid to local authorities. It also has an extensive administrative law function, giving legal advice to local authorities and acting as an appellate tribunal. It supervises industry and commerce, with power to issue warnings and impose fines for breaches of law, appeal from which lies in the ordinary courts. In 1989 six *Länder* were divided into a total of twenty-six government districts in West Germany.

The *Kreis* as a subdivision of the *Land* has been retained in all the area-states, with its two forms of the rural county (*Landkreis*) and county borough (*Stadtkreis*). *Stadtkreise* are now generally towns with a population of at least 80,000. In 1989 there were 91 *Stadtkreise*, and 237 *Landkreise*.

The rural counties are further subdivided into 8,503 municipalities (*Gemeinden*). The principal difference between the *Landkreis* and the municipality is that the municipality has universality of competence, whereas the *Landkreis* only has those functions given to it by law. In general the *Landkreis* performs those tasks which are either beyond the financial capacity of the municipality, or cannot be properly performed in a local framework. In its capacity as an agent of state administration the *Landkreis* is, for example, the housing and highways authority. As an autonomous corporation the *Landkreis* administers savings banks, hospitals, secondary education, vocational training, public assistance, and the provision of gas, water and electricity. The organization of *Landkreis* government varies from *Land* to *Land*, but always contains three elements: an elected council, an executive committee and the executive officer, variously named *Landrat*, *Kreisrat* or *Oberkreisdirektor*. In Saarland and Rhineland–Palatinate he has remained a state official but in all other *Länder* he is now a local official.

The *Landkreis* finances itself by a levy on the tax receipts of municipalities in its area. The *Stadtkreis* is not divided into municipalities and so receives all the revenue which would normally be due to them. Certain tasks of the *Kreis* government are beyond the capacity of all but the largest cities. The commonest solution is for *Kreise* jointly to form public undertakings for specific services, e.g. the supply of gas, electricity or water. Alternatively, the *Land* government can establish multipurpose territorial corporations at the intermediate level between *Land* and *Kreis* and vest the administration of larger projects in them, thereby extending the principle of indirect state administration.

The function of municipalities (*Gemeinden*) can likewise be classified as 'delegated' and 'autonomous'. They are multipurpose authorities, responsible for everything not assigned to other bodies. As in the case of the *Kreis*, single tasks can be delegated to joint authorities. The Bürgermeister is as a rule appointed for a fixed term by the council and his role varies according to the constitution of the municipality.

In the past twenty years there has been a sharp reduction in the number of units of local government. Whereas in 1967 some 24,300 municipalities existed, by 1989 this number had fallen to 8,503. A large number of small municipalities have combined to form administrative unions (*Gemeindeverbände*), which assume tasks of the member authorities. In 1987, 6,013 municipalities belonged to 1,037 administrative unions. In addition to this kind of association, there are some 3,500 administrative associations with a specialized function (*Zweckverbände*), e.g. water supply, secondary education.

THE ORGANIZATION OF THE COURTS

Most courts are *Land* institutions. The cornerstone of a uniform system of courts was laid down by the Judicature Act of 1877 (*Gerichtsverfassungsgesetz*), which came into force on 1 January 1879 and was re-enacted most recently in 1976. It originally established a hierarchy of ordinary (*ordentlich*) courts on four levels:

High Court	(*Reichsgericht*)
Courts of Appeal	(*Oberlandesgericht*, OLG)
District Courts	(*Landgericht*, LG)
Local Courts	(*Amtsgericht*, AG)

The sole federal court was the High Court: all other ordinary courts were *Land* courts. All courts were collegiate except the Local Court, where a single judge presided. Local Courts were grouped under a District Court, and District Courts under a Court of Appeal. Although there were four levels of court, a case could at most be taken through three levels. A first appeal on facts or law (*Berufung*) could be followed by a final appeal on law only (*Revision*). Thus a case originating in a Local Court could go to the District Court on first appeal, and Court of Appeal on final appeal, whereas a case originating in the District Court could go to the Court of Appeal on first appeal and to the High Court on final appeal.

The Emminger Decree of 4 January 1924 made important changes in the jurisdiction and composition of criminal courts and in general reduced the size of panels of judges. The Consolidation Law of 1950 substantially re-enacted the Judicature Act in the new West German state, putting in place of the old *Reichsgericht* in Leipzig a *Bundesgerichtshof* (Federal High Court) – in Karlsruhe. The establishment of the Federal Constitutional Court in 1951 and a European Court of Justice in 1957 have expanded the possibilities of appeal provided under the Judicature Act. The District Court has been increasingly relieved of first-instance jurisdiction, so that the Local Court is becoming a general court of first instance.

The Court of Appeal President, in particular, has important administrative responsibilities. Legal examination offices are attached to Courts of Appeal and applications to be admitted to law examinations and to be admitted to the probationary service as a *Referendar* and *Assessor* are submitted to the Court of Appeal President, from those decisions there is an appeal to the *Land* Minister of Justice and thereafter to the Administrative Courts.

The ordinary courts deal with civil and criminal matters. Besides them have grown up specialist sets of courts modelled on the same hierarchy: Administrative Courts, Tax Courts, Labour Courts and Social Insurance Courts. In each case there is a Federal court of last resort. There has thus been a multiplication of Federal courts: the Federal High Court (Karlsruhe), Federal Administrative Court (Berlin), Federal Tax Court (Munich), Federal Social Insurance Court (Kassel), Federal Labour Court (Kassel) and Federal Constitutional Court (Karlsruhe). The German court system thus combines geographical with functional specialization.

While principally staffed by professional judges, who enter the judiciary as a career service, the commercial courts, Labour Courts and Social Insurance Courts also make extensive use of lay judges who have expertise in the area of the court's competence. The OLG for Berlin bears its historic name, the *Kammergericht*. This court system is now being extended to East Germany.

FEDERAL–LAND RELATIONS

The federal system leaves the state governments with considerable political influence, both at the federal level and within their own governmental areas. The financial system gives them and local authorities their own resources to pursue their own policies. While the rules are laid down in Federal legislation, changes require the consent of the Bundesrat, and the Constitutional Court always stands in the background.

The states have their own central banks, linked with the Bundesbank. Each *Land* also has its own network of local savings banks. The areas of policy which the states determine include education, policing, land use and most transport. Since the 1970s several state governments have developed their own industrial policies. Bavaria and Baden–Württemberg have in particular used their powers to encourage by tax concessions and improvements in infra-structure the growth of new industries in their regions, which has added to the momentum of the north–south transfer of resources.

The powers held and exercised by the Bundesrat make the outcome of *Land* elections important to Federal policy, because they both affect control of the Bundesrat and reflect and influence the national standing of political parties. Each state holds an election every four years, or five years in the case of North Rhine–Westphalia. The national profile of political parties is the major determinant of voting behaviour in *Land* elections. The decline in standing of the CDU/CSU – FDP government contributed to a series of reversals for the CDU and FDP in *Land* elections in 1987–8. Events in the *Länder* will also influence national politics. The CDU's poor performance in the North Rhine–Westphalia *Landtag* election of 1966 precipitated Chancellor Erhard's loss of office. A scandal in the Schleswig–Holstein CDU in 1988, which led to the Minister-President's suicide, both helped the SPD to an absolute majority for the first time in that state, while it also affected adversely the national standing of the CDU, and negated the chances of the Federal government's gaining an absolute majority in the Bundesrat.

Federal and *Land* politics are thus highly interdependent. In consequence, the German federal system has been called 'unitary' or 'cooperative'. As the Report of the Troeger Commission of 1967 put it:

Cooperative federalism is an active principle of the state: it achieves the compromise between a clear delimitation of functions, without which the organization of a federal state would be inconceivable, and the concentration of resources at federal level, which guarantees the most effective utilization of public resources. The organization of our federal state along these lines requires an improvement in the forms of cooperation hitherto employed by means of the creation of new institutions at federal level. Additionally, both parties must be ready, for the sake of the idea, to make use of the newly opened possibilities, whenever the public interest requires it.[14]

In similar vein the Federal Constitutional Court has espoused Smend's doctrine of 'federal comity' (*Bundestreue*) and required that each unit of the Federation should take account not only of its own interests but of the well-being of the whole in formulating and implementing policies.

The most important single means of coordinating the federal system is provided by the political parties. The CDU, SPD and FDP are organized on a local and *Land* basis, but the party units belong to national organizations. The CSU is simultaneously a Bavarian and a national political party. The performance of parties in *Land* and local elections is largely a function of national voting trends. The influence of the parties extends through all three levels of government. The horizontal divisions of federalism are crossed by the vertical links of the party system, which thus serves as an integrating factor. Depending on the degree of unity between a party at national level and its governments at *Land* level, *Land* governments may find themselves in a dilemma as to what their priorities should be: whether they should only represent *Land* interests, as the principles of federalism suggest they should even if that means possibly going against their party at the national level and thus risking damage to the party through internal divisions; or whether they should alternatively follow directives from the national party leadership, even if this happens to be against the better interests of the *Länder* themselves. While in the United States the federal and party systems have been mutually reinforcing, each national party being a mere confederation of state and local party organizations, in Germany they pull in opposite directions. While from the constitutional viewpoint the Bundesrat is a safeguard of *Länder* influence in central government and of the autonomy of regional governments from the party political viewpoint, it is an instrument to be used in the competition for power and influence between the political parties at national level. There is thus a continuous tension between political alignments and regional interests.

The Bundesrat is the institutional expression at the central level of the federal provisions of the Basic Law. The Bundesrat has two functions: it contributes to the legislative process; and it is the organization of the united *Länder*. The original justification for its legislative influence was the need to have a say in the making of laws affecting the vital interests of the *Länder*. However, as was shown in chapter 5, the Bundesrat has developed an independent role in law-making, transcending and superseding its original limited function. Before being introduced in the Bundesrat most federal bills are circulated to the appropriate *Land* ministries for views and comment. In the committees of the Bundesrat each *Land* has only one vote – regardless of size – and the *Land* representative is normally a civil servant. Bundesrat decisions – as in the Bundestag – are almost invariably made on the basis of committee reports and substitution of officials for politicians in committee makes the assembly less partisan than the Bundestag and enables *Land* experience of administration to be fed into the system.[14] In the sphere of administration the role of the Bundesrat is to act as intermediary, linking Federal ministries as policy-makers and the *Land* governments as executants. The Bundesrat conveys to the Federal ministries the interests and proposals of *Land* administrators. This work is discharged by thirteen permanent committees of the Bundesrat, which perform most of the work of the assembly, the plenum simply ratifying the committee proposals. The Bundesrat thus serves to decentralize the creation of national policy.

Amongst the other institutional modes of cooperation between the Federation and *Länder*, and amongst the *Länder* themselves, the following are the most prominent.

Standing conferences   From the early days of the Bonn Republic permanent joint committees of *Land* and Federal ministers have been established. The most important of these is the Standing Conference of Minister-Presidents, which meets once or twice a year and is attended by the Federal Chancellor. Eleven others, dealing with finance, justice, the interior and other areas of administration, meet more frequently and have spawned committees, subcommittees and secretariats. Some have taken on an independent life. The Education Council (*Wissenschaftsrat*) consists of the Federal and *Land* Ministers of Education, and has standardized matters such as schools holidays, examinations and teacher training. The Finance Planning Council (*Finanzplanungsrat*) comprises the Federal and *Land* Ministers of Finance, together with local authority representatives, and has the task of

167

seeking to plan overall limits on public expenditure on a consensual basis.

Inter-Land *treaties*   The *Länder* have always entered into a huge mass of treaties (*Staatsverträge*) and administrative agreements (*Verwaltungsabkommen*) with each other to regulate matters of common concern on a long-term legal basis. By this means the *Land* governments have established the various broadcasting corporations. For example on 1 October 1955 Lower Saxony, Hamburg, and Schleswig–Holstein established North German Radio in Hamburg as a common broadcasting station for the three *Länder*. All the *Länder* participated in the treaties establishing a first and second television channel. ZDF (*Zweites Deutsches Fernsehen*) was created by a treaty between the *Länder* on 2 April 1962, as the Federation lacked the competency to establish a broadcasting institution for transmission for the German public. According to section 1 of its charter it is a public law institution. Its organs are the Television Council, the Executive Council and the Director-General. Financial control is exercised by the Auditor-General of Rhineland–Palatinate, where ZDF has its legal seat. Legal control, which includes political control in order to safeguard observance of the Basic Law, is accorded to the *Länder*, i.e. the government of one *Land* exercises this control for a period of two years.

Joint tasks   The constitutional reforms of 1969 established 'Joint Tasks' (*Gemeinschaftsaufgaben*, Article 91a), which are planned, financed and administered by the Federal and *Land* governments together. Because of the vigorous criticism which this innovation excited, on the grounds that it would undermine and imperil the federal system by departing from the principle of a division of competences between Federation and *Länder*, joint tasks are restricted to the provision of university buildings, the improvement of regional economic structure and the improvement of agricultural structure and coastal defences.

THE *LÄNDER* AND THE EEC

Germany is the sole member state of the EEC to possess a federal constitution. Transfers of national sovereignty to community institutions must be accomplished at the expense not only of the Federation but also of the *Länder*. This has led to the demand by the *Länder* for compensation for this loss of competence in the form of a larger role in the formulation of policy in Community affairs. The Federal government conceded these claims in order to facilitate ratification by the Bundesrat of the Single European Act in 1986. The Office of the Federal Chancellor has been given the task of consulting the *Land* governments before the Federal government decides upon steps in Community affairs. Not content with this consultative role, most of the *Länder* have now established their own delegations in Brussels, basically entrusted with the task of seeking to secure regional aid from Community funds for their respective territories. These developments have militated against the formulation of a consistent and coherent Community policy on the part of Germany.[16]

CONCLUSION

The German system has been called 'quasi-federal' on the grounds that 'the federal principle, though not predominant, is none the less important.[17] The only reason for such a conclusion is that the German system does not correspond to the principle of vertical federalism, which is in any case only exemplified to a limited extent in the American model.[18] Wheare's concept of federalism as a 'coordinate division of powers' questions the status not only of Germany but also of most other systems which are normally regarded as federal. What may be called federal depends less on arrangements of institutions within the system as it does on the manner in which these institutions operate. Federalism provides a formal framework. Most of the German *Länder* incorporate a number of interests, so it is difficult to recognize distinct regional interests. The formal establishment of federal institutions has not been followed by the development of substantial regional groupings. Indeed, the whole trend has been towards the nationalization of politics. Whether this will be qualified in the future by a west–east divide remains to be seen. The federal system has brought a degree of governmental complexity which is at odds with the homogeneous nature of the system. Its successful operation presupposes a basis of consensus and compromise which may render the federal system otiose. The true nature of government does not correspond to the sharp formal separation between federal, *Land* and municipal functions and responsibilities. *Land* and local governments, as well as administering their own immediate functions, serve as the instruments of national government.

Federalism is a relative principle, in which there are two levels of government – national and regional – each based on entrenched constitutional provisions, which define their respective jurisdictions, each neither being entirely dependent on nor serving simply as the agent of the other. The essence of German federalism is that there is a constitutionally protected division of powers between the two levels of government, that the central government cannot disestablish the system or alter it without the consent of the *Länder*, and that there is in consequence a blend of mutual interdependence and co-equal supremacy.[19]

The justification of federalism is that it permits national policies to be adapted to local requirements and gives substantial responsibility and autonomy to regional and local governments. The danger is that it may produce fragmentation of authority and *morcellement* of decision-making. While the positive aspects of devolution have been achieved in Germany, the inherent dangers have been avoided. The clear predominance of the national legislator, the central position of the Chancellor, the transcending of institutional divisions by the political parties, above all a secure political consensus, have rendered the system immune from the debilitating antagonisms between different levels of government which vitiated the Weimar system. The result has been coherent and effective national leadership.

The actual degree of policy uniformity achieved means that much of the formal apparatus of federalism is in practice redundant. Viewed in the context of German politics as a whole, this is a source of neither surprise nor regret. The rapid consolidation of the Federal Republic was bound to work against the federal system. This development was an integral part of the process whereby Germany has become a stable parliamentary democracy. Constitutionalism is the principle of limited government, and federalism that of devolved government and administration. The diminished influence of the *Länder* and the changed role of the Bundesrat bear witness to the circumstance that federalism is no longer needed as a guarantee of constitutional liberty. German federalism has evolved from being an aspect of the constitutional system based on division of competences, to an aspect of a party system based on a broad measure of inter-party agreement. Germany has a federal system, but its politics are not conducted along federal lines.

7   Political Parties

There are few countries in Western Europe where the institution of the political party has had a more traumatic history or such difficulty in establishing itself as an integral part of democratic rule as in Germany. The extension of the franchise throughout Western Europe during the nineteenth century was normally accompanied by the adoption of party government. The Imperial system in Germany remained monarchically based and political parties grew up in a system in which they were divorced from governmental responsibilities.

The establishment of democratic rule in the Weimar Republic brought with it the formal adoption of the party government model. In practice, however, it laboured under insurmountable difficulties. The fragmentation of the party system, reinforced but not created by the electoral system of proportional representation, meant pervasive governmental instability. This ensured that government was effectively in the hands of the pre-democratic military and bureaucratic elite. The dominant intellectual tradition remained state-centred and envisaged only a subordinate role for political parties. The Russian Revolution of 1917, the adoption of the republican form of government and the Versailles Treaty of 1919 led to the creation of very powerful anti-system parties of left and right which posed a permanent threat to the established parties. The onset of global depression in 1929, which struck particularly hard in Germany, exposed the weakness of the Weimar system, which collapsed in 1933.

The succeeding system, that of the Third Reich, was one which apparently gave the dominant position to a political party, the National Socialist German Workers Party (NSDAP). All the other parties were barred and office-holding in state positions was exclusively associated with membership in it. The NSDAP was a mass party which was extraordinarily successful in mobilizing the German population though there is a great deal of controversy as to the degree to which it actually determined policy rather than merely provided support for the system of the Third Reich.

The collapse of the Hitler regime meant the demise of the Nazi party and its associated organizations. Democratic parties were gradually re-established under the aegis of the Allies. The nascent party system which emerged under Allied tutelage has proved to be extraordinarily stable. Political parties in the occupation period were granted licences by the occupation authorities. Licences were only granted to parties which appeared to be democratic in form and intent and were normally refused to extreme nationalist parties. Parties which had exclusively regional aspirations were also unlikely to be licensed by the Western Allies. The parties that emerged in this protected party system, the CDU/CSU, SPD, FDP and KPD, were to provide the major actors in the party system of the Federal Republic, with the exception of the German Communist Party (KPD) which was barred in 1956.

The total collapse of the system in 1945 and the discredit the Nazi regime had brought on the elites who had been in varying degrees associated with it, meant that, unlike Weimar, there were no anti-system competitors. The territorial base of the Prussian elite had been destroyed by the war, and by the subsequent Russian and Polish occupations. Bonn has thus been a party state and quite different from any past German regime. The legitimacy of the state is not superior to, but identified with, the legitimacy of the political parties. This has meant that when the parties appear to attract less support, when there is a climate of *Parteiverdrossenheit* (alienation from parties), commentators immediately begin to talk of *Staatsverdrossenheit* (alienation from the state).

THE DEVELOPMENT OF THE WEST GERMAN PARTY SYSTEM

The Genesis of the Party System

The party system which emerged in the protected environment of Allied occupation after 1945 was relatively very concentrated in contrast to the fragmented party system of Weimar. The disenfranchisement of former members of the NSDAP and the system of licensing by the Allies excluded extreme right-wing parties. The Allies were also at pains to prevent the emergence in the early years of occupation of parties based on the interests of the refugees or regional interests. The total collapse of the

Third Reich meant that in any case the appeal of extreme nationalist parties was likely to be small though extreme nationalist candidates had some local successes where they were allowed to stand in the period before the economic miracle got under way. The British authorities were more lenient than the American or French and most of the nationalist successes occurred in the British zone, e.g. the DRP polled 10 per cent in Göttingen in the April 1947 Lower Saxony election and 70 per cent in the Wolfsburg Town Council election of March 1949. The mass exodus from the east and the reduction in territory also meant a reduced scope for regionally based parties. Contrary to earlier expectations, the post-war period also proved to be an infertile one for left-wing parties. The scale of the defeat left the German population numbed and the circumstances of post-war Germany meant that there was an almost universal focus on individual survival rather than collective solutions. West Germans were also influenced by the manifest lack of enthusiasm of the United States, the dominant occupying power, for left-wing parties and solutions.

Temporary Multi-partyism

The transition to the Federal Republic ushered in a short phase of multi-partyism. Regional parties had been licensed in the last period of occupation. The most successful of these parties was the *Bayern Partei* (Bavarian Party). Had it been licensed earlier it would have been likely to have achieved even more support than it in fact did. Ex-Nazis were also by then enfranchised.

The result of these developments was that ten parties were represented in the first Bundestag. The largest party was the CDU/CSU. The Christian Democratic Union (CDU) is a Christian democratic party which operates in all states except Bavaria. The Christian Social Union (CSU) is restricted to Bavaria. The major opposition party was the German Social Democratic Party, the SPD. The liberal party, the Free Democratic Party, formed a coalition with the CDU/CSU. Alongside these parties was an extreme right-wing party, the *Deutsche Reichspartei*, the Centre Party, regionally based parties like the Bavarian Party, and the South Schleswig Voter's Association (the party of the Danish minority in Schleswig–Holstein) and the Economic Reconstruction League (WAV) which had emerged in the occupation period.

CDU/CSU Dominance

The return of multi-partyism which had been feared by the framers of the Basic Law proved to be of extremely limited duration. The CDU/CSU quickly emerged around Chancellor Adenauer as the dominant party. Supporters and voters were drawn to the party by the performance of Chancellor Adenauer and his team as the first government of the Federal Republic. The CDU absorbed other parties, like the refugees party the GPBHE which was created in 1950, by drawing them into coalition and eventually taking over their supporters. The Bavarian Party was eliminated at the federal level by a change in the electoral law which required for the 1953 and subsequent elections that a party win three direct seats or five per cent of the federal vote. (For details of the election system see pp. 181–4.)

The FDP, which at that time sat to the right of the CDU/CSU in the Bundestag, was little more than an appendage of the CDU/CSU for conservative voters who were worried by what they saw as the clerical bent of the CDU/CSU. It was often referred to at that time as 'a reserve platform for dissatisfied CDU/CSU voters'.

The system that emerged was one of a bourgeois bloc of parties overwhelmingly dominated by the CDU/CSU. Ranged against this bloc was an internally antagonistic opposition of left-wing parties, the Social Democratic Party and the Communist Party. The Communist Party had very little support and, after failing to gain representation in the second Bundestag in 1953, was banned by the Federal Constitutional Court in 1956. The party system was in a state of imbalance in this period since the CDU/CSU-led bloc was numerically so much larger than the SPD.

The Transition: 1966–1969

The period 1963–72 has been referred to by Peter Pulzer as 'the second founding of the Federal Republic'.[1] In this period the CDU/CSU, which had been plagued by a chronic leadership crisis after Adenauer's reluctant retirement in 1963, lost its position of dominance. Of more long-term significance was the change in the position of the SPD. By adopting the moderate Bad Godesberg Programme in 1959 the SPD both increased its own electoral appeal and made it possible for bourgeois parties to consider entering into coalition with it. Until then the SPD's ideology had been strongly influenced by Marxism and was unacceptable to the CDU/CSU and the FDP.

This period, in which the CDU/CSU and the SPD joined together in the Grand Coalition, presented the West German party system with its first test of legitimacy. The concentration around the centre of the political spectrum left room for anti-system movements on both the left and right. On the right the Neo-Nazi party, the NPD, attracted some support and narrowly failed to get into the Bundestag in the 1959 election (4.3 per cent). The decision of the SPD to form a coalition with the CDU/CSU led to the alienation of many on the left of the party who joined together with other disaffected left groupings to form the APO, the Extra-Parliamentary Opposition. Despite its name, it did form a party, the ADF, to contest the 1969 election but it made very little impact.

A Balanced Party System: 1969–1982

After the Federal Election of 1969 the SPD ruled in coalition with the FDP until September 1982. This represented the culmination of developments associated with the SPD's adoption of the Bad Godesberg Programme. Without it, the FDP would never have been able to contemplate coalition with the SPD. This was the first time that the CDU had not provided the Chancellor and the party system had thus successfully demonstrated that it could provide for an alternation of power.

The CDU/CSU remained a very strong grouping and gained more votes than any other party in the elections of 1969, 1976 and 1980. The party system between 1969 and 1982 showed all the hallmarks of a well-functioning and balanced system.

A Reversion to Party Blocs

The decision of the FDP to change coalition partners in the early autumn of 1982 might have pushed the system into obvious imbalance. This has only been partially true, however, since a new left-wing party, the Greens, gained representation in the Bundestag election of March 1983. What emerged with the breakdown of the SPD–FDP coalition and the addition of a fourth party was a reversion to a two-bloc party system with a relatively small arithmetical gap between the two blocs. The FDP had kept the option of coalition with the CDU at *Land* level relatively open from 1969 to 1982. It now has only one coalition (Hamburg) with the SPD. Clearly the Greens are totally unacceptable to the CDU/CSU and the FDP as coalition partners. At present a governing coalition of the right of centre is counterbalanced by an opposition of two left-of-centre parties. The system is thus more polarized than at any point since the 1950s. It is also in partial imbalance since the left bloc is much weaker than the right. In the right bloc, the FDP is the automatic coalition partner of the CDU/CSU. The SPD has, with the exception of 1972, always been electorally weaker than the CDU/CSU, but the major weakness of the left bloc has been the problem of coalition. This is a problem for both parties. Those on the right of the SPD argue that coalition with the Greens would simply lose the SPD votes at the centre while giving votes to the Greens on the left end of the spectrum by inflating their importance. Coalition has been a problem for the Greens since they could not at the federal level accept the minimal conditions that would have been imposed on defence and security by even a left-led SPD, but this barrier now looks less high as SPD security policy adapts to the Gorbachev agenda. Coalition has been possible, however, at the *Land* level but many within the Greens remain opposed to this, and it has only occurred twice, in Hessen in 1985 where it broke down just over a year later and in 1989 in West Berlin. The left bloc has thus appeared weaker than in the 1950s. Then the KPD was unacceptable as a coalition partner for the SPD but it failed to get into the second Bundestag and the SPD picked up nearly all its votes. In the 1980s the left is also divided but there it little chance of the SPD absorbing the Greens as it did the KPD. The success of the FDP and the Greens in the last two elections, especially in 1987, means the system is now best regarded as a two-and-two-halves party system rather than a two-and-a-half party system. This mild fragmentation of the party system is reflected in the declining share of the vote obtained by the major parties. In 1987 it was 81 per cent, its lowest level since 1953 (see table 7.1).

Table 7.1 Percentage of votes obtained by the major parties (CDU/CSU and SPD), 1949–1987

1949	53	57	61	65	69	72	76	80	83	87
60.2	74	82	81.5	86.9	88.9	90.7	91.2	87.4	87	81

ELECTORAL PATTERNS

The electoral relations of the West German parties can be regarded as typical for contemporary Western Europe, i.e. a shifting balance between the persistence of old cleavages and marked electoral volatility. These traditional cleavages are based on social class and religious affiliation. The territorially restricted character of the Federal Republic, in comparison to past German polities, ensures that regional voting loyalties hardly play a role, except to the extent that Bavarian loyalties work to the benefit of the CSU. The permanent alliance between the CDU/CSU means, however, that the CSU has always been more than a vehicle for purely regional interests.

Patterns of Class Voting

Class, defined according to occupation, remains the most significant line of cleavage in the West German electorate. The manual working class provides the core electoral support for the SPD whilst the self-employed (including farmers) vote overwhelmingly for the CDU/CSU. The salaried middle class has divided its support much more equally since the mid-1960s, with swings in both directions, and the SPD lost appreciable support in this group in the 1983 election. The SPD devoted a great deal of effort to wooing the so-called 'technical intelligentsia' in the run-up to the 1987 election.

Electoral support for the SPD by manual workers is very strongly associated with membership of a trade union. The closed shop is outlawed in West Germany and it is thus reasonable to take trade union membership as an indication of identification between the manual worker and his occupational group. This identification is then reinforced by actual membership of a union, although about one-third of union members normally vote CDU/CSU. The pattern of support for the SPD has remained strikingly consistent. The rapid decline in the size of the manual working class relative to the population as a whole makes it an increasingly less promising base for an SPD majority.

The connection between a middle-class occupation and voting for an anti-socialist party has in recent decades been much less marked in Germany than in Britain. In the first years of the Federal Republic two-thirds of the middle class still voted for the centre right. The term 'middle class' covers a very amorphous group from lower grade clerical workers to top level civil servants. It is important to remember also that parties have very important patronage functions in relation to public service employees such as teachers. Teachers are civil servants in Germany and the parties do exercise some patronage functions. The middle class is now the largest single social group as the categories of self-employed and manual working class have shrunk as a proportion of the electorate. Growth has been particularly striking in the new middle class of service employees. It is in this group that electoral volatility has been highest and party identifiers most sparse. As one commentator has noted.

Consequently, the new middle class finds itself with a position in the social structure and a life-style that places it between the working class and the old middle class. As a result its loyalties are divided between these other two strata and its votes are split between the parties of the left and right.[2]

The groups identified by Klingemann tend to respond less to traditional social cues and much more to their perception of the issues and the parties' competence to govern. This helps to explain why the parties, with the exception of the Greens, stress their governmental vocation and why they conduct very expensive electoral campaigns.

A great deal of attention has been focused on electoral change among a part of the middle-class electorate. There are a number of indications that at least since the late 1970s the dominant political values of the Federal Republic have become less relevant to sections of the younger, highly educated middle-class electorate in non-industrial occupations. For these voters adherence to the traditional values established by the post-war generation of economic well being and security have been replaced by adherence to 'post-materialist' values, i.e. those which stress participatory and environmental concerns. The SPD is particularly affected by this development since it has traditionally polled well among the 18–35 age range.

The Religious Cleavage

The West German electorate was divided in more or less equal

179

proportions between Catholics and Protestants. The CDU electoral dominance of the 1950s rested on its being able to attract overwhelming support among Catholic voters and a significant level of support amongst Protestant voters, Catholic identification with the CDU/CSU transcending class barriers was an inheritance from the old Catholic Centre Party. Catholics had been mobilized as Catholics into politics at the inception of the age of mass politics by Bismarck's attack on the church in the so-called *Kulturkampf*. This identification was then reinforced by the anti-socialist stance of successive Popes.

This situation began to change in the 1960s as a result of three factors. The changed policy of the Vatican under Pope John XXIII corresponded to a change in the SPD, which, in the Bad Godesberg Programme of 1959, had abandoned both its theoretical adherence to Marxism and its historical anti-clericalism. This now made it possible, in theory at least, for Catholics to vote SPD without incurring priestly censure.

More important in the long run, however, was the beginning of a process of secularization in the 1960s. Church attendance in the Federal Republic fell quite dramatically after 1965. This fall was most marked in relation to Catholics since church attendance and the taking of communion had been an obligation for Catholics in a much stronger sense than for Protestants. Regular and frequent church attendance declined from 60 per cent of all nominal Catholics in 1965 to 36 per cent in 1980 (still quite high in comparative terms). This decline in church attendance was most marked among the new middle class.

Catholics who continue to attend church regularly overwhelmingly support the CDU/CSU. The CDU/CSU also enjoys a clear majority among Catholics who attend church infrequently. Among Catholics who have been secularized a clear majority voted for the SPD until the 1983 election when a majority voted for the CDU/CSU. The CDU/CSU also enjoys a clear majority among church-going Protestants. They, of course, represent a much smaller proportion of the Protestant half of the population than regular church-going Catholics do of the Catholic population.

The cleavage line between the secular and the religious is thus still a major though declining factor in predetermining electoral choice in the Federal Republic. In the 1972 election in which the SPD for the first and only time became the largest party in the Federal Republic, it appeared to be on the way out since Catholic workers supported the SPD in large numbers. The introduction by the SPD/FDP government of new legislation on divorce and abortion pushed church-going Catholic workers back into support for the CDU/CSU in 1976. It is possible that this support will be eroded less by continuing secularization than by the anti-union policies of the CDU/CSU–FDP government and by continuing high levels of unemployment. It was the extreme pro-business electoral campaign of 1972 that played a major part in persuading Catholic workers to vote according to their class position rather than their religious affiliation.

Until the Federal election of 1972 there was also a clear contrast in the voting preferences of male and female voters. This difference largely disappeared at the 1972 election and since then there is no significant difference in voting behaviour according to gender. Although class and confession are still the major determinants of voting choice in the Federal Republic their pull is declining as class patterns alter and society becomes more secular. Volatility is therefore increasing as voters respond less to traditional social cues and orient themselves more to perceptions of competence and to political issues.

PARTIES AND ELECTIONS

The outcome of elections in the Federal Republic as elsewhere reflects not only long-established party preferences and the voters' reactions to particular issues but the impact of the kind of electoral system employed.

The West German Electoral System

Normally the Bundestag has 656 directly elected members. (N.B. From 3 October to 2 December 1990 the Bundestag has 663 members: 497 from West Germany, 22 from West Berlin and 144 from the former DDR.) The electoral system is a mixed one in which half the representatives are elected on the simple majority plurality principle but the other half are selected on the basis of party lists so that the overall system is proportional.

The aim of this dual system is to combine accurate representation without losing the link between the voter and his deputy. A possible disadvantage of the system would be the creation of two classes of deputies; those elected by constituences, who concentrate on representing their voters, and deputies elected on the list basis, who are almost exclusively creatures of party. In practice this gulf has not emerged. Constituency deputies attempt to reinsure themselves on the lists and list deputies often shadow a particular constituency. Both types of deputies attempt to associate themselves with constituency activities to maintain the activists' support at both selection processes and the rather less demanding timetable of the Bundestag allows both types to spend more time in their home area than is the case in Britain. As in Britain, deputies often raise constituency or regional issues in the Bundestag, but individual grievances are much more likely to be dealt with through the system of administrative courts.

An argument often advanced in favour of the list system is that it facilitates the representation of minorities, or even of a majority like women since it is much easier to translate party declarations in favour of such a policy into practice than where it is dependent on decisions by individual constituency selection committees.

In voting in a Federal election the elector is given a ballot paper divided into two columns (figure 7.1). The left-hand column is made up of party lists of candidates. These lists are *Land*- rather than Federal-based since the architects of the electoral system wanted to avoid repeating the deficiencies of Weimar where the central party leadership drew up nationwide lists, a procedure which clearly strengthened centralizing tendencies in the political parties.

The elector thus casts two votes, one for an individual candidate and the second vote for a party. There is no requirement to be consistent and, since the early 1970s, there has been a significant increase in 'ticket splitting', i.e. voting for a candidate of one party with the first vote and for a different party with the second. The possibility of splitting provided by the electoral system encourages tactical voting and allows the elector in certain situations to express a preference both for a particular form of coalition and against a particular faction in a party. Thus, during the SDP/FDP coalition a number of voters voted SPD with their first vote and FDP with their second. Such voters were expressing a preference for a coalition with the FDP and were also expressing a negative preference against a too complete victory for the SPD which would have strengthened the left. In 1983 and 1987 a number of CDU voters cast a second

Stimmzettel

für die Bundestagswahl im Wahlkreis 129 Fritzlar
am 3. Oktober 1976

Sie haben 2 Stimmen

hier 1 Stimme ⊗	⊗ hier 1 Stimme
10r die Wahl	10r die Wahl
eines Wahlkreisabgeordneten	einer Landesliste (Partei)
(Erststimme)	(Zweltstimme)

	Erststimme				Zweltstimme	
1	**Dr. Kreutzmann, Heinz** Reg.-Direktor a. D. Borken Kellerwaldstraße 7 **SPD** Sozialdemokratische Partei Deutschlands	◯		◯	**SPD** Sozialdemokratische Partei Deutschlands Leber, Bömer, Frau Dr. Timm, Matthöfer, Wuttke	1
2	**Stahlberg, Hermann** Prokurist Fritzlar 1 Paulstraße 3 **CDU** Christlich Demokratische Union Deutschlands	◯		◯	**CDU** Christlich Demokratische Union Deutschlands Dr. Dregger, Zink, Dr. Wallmann, Dr. Schwarz-Schilling, Frau Dr. Watz	2
3	**Kohl, Heinrich** Staatssekretär Frankenau 1 Bärenmühle **F.D.P.** Freie Demokratische Partei	◯		◯	**F.D.P.** Freie Demokratische Partei Mischnick, Wurbe, von Schoeler, Hoffle, Dr. Solma	3
				◯	**AUD** Aktionsgemeinschaft Unabhängiger Deutscher Schlingelhof, Frau Fleißig, Kraußer, Frau Bomka, Dolenschall	4
				◯	**AVP** Aktionsgemeinschaft Vierte Partei Dr. Consillus, Kayser, Hambech, Dr. Lips, Frau Pesina	5
6	**Pschera, Otto (jun.)** Elektroinstallateur Burgwald-Bottendorf Wolkersdorier Str. 21a **DKP** Deutsche Kommunistische Partei	◯		◯	**DKP** Deutsche Kommunistische Partei Mayer, Knopf, Frau Dr. Weber, Schröder, Frau Schuster	6
				◯	**EAP** Europäische Arbeiterpartei Friesecke, Frau Leffek, Schauerhammer, Rumpf, Frau Horn	7
				◯	**KPD** Kommunistische Partei Deutschlands Harterich Horiemann, Frau Koch, Beck, Dr. Schneider	8
				◯	**KBW** Kommunistischer Bund Westdeutschland Klocke, Frau Mönich, Koenen, Geike, Ohmer	9
10	**Hoffmann, Ralph** Student Gießen Großer Steinweg 21 **NPD** Nationaldemokratische Partei Deutschlands	◯		◯	**NPD** Nationaldemokratische Partei Deutschlands Quintus, Dr. Buck, Frau von Woizogen, Dr. Anrich, Fuhirott	10

Figure 7.1 Standard ballot paper for a Bundestag election.

vote for the FDP. This again expressed a coalition preference but in 1987 it was also frequently a vote to prevent an absolute majority for the CDU/CSU which looked possible in the first phase of the election campaign. A number of CDU supporters were concerned that in a CDU/CSU government the CSU, without the FDP to act as a brake, would play too great a role.

The distribution of seats is arrived at in a manner designed to achieve a proportional distribution of seats overall. Half the seats are allocated on the basis of the result in each of the 328 individual constituencies. The remaining half is made up of candidates drawn from the parties' lists in each *Land*. The seats are then allocated by the so-called Niedermeyer method (introduced in 1984, before that the D'Hondt method was used). The system uses the following formula to calculate the allocation of seats.

$$\frac{\text{Party's total number of votes} \times \text{number of seats available}}{\text{Total number of votes of all parties polling more than 5 per cent}}$$

These calculations will result in the ascription of virtually all the seats in the Bundestag and any remaining seats are given to the party/parties with the highest remainder.

Once each party has been allocated its share of the 656 seats in the Bundestag, its votes are divided up into *Land* totals and the Niedermeyer calculations are used to determine how many of these seats each party is entitled to in each *Land*. The number of seats that each party has won in the constituency elections is then subtracted from the total entitlement in each *Land* and each party is then allocated additional seats from their party lists to make up the total number. The system has thus an overall proportionality. On the rare occasions where a party has won more direct seats than its proportional share of the vote in the *Land* would entitle it to, it is allowed to keep the extra seats (*Überhangsmandate*). This situation prevailed in the Bundestag elected in 1987 (see table 7.4). It is obviously rare since it means that a party has to exceed, on the basis of one list of half the seats, its overall proportional total.

There are two further points to note. There is a 5 per cent threshold. A party has to win 5 per cent of the Federal total or three direct seats to be represented. This makes representation next to impossible for a regional party like the *Bayern Partei*. The CDU's total is not combined with the CSU. The CSU's list therefore competes with the total of all the other parties. There are no by-elections in Germany. If a deputy dies or resigns he is simply replaced by the next name on the list from the preceding election. In the December 1990 election West and East Germany had separate 5 per cent clauses (pp. 14–15).

The 1987 Election

The 1987 election was won convincingly by the governing coalition. This is in line with long-term trends, no government of the Federal Republic has yet lost an election (see tables 7.2–7.4).

There are a number of interesting features of the 1987 result of which the first is the relatively poor performance of the two major party groupings and their declining share of the vote

Table 7.2   Federal elections 1949–87

	1949	1953	1957	1961	1965	1969	1972	1976	1980	1983	1987
Turnout	78.5	86.0	87.8	87.7	86.8	86.7	91.1	90.7	88.6	89.1	84.4
CDU/CSU	31.0	45.2	50.2	45.3	47.6	46.1	44.9	48.6	44.5	48.8	44.3
FDP	11.9	9.5	7.7	12.8	9.5	5.8	8.4	7.9	10.6	7.0	9.1
SPD	29.2	28.8	31.8	36.2	39.3	42.7	45.8	42.6	42.9	38.2	37.0
Greens	—	—	—	—	—	—	—	—	1.5	5.6	8.3

Table 7.3   Distribution of seats 1961–87

Party	1961	1965	1969	1972	1976	1980	1983	1987
CDU/CSU	242	245	242	225	243	226	244	223
FDP	67	49	30	41	39	53	34	46
SPD	190	202	224	230	214	218	193	186
Greens	—	—	—	—	—	—	27	42
Total	499	496	496	496	496	497	498	497

Table 7.4   Result of 1987 Election (1983 in brackets)

	Votes (m)	Votes (%)	Gain/loss (%)	No. seats
CDU/CSU	16.7 (18.9)	44.3 (48.8)	−4.5	223 (224)
SPD	14.0 (14.8)	37.0 (38.2)	−1.2	186 (193)
FDP	3.4 (2.7)	9.1 (7.()	+2.1	46 (34)
Greens	3.1 (2.1)	8.3 (5.6)	+2.7	42 (27)

Turnout: 84.8% (89.1%). Up until 1990 there were 496 seats in the Bundestag. The number of seats in the Bundestag 1986–90 was 497. The extra seat occurred because the CDU won one more seat directly in Baden–Württemberg than the proportion of its second votes entitled it to. The CDU has 174 seats (191). The CSU has 49 (53).

(table 7.4). The reasons for this decline differ as between the parties.

The CDU/CSU

There are two major explanations for the CDU/CSU's losses. The first relates to the transfer of votes to the FDP. This transfer from the major coalition partner to the FDP has been a marked feature of a number of West German elections – a process facilitated, as we have seen, by the two-vote system which allows electors to cast the first (direct) vote for the major coalition partner and the second (list) vote for the FDP). In past elections, e.g. 1983, this practice of 'ticket splitting' occurred when voters of the major party had reason to fear that the FDP might not surmount the 5 per cent hurdle. In 1987 it always appeared probable that the FDP would clear the 5 per cent hurdle, and yet a considerable number of CDU/CSU voters cast their second vote for the FDP.

There are two obvious explanations for this behaviour. First, opinion polls in December 1986 were forecasting a very high poll for the CDU/CSU, and the prospect of an absolute majority for the CDU/CSU was widely canvassed. Peter Pulzer pointed out as early as 1962 that a section of the German electorate was opposed to the idea of a majority party (*horror majoritas*) and was therefore likely to cast its second votes tactically for the FDP to frustrate the emergence of a majority party.[3]

This impulse was much strengthened in the 1987 election by the actions of Franz Josef Strauss, who vigorously attacked the FDP on law and order and foreign policy in the closing stages of the campaign. These attacks misfired badly since the FDP foreign policy of detente was widely popular. The FDP responded to the attacks by suggesting that Strauss's campaign was motivated by a desire to replace Hans-Dietrich Genscher by himself as Foreign Minister, a change likely to cause alarm at the centre of the West German political spectrum. The CDU/CSU also suffered severe losses due to abstentions. This is largely to be explained by widespread complacency due to the very high rating of the CDU/CSU in the opinion polls before Christmas. These abstentions due to complacency were accompanied by protest abstentions from farmers annoyed by developments in the Common Agricultural Policy, especially dairy quotas.

The SPD

The result for the SPD was arguably worse than that for the CDU/CSU. The SPD vote only declined from 38.2 to 37 per cent, but 1983 was already a major reverse (its average poll between 1969 and 1980 had been 43.3 per cent), and 37 per cent took the Social Democrats back to the level they had been before the breakthrough of the Bad Godesberg Conference of 1959. In 1987 the SPD losses largely accrued to the Greens who were estimated to have won 500,000 votes from the SPD. The strength of the Greens *vis-à-vis* the SPD was also reflected among young voters, traditionally a group in which the SPD has been very strong. Some four months after the election in Germany an official analysis is published based on an analysis of a sample of completed ballot forms. The representative figures for 1987 indicate that of the 18–24-year-olds who voted 37.5 per cent voted CDU/CSU, 38.1 per cent SPD, 8.3 per cent FDP and 15.5 per cent Greens. The SPD polled above its overall percentage in three states belonging to 'the rust belt' and in which it had recently polled well in state elections. In the Saarland its share went down marginally from 43.8 to 43.5 per cent. In Lower Saxony it increased its poll from 41.3 to 41.4 per cent. Most importantly, in West Germany's largest state, North Rhine–Westphalia, the home state of Johannes Rau, the SDP share increased from 42.8 to 43.2 per cent. The SPD had run a special campaign in North Rhine–Westphalia which based itself more squarely on Rau.

Worryingly for the SPD, it not only failed to make any impression in the prosperous south, Bavaria and Baden–Württemberg, but its support slipped in Hamburg and Bremen, two of its traditional safe areas. The drop in support in Hamburg of 6.3 per cent was especially high.

The electoral weakness of the SPD and the difficulty it had in devising an electoral strategy to win votes both at the centre and from the Greens was already a major feature of the 1983 election. The increasing strength of the Greens, especially after the Chernobyl nuclear disaster, merely exacerbated a pre-existing set of difficulties. The SPD attempted to meet these difficulties in two ways. Its electoral programme as agreed at the party conference in Nürnberg in August 1986 and electoral conference in Offenburg in September 1986 was more radical than previous SPD programmes, most notably on defence and in its commitment to cease using nuclear energy within a decade. If the programme was designed to attract voters on the left, the Chancellor-candidate, Johannes Rau, was clearly designed to appeal primarily to the centre while attempting not to alienate those on the left. This dual strategy of the SPD also entailed a relative playing down of issues in the campaign. The assumption was that Rau's personal popularity, complemented by Kohl's low standing in the opinion polls, would pull the SPD to victory and that Rau would repeat his 1985 victory in North Rhine–Westphalia. This was always a very optimistic assumption. The SPD is much stronger in North Rhine–Westphalia than in the Federal Republic as a whole. In a Federal election Rau's disinclination to be identified with specific policies was much more of a handicap than in running as the incumbent in a state election. It was also a handicap in running against Kohl who shared a similar disinclination to address issues.

The SPD campaign was also marked by very severe strategic and tactical failures. At a strategic level, the decision made by Rau and his staff to proclaim the SPD's electoral goal as an absolute majority was an error. It was meant to head off damaging discussions of a coalition with, or governmental dependence on, the Greens. In fact, it simply lacked credibility. This became more and more apparent from the early summer of 1986. After the SPD failed very badly in the Hamburg election of November 1986, Brandt attempted to contain the damage by lowering the target to 43 per cent. By that time even that looked far too high a figure, and the credibility problem which had dogged that SPD campaign continued.

Background events conspired against the SPD as well. The trade union/working-class core of the party was weakened by the collapse of *Neue Heimat*, the trade union housing body, in the autumn of 1986. The circumstances of the collapse greatly annoyed the many working-class tenants of *Neue Neimat*, and the way in which it had conducted its affairs reflected very badly on the trade union leadership. This meant that alliance with the trade unions was less of an advantage than in the past but the SPD could not afford to be too critical of the trade union leadership.

The series of chemical spillages into the Rhine in November and December 1986, although an embarrassment to the government, failed to bring the SPD electoral benefits. The SPD's chemical policy is concerned primarily with more stringent regulations for the marketing of chemicals rather than with the problems of aquatic pollution. Thus the benefits of the considerable public disquiet about the chemical scandals were reaped by the Greens, who were seen as being more wholehearted about environmental pollution than the SPD. The SPD vote held up relatively well among its working-class supporters. As already noted, it was able to increase its vote in North Rhine–Westphalia and polled especially well in the Ruhr.

The SPD's major losses were to the Greens. Since it seemed extremely unlikely that the SPD would form a government many on the left/post-materialist wing of the party felt much less inhibited about voting Green. This propensity was clearly strengthened by the environmental scandals (Chernobyl and the Rhine pollution) to which the Greens were able to respond more unequivocally than the SPD. After 1983 the SPD had placed great hopes of electoral advance among 'the technical intelligentsia'. These hopes were not realized in the 1987 election.

The FDP

The success of the FDP appears to be highly dependent on what Anglo-Saxons call 'tactical voting' and Germans more weightily describe as 'strategic voting'. In the section below on individual parties we point out a number of functions performed by the FDP in the party system and, given that the core support of the FDP is about 3 per cent, it appears that many of the extra votes it attracts are from voters who are voting for a function rather than a programme. Strategic voting is made easier because of the electoral system which allows voters to split their votes.

In the 1987 election two considerations appear especially relevant, that of the prevention of the emergence of a majority party and ideological behaviour within the coalition. A number of voters appeared to vote FDP in the election precisely because there had been much speculation in the preceding month about the CDU/CSU winning an absolute majority. They were also moved to vote FDP by a desire to affect the coalition balance, in particular to curb the CSU, which is seen as extreme right. Not all the FDP increase can be explained in this way and they clearly benefited from the votes of dissatisfied farmers.

The FDP vote, resting as it does on neither one of the great social cleavages nor its articulation of a particularly tightly drawn ideology, has historically been subject to much more oscillation than the other parties. It has proved especially vulnerable at *Land* level, where the lack of a two-vote system and the absence of the *horror majoritas* that some German electors have about the federal level, means they can rely much less on strategic voting. The changing occupational structure of German society and the continued expansion of the service sector may mean the FDP has a larger core support in future. Until then it seems likely that its functional role will always take it over the 5 per cent hurdle in Federal elections.

The Greens

The Green vote had shown distinct signs of stagnation in 1985. They were aided in 1987 by the strategic errors of the SPD campaign and the effects of two ecological disasters, Chernobyl and the Rhine spillages in 1986.

The Greens polled particularly well among younger well-educated voters under thirty-five. Interestingly, they did not poll especially well among female voters despite their many commitments to bridging the gender gap and their commitment to the 'zip principle' i.e. alternating male and female candidates on party lists. There was also a slight decline in the number of first time voters voting Green.

INDIVIDUAL PARTIES

The Christian Democratic Union

In an important sense the Christian Democratic Union is the most novel of the original Bonn parties and arguably for that reason the party best attuned to post-war realities. Historically, the strength of the religious cleavage had made the formation of a biconfessional party impossible. The decision of the Catholic Centre Party to vote for 'the Enabling Law' in March 1933 would have made the prospects of a purely Catholic party very unpromising in 1945. But the very marked religious revival after 1945 made the formation of a party based on religious values very likely. An added impetus to the formation of such a party was given by the anxiety of both Catholic and Protestant politicians that socialism would triumph unless faced by a biconfessional party.

> The religious revival in post-war Germany runs like a bright thread through most of the distinctive phenomena of the intellectual and political scene; the spontaneous foundation of the great 'Christian' party encompassing both major faiths, the new appreciation for democracy and the dignity of the individual, the anti-Bismarckian reappraisal of German history, the return to federalism within and hope for other federal union with other European countries in place of nationalism, and the high prestige of the churches, which more than any other German institution had emerged untarnished from the Nazi area.[4]

The rejection of atheistic, materialistic values contained in the endorsement of Christian values allowed the Christian Democrats simultaneously to attack the Nazi regime and the emerging communist regime in East Germany. The division of Germany also contributed to the success of the CDU/CSU. It cut off the overwhelmingly Protestant areas of central and eastern Germany. Catholics who had formed slightly less than one-third of the pre-war German population, now made up 45 per cent of the inhabitants of post-war western Germany. The historical record of Protestant conservative parties and the destruction of their major territorial base in Prussia now made a biconfessional conservative party an attractive option for conservative Protestants for the first time.

The CDU quickly emerged after 1949 as the strongest party. This advance was associated with its performance in government and with the dominant figure of the first Federal Chancellor, Konrad Adenauer. His foreign policy priorities of anti-communism and solidarity with the Western democratic allies corresponded to the views of most West Germans. The success of the social market economy internally and the resulting prosperity was perhaps even more important in consolidating the popularity of the CDU/CSU.

In retrospect, the difficulties the CDU suffered in the two decades from the early 1960s were inherent in its success. Its overwhelming success in the 1950s persuaded the SPD to drop its character as a 'class party' and to adopt the *Volkspartei* (catch-all) model of appealing across class and confessions. The dependence on and identification with Adenauer also began to be a handicap and he was persuaded to retire in 1963. His reluctant retirement as Chancellor heralded a period of intensive struggle to succeed him which resulted in the resignation of his successor as Chancellor, Ludwig Erhard, in October 1966. Electorally, the CDU was weakened by the trend towards secularization and the emergence of a new middle class often employed in the public sector, who were much more open to appeals from the SPD than the traditional middle class. Its major weakness was its loss of an ally, the FDP, with whom the SPD formed a governing coalition until September 1982.

The loss of governmental office in 1969 came as a severe shock to the party and it invested a great deal of effort in the late 1960s and 1970s in strengthening the party apparatus. As Christian Hacke wrote,

Under Adenauer the CDU could hardly be called a party: it was, rather, a dependent branch of the parliamentary group in the Bundestag, which in its turn was only a body dependent on the chancellor. The party had no effective party headquarters but was at most an organization for fighting elections.[5]

Even this description flatters the party since Adenauer relied very heavily on the Chancellor's Office and the Federal Press and Information Office for assistance in his electoral campaigns. The most important long-term reform was the creation in the mid 1960s of the post of Secretary General of the CDU. The establishment of this post meant that for the first time the Bonn head office had a full-time administrator whose job it was to establish links with the party organizations in all regions and at all levels throughout the Federal Republic. Until then the Bonn Office had contact only with the regional CDU organizations, who had monopolized access to district and local branches. The party thus ceased to be in the hands of the *Ländesfürsten* (regional notables) in the way it had been hitherto.

The creation of this post led to the recruitment of a number of brilliant staff members who have given the CDU electoral machine a technically gifted and pragmatic cutting edge quite different from the CDU in the past and the contemporary SPD. The core group included Wanfried Dettling, Peter Radunski, Wulf Dieter Schonbohm, Hans-Joachim Kierey and Wolfgang Bergsdorf. They had all studied political science at the Free University of Berlin and taken the distinctly unfashionable step at that time in university circles of supporting the CDU. They now occupy the most senior posts in the CDU administration and meet regularly in a group known as the Pentagon.

Rainer Barzel was replaced as Chairman of the CDU by Helmut Kohl in 1973. Helmut Kohl fought a very creditable election as CDU/CSU candidate for Chancellor in 1976 and achieved the CDU/CSU second best result up until then. His subsequent performance as parliamentary party leader was widely regarded as ineffectual and he was replaced by Franz Josef Strauss as the candidate in 1980. Franz Josef Strauss fought a very aggressive campaign which alienated many moderates, especially in Northern Germany, and the result of the election was a marked setback for the CDU.

Strauss's unequivocal defeat allowed Kohl to pursue a policy of cultivating the FDP with a view to detaching them from the coalition. The coalition collapsed in September 1982 and Kohl formed a CDU/CSU–FDP government after toppling Helmut Schmidt by a constructive vote of no confidence. The CDU/CSU won the subsequent election of March 1983 with ease.

Kohl's relaxed chancellorial style and indecisiveness in crisis situations has led to a great deal of media criticism but his dual position as Chancellor and Party Chairman has inhibited public expression within the CDU about his performance.

His achievement in winning the January 1987 election, albeit on a much reduced share of the poll, should have ensured that he continue to lead the CDU but a run of poor *Land* election results since then put him under increasing pressure. Criticism of his policy grasp ignores his ability as a party manager. His tough foreign policy rhetoric appeals to the right of the party, while in practice he has proceeded cautiously in internal policy. He devotes a great deal of policy attention to personnel matters and potential rivals like Kurt Biedenkopf found themselves outmanoeuvred. His handling of unification in 1989–90 transformed his Chancellorship.

Party Groupings   The CDU has a stronger claim to be regarded as a *Volkspartei* than the other major parties. It has not only consistently pursued an electoral strategy of attempting to appeal to all social strata, but different groups have a major role in both the party at large and the *Bundestagsfraktion*. The major groups are those based on confessional and economic interest groups. The Protestant Working Circle (*Evangelischer-Arbeitskreis*), founded in 1952, has safeguarded Protestant interests within the CDU and provided the basis of Gerhard Schroeder's 'Hausmacht' (power base) in the CDU, while he was Foreign Minister between 1963 and 1966.

The most influential economic interest group is the *Wirtschaftsrat*, the employers' organization, which has given very consistent support to the principles of the social market economy. Its very considerable influence has been helped by its role in securing external financial support for the party.

Smaller and more protectionist business interests are represented by the *Mittelstandsvereinigung*. The influence of this grouping probably reached a high point during the SPD–FDP coalition. Since the formation of the CDU/CSU–FDP government some of the political activities of small businesses have been refocused on the FDP.

The last major grouping in the CDU is formed by the Social Committees of the Catholic trade unionists. In the 1940s this grouping played a major role and, even into the 1960s, leading figures like Hans Katzer played a major role in the CDU/CSU. In recent years their influence has declined considerably. The further decline of the trade unions is likely to reinforce this trend. They still have some influence, however, as the CDU cannot afford to forgo the support of Catholic trades unionists and the present Minister of Labour, Norbert Blüm, is the Chairman of the Social Committee.

Christian Social Union

The strength of Bavarian particularism has meant that Christian democracy has been represented by an autonomous party, the Christian Social Union, which has been united with the CDU to form a joint *Bundestagsfraktion* since the first Bundestag of 1949. The CSU is the successor party to the Bavarian People's Party (BVP), the Bavarian affiliate of the Centre Party. Like the BVP it had the difficult task of uniting the political aspirations of backward-looking rural voters who were often particularist, and urban Catholic voters who, while laying some stress on a Bavarian dimension, wanted to participate in a wider German political framework.

The CSU was much aided in its formation and rapid growth after 1945 by an initial Allied refusal to license regionalist parties. Without this inhibition it is likely that a purely Bavarian party would have done very well in 1945 given the Bavarian experience of united Germany 1871–1945. By 1948 when the *Bayern Partei* (Bavarian Party) was licensed economic recovery was under way and it was quite clear that the United States was determined to form a West German state. Nevertheless, the formation of the *Bayern Partei* led to the loss of half the CSU membership in 1948 and to the reinstatement of a more particularistic and backward-looking appeal in order to counter the attraction of the *Bayern Partei*. It was a very strong advocate of a states-rights position in the debate on the drafting of the Basic Law (see p. 125).

The modern electoral success of the CSU has its origins paradoxically in its unexpected loss of power in Bavaria in 1954 when a four-party coalition was formed against it. The shock of loss of office led to a comprehensive reorganization and a strengthening of the party headquarters, including the creation of the office of Secretary General. The CSU became, and has remained, the most intensively organized party in the Federal Republic. Its electoral dominance has rested on its performance as the governing party in Bavaria itself since the late 1950s and its influence at the federal level as part of the CDU/CSU.

In Bavaria itself it has had to devise a policy mix which would satisfy both rural agricultural interests and urban industrial interests. The creation of the Common Agricultural Policy was an important window of opportunity for the CSU since it meant that the costs of supporting the very uneconomic Bavarian agricultural sector were not borne by the state finances of Bavaria, which would have implied passing some of the costs on to local industry. The maintenance of the CAP and of high agricultural prices has therefore been a key CSU policy.

As a state government with considerable influence in Bonn and freed from the need to subsidise agriculture, the CSU has been very successful in attracting industry. The state government offers a whole battery of infra-structural advantages and the industrial relations climate of Bavaria with its low level of unionization has made Bavaria a very attractive site for industry. Under a succession of CSU governments Bavaria has been transformed from a poor, largely agricultural land to a *Land* whose industrial health and prosperity is rivalled only by that of its neighbour Baden–Württemberg.

Christian democracy has been, and continues to be, stronger in southern Germany because of the confessional balance. Despite the influx of post-war refugees, Bavaria remains overwhelmingly Catholic since the refugees from contiguous areas like the Sudetenland were also Catholics. CSU policies successfully mobilized rural and urban Catholics but until the mid 1960s the CSU had made little inroads into the Protestant minority. The Bavarian Protestant minority was traditionally anti-clerical but the same impulse made them very Pan-German since they wanted to escape Catholic domination in a particularist Bavaria. In opposition from 1969 to 1982 the CSU, and most notably its leader, Franz Josef Strauss, was a bitter opponent of *Ostpolitik* (see chapter 10), though it moderated its tone once in government. The decidedly nationalist stance of Strauss during these years was designed both to establish the CSU as a conservative force throughout the Federal Republic and to appeal to the Protestant minority in Bavaria, an aim in which it has been successful.

A final factor which helps account for the CSU's electoral strength is the weakness of the SPD. Unlike the CSU, which has been able to identify itself successfully with Bavarian cultural and political symbols, the SPD is merely the SPD in Bavaria. It suffered from the support of the Roman Catholic Church for its opponents. It failed to share in the general electoral advance of the SPD in the 1970s. Not only did it continue to suffer from its traditional handicaps of a secular and un-Bavarian identity, but the already weak SPD in Bavaria was peculiarly marked by factional strife. Munich has the largest concentration of students in the Federal Republic and the Munich SPD was taken over by the far left of the party. Outside Munich the SPD in Bavaria remained in the tradition of Bavarian SPD moderation. The contending camps were of roughly equal weight with the result that neither side was able to dominate the other and the Bavarian SPD was characterized by immobilism and paralysis. The most prominent figures, like Hans-Jochen Vogel and Peter Glotz, abandoned their political careers in Bavaria and concentrated on making their way at the federal level.

The CDU/CSU Relationship

Since 1949 the CDU/CSU have had a joint parliamentary party, though the CSU *Landesgruppe* (parliamentary group) has understood this as a permanent alliance whose terms have to be renegotiated at the start of every legislative period. The most serious threat to this cooperation occurred in 1976. The election results of 1976 had had a contradictory effect on the balance of power in the CDU/CSU. Helmut Kohl's position was initially strengthened by the CDU's impressive performance in the election. However, the even more marked success of Franz Josef Strauss and the CSU led the CSU to expect even greater influence for the CSU *Landesgruppe* in the joint *Bundestagsfraktion*.

Moreover, the failure of the CDU/CSU to obtain an absolute majority in a situation in which the FDP was pledged to continue in coalition with the SPD, meant that, although the CDU/CSU was by a considerable margin the largest party, after the election it would not be able to form a government. Strauss and the CSU were not in favour of moving to the centre and cultivating the FDP. A strong tension between the CSU and the FDP has existed since the *Spiegel* affair of 1962 in which the FDP pressed for Strauss's resignation after Strauss had been shown to have acted unwisely and possibly illegally in launching a series of actions against the weekly magazine *Spiegel* which included having the Editor arrested. Strauss advocated an alternative strategy in which the CSU would establish itself on a federal basis and attempt to mobilize the right and extreme right whilst the CDU would mobilize the centre and on 18 November 1976 the CSU *Landesgruppe* meeting in Wildbad Kreuth in Bavaria voted to end their joint parliamentary arrangement with the CDU. But, in the following three weeks the costs of this step became increasingly apparent to the CSU. In the first place Kohl took an uncompromising stand: either the alliance would continue or the CDU would extend its organization into Bavaria and public opinion polls indicated that such an extension would hit the CSU badly, particularly in Franconia. In the second place there was considerable resistance to the decision in some CSU local branches. As a result, the disagreement was hastily papered over.

The relationship remained strained. Strauss was still convinced that the CSU success could be repeated throughout the Federal Republic if he were to lead the CDU/CSU, a view which ignored the fact that Christian democracy was stronger in south Germany than in the north, not so much because of any failure by the CDU leadership, but because of deep rooted factors like the religious divide.

Franz Josef Strauss succeeded in imposing himself on the CDU/CSU as Chancellor-candidate for the 1980 election. His appeal north of the Main proved extremely limited, however, and the CDU/CSU suffered a crushing defeat. This left the way free for Kohl's alternative strategy of detaching the FDP from the coalition. This strategy had succeeded by September 1982 but continued to be opposed by Strauss, who pressed strongly for new elections when the Schmidt government fell on 1 October 1982. If an election had been held at that time, public disapproval of the FDP, who were held responsible for bringing Schmidt's popular chancellorship to an end, would have made it almost inevitable that the FDP would have fallen beneath 5 per cent. Kohl resisted Strauss's pressure and called the elections in March 1983 when the FDP surmounted the 5 per cent barrier.

Helmut Kohl continued to fear an absolute majority for the CDU, since it would have raised intractable problems of coalition management given Strauss's oft repeated allegations of Kohl's incompetence. Paradoxically, when an absolute majority looked a possibility in December 1986, Strauss reduced the chances considerably by attacking the FDP on its very popular foreign policy of detente, thereby helping to undermine the chance of an absolute majority for the CDU/CSU and reinforcing the chances of the CDU/CSU–FDP coalition.

The poor performance of the CDU/CSU and Strauss's contribution to it weakened the position of the CSU more than the CDU. Politically, the result was favourable to Kohl since it meant a strengthening of the FDP who would, he calculated, sustain him in power and contain the CSU.

On a number of issues in the summer of 1987, e.g on granting asylum to Chilean refugees and in his final position on the INF Treaty (see chapter 9), Kohl reflected the view of the FDP rather than the CSU. Strauss reacted with furious denunciations but was condemned to remain in permanent coalition with the CDU. Strauss's position was further weakened by a furious controversy in 1988 over a decision to exempt aircraft fuel for private pilots from a proposed tax increase on aircraft fuel in general. This exemption was inserted at Strauss's insistence. He was a keen amateur pilot but controversy over this issue further undermined his popularity. After Strauss's sudden death in the autumn of 1988, Theo Waigel continued as the leader of the CSU parliamentary group and succeeded Strauss as Chairman of the CSU, while Max Streibl became Minister-President of Bavaria. They are much less likely to pursue a confrontational strategy with Chancellor Kohl in the Strauss manner.

The SPD

The German Social Democratic Party (SPD) is by far the oldest German political party and it is very conscious of being part of a historical tradition which dates back to the 1840s and Ferdinand Lassalle. The modern history of the party really begins with the creation of the Socialist Labour Party. This was formed at Gotha in 1875 through the fusion of the *Allgemeiner Deutscher Arbeiterverein* (German General Workers Association) founded by Ferdinand Lassalle, with the *Sozialdemokratische Arbeiterpartei* (Social Democratic Workers Party) led by August Bebel and Wilhelm Liebknecht. The prolonged persecution of the SPD by Bismarck helped to consolidate the party and to increase its support. In 1891 the party adopted a new programme and its present name. The Erfurt Programme was divided into two parts, the first outlining a theory of social development and long-run objectives in Marxist terms, the second laying down a relatively modest set of aims that the SPD would try to realize within the status quo of capitalist society. The programme, with its uneasy synthesis of revolutionary and reformist tendencies, faithfully mirrored the tension between contending groups in the SPD.

The left wing of the SPD quit the party at the end of the First World War to form the German Communist Party (KPD) and factional conflict within the SPD lost much of its intensity and bitterness. It was replaced by very bitter inter-party conflict between the SPD and the KPD. The SPD played the leading role in a number of Weimar governing coalitions but it faltered in the face of the world depression and the last social democratic led government collapsed in 1930. The intensive conflict with the KPD which divided the well-organised and powerful German labour movement ruled out any cooperation between the KPD and SPD to resist the rise of the NSDAP. Once in power the Nazis quickly banned the SPD and imprisoned those of its local and national leaders who had not fled into exile. The SPD had initially assumed that the party would be successfully led from abroad, as in Bismarck's time. The all pervasive nature of the instruments of repression available to the regime and disillusionment with the less than heroic conduct of some of the exile leadership meant that the exiled party leadership gradually lost contact with those who continued to support the SPD inside Germany.

The weakness of the exiled Executive Committee in London meant that the post-war leader of the SPD was likely to be someone who had endured the Nazi years in Germany. There were two candidates, who represented sharply differing orientations. Otto Grotewohl had emerged as leader of the so-called Central Committee (*Zentralauschuss*) of the SPD in Berlin. Grotewohl and the Berlin group inevitably were much affected by developments in the Soviet zone and they advocated fusion with the KPD. Kurt Schumacher, the most prominent of the leaders in the Western zones, was bitterly opposed to fusion with the KPD. At a conference in Wennigsen near Hannover in October 1945 the representatives of the exiled Executive Committee and most of the delegates supported Schumacher. In April 1946 Grotewohl led the SPD in the Soviet zone into a new fused party, the Socialist Unity Party, SED.

The re-established SPD after 1945 was dominated by Kurt Schumacher. The stress was on continuity and party organization and membership was reconstituted with breathtaking speed. Schumacher rejected attempts to produce a new programme to replace the Heidelberg Party Programme of 1925 though he introduced a modest revisionism while not directly attacking the traditional ideological tenets of the SPD. Marxism was rejected by Schumacher as the sole legitimate basis for the party: 'It is no matter whether someone becomes a social democrat through the methods of marxist analysis for philosophical or ethical reasons, or out of the spirit of the Sermon on the Mount.'[6]

In the immediate post-war period it looked as if the SPD would emerge as the strongest party in any political system set up to cover the Western zones. By the time the Federal Republic had been established the party had lost a lot of ground and was to be relatively weak in the first decade of the Bonn Republic's existence. There were a number of reasons why the SPD's initial hopes proved illusory. The straitened conditions of post-war German existence led to what Kirchheimer has called 'the privatisation of German life', to a concentration on individual advancement and neglect of public questions. Paradoxically, despite the bitter anti-communism of Schumacher and the SPD, the unpopularity of the Socialist Unity Party hindered the SPD since many of the SPD policies, e.g. on economic matters, could be associated with similar sounding and extremely unpopular policies in the Soviet occupied zone. The division of Germany also robbed the SPD of some of its strongest support in areas like Saxony and Thuringia and the changed confessional balance which benefited the CDU/CSU clearly weakened the SPD. Much to its disappointment, the SPD did not receive the backing from the British Labour Government it expected and the Americans, who especially after 1947 were by far the most powerful of the occupying powers in the Western zones, clearly signalled their preference for the CDU/CSU and their dislike of the SPD.

Schumacher and the SPD also made some important strategic errors. Schumacher went into opposition in the Frankfurt Economic Council in 1947 calculating that the SPD would benefit from opposition to what he assumed would be the necessarily unpopular policies of the Western Allies. In the event, fear of the Soviet Union, massive American economic help through the Marshall Plan, and the successful currency reform of 1948 meant that association with Allied policies proved to be a bonus rather than a handicap to the CDU/CSU. Schumacher's other major strategic error was to attack the leadership of the Roman Catholic Church very bitterly in the 1949 election. This left Catholic workers with little alternative but to vote CDU/CSU and the SPD missed an important opportunity to recruit an important group in German society that it had always regarded as rightfully part of its own patrimony but which had been snatched from it by the repercussions of the *Kulturkampf*.

The road to Bad Godesberg   Major electoral reverses in 1953 and 1957 accelerated the efforts of the party to adopt a revisionist programme. This was easier to carry through than for social democrats elsewhere since the banning of the KPD in 1956 removed all electoral competition on the left. The anti-model of the GDR also undermined attachment to Marxist analysis in a way that appeared to leave the SPD little alternative but to drop its historic position of Marxist analysis and reformist practice.

The Bad Godesberg Programme of 1959 failed to mention Marx and dropped long-standing commitments to nationalization. The SPD formula of 'as much competition as possible, as much planning as necessary' represented a commitment to improving and reforming rather than abolishing the social market economy. A year later in a famous speech in the Bundestag on 30 June 1960 Herbert Wehner accepted the basic foreign and security policy positions of the Federal government.

The Bad Godesberg Programme was accompanied by the drop-ping of many traditional SPD symbols and the adoption of the 'peoples' party' model which had hitherto been identified with the CDU/CSU.

On Schumacher's death in 1952 he had been replaced by the rather lacklustre Erich Ollenhauer. The adoption of the Bad Godesberg Programme indicated the SPD's commitment to electoral priorities and Ollenhauer was replaced as Chancellor-candidate for the 1961 election by the young mayor of West Berlin, Willy Brandt. The SPD improved its electoral perform-ance in 1961 and 1965 but its opportunity to enter government came in 1966 when the CDU/CSU–FDP government collapsed and a Grand Coalition of CDU/CSU–SPD was formed in November 1966.

The SPD in government 1966–1982 The formation of the Grand Coalition disillusioned many younger and more left-wing mem-bers of the SPD and the decision to join the Grand Coalition remained a controversial one throughout the life of the govern-ment (1966–9). Unease about the Grand Coalition was deepened by the debate about the introduction of the so-called Emergency Law to provide for continued government in ex-treme situations like wartime. Young and left-wing members of the SPD joined with many outside the SPD in the APO (Extra-Parliamentary Opposition). This movement was able to mobilize very large numbers for demonstrations but by 1969 was collaps-ing due to internal conflict between the values of the adherents of the newly legalized Communist Party, the DKP, and the anti-authoritarian values of the rest.

After the Federal election of 1969 the SPD and FDP were able to form a coalition and their partnership in government was to last thirteen years. This seemed to many observers a triumphant vindication of the party's 'catch-all' strategy. There was always a considerable minority inside the party who were critical of the compromises inherent in such a coalition. In the period between 1969 and the mid 1970s the criticism was concentrated in the JUSOS (*Jungsozialisten*), the party's youth section. The JUSOS were affected by the revival of an interest in Marxism at German universities which characterized the late 1960s and by the experiences of many of them in the APO. Their principal aims were to steer the party in a leftward direction and perhaps even more importantly to introduce in practice a very real degree of inner party democracy. There was little chance that governmental policy could be moved leftwards given the exigencies of coalition and Brandt as Party Chairman tried to absorb these demands by producing a long-term programme which was supposed to guide SPD policy in the 1980s.

Much of the conflict between the JUSOS turned on their attempts to carry through the principle of 'the imperative mandate'. The basic principle of the imperative mandate is to transform representatives into delegates by binding members of parliament to follow decisions of the local level of the party which selected them. It was objected to by a number of SPD deputies as being against the Basic Law and never became party policy. There was also a great deal of bitterness when the JUSOS were successful in capturing the party in some local areas and effected changes in policy and personnel. At the Federal level they were never more than a minority voice.

Brandt's major achievement was his policy of detente, of *Ostpolitik* – a policy which united the left and right of the party. Brandt was all the more bitter when the exposure of his personal assistant in the Chancellor's Office, Gunter Guillaume, as an East German spy so undermined his position in May 1974 that he had to resign as Chancellor.

Willy Brandt was replaced as Chancellor by Helmut Schmidt, but he remained as Party Chairman. In the succeeding period 1974–82 the SPD was run by Schmidt as Chancellor and Deputy Chairman of the party, Willy Brandt as Chairman and Herbert Wehner as leader of the *Bundestagsfraktion*. Initially this arrangement worked well and the SPD revived electorally after the mid-term trough of 1974 and factional conflict diminished.

The Chancellor meets the public's need to be governed efficiently and, indeed, perfectly; the Party Chairman absorbs and channels everything that goes beyond matters of state, he preserves the identity of the party and keeps the Chancellor free for his task, and finally, the parliamentary party leader reconciles the necessities of government and conflicting trends within the party. Despite internal conflicts and tension, this trio, which can be taken as representative of the party as a whole, has proved itself splendidly.

However, shadows were beginning to encroach on this enviable picture. Helmut Schmidt's pragmatic governmental orientation was electorally popular but some aspects of his style and policies were to have severe, even crippling, consequences for the SPD in the long run. His impatience with intra-party discussion and his expectation that the party was there to support him led initially to a decrease in factional conflict but the longer-term result was to force many younger and more left-wing members to conclude that the SPD could never reform itself in the direction of realizing intra-party democracy and they began to leave and sink their energies in various citizens' initiatives and alternative groups.

Schmidt's policy preferences encouraged younger left-wing members to leave the SPD. Schmidt's priorities were shaped by a concentration on keeping the West German economy internationally competitive. The Federal Republic's dependence on external energy sources had been underlined by the oil price crisis of 1973/4 and Schmidt launched a vast long-term programme for the expansion of nuclear energy provision in order to safeguard the Federal Republic's position. A concern with West German competitiveness also made him reluctant to impose costly environmental measures on German industry (see chapter 8).

Given the SPD's coalition with the FDP and the SPD's close identification with the unions there was probably no real alternative at that time. The long-term impact inside the SPD was extremely damaging. The events of 1968 and the prosperity of the Federal Republic led to a profound value shift among the better educated younger generations in favour of quality of life issues. Often referred to in convenient shorthand as 'post-materialists', holders of these political values were particularly well represented in the SPD.

From the late 1970s onwards there was a running battle on nuclear energy and environmental issues between the left and the party leadership who supported Helmut Schmidt, though Brandt, aware of the strength of support for these views, distanced himself somewhat from Helmut Schmidt between 1980 and 1982. As well as promoting intra-party discord, Schmidt's clear rejection of the environmental position helped persuade many younger people to leave the SPD and help in establising the Greens.

Helmut Schmidt was also the father of NATO's dual track decision. Helmut Schmidt first proposed it at a London meeting of the International Institute for Strategic Studies and as adopted by NATO it envisaged negotiation with the Soviet

Union to persuade it to remove its SS20 missiles in Eastern Europe, but if this failed then NATO would deploy intermediate range nuclear missiles in Western Europe, including 108 Pershing 2 and 96 Cruise missiles in the Federal Republic.

In the event the Soviet Union refused to withdraw its SS20 missiles. The prospect of the deployment of Cruise and Pershing missiles gave enormous impetus to the Peace Movement in the Federal Republic and within the SPD opposition to governmental policy mounted steadily after 1980. Opponents of governmental policy were probably in a majority from 1981 onwards and a possible defeat for government policy at the Munich Party Conference of April 1982 was only prevented by a compromise formula which left the final decision to a special party conference to be held in November 1983. At this conference on 18–19 November 1983 the delegates voted overwhelmingly to reject the deployment of new NATO missiles on German soil. The isolation of Helmut Schmidt on this issue was brutally apparent in the final vote in which his policy was defeated by 400 votes to fourteen.

The years since the collapse of the Schmidt government have been very difficult ones for the SPD. In the three Federal elections since then it lost decisively and its share of the poll is now once again approximately equal to its share after the passing of the Bad Godesberg Programme. It is weak at *Land* and communal level though it was successful in the spring of 1988 in taking Schleswig–Holstein for the first time since the 1950s, after the CDU had been discredited by a corruption scandal.

The SPD leadership which was associated with its electoral success has now left the stage. Helmut Schmidt ceased to play any prominent role in the party after losing the Chancellorship. Herbert Wehner retired after the 1983 election to be replaced as leader of the *Bundestagsfraktion* by Hans-Jochen Vogel, the unsuccessful Chancellor-candidate in 1983. Willy Brandt resigned as Party Chairman in April 1987 after his attempt to appoint a Greek woman, who was not a member of the SPD and was engaged to a CDU politician, to the position of party spokesman provoked a storm of dissent in the party. Hans-Jochen Vogel was then appointed Party Chairman with Oskar Lafontaine, the Minister-President of the Saar and the candidate for Chancellor in 1990, being designated as a Vice-Chairman of the party.

Throughout the 1980s the SPD has been plagued by the

dilemma of either concentrating on its core support or pursuing some sort of accommodation with the Greens. A concentration on its core electorate suffers from a number of disadvantages. Industrial change in West Germany as elsewhere is reducing the number employed in manufacturing industry. This strategy is also weakened by the difficulties of the unions. The increase in unemployment in the 1980s weakened the position of the trade unions. The capacity of the trade unions to help the SPD was further undermined by the *Neue Heimat* scandal which weakened the credibility of the unions and has meant that they are likely to be concerned with their own considerable problems rather than mobilizing the SPD electorate. A concentration on the SPD's traditional core electorate would be likely to give it a permanent minority status and an identification with organized labour would give the FDP, even in the long term, little incentive to form a coalition with the SPD.

The alternative orientation is to stress environmental and ecological concerns. Such an orientation is attractive to the considerable body, especially of younger members, in the party who adhere to post-materialist values. The SPD leadership was badly shaken by the electoral success of the Greens in March 1983 and in the legislative session 1983–7 a considerable 'Greening' of the SPD took place, most notably its post-Chernobyl commitment to dispense with nuclear energy within a decade. The more ecological face of the SPD did not, as many in the leadership had hoped, succeed in draining 'the Green Marshes'. The increased success of the Greens in 1987, which as in 1983 was largely at the expense of the SPD, has provided a powerful impetus to exploring the possibility of coalition with the Greens. Such a course is fraught with difficulties. Even at the *Land* level it has been very difficult to form a coalition. The Hesse coalition of December 1985, one of only two examples of a SPD–Greens coalition, collapsed in February 1987. Significant opposition to being involved in government exists in the Greens, and within the SPD there remain many who are opposed to coalition with the Greens. At the federal level the Greens outright opposition to NATO and its defence and security policies generally render a coalition extremely difficult. Even were such a coalition possible then many fear that it would alienate many votes at the centre and the SPD would be just as far away from power as ever.

In the wake of the 1987 defeat there was a great deal of enthusiasm for exploring the possibility of coalition with the

Greens, and Johannes Rau, the unsuccessful Chancellor-candidate, was much criticized for having excluded coalition with the Greens. At that point support coalesced behind Oskar Lafontaine, the Minister-President of the Saar, who had criticized Johannes Rau for excluding the coalition option. Lafontaine was made a Vice-Chairman of the party. Lafontaine's supporters pointed to his success in the Saar where he successfully combined a stress on radical environmental policies and on the preservation of employment in a state dominated by declining heavy industry. This was seen as giving him the chance to demonstrate the popularity and practicability of his appeal before the SPD decided on its next Chancellor-candidate, something usually decided only in the year before the election. The unexpected result in West Berlin in January 1989 put the option with Greens at the federal level back on the agenda for a period; only to disappear with the defeat of the West German Greens in 1990 (see conclusion).

The Freie Demokratische Partei *(FDP)*

The FDP, although small with a core electoral support of between 3 and 4 per cent, has participated in the overwhelming majority of Federal and *Land* governments in the Federal Republic. The key role of the FDP is created by the absence of a majority party in the Federal Republic; only once in 1957, when Adenauer led the CDU/CSU to an absolute majority, has one of the two major parties been in a position to form a government on its own, and even then Adenauer chose to rule with minor party support. The FDP had chosen to go into opposition in the preceding year but, in normal circumstances, the FDP is the obvious partner for one or other of the two major party groupings.

German liberalism has traditionally been divided between right-wing national liberals and a more progressive liberalism, and in Weimar these two tendencies had been represented by separate parties. It had been possible to form a single party in 1948, but the two tendencies remained.

In the 1950s the FDP was on the right of the political spectrum. It sat to the right of the CDU/CSU in the Bundestag and its German Programme of 1954 was decidely nationalistic and conservative. It was often described as 'a reserve platform for dissatisfied CDU/CSU voters' who basically accepted Adenauer's programme but found the CDU/CSU too clerical.

The FDP was in coalition with the CDU/CSU between 1949 and 1956; when, after an internal party struggle, it withdrew from the coalition. Its new party leader, Thomas Dehler, was decidely nationalist and the FDP alone among German parties opposed German entry into the EEC. In 1961 the FDP rejoined the coalition with the CDU/CSU but withdrew in the autumn of 1966 after disagreements on economic policy. The CDU/CSU then formed the Grand Coalition with the SPD.

The years of the Grand Coalition were crucial for the FDP. Erich Mende, who had been leader since 1961, was replaced by Walther Scheel in 1967, a representative of progressive liberalism. The party faced the prospect of extinction since the CDU/CSU and SPD were very close to changing the electoral system to a first past the post system. This would have condemned the FDP to oblivion at federal level, but at the last moment the SPD drew back and the electoral system remained in place.

Willy Brandt had a long-term preference for coalition with the FDP but negotiations in 1966 had convinced him that the FDP were not yet reconciled to coalition with the SPD. In 1969 the FDP did go into coalition with the SPD; a coalition that was to last thirteen years. The decision to enter a coalition with the SPD imposed a considerable strain on the FDP and many party members left; in the first legislative period six prominent FDP deputies crossed party lines to join the CDU/CSU. Together with those who had left the SPD they robbed the coalition of its majority and precipitated the election of 1972.

In the early 1970s the social liberals dominated the party and the adoption of the Freiburg Theses in 1971 with its central concept of 'reform capitalism' represented a major victory for their view that market mechanisms had to be restrained by social considerations. Despite its adoption of the Freiburg Theses, the FDP remained very distinct from the policy positions of the SPD. The FDP, despite Freiburg, was much more enthusiastically committed to the market economy and remained bitterly opposed to any extension of the formal powers of organized labour. It tended to agree with the SPD on the necessity for reform of the educational system, liberalization of the criminal law and the law on abortion. The major point of agreement was, however, on *Ostpolitik*, on detente which both united the divergent wings of the SPD and served as the coalition buckle between FDP and SPD.

By the early 1980s the SPD–FDP coalition was beginning to fray, the FDP were increasingly worried by deficit spending and the pressures on the SPD to adopt a more reflationary policy. They were also worried about the long-term electoral prospects of the SPD and the electoral penalties they suffered from being identified with it. They began to distance themselves from the SPD in early summer of 1982. Count Lambsdorff, the Economics Minister, was bitterly critical of SPD economic policy and indicated that the FDP wanted to pursue a much more market-oriented policy. At the *Land* level the FDP had formed coalitions with the CDU in the Saar and Lower Saxony in order to sustain CDU governments in power and in the early summer of 1982 the FDP indicated that it wished to drop its support of the SPD government in Hesse for the elections to be held in September 1982 and transfer it to the CDU. This was a clear signal that the FDP leadership regarded the federal coalition as doomed. A CDU–FDP victory in Hesse would then have been the occasion to leave. These plans were rudely short-circuited by Helmut Schmidt who brought the coalition to an end on 17 September 1982.

The FDP has been in coalition with the CDU/CSU since October 1982. This precipitated a major turnover and loss in membership and a marked turnover of Bundestag deputies in the ensuing election of March 1983. The problem of identity in coalition with the CDU/CSU is a much sharper one for the FDP since the policy differences with the CDU/CSU are much less salient than with the SPD. In domestic policy the FDP is, if anything, to the right of the CDU and presses for tax reductions. This right-wing stance on issues of distribution is complemented by some attempt to remain liberal on issues of public order though the loss of the interior ministry to the CSU after the March 1983 election has hampered the FDP's role as flag bearer for liberal values, and in 1988 it has had to agree to a much tighter law on demonstrations than it would have liked. Its main identity has been on foreign policy issues where Hans Dietrich Genscher has pursued a consistent policy of detente. The FDP has profited greatly from its policies in this area since they reflect public opinion and continuous attacks from Franz Josef Strauss ensured that voters identified them with the FDP. It was, for instance, a major factor in the 1987 election.

The FDP in the West German party system   The key role of the FDP is less to do with its representing an ideology than its functional utility in the Germany party system. In the development of the West German party system the party has performed four main functions. Its most characteristic function is as *majority provider*. As already mentioned (p. 180) a proportion of West German electors have a *horror majoritas* and have a propensity to vote FDP if a single party appears likely to attain a majority.[8] The FDP then benefits twice since in the absence of a majority the victorious party will normally turn to the FDP in order to form a coalition majority.

A second function is as an *agent of transition*. No opposition has proceeded directly to government in West Germany. There is no habit or expectation of alternation of power, of the replacement of the 'ins' by the 'outs'. Change takes place not as a result of electoral victory but of a change of partners by the FDP. The transition from CDU/CSU-led government to SPD-led government came about as a result of the FDP's decision in 1969 not to form a coalition with its former natural ally the CDU/CSU but with the SPD. A more rapid transition occurred in 1982 when it changed back to the CDU/CSU. The performance of such a function is not without risks and costs to the FDP but an inability to perform this function would result in extinction by absorption into one of the larger parties as the large partner goes through an electoral trough – a real possibility for the FDP if it had remained in coalition with the SPD in 1982. The FDP normally guards against absorption by preserving one or two coalitions at the *Land* level with the party that it is not in coalition with at the federal level. In the summer of 1987 it formed a coalition with the SPD in Hamburg.

The third main function is that of a liberal corrective. This was least pronounced in the coalitions with Adenauer in the 1950s where Adenauer's conception of 'Chancellor Democracy' left little room for a 'liberal corrective' though on education the FDP argued for a more secular and in foreign policy for a more nationalist approach. The liberal corrective function was most pronounced in coalition with the SPD. In the 1950s the party system was divided into two blocs and there was no possibility of the FDP coalescing with the SPD – a situation only changed by Bad Godesberg. In the social–liberal coalition the FDP exerted enormous leverage since its presence was absolutely necessary to the coalition's survival and it would have been possible for the

FDP to switch partners, as a minority continually urged, and as the party eventually did. The FDP concept of a liberal corrective was often successfully involved against an extension of codetermination or progressive taxation.

It is less effective in the CDU/CSU–FDP coalition since the party system has again more of a bloc character and it is difficult to envisage the FDP changing partners again. It is, however, involved in relation to immigration, abortion and legislation on demonstrations though the loss of the Interior Ministry has removed its most important instrument for effecting a liberal corrective on issues of civil liberty.

Its fourth main function has been a derived one as *ideological balancer in governmental coalitions*. This function is distinctive in that it is one assigned to them by the leader of the main governing body rather than a function they decide to perform independently though they have to go along with the role. This role existed in a muted form in Brandt's period as Chancellor. It is significant here that he advanced the concept of the New Centre (*Neue Mitte*) after the SPD's striking electoral advance in 1972 when they were uniquely in the Federal Republic the largest single party. The invocation of the New Centre and the special role of the FDP was designed to curb the SPD left.

The notion of *ideological balancer* was most developed by Helmut Schmidt, who continually used the FDP to contain his own left wing. There was very widespread agreement between Schmidt and the FDP except on the role of the labour unions and a few other issues and the presence of the FDP in the Cabinet allowed Schmidt to defeat the left wing of the SPD.

It is, however, also a major feature of Helmut Kohl's style. An absolute CDU/CSU majority would make it much more difficult for Kohl to contain the CSU. On a number of civil liberty and foreign policy issues the FDP is used quite explicitly by Kohl to contain the CSU. The close identification of the FDP with Helmut Kohl has proved to be an electoral disadvantage in 1988–9 as Kohl's standing is dubious.

The Greens

Until the last decade the parties representing three of the four great families of Western European politics, the Christian democrats, the liberals and the social democrats, monopolized political representation in the Federal Republic. The foundation of the Greens in 1980, their successful entry into the Bundestag in March 1983 and their consolidation of this position in January 1987 thus make a very significant addition to the party system.

The formation of the Greens in 1980 represented the culmination of a number of years of activity on the left. From the mid 1970s one of the most striking developments in West German politics had been the formation of citizens' initiatives (*Bürgerinitiativen*) to deal with a range of issues, but especially environmental issues.

These initiatives, which were usually locally based, represented both a reaction to governmental policies and the outgrowth of rather longer-term social developments.

The SPD governments of Helmut Schmidt had embarked on a very ambitious programme of expansion of the provision of nuclear energy. In opposition to the building of these plants the left inside and outside the SPD found they could mobilize support over a very much wider spectrum than on any previous issue. They were able, as in the opposition to the building of the nuclear plant at Whyl in Rhineland–Palatinate, to mobilize farmers and winegrowers in the affected areas.

The Greens first came together to fight the European Elections of 1979 and it was the income that they derived from the state subsidies received for campaigning in that election that both made practicable and desirable the step of becoming a political party, which they took in 1980. We shall see in the section on party finances that the Greens were the party most dependent on state finance.

The decision to establish themselves as a political party was a difficult one and the Greens continued to think of themselves as 'an anti-party party', as being the interface between extra-parliamentary opposition and a political party. They continually used the metaphor of the two legs, i.e. one leg in parliament and the established political system and one leg in the new movements and extra-parliamentary activity. Such a metaphor, of course, leaves a lot of scope for interpretation as to what the distribution of weight on the respective legs is to be.

The Attempt to Realise Party Democracy   Their enthusiasm for participation and the negative experience of many of the founder members in the SPD meant that the Greens were determined to replace the pyramidal top-down Bonn-centred model characteristic of the established political parties by structures based on the rights of ordinary local party members (*Basis Demokratie*). They were also concerned to assert the legitimacy of extra-parliamentary activity – an aim which seems to the established parties to represent a failure to learn from the collapse of Weimar.

The structures devised by the Greens are novel and were constructed to realise three aims; of preventing the emergence of a professional class of politicians and functionaries, encouraging participation and dramatically reducing the autonomy of the parliamentary elite. The desire to inhibit the emergence of a class of professional politicans is reflected in a number of provisions. Office-holding in the party is unpaid beneath the federal level. Parliamentary representatives were expected only to draw the salary of a skilled worker with the residue to be paid into party funds during their tenure of office. They were also expected to 'rotate' and make way for a designated successor (*Nachrücker*) at the midway point in a legislative session.

Participation was to be encouraged by very loose membership structures. All meetings were in principle open and all party members could participate in party conferences. The holding of multiple party office, which is very widespread in the other parties, was expressly forbidden.

The autonomy of the parliamentary elite was to be constrained in a number of ways. Rotation was designed permanently to refresh the parliamentary elite from the *Basis*. The key concept designed to reduce the autonomy of the parliamentary elite was the imperative mandate, a favourite idea of the left in the SPD in the 1970s, which envisaged that Bundestag deputies (MDBs) should be bound by instruction from the local party that had sent them to the legislature.

The Practice The Greens organizational principles represent a very optimistic reading of human nature and practice has proved difficult. Rotation, which was the principal device to prevent the emergence of a class of professional politicians, proved extremely difficult to endure. It also proved to be extremely controversial, though all but Petra Kelly and Gert Bastian, who resigned and rejoined the Greens, were eventually rotated. The experience of the Greens was, however, that once rotated MDBs rarely retired into private life, but remained active in a number of capacities awaiting the chance to return to the political stage, e.g. Joschka Fischer, a notably reluctant

213

rotatee, became a driving force to form a coalition between the Greens and the SPD in Hesse. The practice of having both members and their designated successors in the *Bundestagsfraktion* simultaneously was not a happy one and led to intense rivalries. Rotation has now been dropped and, although there is an expectation that members will not serve more than one term without a break, the presence of Petra Kelly and Otto Schily in the new *Fraktion* after 1987 suggests that this will not be pursued vigorously.

Membership and activity are not strikingly higher in the Greens than in other parties. The loose structures place little premium on joining and the membership ratio is by far the lowest of the parties represented in the Bundestag. The Greens are also the party most dependent on state subsidies. Surveys also indicate that the active membership is not significantly higher. The major success of the Greens in terms of participation is the much higher participation by women in the Greens at all levels, including the *Fraktion*.

The attempt to reduce the autonomy of the parliamentary elite has been a conspicuous failure. The imperative mandate was largely ignored because, whilst apparently binding MDBs to instruction from the local level, it could, because these instructions were likely to conflict, potentially increase the autonomy of the parliamentary party. Given the loose membership structure, the *Basis* was subject to large fluctuations and would have found it difficult to pursue a consistent policy of imposing its will on its representatives. One could also argue that there is an inherent tension between the principle of rotation and the desire to make the parliamentary elite more responsive. The fact that an MDB knows that, as a matter of principle, he/she will be rotated half-way through the legislative period, is likely to make him/her less and not more responsive to 'the *Basis*'. Lastly, in a party in which resources and paid jobs are concentrated at the parliamentary level, it was always unlikely that the end result would be a party that was much more decentralized than its conventional rivals.

The Greens in the Party System The Greens are an extremely heterogeneous party and, indeed, in some areas like West Berlin, they are known as the Alternative List. Right-wing ideologists who took part in the formation of the Greens left after a short period and the party has clearly been located to the left of the SPD.

There are a number of different ideological positions within the party but the basic distinction has been between the so-called *'Realos'* (realists) and 'the *Fundis'* (fundamentalists). The *Realos* are prepared to contemplate alliances and, even under certain circumstances, coalition with the SPD. From December 1985 until February 1987 the Greens formed a coalition with the SPD in Hesse in which Joschka Fischer a leading *Realo* was Minister of the Environment. The *Fundis*, as the name suggests, represents a more comprehensive rejection of the established system. Unlike the *Realos*, they are very reluctant even to contemplate coalition with the SPD since they fear that this would end with their being absorbed back into the established system. The *Fundis* dominate in areas such as Hamburg and prominent *Fundis* such as Jutta Ditfurth, Thomas Ebermann and Rainer Trampert were in the *Fraktion* elected in January 1987, though the majority of ordinary members are usually counted as *Realos*.

The boundary between these positions is not fixed and individuals cross from one position to the other. The open nature of Green decision-making bodies moreover often means that participants in conferences and meetings change fairly frequently. This results not surprisingly in the balance between the two positions changing from conference to conference.

Party strategists in established parties, especially the SPD, are alternately baffled and annoyed by the Greens' ability to secure parliamentary representation despite policy incoherence, continual unfavourable media comment, bad relations between the *Fundis* and *Realos*, and their lack of professional electoral machines. Three explanations suggest themselves. The Greens continue to benefit from the new issues of environment and defence that emerged in the 1970s. These are both issues which have a considerable appeal, but which the established parties, including the SPD with their investment in the status quo, are much more inhibited in appealing to than the Greens. In relation to the environment, the SPD has to take the unions, whose main concern is employment, along with it, and in relation to defence the SPD could not articulate an anti-NATO policy in the manner of the Greens. On both these issues the Greens have been helped by developments in the 1970s. Their views on the environment have been given greater credibility by the highly dramatic and, for Germans, deeply emotional problem of the 'dying forest' and the twin disasters of Chernobyl and the Rhine spillages.

The Greens are able to compensate for their weak organization by the middle-class, highly educated character of their support. Their core clientele have a high level of political interest and awareness and therefore do not need to be mobilized into voting by party electoral machines. Lastly, although the Greens lack the conventional organizational apparatus of the established parties, they are sustained by a dense network of communication based on alternative economic enterprises.

Women's Issues   Another central area of concern to the Greens has been women's issues. This concern has been reflected in a number of different ways beginning with the issue of participation of women in the party itself. Green candidates' lists for party and public office are ideally put together on the zip principle, i.e. alternating female and male candidates, and this was made official party policy at their party conference in May 1986. This policy has certainly increased women's representation, which has increased from 35.7 per cent of the 1983 *Bundestagsfraktion* to 57 per cent after the 1987 Federal election. This quota has sometimes been exceeded, as in the 1986 Hamburg elections, where all the Green candidates were women.

In the membership as a whole every third member is female as compared with one in four in the established parties. The difference then lies less in the participation rate in the membership as a whole but in the inversion of the normal rule of West German politics that female participation decreases as one ascends the party pyramid towards Bonn. Female membership in the Greens' *Bundestagsfraktion* was strikingly higher than in the party as a whole and between 1985 and 1987 women held all the leadership positions in the *Fraktion* and at time of writing occupy two-thirds of them.

This successful representation of women is all the more striking since the almost complete absence of paid posts, apart from the *Fraktion*, means participation is a very costly activity and this is generally held to affect women more adversely since they are more likely to have to pay the costs of looking after children while they involve themselves politically.

The striking success in terms of representation is less apparent as an electoral effect. Paradoxically the FDP, which made no concessions towards women's representation, and the CDU/ CSU, which made minimal concessions, attracted more female than male voters whilst the SPD, who made considerable efforts to increase female representation and the Greens who made it a central organizational principle, both attracted more male than female voters in the 1987 election. However, the Greens did make significant gains in a key target group of women between 25 and 45 with an unprecedented gain of 7 per cent among 35–45-year-old women. A potentially hopeful development for the Greens was the high degree of abstention of 18–24-year-old women based to some extent on distrust of the established system. This could well be a platform for Green gains among the succeeding generation of women voters. In the 1990 election the West and East German Greens fought on separate lists and while the East German Greens gained entry to the Bundestag, the West German Greens lost votes to the SPD and failed to enter the Bundestag.

THE FINANCING OF WEST GERMAN POLITICAL PARTIES

Historically, German political parties were financed in two ways. The classic mass membership parties, the SPD and the Catholic Centre Party were financed on the basis of subscriptions by the membership. The practice of paying monthly dues on a graduated scale was established by the SPD at a very early point in the party's history and acquired a deep symbolic and emotional dimension during the period when the party was banned between 1878 and 1890. The paying of these dues to the party was taken as a symbol of commitment which was duly registered in the party book carried by every party member. The collecting of these dues was seen as one of the central tasks of the party and provided the basis for the extensive bureaucracy and 'cradle to grave' services then characteristic of the SPD. The Catholic Centre Party adopted many of the SPD's practices in relation both to the funding of party activities and techniques of mass mobilization.

The narrow base of most bourgeois German political parties meant that they were unable to rely on the financial contributions of members. They were largely *'Honorationenparteien'* (notables' parties) with a very low ratio of members to voters. Their major source of support was from business. It proved impossible

217

to organize a conservative party in Germany which could command a mass following. Business thus felt particularly weak and attempted to buy political influence by supporting a range of bourgeois parties. It was particularly concerned historically to prevent alliances between left liberals and the SPD.

In the first decade of the Federal Republic, party finance was re-established on the traditional basis of the SPD being financed by membership subscriptions and the bourgeois parties by business. At that time the SPD derived 80 per cent of its income from membership contributions. Despite the emergence of an 'industry-friendly' majority party – the CDU/CSU – business continued to invest heavily in political parties. Between 80 and 85 per cent of CDU, CSU and FDP funds were provided by business. As in the Weimar Republic, industry spread its donations among the anti-socialist parties with the FDP, the most industry-friendly party, receiving a disproportionately high percentage. The willingness of industry to contribute was strengthened by the introduction of tax concessions in 1954. The ability to receive tax concessions was facilitated by the creation of intermediate associations to channel funds to the political parties. These *Fördergesellschaften* (support organizations) have remained a permanent feature of the West German party political landscape.

The continued support of industry to the political parties was strenuously opposed by the SPD, who derived nearly all their income from membership contributions and the profits of party enterprises like newspaper publishing. The SPD government of Hessen lodged an objection with the Federal Constitutional Court in 1958. The court then ruled that tax concessions for donations to political parties offended against the principle of equity since equal opportunities could not be ensured for all political parties[9] This ruling had a depressing effect on the readiness of industry to contribute to political parties. Adenauer, the then Chancellor, was also becoming increasingly concerned about the expectations entertained by industry in relation to governmental compliance with their demands. These demands constituted a potential threat to the CDU/CSU's character as a *Volkspartei* (catch-all party), seeking to attract electoral support from wide strata of society. The result of these twin pressures was the introduction of a system of state financing of political parties in 1959. The first law of 1959 was based on the para-constitutional position of the parties in Article 21 of the

Basic Law and awarded the parties represented in the Bundestag DM 5 million in the first year to carry out political education.

The law was opposed by the SPD, and the Hessen government again appealed to the Federal Constitutional Court in 1966. The court ruled that taxpayers' money could not be used to finance the general functions of political parties but could be used to finance the cost of elections.[10] The SPD was by this time in 'the Grand Coalition' with the CDU/CSU and henceforward abandoned its opposition to the state financing of political parties.

The Parties Law of 1967 has provided the basis for all subsequent legislation on state finance for political parties. The central provision was a formula by which each party that won over 2.5 per cent of the vote was given DM 2.5 from public funds for each elector who had voted for the party in the preceding election. The 2.5 per cent hurdle was reduced in a subsequent decision of the Federal Constitutional Court to 0.5 per cent in order not to discriminate against new parties. The amount allocated per voter has twice been revised upwards, first to DM 3.50 and then to DM 5. These provisions have been extended to cover *Land* and European elections. In the 1984 European election all five major parties (CSU is counted as a separate party for the purposes of an electoral campaign) spent far less on the electoral campaigns than they received as subsidies.

There are three further sources of public support for party finance. A proportion of the money allocated by the Bundestag to support the work of the parliamentary parties is used by the parties to support the general work of the parties. In 1977 the parties received DM 34.999 million from Bundestag funds, of which only one-half was retained by the parties in the Bundestag, the remainder being used to finance the general work of the parties. All the established parties have parallel political foundations which are meant to be juridically separate but which were shown to have indulged in large-scale tax evasion in the evidence presented during the Flick affair, where two FDP ministers, Lambsdorff and Friderichs, were charged with making tax concessions to the Flick Company in return for large donations.

Political parties also expect that MDBs contribute a proportion of their salaries to the general party treasuries. In 1977 SPD MDBs contributed DM 500 out of their basic monthly salaries of DM 9,013.

Further contributions are made to the local and regional levels of the parties. In the case of the Greens the MDBs are allowed to retain only the salary of a skilled worker, DM 1,920 a month, though allowances are made for children. The rest of the salary is used to finance the work of the party and various ecological funds. Fees paid by MDBs make a considerable contribution to party income and in 1981 accounted for 9.1 per cent of FDP income and 13.5 per cent of CDU income.

The parties are required to produce a set of accounts of income yearly. The accounts for 1984, published in October 1985, are presented in table 7.5.

Table 7.5 Party finance in West Germany 1984

Total income (DM m)	Attributable to membership contributions (%)	Attributable to donations (%)	Attributable to subsidies (%)
CDU 217.7	43.2	12.5	37.2
CSU 43.4	34.4	29.1	32.2
SPD 209.7	49.5	8.2	33.8
FDP 29.9	27.7	30.5	36.9
Greens 43.3	8.7	12.7	58.2

These accounts contain little that is surprising. The FDP remains the party that is most dependent on donations, closely followed by the CSU. The SPD is, as one would expect, least dependent on donations. The trade unions are specifically debarred by law from making contributions to political parties. It is also noticeable how dependent the anti-system party, the Greens, is on state subsidies.

In a political/administrative culture where legalism and legal values normally predominate, the question of party financing has brought all the established parties into conflict with the Federal Constitutional Court and tempted many politicians into illegality. Many observers had expected the Federal Constitutional Court to maintain a firm line on party financing in keeping with their previous rulings and to overturn the 1983 law on party finance. However, in an unexpected and controversial decision in July 1986 the Federal Constitutional Court ruled that restrictions on party foundations should not be tightened and that tax deductions of up to DM 100,000 were permissible. This is widely held to have increased the tax-deductible threshold, which the 1983 law had set at 5 per cent of income. This decision will reinforce the status quo and the Greens look likely to emulate the established parties and set up at least one Green Foundation (see p. 116).

PARTIES AND THE MAKING OF PUBLIC POLICY

German political parties appear at first sight to be in a much more favourable position than British political parties or indeed their own historical predecessors to influence public policy. Comparatively speaking, German parties are extremely well resourced. This enables them and their associated foundations to employ large research staffs to work on the formulation of alternative policies. The conventionally observed distinction between politics and administration rarely applies in Germany where, as we have seen, positions, especially senior positions, in the public service are increasingly partisan appointments. Ministers themselves, in contrast to previous German practice, are drawn from the ranks of senior politicians in the governing parties – normally from the *Bundestagsfraktion*, but occasionally, as happened in the case of the newly created Ministry of the Environment in June 1986, the minister is drawn from the *Land* level. In 1988 Chancellor Kohl appointed as Health Minister a university professor, Ursula Lehr, who at the time of appointment held no official post. In such a case the earliest opportunity is taken to find the Minister a Bundestag seat. The key point for our argument is that ministers are, in contrast to the past, invariably drawn from the political parties.

The preconditions for party governments are clearly present in Germany. It remains a matter of debate, however, as to whether the impress of political parties on public policy is, in practice, much greater than in the United Kingdom. To understand this we have to look at the constraints that operate to impede the policy impact of political parties.

Systemic Constraints

The principle of government by parliamentary majority is qualified by the existence of a dual majority at federal level. Since it can happen, as between 1969 and 1982, that the opposition party to the Federal government is more strongly represented among the *Länder* governments, and thus disposes of a majority in the Bundesrat, there is a structural imperative for the government to cooperate with *Länder* elites. Even where parties sympathetic to the government constitute the majority in the Bundesrat, the principle of 'cooperative federalism' implies an approach based on an attempt at consensus rather than pushing a too sharp party line.

The primacy accorded to party policy is also constrained by the theory and practice of judicial review as operated by the Federal Constitutional Court. The institution of judicial review means that possible objections by the Court have to be taken into account in the preparation of every bill. The broad scope of the Basic Law, which is notable for enshrining goals and values as well as prescribing the mechanisms of government, means that this anticipated reaction acts to reduce the margin for the implementation of party goals over quite a wide area.

Party System Constraints

German governments are almost invariably coalition governments and the priority given to party policies has often to be sacrificed to the exigencies of coalition agreement. The formation of governments is normally preceded by a fairly detailed working-out of a coalition agreement and all governmental policies must command the agreement of the coalition partner.

The Party Dimension

The close relationship between the political parties and the bureaucracy is a two-way process in which, while the administration is now staffed by party-card holders, especially in senior positions, administrative values are often decisive in party discussion. In all political parties the percentage of public officials in the membership has grown. Whilst public officials constituted 4 per cent of the West German population in 1973, they made up 13 per cent of the membership of the CDU (1976), 12 per cent of the CSU (1976), 14 per cent of the FDP (1977) and 10 per cent of the SPD (1977).[11] This rise in the number of party members who are public officials has been accompanied by an even stronger trend for these same officials to win public office. In 1968 Beamten accounted for 9.9 per cent of the membership of the SPD but 19.7 per cent of those elected to public office.[12]

In many state parliaments over a half of the parliamentarians are public officials. The prevalence of public officials among party and governmental office-holders, together with a system which elevates the expert and provides a high level of access for interest groups, necessarily reduces the space for party impact (see chapter 5).

The Law-making Process

In the law-making process in the Federal Republic the demands generated by political parties tend to be crowded out by a culture of expertise. Policy proposals normally originate in a dialogue between the bureaucracy and relevant interest groups and experts. The government organizes policy around 'cooperative, trustworthy "professional" organizations which acquire privileged institutional status'.[13] At parliamentary level the impact of administrators and administrative values is very marked and is normally combined with penetration by interest groups. All three established parliamentary parties have a series of major and minor policy-making committees. The members of such committees are, or become, experts. These experts are, moreover, often the representatives of interests. Klaus von Beyme cited the example of the Bundestag Committee on Labour and Social Order, 70.3 per cent of whose members belong to trade unions, and the Agricultural Committee, of which 77.7 per cent of the membership were farmers.[14]

The Federal Bank

The key central agency insulated from party politics is the Federal Bank (*Bundesbank*) and indeed this is often contrasted favourably with the position of other central banks which are directly subordinate to political control. The key role of the Federal Bank in economic policy-making in the Federal Republic significantly reduces the scope for party input into the policy process.

Attitudinal Homogeneity

The traumatic political experience of the Germans in the twentieth century has created an homogeneity of attitudes which reduces the scope for the development of alternatives. There is a very wide consensus on the negative connotations of the ideological eras of German politics, a hypersensitivity to inflation as a result of the Weimar experience, a belief in institutional pluralism as a reaction to the centralization of power in the Nazi period. The anti-model of East Germany remains a most pervasive constraint on the articulation of policies of a left-wing character.

Taken together, these factors have induced a very broad consensus behind what is sometimes called 'the West German model'. This consensus acted as a very powerful solvent on party political conflict. It is now beginning to be eroded as historical memories become less sharp and the political agenda changes. The most obvious manifestation of this is the Greens. Nevertheless, it remains a very important explanation of the unexpected lack of impact of the political parties.

Table 7.5 Result of 1990 Bundestag Election
(1987 votes and October 1990 seats in brackets)

Party	Votes (M)	Votes (%)	1987	+ (−)	Seats	Oct. 1990
CDU/CSU	20.4	43.8	(44.3)	(0.5)	319	(305)
SPD	15.5	33.5	(37.0)	(3.5)	239	(226)
FDP	5.1	11.0	(9.1)	1.9	79	(57)
Greens	1.8	3.9	(9.2)	(5.3)	−	(51)
PDS	1.1	2.4	−	−	17	−
Bundnis 90/Green	0.6	1.2	−	−	8	−
Others	2.0	4.2	(0.4)	−	−	−

Qualified to vote	60,373,753
Voting	46,996,733
Turnout	77.8% (1987 − West Germany 84.8%)

The election of 2 December 1990 − the first post-war elections in a united Germany − confirmed that the existing party system could be adapted to the new framework of politics.

8　The Political Economy of the Federal Republic

THE EMERGENCE OF THE SOCIAL MARKET ECONOMY

After 1945 economic policy was initially very largely the responsibility of the Allies, and the economy was run on a planned basis. Food and essential commodities were rationed, prices and wages were controlled and foreign trade and exchange were regulated. The Allies had continued with a command economy because of the devastation they had encountered and the sheer difficulties of feeding the population, especially in the British zone, as the expected supplies from Germany's traditional agricultural hinterland in the east failed to arrive.

The planning system was initially supported by most Germans with the exception of the FDP. However, a group of influential Freiburg economists had advanced a series of arguments in favour of freedom of markets since the 1930s, as the Third Reich moved to greater state intervention and they were to be the nucleus of post-war support for market philosophies.

By 1948 market ideas had again collected a lot of support from economists. Alfred Müller-Armack, generally thought of as the father of 'the social market economy', accepted the Freiburg arguments in favour of the market but argued that government should redistribute the results of market processes if the social consequences were unacceptable. Müller-Armack found a key ally in Ludwig Erhard, a veteran market economist, who had by 1948 become Economics Director of Bizonia. Erhard then set about liberalizing the economy. The military governments had put through a currency reform on 20 June 1948 by introducing the Deutschmark. This act is often associated with the start of the 'Wirtschaftswunder' (the economic miracle) as shop windows suddenly filled with goods which had already been produced but which producers had thought it not worthwhile to bring on to the market in the absence of currency reform.

On 26 June 1948, Erhard took the decisive step in the

direction of the social market economy by promulgating the law on the liberalization of markets and the removal of central planning. The social market economy established by Erhard has been well characterized by Horn as:

1 The highest possible economic welfare through competition, steady economic growth, full employment and free international economic relations.
2 An efficient monetary framework – and in particular a stable average price level achieved through an independent central bank, stable budgets and balanced foreign accounts.
3 Social security and progress through maximization of the national product, effective competition and adequate redistribution of income and wealth.[1]

The aspect of the social market economy which was most imperfectly realized was competition. It took until 1958 for a Cartel Act to be passed and it was notably weak, except by previous German standards. Those large firms which had been split up by the Allies largely reformed, though not in the chemical industry where BASF, Bayer and Hoechst retained an independent life after the breakup of IG FARBEN in 1951. Initially, the introduction of the social market economy led to a very sharp increase in industrial production but unemployment remained high until 1953. As the impact of the boom occasioned by the Korean War fed through the economy, full employment was restored and the *Wirtschaftswunder* became an important source of political stability to the nascent republic.

Contemporary observers had not predicted the scale of the success and indeed many had predicted disaster. In retrospect, it looks less surprising. Among the favourable conditions were American Marshall Aid after 1947; the availability of a large supply of cheap, reliable labour escaping from East Germany and from areas occupied by the Russians (sometimes whole factories were rebuilt by their owners in the West); the presence of large numbers of Allied forces which boosted the economy and the balance of payments; and the undervaluation of the German mark until the world monetary upheavals of the early 1970s. Moreover, it should be noted that, despite the use of such phrases as *der Zusammenbruch* (collapse) and *die Stunde O* (zero hour) to describe the end of the war, much of Germany industry escaped unscathed. Lawrence estimates that around one-quarter of Germany's industrial capacity was destroyed or dismantled: a considerable proportion, but something short of complete devastation of the kind which the phrases quoted conjure up.[2] Finally, it should be noted that after 1958 membership of the EEC conferred considerable advantages on West Germany; advantages, one might even suggest, greater than on other member states. German industry benefited from access to a wider market, whilst German agriculture was protected from undue disruption.

The economic miracle of the 1950s represented a conscious reversal of the priorities of the political economy of the Third Reich. During the Third Reich the German economy had been partially decoupled from the wider world economy and the emphasis had been on self-sufficiency and autarky. The post-war miracle depended on West German acceptance of the rules of the game of the liberal international economy. After some reluctance in the 1940s, these were embraced with gusto by German industrialists in the 1950s, and the economic miracle was built on a very marked export orientation in manufactured goods which accounted for about 30 per cent of West Germany's GNP.

The 1960s

In the 1960s there was some growth in state intervention. In 1963 the Council of Experts (*Sachverständigenrat*), made up of five economists, was established to report to the government each year on economic trends. The mild recession of 1966 and the advent of Karl Schiller as Economics Minister during the Grand Coalition, led to the introduction of a mild form of Keynesianism. The 1967 Stability and Growth Act required the government to seek to maintain a stable price level, full employment and a foreign trade equilibrium and to fine tune the economy where necessary through the use of fiscal indicators. The adoption of Keynesian techniques was paralleled by the establishment of *Konzertierte Aktion* (concerted action), a tripartite framework for consultation between government, industry and unions, through which it was hoped to influence the behaviour of the non-governmental actors by acquainting them with as much information on the state of the economy as possible.

The resulting system has been characterized as a unique blend of medium-term financial planning, which achieved much greater government control over spending; close coordination between federal and state (*Land*) economic and fiscal policy through the Financial Planning Council (*Finanzplanungsrat*) and Countercyclical Advisory Council (*Konjunkturrat*); and close consultation between government, industry and unions about economic conditions and prospects through the Concerted Action system (*Konzertierte Aktion*). At its best, this mildly corporatist, distinctly interventionist (by German standards) system worked rather well.[3]

1973 – The End of an Era

Economic policy-making for the Federal Republic became much more difficult in the 1970s. The economy of the Federal Republic was highly dependent on imported energy and was therefore especially vulnerable to the rise in energy costs after the oil price rise of 1973. Worse still the rise in energy costs was accompanied by a falling off in world trade. Schmidt, until May 1974 both Economics and Finance Minister, responded by introducing a fairly vigorous regime of deficit spending. In 1972 the Federal Budget had a deficit of DM 4 billion but by 1976 the budget was registering a DM 26 billion deficit. Although exports had recovered by 1976 the budget deficit was to remain a problem as social spending steadily increased under the SPD–FDP government. Between 1969 and 1981 public expenditure (principally the cost of the welfare state) had risen from 38 per cent of GNP (low by West European standards) to 51 per cent in 1980. Budgetary stability had been an important agreed goal, part of a continued reaction to the 1923 inflation, and these deficits made the SPD–FDP government very vulnerable to attack. The existence of these deficits proved less decisive than one might have predicted for two reasons. Helmut Schmidt was seen by West Germans as a massively reassuring figure. Personally austere and an acknowledged economics expert, his personal credentials as managing director of the Federal Republic Limited seemed beyond question, despite reservations about other board members. Moreover, the level of employment, another very important goal, remained high by international standards.

The situation of the government deteriorated sharply after 1980 in the wake of the second oil crisis occasioned by the Iranian revolution of 1979. The Federal Republic recorded its first trade deficit for fifteen years in 1979, unemployment more than doubled between 1980 and 1982, rising from 4.1 per cent (1 million) to 8.5 per cent (circa 2 million) and industrial production fell by 5.5 per cent in 1980, stagnated in 1981 and fell again by 5.5 per cent in 1982. Even more threateningly given West German sensitivity to inflation, the inflation rate rose to 5.5 per cent in 1980 and 6.5 per cent in 1981.

These developments played a major part in the dissolution of the SPD–FDP coalition. Helmut Schmidt, the governmental wing of the SPD, and most of the FDP wanted to give priority to cutting the budget deficit, despite the probable effect on unemployment. The SPD left, the trade unions and the social liberals united around the defence of 'the welfare net' and the maintenance of high levels of employment. The tensions over these issues were a major factor in the break up of the SDP–FDP coalition.

The CDU/CSU–FDP Government

Otto Lambsdorff (Economics) and Gerhard Stoltenberg (Finance), the key figures in the economic policy formulation of the new government, gave priority to the restoration of budgetary stability by the introduction of relatively tight fiscal policies. This proved very effective and by 1986 the budget deficit stood at 1.5 per cent of GNP as compared with 4.5 per cent in 1982. By that time inflation had been reduced to zero and for periods was actually negative. Industrial production, which had initially fallen after the collapse of the SPD–FDP government, quickly picked up and rose 14 per cent between 1983 and 1986. Export performance was very impressive and profits from trade with North America reflecting an overvalued dollar were especially high. The only economic indicator that remained negative was the level of unemployment, which remains about 2 million.

This generally very optimistic picture began in 1987 to look a little less rosy. The continued rise in the value of the Deutschmark, in itself a reflection of the success of the West German economy, and the rise in German labour costs, was beginning to make some German products less competitive in key markets and the level of exports had fallen away from its recent very high levels. This reverse proved to be temporary and boom conditions prevailed from 1989.

GOVERNMENT AND INDUSTRY

The core responsibility for the performance of the West German economy lies with the Bundesbank and the three ministries of Economics, Finance and Research, and Technology. Unlike the Bank of England, the Bundesbank has a constitutionally anchored and zealously guarded autonomy. This autonomy has not prevented it from exercising a major role in the development of German economic policy and its representative is often invited to attend Cabinet meetings of the Federal government. The Bundesbank has also been aided in promoting a consistently cautious fiscal policy by very widely shared public anxieties about inflation, traceable ultimately to the German experience of catastrophic inflation in the early 1920s. Since 1974 the Bundesbank has published annual money supply targets in a conscious attempt to influence the level of wage settlements and government fiscal policies.

However, the major governmental actor in relation to industry is the Ministry of Economics. The Ministry of Economics sees itself, and is seen by industry, as the *Anwalt* (attorney) of German industry. This means that it sees itself as the spokesman for industry and will attempt to defend industry in interministerial disputes, e.g. on environmental regulation. It will also advance the interests of German industry at the European Community level. It is especially well placed to carry out this function since it shares responsibility for European policy with the Foreign Ministry and carries the major responsibility for day-to-day policy, its preparation and transmission to Brussels. In its Division Four, the Industrial Division, the Ministry has a number of specialized *Referate* (sections) dealing with each of the main industries. The Ministry has, however, been less interventionist than its British equivalent. It acts rather as spokesman for the 'social market economy' with the emphasis on the market aspects. Its adherence to the social market economy is such that this theory is often referred to by Ministry officials, only half in jest, as *'die reine Lehre'* (the true doctrine). Since 1974 the Minister has always been a member of the FDP.

Although the Ministry is, in theory, non-interventionist and at the declaratory level at least ruled by market principles, exceptions are made. These exceptions to the true doctrine are often referred to as *Sündenfälle* (occasions of sin). Subsidies and protective measures have been allowed where a sector is in crisis, like shipbuilding and steel. Subsidies are also much more likely to be given where there is a high incidence of small business interests (*Mittelständische Interessen*). This practice can partially be explained by the fact that the minister and some of his leading officials, especially in the policy planning section (*Grundsatzreferat*), are FDP adherents. The FDP is committed to the market economy but is also crucially dependent on the support of small business.

The established attitudes of the Economics Ministry were perceived as an obstacle by some leading members of the SPD in the early 1970s, and in 1972–3 the former Atomic Energy Ministry was transformed into a new Ministry for Research and Technology. It is this ministry that has implemented the nearest equivalent to an industrial policy in the Federal Republic. This policy has taken the form of providing massive financial resources in certain key sectors, especially electronics and nuclear energy, to finance research and development. The giant electrical firm Siemens has been the most notable beneficiary of this policy.

The policy has been accompanied by a great deal of controversy. Critics have pointed out that much of the investment, especially in electronics and computers, appears to have been misplaced. They draw attention to the fact that firms like Siemens are conspicuously liquid and could well and should undertake the investment in research and development themselves. The Ministry also attracted a great deal of criticism from some sections of industry. The chemical industry, which is conspicuously successful in research and innovation, is very strongly committed to market principles. It accepted very little money from the Research and Technology Ministry and pressed instead for a policy of supporting research by a generous tax regime.

The Research and Technology Ministry survived the transition from an SDP–FDP coalition to a CDU/CSU–FDP coalition and continues to support research and development on a massive scale, e.g. the German space programme.

Despite the above-mentioned differences in philosophies and practice, the Economics and the Research and Technology Ministry are alike in being much more likely to look to industry to supply them with information than their British counterparts. The principal explanation is that the specific German form

231

of 'cooperative federalism' in which policies are almost exclusively implemented by *Land* (state) bureaucracies has meant that normally the Bonn ministries have often found it easier to get information direct from industry rather than relying on the necessarily time-consuming procedure of consulting *Land* bureaucracies. They are particularly likely to turn to industry when time constraints are short, e.g. in preparing a reply to parliamentary questions. Whitehall in similar circumstances would usually rely on information already available in the ministry.

The Bonn ministries, in approaching the industry for information, would in most cases use the relevant trade association. There is a general political-administrative culture of reliance on consultation with the extremely well-organized interest groups. In exceptional cases where the government is a major customer and one firm is totally dominant, they might approach a single firm rather than a trade association, e.g. Siemens. In the chemicals sector for instance they would invariably approach the *Verband der Chemischen Industrie* (Chemical Industries Association).

THE REPRESENTATION OF BUSINESS INTERESTS

By international standards capital and labour are very highly organized in the Federal Republic, but the degree of organizing differs between the two sides of industry. Business interests have a much higher organizational density and command much greater resources than their labour counterparts.

Peak Associations

Business interests are represented in the Federal Republic at the federal level by three principal peak associations, the BDA (*Bundesvereinigung der Deutschen Arbeitgeberverbände*), the BDI (*Bundesverband der Deutschen Industrie*), and the DIHT (*Deutscher Industrie und Handelstag*). Following traditional German practice, a distinction is made between an employers' association, the BDA, and the general interest association for business, the BDI. The BDA is concerned with all aspects, including wages and social policy. Unlike the BDI, which is restricted to industry in its narrower sense, the BDA covers all the main sectors of the economy. It has a very high organizational density with over 80 per cent of German employers belonging to the BDA through its member organizations. Despite this very high density, the BDA is dominated by the representatives of the very large firms through their dominant role in the two most influential sectoral organizations, *Gesamtmetall* (everything connected with the production and working of metal), and the *Verband der Chemischen Industrie* (Chemical Industries Association). The making of collective agreements in Germany is the responsibility of the sectoral employers' organizations but the BDA ensures that agreements within the different sectors are concerted and that no one sector concludes agreements which are out of line. This constraint applies not only to the level of wage agreements but also to hours of work and codetermination. The BDA and its member organizations are extremely well funded and they have developed an impressive and increasingly centralized system of funds to compensate firms and sectors which lose through industrial disputes. This has two implications. First, German employers are much more ready than other Western European employers to contemplate and practice 'lockouts'. Secondly, although much collective bargaining is still done on a regional level, it is in practice becoming increasingly centralized, since employers' strike funds are centrally held and any regional association making a settlement that was out of line would not receive payments from the fund. The high organizational density of the BDA, the marked capacity of the German employers to act collectively and a labour law which makes striking difficult and lockouts comparatively easy, combine to place German employers in a very powerful position.

The BDI represents the interests of German industry. It has thirty-five member associations and its membership is normally reckoned to comprise about 95 per cent of the firms in the industrial sector. Like the BDA, the BDI is generally identified with the interests of large business.

The DIHT, the organization representing the chambers of commerce, is a more specifically German type of organization than the BDA and BDI. Unlike the BDA and BDI, it is not a voluntary organization. Membership is compulsory for firms and the chambers of commerce perform a number of public functions, e.g. in relation to vocational training. Despite its parastatal character, the DIHT is an energetic representative of business interest with a much heavier accent than the BDA or

BDI on the interests of small and medium sized business (*Mittelständische Interessen*).

Other Channels

In previous accounts of business representation in West Germany attention has been focused only on the peak associations. In our view this is seriously misleading. It is true that in the early years of the Federal Republic the BDI in particular did dominate business representation. There were two major reasons for this. First, business had a strong collective interest in laying down the framework conditions (*Rahmenbedingungen*). There were key issues like the Codetermination Law and the Competition Law where the BDI was able to exert a major influence in the direction of a pro-business outcome. Secondly, in an era in which the system was being established, personal networks were important and a number of key figures in the BDI cultivated close friendships with Konrad Adenauer.

The peak associations were again of crucial importance during the SDP–FDP coalition, where there were general areas of disagreement between the Federal government and the business and industry community. The SPD–FDP government has been succeeded by an industry-friendly (*Industriefreundlich*) government and there are no major issues at stake between business and government. In this situation, interests become increasingly sectoral and a more and more important role is played by the very well organized sectoral associations, e.g. the *Verband der Chemischen Industrie*. These associations maintain a Bonn presence and, while industry-friendly governments are in power, they, rather than the BDI, would, taken together, do the bulk of the work of representing business though, of course, some collective interests, like pro-business tax reforms and the struggle against over-stringent environmental regulation, continue to be pursued at the collective level. The BDA's importance is less subject to fluctuation than is the BDI's since the issues it handles remain ones in which business has a strong collective interest.

Large firms also take part directly in the political process although they normally lack the specialized government relations divisions of large British firms. These large firms normally also maintain a Bonn office as a base for lobbying. This is a common feature in sectors where the government is the principal customer (e.g. defence and telecommunications), or where it subsidizes research (Siemens). It is not the case in the chemicals sector and other sectors where the government is neither a major customer nor a major research sponsor. In these sectors the sectoral association is responsible for the great bulk of contacts with government, and the firms do not maintain a Bonn base.

The German Farmers Union (Deutscher Bauernverband)

One of the marked peculiarities of modern German historical development has been the way in which business interests were happy to tolerate and indeed come to an accommodation with the agricultural sector. There was no German equivalent to the repeal of the Corn Laws, instead an alliance was forged in the Imperial period between 'rye and iron' (*Roggen und Eisen*).

In the Federal Republic the cohesion of the industrial and business community is matched and indeed surpassed by the agricultural community organized in the German Farmers Union (DBV). It has approximately 750,000 members and represents over 90 per cent of those engaged full time in agriculture. This is the highest ratio of membership of any interest group in the Federal Republic. Unlike the situation in the Weimar Republic and unlike that in a number of other continental countries, there are no significant regional or religious cleavages.

This amazingly cohesive group is also helped by a very favourable mass and elite opinion. West Germans do not rate agricultural surpluses highly as a major problem. The favourable view of farmers has a number of roots. These include the long-term effects of the *'Blut und Bodenmystik'* (blood and soil mysticism) of the Third Reich, fear of rural radicalism engendered by the collapse of Weimar, the close relations between urban and rural dwellers fostered by the food shortages of the early post-war period, the fact that one-quarter of the population of West Germany have fled from the overwhelmingly agricultural areas of eastern Germany and the feeling present in the early years of the Federal Republic that the loss of these agricultural lands in the east would necessarily mean subsidizing agriculture in the Federal Republic for the indefinite future in order to make good the deficit. This deficit had produced extreme hunger in the years after the war and the subsidization of the farming interest was part of the founding compact of the

Federal Republic given formal expression in the Lübke Plan of 1953 and the Agricultural Act of 1955.

The high levels of cohesion and of public and elite acceptance of the DBV ideology that farmers perform a vital service to the economy and to the maintenance of the countryside are clearly major political resources for the DBV and the agricultural interest in the Federal Republic. The DBV seeks to use these favourable background conditions in a number of ways. First and most important it cultivates a close relationship with the Ministry of Agriculture. It has been notably successful in this area and the ministry is often spoken of as an example of 'clientelism' or agency capture. It also directs its attention to the Bundestag. Its attention here is focused on controlling the Bundestag Agriculture Committee. In the Agricultural Committee for the legislative period 1980–2, sixteen of the twenty-six members were directly engaged in agriculture and the viewpoint of this committee is normally very close to that of the DBV. Our argument here is that the Bundestag is thus unlikely to act as a countervailing power to the Ministry of Agriculture since it delegates powers to the Agriculture Committee which is securely dominated by the agriculture interest.

The DBV has also been notably successful in getting its supporters into key positions in the CDU/CSU and the FDP. The present Minister of Agriculture, Ignaz Kiechle (CSU), has for long been a prominent member of the DBV and, but for the requirements of coalition balance, the job would have gone to von Heeremann the DBV president who had been Kohl's choice in the post. Relations with the SPD have never been as close, and very few full-time farmers vote SPD.

German farmers' incomes have been threatened since 1984 by the very minimal reforms, particularly the introduction of milk quotas, made in the Common Agricultural Policy. This led to abstention by farmers in the 1984 European election and the 1987 Federal election. The response of the Federal government has been to allow Herr Kiechle to veto any attempts at far-reaching reform of the CAP whilst calling without much conviction for the reduction of EC spending. At the same time the Federal government has reintroduced national subsidies for farmers on an appreciable scale. This will have some impact on costs but business has expressed no criticism and simply views it as a small sacrifice for the maintenance in power of the industry-friendly parties, the CDU/CSU and the FDP.

THE ORGANIZATION OF LABOUR

Although the trade union movement is well resourced by international standards, it organizational density is comparatively low. Just under 40 per cent of the German workforce is organized in unions. Whilst this is comparable to the rates of other industrial economies, it compares very unfavourably with the rates achieved by the employers' organization of around 80 per cent.

The German trade union structure was rebuilt with a great deal of British guidance after 1945. Its rebuilding also reflected a desire not to repeat the mistakes of Weimar when an apparently powerful labour movement had proved totally unable to stop Hitler's rise to power and its own subsequent destruction. The reconstituted trade union movement was guided by the two major principles of the unitary trade union (*Einheitsgewerkschaft*) and the industrial union (*Industriegewerkschaft*). The principle of the unitary trade union is an attempt to overcome the confessional and political divisions which characterized the trade union movement in Weimar. It involved a less close relationship with the SPD than had formerly obtained. There is no equivalent in Germany of collective membership and the bloc vote as with the British Labour Party and the unions. The Catholic trade union movement was not restarted though a small Christian trade union was formed in the mid 1950s when the union movement was split over the issue of German rearmament. A final dimension of the unitary concept involved keeping communist influence in the union movement to an absolute minimum since the communists were held liable for the division in the Weimar labour movement.

The concept of the industrial union involves the ending of inter-union strife by only allowing one union per industry. Although the intention of this reform was to strengthen the labour movement by abolishing competition, its effect has arguably been to weaken the union movement as a whole since individual unions identify very strongly with the interests of their own industry sometimes in opposition to the interests of the wider labour movement.

The unions are organized in the *Deutscher Gewerkschaftsbund* (DGB), a peak association of seventeen unions. The DGB has relatively modest powers and cannot steer or direct individual unions. The German union movement with only seventeen members of the DGB is thus concentrated but not centralized. The most influential union is IG Metall, the metal workers' union, which is by far the largest. Influence is not domination, however, and although there have been periods when IG Metall appeared to dominate the DGB, this has not been true for some time and, as we shall see later, there is not inconsiderable opposition to the present strategy of IG Metall among a section of unions affiliated to the DGB.

DGB and Government

In the Adenauer period, the DGB had very little access to government. During the Grand Coalition and up until the unions withdrew in 1977, the unions participated in tripartite consultation with the government through the so-called 'Concerted Action'. This could never have developed into full-blown corporatism since the DGB is too decentralized and simply lacks the steering capacity to work corporatist-type arrangements.

Despite the collapse of Concerted Action, the unions enjoyed a high level of access to government and a number of prominent trade unionists served in Schmidt cabinets. Under Helmut Kohl tripartite meetings have been dropped and the union leaders have been marginalized. They have also contributed to this situation – a sort of self-marginalization – by a series of scandals which have done a great deal to delegitimize the trade union leadership. The central scandal, as already indicated, involved the collapse of the *Neue Heimat*, the trade union organization for constructing workers' houses. This organization collapsed with considerable ignominy in circumstances which reflected a great deal of discredit on some union leaders. Not only was there widespread corruption but the trade union management of *Neue Heimat* had conspicuously failed to invoke the procedures required under codetermination to inform its own workforce. The difficulties involved in clearing up *Neue Heimat* and other trade union enterprises are likely to absorb much of the energies of the trade union leaders for a number of years rather than those energies being expended to institute new strategies for the DGB. Another major scandal involving the retail branch of the cooperative movement in 1989 was a further blow to the DGB.

Unlike the BDA, the DGB is not even an informal party to collective bargaining. Wage agreements are negotiated by individual unions. However, although there is no centralized system of collective bargaining in the Swedish mode, individual unions increasingly conduct bargaining in a centralized manner although many agreements continue to be negotiated at the regional level. The bargaining strategy is planned centrally and institutional devices have been devised to overrule a regional organization intent on concluding an agreement out of line with the central union strategy, or rejecting one in line with it.

The bargaining position of the unions has been severely weakened by five developments. The first is not new. German industrial workers often develop a high identification with the firm than employs them and union officers in a particular plant often identify more strongly with the firm and its aspirations that with the goals of the union in general. Secondly, the rapid development of industry in South Germany, especially in Bavaria and Baden–Württemberg, the 'sun belt' states, weakens the unions. In the 'rust belt' union loyalties and unionization remain high (50 per cent in the Saar, 40 per cent in North Rhine–Westphalia), but in the rapidly expanding regions it is much lower (Bavaria 25 per cent). Thirdly, the onset of high-level unemployment in the early 1980s weakened the unions' negotiating position. Fourthly, their negotiating position has been weakened by unresolved policy differences between leading unions. A majority led by IG Metall and IG Druck (the printing union) want to pursue what is by German standards a relatively conflictual strategy of responding to unemployment by pressing for significant cuts in the working week. A minority, often referred to as the Gang of Five (chemicals, foodstuffs, mining, construction and textiles), wish to pursue a strategy of maximum accommodation. IG Chemie (chemicals) was the first German trade union to invite a CDU Chancellor (Helmut Kohl) to address its annual conference. The understandable reluctance of East German workers to join trade unions after their negative experience of communist led unions is a final source of weakness.

IS THE WEST GERMAN SYSTEM CORPORATIST?

The relatively concentrated nature of West German interest groups and labour unions, the formal tripartite structure of Concerted Action (1967–77) and informal tripartism of the later Schmidt years led some observers to describe West Germany as corporatist. This view overlooked the limited scope of 'Concerted Action' which was restricted almost exclusively to the area of incomes policy. As a body its deliberations had no binding force, indeed its purpose, as conceived by Karl Schiller, was not to act as a direct forum in wage bargaining but for the government with the aid of macroeconomic projections to inform business and labour about the expected consequences of their own policies and about the probable result of the government's policies. Any residual corporatism disappeared after 1982. Moreover, whilst interest associations, both business and labour, are relatively concentrated, i.e. few in numbers, they are not highly centralized, i.e. the peak associations cannot command member groups and corporatist steering is thus largely excluded. The unity that is certainly present in the German industrial policy community owes less to corporatist structures than to the homogeneity of attitudes described at the end of the previous chapter. If the role of overarching corporatist institutions has been exaggerated, the central importance of corporatist arrangements at the sectoral level (meso-corporatism) where employers, unions and the relevant ministry normally act together and impose their collective decisions on their members cannot be overstressed.

Codetermination

A distinctive feature of the German system of industrial relations is the institutionalized participation of workers' representatives in the management of companies through a system known as 'codetermination' (*Mitbestimmung*). In 1952 this system was adopted for heavy industry (*Montanmitbestimmung*). German firms normally have a small executive board which reports to a rather larger supervisory board. In the heavy industry model the supervisory board has an equal number of representatives of capital and labour and one 'neutral' member. Moreover, the personnel director on the main board has to have the support of the labour side in the supervisory board. This form of codetermination reflects the strengths of the unions in heavy industry and the delegitimization of the employers' side by their actions in the Third Reich. Its importance has decreased in recent years as heavy industry has continued to contract in size and influence. In the SPD–FDP coalition, a new codetermination law was introduced to cover firms with more than 2,000 employees. This is a much weaker system. Again capital and labour are equally represented on the supervisory board.

However, there is no neutral member and the chairman of the supervisory board is nominated by the employers' side. Moreover, the labour side must contain one under-manager (*Leitender Angestellte*) who might vote with the employers' side when there is a conflict. There is no requirement for the personnel director to be approved by the labour side of the supervisory board.

Despite these concessions, which were inserted as a result of pressure from the FDP, the act was opposed by industry, especially by multi-national firms. They took the resulting act of 1976 to the Federal Constitutional Court, where it was upheld. The unions were so incensed by this, since in their view the act was not nearly strong enough, that they withdrew from the 'Concerted Action' system in 1977.

The third form of codetermination applies to all firms employing more than five people. It allows the workers in these firms to elect works councils (*Betriebsräte*) which have extensive consultative rights further strengthened in 1972. The unions attempt and to a large extent succeed in dominating these elections. Nevertheless, differences often appear between works councillors who identify with the firm and the wider union. The works councillors negotiate conditions of work rather than wages but these can be vitally important since they cover issues like fringe benefits, pensions, overtime etc. In the chemical industry there are very significant differences between the wages and conditions offered in one of the prosperous giants and the agreed minimum wage paid by a less prosperous firm. The firm of Bayer Chemicals supports two *Bundesliga* football teams and sports facilities are so good that twenty-three members of Bayer works sports clubs have won Olympic medals.

The codetermination system in its various forms has had some successes in recent years. In the general rationalization process of the 1980s, the system gives the workforce valuable rights of information and consultation in relation to proposals for plant closure. It can for instance demand the adoption of a 'social plan' to provide for financial compensation for employees who are redeployed or lose their jobs. It can further be argued that it does force the unions into a more responsible attitude. Members of IG Metall play a key role in Volkswagen and they agreed in the 1970s to extended lay-offs and rationalization till new models like the Golf came on stream and restored the market position of Volkswagen.

241

POLITICAL PARTIES AND ECONOMIC INTERESTS

The fit between economic interests and political parties, while close, is less exclusive in the Federal Republic than in Britain. Business has close relations with the CDU/CSU and the FDP. Historically indeed there has been a closer fit between business ideology and that of the FDP. Business was also very close to the FDP in the period of the social/democratic–liberal coalition of 1969–82 where the FDP were able to block far-reaching legislation on codetermination and environmental protection. The CDU has always contained a union-oriented Catholic social wing, the so-called 'Social Committees', which has prevented the CDU/CSU being an articulator of business views in the relatively unambiguous manner of the British conservative party. The decline in the influence of the 'Social Committees' and the greater influence of neo-conservative ideology in the CDU has led to a much closer fit between the CDU and business than in the past. Agricultural interests, despite very considerable subsidies, feel less close to their traditional allies in the CDU/CSU and have stepped up the pressure on the CDU/CSU by large-scale electoral abstention. This has been fairly effective in producing more subsidies.

The relationship between the SPD and the trade unions has often been an ambiguous one in the Federal Republic. When the united trade union movement (the *Deutscher Gewerkschaftsbund*) was formed in 1949, it was officially neutral on party political questions. Despite an extensive common membership with the SPD, its first Chairman, Hans Böckler, actually steered it in a direction where it could reasonably be seen as supporting the Christian Democratic government, particularly over the issue of European integration. The importance of the rearmament issue led in 1952 to the removal of Böckler's successor, Fette, and his replacement by Walter Freitag, an SPD deputy. During Freitag's period as Chairman in 1952–5, the DGB was very closely identified with the SPD.

Relations with the SPD were close after 1969, partly on account of the unions' support for Brandt's *Ostpolitik*, but principally because the SPD was more sympathetic, if not much more successful, in practice than the CDU/CSU in responding to demands for an extension of industrial codetermination beyond the coal and steel industry. The German unions do not have the same institutionalized access to the SPD that their British counterparts enjoy to the Labour Party, nor are they an important source of finance. Yet they can be, and often are, an important source of support to the SPD in various ways.

How valuable this support can be in electoral terms can be seen in the 1972 election. The DGB gave more decisive support to the SPD than in any previous campaign, including that of 1953. The DGB's action was the product of four main factors. There was first the tremendous sympathy for Brandt and his government as the grass roots demonstrated in the spontaneous pro-government strikes, particularly in the Ruhr, at the time of the no confidence motion by the CDU/CSU opposition on 27 April 1972. There was also the hope that an SPD victory would increase the chance of codetermination on the basis of parity being extended to all industries. The visible decline in the influence of the Catholic Social wing in the CDU made it seem much less likely that the CDU would be accommodating in this respect. Finally, the clear identification of the business lobby with the CDU/CSU opposition helped to provoke the DGB support for the SPD. The backing by the DGB was very effective and was a major factor in the high degree of support that the SPD gained among working-class voters.

This backing was largely absent in the 1976, 1980 and 1983 elections. In 1976 the then General Secretary of the CDU, Professor Kurt Biedenkopf, waged a campaign against '*Filzokratie*', i.e. using trade union resources for the electoral benefit of the SPD. This campaign placed the DGB on the defensive given its formal commitment to party political neutrality and, while many obviously worked as individuals for an SPD victory, there was very little in subsequent elections of the public display of solidarity so characteristic of the 1972 election.

The DGB support is important to the SPD in two further ways. First, some of the SPD Cabinet members have had backgrounds as trade union leaders. In the Schmidt Cabinet of 1974–6 there were five: Georg Leber (Defence), Walter Arendt (Labour), Helmut Röhde (Education), Kurt Gscheidle (Traffic and Post), and Hans Matthöfer (Research). Secondly, their support in not pressing for inflationary wage settlements was essential to the survival of the SPD government. One of the factors in Brandt's resignation as Chancellor was his inability to get his view of the correct level of wage settlements accepted by ÖTV, the public service union.

Although the DGB as such plays no recognized role in the factional balance inside the SPD, the role of trade unionists and trade union functionaries is a crucial one. At the local level many of the party office-holders are trade union functionaries. At the national level the major trade unions and the DGB are in a strategic position to influence the SPD leadership when the SPD is in government. Reflecting the generally conservative nature of the values held by the German trade unions, this weight is almost invariably exercised, as in the past, against the left of the Party. They are able to make their influence felt through the Working Group for Employees' Questions (*Arbeitsgemeinschaft für Arbeitnehmerfragen*, AFA). This working circle was founded in 1972, partly as a counterweight to the JUSOS.

After 1980 the relationship between the SPD and the DGB deteriorated. There were two main reasons for this. First, the trade union leadership pressed for a much more Keynesian response to mounting unemployment than the SPD–FDP government was prepared to contemplate. Secondly, there was increasing anger in the trade unions at the budgetary cuts suggested by the government. In November 1981, Franz Steinkühler, then IG Metall leader in Baden–Württemberg, had been able to mobilize more than 70,000 workers against governmental budgetary cuts. Union anger grew considerably in the early months of 1982 and a 'hot autumn' was promised for the SPD–FDP government which, as we have noted, collapsed in September 1982. The growing strains between the SPD and the trade unions caused a great deal of alarm inside the SPD. Wolfgang Roth managed to get the party executive's proposals on the economy rejected at the Munich Conference and the resolutions that were finally passed were much friendlier to the unions. In the period between the end of the Munich Conference and the collapse of the Schmidt government there were frequent expressions of concern at the strains being imposed on SPD–trade union relations by governmental policy. Subsequently relations were more harmonious, but were not without problems. At the time of the collapse of the Schmidt government many in the SPD calculated that the CDU/CSU would make sweeping budgetary cuts and thus drive the trade unions and the SPD closer together.

In practice, things have turned out to be much more ambiguous. The CDU/CSU–FDP coalition has made some budgetary cuts but much less than many of both their adversaries and supporters had expected. This might have been expected to delay the re-establishment of very close relations between the DGB and SPD. However, the government has alienated the bulk of the DGB leadership by ending the practice of fairly frequent meetings with DGB leaders and by taking a very tough line on the payment of unemployment pay during strikes.

The generally poor relations with the CDU/CSU–FDP government have not led to a totally harmonious relationship with the SPD however. The SPD is now less convinced of the unambiguous merits of growth. It has also had to adopt a large number of environmentalist positions as a result of its electoral competition with the Greens. This has sometimes caused problems. Many union leaders were unhappy about the SPD's adoption in 1986 of an anti-nuclear policy and the chemical workers' union has fought a continual rearguard action against measures which they see as damaging to the interests of the chemical industry. The SPD has given some priority to reconciling the objectives of employment and environment but this has sometimes led to compromises which lead to greater support for the Greens.

Union leaders were greatly angered by a series of public statements by Oskar Lafontaine, the SPD Vice-Chairman, in the spring of 1988, where he backed the union demands for a shorter working week to combat unemployment but suggested to the immense annoyance of the unions that should this happen, it should be accompanied by a reduction in wages.

THE EROSION OF CONSENSUS

The comparatively harmonious relationships which have prevailed in West German economic life around agreement on 'the magic quadrangle of stable prices, a high level of employment, a balance of payments surplus and a policy of growth' were reinforced by the absence, especially after the late 1950s, of real division between the parties on these goals. The relationship between the two sides of industry became more tense with the onset in the early 1980s of higher levels of unemployment than known since the post-war recovery. A great deal of consensus remains, however, and it is unlikely that industrial tensions will feed into greater party political polarization. What is more striking is the emergence of a new line of cleavage running

245

between those who support the traditional primacy of economic values (CDU/CSU–FDP and part of the SPD) and those largely younger citizens who stress environmentalist values, the so-called post-materialists (part of the SPD and the Greens).

The Greens represent a fairly radical break with the post-war consensus on economic policy and we shall look in detail later at the emergence of environmentalist positions. The Greens reject nearly all aspects of the present economic structure and wish to reverse much of industrial society. Their ideal is of relatively small-scale, environmentally friendly production units. Unlike the other parties, they have no established relations with orga-nized economic interests. They are, however, inextricably in-volved in an economic counter-culture of small cooperatives, service organizations and wholefood shops. This sector is econo-mically insignificant but is an important source of support to the Greens. The Greens are nearest to the consensus on agriculture where they are fervent supporters of small farming units despite their opposition to large-scale agra-business and the chemica-lization of agricultural production.

THE BANKS AS THE EFFICIENT SECRET OF WEST GERMAN INDUSTRY

In the old days, it used to be said that 60 per cent of the representatives on the boards of German firms were from the Deutsche Bank, 20 per cent were people close to it and 20 per cent were from other banks. The view that banks are 'the efficient secret of organized private enterprise' in the Federal Republic stretches back in English writings to Andrew Shonfield. It has become a major theme in the analysis of Dyson and others.[4]

The argument that banks play an important role in guiding and coordinating the strategies of West German industrial companies is based both on their historic relationship and on some observable present-day realities. The late industrialization of Germany, and the absence of the sort of relations that Britain possessed with the United States and the Empire, meant that German capital was largely invested at home. The stock ex-change in Germany was a much less important provider of capital for industry than its counterparts in Anglo-American countries. In this situation the banks played a major role in lending capital to industry. The system of having representatives of the banks, especially the Deutsche Bank, on the boards of industrial firms dates back to the Imperial period, as does the system of interlocking directorships.

The close relationship between the banks and industry continued in the post-war period. Dyson has argued that in some areas it has been strengthened – for example, in construction where outstanding credits after 1945 were converted into bank-held shares and bonds to assist reconstruction.[5] Much has been written on the role of Hermann Abs and other prominent bankers who played an important part in post-war German industry. It is often pointed out that the share of equity capital in the corporate capital structure of West German companies is less than in American and British counterparts, and they are, therefore, heavily dependent on the banks for loan finance.[6] It is further argued that it is not so much the proportion of shares actually held by the banks themselves (8 per cent in 1983) that is important but that West German shareholders still continue to deposit their shares with the banks. Zysman has claimed that 85 per cent of all privately held shares are held in proxy by the banks.[7] The possession of these 'proxy shares' means the banks play a dominating role at shareholders' meetings through the exercise of their *Depotstimmrecht* (proxy voting right). In particular, this secures a major representation for the banks on the supervisory boards of the firms and by extension allows them a major say in the choice of personnel for the executive board.

Banks occupied about 15 per cent of all seats on the supervisory boards of the 100 biggest joint-stock companies in the FRG in 1974 and were represented on the boards of 75 of them. Some 57 per cent of these seats were occupied by representatives of the three biggest banks. The Deutsche Bank is represented on the supervisory boards of 38 of the 100 biggest companies, the Dresdner Bank on 23 and the Commerzbank on 14. According to the Monopolkommission, a fifth of all the chairmen of the above firms' supervisory boards in 1978 come from the banks, three-quarters of them from the big three and 60 per cent from the Deutsche Bank alone.[8]

Attention has also been paid to the role of the 'House bank', i.e. an exclusive and intensive relationship with one bank. It is often argued that the close relationship with a particular bank aids the firm by providing a form of industrial early-warning system, and that it plays an important role in pressing economic rationality on a firm during the process of *Sanierung* (rationalization).

This view that West German banks control West German industry and that industry benefits from this relationship has become an almost unchallenged piece of conventional wisdom in Britain where it is constantly contrasted with an alleged lack of interest by the City of London in British industry. Like many pieces of conventional wisdom it is partly true. West German banks do invest much more heavily in West German industry than their British equivalents and their expectations of return on their investment are somewhat lower than normally prevails when credit is raised on the equities market.

However, British enthusiasts do seem to have ignored a number of problems and qualifications. First, the view of the banks' role that they adopt is by no means uncontentious in Germany itself. It is a view with firm roots in left-wing ideology reaching back to Hilferding but its empirical basis is less convincing. The German proponents of the power of the banks thesis have usually been Marxists and have given a lot more attention to theory than empirical evidence. Secondly, there is a wide divergence between sectors and this is not new. By the late nineteenth century the steel industry was characterized by close relations with the banks. The very high rate of profitability of the chemicals industry meant that its external credit needs were comparatively modest and the relationship with the banks was much looser. The role of the banks is also affected by the type of leadership in a particular industry, e.g. until recently the West German chemical industry has been led exclusively by chemists. The common background in chemistry, normally with a distinguished background in research, strengthens the view of the leaders of the chemical industry that they know best.

The degree of bank involvement also varies according to whether a firm stays in its own sector as is true of the three chemical giants, BASF, Hoechst and Bayer, or has expansionist ambitions. The Deutsche Bank has been much involved in terms of both credit and advice in the expansionist course of Daimler Benz, the motor engineering group which has expanded into electronics, aerospace and advanced weapons systems.

Not only have proponents of bank influence overlooked sectoral differences they have also underestimated the changes at work as the West German economy becomes more internationalized. West German shares are now much more attractive both to foreign buyers and to the Germans themselves. More importantly, the argument that the relationship with the banks gives West German firms an edge is not self-evidently true. Despite expansion overseas in the 1970s and 1980s, the West German banking system remains less international than its British and American counterparts. Precisely because of this, the advice it offers may not always be appropriate; the West German banks know German markets very well but their relative Germano-centrism may make them less prescient guides to international markets. Indeed, it could well be argued that the bank connection is one of the factors contributing to 'the rigidities' analysed by Jonathan Carr.[9] It is also by no means the case that the banks are always successful in promoting the restructuring of an industry. They failed in their attempts to bring about a rationalization of the German tyre sector through a merger between Continental Gummi Werke and Phoenix. The Deutsche Bank, which is heavily involved in Volkswagen, was also embarrassed by revelations of massive currency frauds at Volkswagen in early 1987 only months after it had led a DM 2.1 billion rights issue.

The question of bank involvement in industry has now become an important political issue. In 1986 Daimler Benz completed a round of expansion by taking over AEG, the electronics giant, and consolidated its position as the Federal Republic's largest company by a significant margin. The Daimler Benz expansion has been charted and, to a large extent, financed by the Deutsche Bank and the acquisition of AEG led to a great deal of criticism of the Deutsche Bank. The Monopolies Commission recommended that banks should not be allowed to hold more than 5 per cent stakes in non-banking concerns. (In 1987 the Deutsche Bank had an equity share of 25 per cent in Daimler Benz.)

The State Secretary of the Economics Ministry, Otto Schlecht, publicly queried whether banks had acquired powers for themselves that were economically and socially undesirable. It is unlikely, however, that the Monopolies Commission recommendation will be implemented. The Deutsche Bank will be a little more circumspect. The amount directly lent by banks will continue to decline and be replaced by equities and securities. This will still leave room for the banks, as the banks control the buying and selling of shares on the stock market rather than separate stockbroking firms as is the case in a number of other

249

countries. The influence of the German banks is likely to be reduced not by internal changes but by the further globalization of markets. The demands for liberalization in order to make West Germany a finance centre (*Finanzplatz Deutschland*) commensurate with its industrial status are beginning to have some effect and competition from foreign banks is increasing. The demand to make the Federal Republic a financial centre reflects fears about West Germany's over-concentration on manufacturing industry and the need for financial services for the new corporate giants now being created.

THE GROWTH OF ENVIRONMENTAL PRESSURES

Throughout the early history of the Federal Republic the primary concern of industry was to expand production. In this view the function of the state was to facilitate this and environmental protection was accorded a relatively low priority. This view was shared by all CDU/CSU led coalitions and also by the Grand Coalition (1966–9).

The advent of a social democrat led government in 1969 brought a shift in priorities. Quality of life issues such as participation and protection of the environment moved sharply up the scale of priorities. The change in policy reflected a general value shift associated both with the very high standard of living the West Germans had achieved and the expansion of opportunities in higher education.

Despite the reform rhetoric, the environmental measures actually passed by SPD–FDP governments were designed not to impose too heavy costs on industry. There were three principal reasons for this limitation. First, the junior coalition partner, the FDP, has always seen itself as the most industry-friendly party. The FDP held the two most important ministries in relation to environmental policy, those of Economics and the Interior. The desire of Gerhart Baum's Interior Ministry, which was responsible for nearly all environmental regulation, to institute ambitious reforms was checked by the Economics Ministry which has been seen as the attorney for German industry. Helmut Schmidt, the Federal Chancellor from 1974– to 1982, was as close to industry as is possible for an SPD Chancellor to be. His preferences, whether in relation to expansion of the provision of nuclear energy or the environmental regulation of industry, were determined by considerations of economic rationality rather than by a desire to improve the quality of life in a wider sense. This position was buttressed by a close relationship with the trade union movement expressed *inter alia* in a record number of leading trade unionists holding ministerial portfolios in the first Schmidt Cabinet. Although relations with the trade union leadership soured as unemployment climbed, they remained allies in opposition to any environmental measures which would seriously affect the competitiveness of West German industry. In a recent interview, Albrecht Müller, one of Schmidt's closest confidants and former head of the Planning Division in the Chancellor's Office, said that Schmidt's opposition to environmental regulation of the chemical industry rested on his talks with top management and senior union men at Bayer.

Helmut Schmidt's hostility to far-reaching environmental measures did not inhibit a further shift in public attitudes. Environmental consciousness and an attachment to what are often called 'post-materialist values' had been steadily climbing in West Germany since the mid 1970s. The impact of this consciousness had been limited by the fact that the countervailing forces in the governmental parties, already referred to, inhibited anything other than a very partial articulation of environmentalist positions. In particular, the SPD, a far higher proportion of whose adherents were sympathetic to post-materialist values than in the other established parties, was inhibited from giving unequivocal expression to them by the views of Helmut Schmidt and the almost united opposition of the major trade unions.

This situation changed dramatically after the March elections of 1983. The SPD was now in opposition. Helmut Schmidt had ceased to be Chancellor after October 1982 and thereafter ceased to play any significant role in steering party opinion. The unity of the trade unions also began to show signs of strain. IG Metall, the largest union, had become much less opposed to environmental measures. IG Chemie remained very suspicious of environmental measures and was often in conflict with the new policy of IG Metall and the unions who followed IG Metall's lead in the DGB. The new disunity in the trade union movement, however, left more leeway for SPD policy-makers since a united union view no longer constituted the veto it had done in the past.

Perhaps the most significant change, however, was the entry of the Greens into the Bundestag after the election of March 1983. This undermined one of the SPD leadership's principal arguments that a vote for an ecological party was a wasted vote since such a party would not secure representation in the Bundestag. Henceforward, a major element of SPD strategy was to be concerned with winning back these 'lost children of the SPD' (Willy Brandt). This necessarily involved a much greater stress on environmental regulation. The effect was not restricted to the SPD. The saliency of the environmental issues in West Germany, reinforced but not created by the alleged effect of acid rain on German forests (*der sterbende Wald*), meant that the CDU/CSU and FDP could not ignore these issues. There is thus a very marked contrast between the lack of impact of the Greens' ideas on party democracy and enthusiasm for its environmentalist positions – a phenomenon described by Greens as *Themenklau* (issues robbery). In 1986 environmentalist pressures were further strengthened by the creation of an Environmental Ministry.

The parties' commitment to environmentalist positions is kept under constant scrutiny by the more than one thousand environmentalist organizations established in the Federal Republic. Environmentalist pressures were moreover greatly strengthened by two major incidents in 1986. The Chernobyl nuclear accident had a much greater impact in the Federal Republic than in any other Western European country. The second incident or series of incidents was a whole series of major chemical spillages into the Rhine both in Switzerland and at the sites of all three West German chemical giants during the campaign for the 1987 Federal election.

The Impact of Environmental Pressures upon Industry

Pressures for stringent environmental regulation which are arguably stronger than in any other major Western European economy have had a major impact on the conditions under which industry operates in the Federal Republic. This impact is at its starkest in the case of the nuclear energy industry. Under the impact of the oil-price rise of 1973 the Schmidt government launched a massive programme for the construction of nuclear power plants in order to weaken West German dependence on the unpredictable Middle East. The programme was to prove extremely contentious and excite enormous opposition, not least within some SPD area organizations. By 1980 only fourteen plants had been built and even by 1986 only eighteen were actually producing electricity (30 per cent of German needs).

The Chernobyl incident tipped the SPD into outright opposition to nuclear power. The government parties did not follow the SPD but any future expansion of the nuclear industry in the Federal Republic looks extremely unlikely. West German industry continues to be dependent on imported energy but has become much more efficient at using it. Moreover Britain has since 1982 been the largest single supplier of oil rather than Saudi Arabia.

West German industrialists constantly point to the impact of environmental measures on industrial costs. The steel industry for instance has been especially vociferous about the cost of emission filters. However, it can be argued that these pressures may work to the long-term benefit of West German industry. It has a clear lead over its European competitors in 'clean production' technology. These pressures are now much more apparent in other Western European countries and the Single European Act has given the EC explicit powers in relation to the environment. The more other Western European countries emulate West German environmental standards, the more they are also likely to be buying West German technology.

The West German economy in the first two decades of its existence was essentially a manufacturing economy centred around the steel, automobile, engineering, machine tools, chemical and electrical industries. Its key features were its concentration of manufacturing and its very marked export orientation. This export orientation was primarily towards Western Europe – the destination of over two-thirds of German exports. Western Europe is regarded by all German major companies as the domestic market.

Changes in the global economy in the 1970s and 1980s, especially increased competition from 'new technology' competitors in the United States and Japan, have brought important changes. The key sectors remain crucial but subject to some erosion. The steel industry is caught in a declining spiral of heavy industry as shipbuilding and other outlets for its products contract. The electrical and electronic industries have lost some of their competitiveness.

West German industry has responded in two very marked ways to the new challenges. There has been a very great increase in outward investment. Until the late 1970s industry in the Federal Republic was very largely domestic based with a level of direct foreign investment less than one-third of its share of world trade. An appreciating Deutschmark and rising labour costs impelled a major change. Between 1976 and 1983 the value of foreign direct West German investments doubled. In recent years the chemical industry, for instance, has made huge acquisitions in North America.

The second major change is the growth of diversification and huge conglomerates. Post-war German firms were manufacturing oriented and remained based in their own sectors. Now some of the major firms, conspicuously Daimler Benz, have set out on a path of expansion and acquisition. Daimler Benz is now by far the largest German company. It remains to be seen whether management structures, which were so conspicuously successful in producing and selling in one sector, are equally successful at managing diversified conglomerates. Despite these changes the Federal Republic remains a predominantly manufacturing economy with more than 40 per cent of the workforce still employed in the manufacturing industry.

The Federal Republic remains also a country of small and medium-sized businesses which have been accorded a great deal of political protection by the CDU/CSU–FDP. The skills of these small businesses and of their highly trained workforces remain an important part of West German economic success. Medium-sized firms of less than 5,000 employees produce half of West Germany's export of capital equipment.

All firms in the Federal Republic benefit from a remarkable emphasis on training and skills which has made the Republic's workforce much better able to adapt to new technologies than most of its competitors, e.g. a major development in the chemical industry has been the trend away from relatively low value bulk chemicals to high value 'speciality' chemicals. These are produced in much smaller quantities and a very high level of skill is required in their production. This has been reflected in the success of the German chemical giants in this area.

SOCIAL CHANGES

West German political stability has been crucially dependent on its continued economic success. The argument of this chapter has been that, despite a more difficult economic environment, this success is continuing. The development of the economy has not only encouraged stability within the Federal Republic, it has also brought about important changes in West German society.

The scale of West German economic revival in the 1950s led to a vastly increased demand for labour. Until the 1960s this demand was largely met by refugees from the East, the participation of increasing numbers of women in the labour market and the transition from agricultural to industrial employment. From the late 1960s onwards a key development was the use of large numbers of foreign labourers from Southern Europe, Turkey and North Africa. The intention on the part of German employers, indicated clearly by their appellation for the foreign labourers – *Gastarbeiter* (guest-workers) – was that their stay in West Germany would only be temporary, that they would be a source of labour tied to the business cycle, able to be turned off when demand slackened and turned on again when it revived. In practice, this has proved very difficult to achieve. Many guest-workers have brought their families and have signed extended labour contracts. The whole question of foreign labour became a political issue with the onset of large-scale unemployment. The Kohl government has attempted to devise schemes to reduce the numbers of these labourers. Such schemes are constrained, however, by the need to avoid any policy measure that would remind international opinion of the past and by the commitment of the FDP to a liberal solution to the immigration issue. The government has introduced some financial inducements to persuade guest-workers to return home but the take-up has been relatively modest. There are still more than a million and a half registered foreign workers and their share of the workforce amounts to 7.6 per cent. Relatively few foreign workers have been accepted as West German citizens and the *Gastarbeiter* remain much less integrated into German society than immigrant workers in Britain and France. It seems likely that the children of the *Gastarbeiter* who have grown up in the Federal Republic will be much more assertive in pressing for their rights than their parents have been and this problem looks like remaining an area of concern to West German society.

The North–South Gap

Regional differences in wealth and income were a much less marked feature of the Federal Republic in the 1950s and 1960s than the North/South divide in Britain and Italy. The richest regions were North Rhine–Westphalia, which contained the Rhine–Ruhr coal and steel belt, and parts of Hamburg and Bremen. The southern states of Baden–Württemberg and Bavaria were still predominantly agricultural with industrial centres in Stuttgart and Munich.

One of the most marked features of the past two decades has been the successful strategy of Baden–Württemberg and Bavaria to industrialize themselves. This industrialization has been a conscious strategy by the *Länder* governments who set out to offer incoming industry all kinds of selective benefits. The benefits have been a subtle mix of a lesser degree of regulation on the one hand and tax concessions and infrastructural support on the other. The *Länder* governments were enormously aided in this strategy by not having to bear the financial costs of subsidising agriculture, which had been unloaded on to the EC Common Agricultural Policy. Industry was attracted south not only by government inducements but by a relative absence of union influence as compared with traditional industrial areas and the quality of the universities and research institutes in Baden–Württemberg and Bavaria. Many of the firms that have flourished in the south have been small and medium-sized business in high tech areas, but some large firms have also moved south, e.g. Siemens has transferred the bulk of its operations from Berlin to Munich. The result has been that these southern states have topped the *Länder* growth league every year since the late 1960s and income levels are now higher. The southern states have become the Federal Republic's 'sun belt'.

Developments in the northern states have run counter to those in the south. Mortgaged to traditional industries, with a much higher level of unionization and less attractive to capital, they have lost out to the south. Bremen and Schleswig–Holstein (shipbuilding), the Saar (coal and steel) and parts of North Rhine–Westphalia and Lower Saxony have been particularly badly affected and are now sometimes referred to as Germany's 'rust belt'.

The disparity, though increasing, is of a much lesser order of magnitude than in Britain. Most of the central sectors of German industry remain healthy and they are still strongly represented in the north. Moreover, there is no equivalent to the magnet effect of London and the south-east in Britain, with its concentration of political and economic power. The Federal Republic remains a political and economic system where political and economic power is geographically dispersed, despite the perceptible movement to the south.

The East–West Divide

The difference between the northern and southern states look very modest in comparison to the stark divergence between economic conditions in the five new Laender and the other Laender of the Federal Republic. In the former GDR territory all sectors are weak, unemployment is high, and complete collapse is only prevented by massive subsidies from the Federal government. The Treuhand-Anstalt – the government agency to privatize East German industry – has had considerable difficulties. Over the slightly longer term, it can be expected that German industry's genius for organization and industrial training, combined with massive capital flows from western Germany, will transform the economic situation of the former GDR.

9 The Federal Republic and the West

External relations have always assumed a peculiar importance in the Federal Republic. In chapter 10 we will look at the interlinked issues of the unresolved national question and policy towards the East. This chapter will focus on relations with the West, which is seen as the key arena of the foreign policy of the Federal Republic.

The establishment of the Federal Republic in 1949 left the newly founded state with a number of daunting problems, of which three were absolutely central. The first was the question of how to re-establish national unity. The second was to find a way both of lifting the discriminating provisions imposed on German economic production and of securing access to the markets of the developed industrial economies. The third policy imperative was to find an answer to the security problem posed by the external threat from the East.

Adenauer found the answer to all three policy problems in a close and unquestioned identification with the Western powers. National unity would be re-established by a close identification with an 'American Policy of Strength' which would bring about the disappearance of the GDR. The economic policy dilemmas were to be resolved by European integration. The security dilemma was resolved by reliance on the United States.

A key feature of the foreign policy of the Federal Republic has been the way in which foreign policy has been formulated within the parameters set by answers to these policy dilemmas, rather than by a historically conditioned perception of national interest. This leads to a further feature in the way that foreign policy towards the West has been and continues to be formulated in the context of transnational institutional structures. The low politics of German foreign policy is bound up with the European Community and the high politics of security is determined within a NATO framework.

THE FEDERAL REPUBLIC AND WESTERN EUROPEAN INTEGRATION

In the beginning was Adenauer.
Arnulf Baring, *Aussenpolitik in Adenauer's Kanzlerdemokratie*

The central importance given by the Federal Repubic in its early years to the integration of Western Europe has a number of explanations but a dominant theme is provided by the foreign policy programme of Konrad Adenauer. In domestic policy, support was attracted to the CDU/CSU by a whole range of personalities and policies; in foreign policy only one personality, one policy mattered. The Federal Republic was at that time not fully sovereign and the Allies still exercised important rights in relation to foreign policy. In practice, however, the West German government came to play an increasing role as the Western powers thought it unwise to appear to be imposing decisions on the Germans. As the sole interlocutor with the Allied High Commissioners, Adenauer was in a position of enormous strength *vis-à-vis* his Cabinet colleagues. He was further aided by a brilliant and devoted staff in the Chancellor's Office. These close aides, including Walter Hallstein and Herbert Blankenhorn, became the principal officials in the Foreign Ministry when it was created in 1951. Adenauer acted as his own Foreign Minister until June 1955. Even after Heinrich von Brentano was appointed Foreign Minister, the key officials took their cue from and reported to the Chancellor.

Adenauer was a deeply committed European. His Europe was the catholic 'Abendland' of Western Europe, radiating out from his native city of Cologne. His concept of Europe had at its centre a Franco-German entente, a policy which he had consistently advocated since the early days of the Weimar Republic. He was a very firm anti-communist and was closely identified with successive US administrations and was bitterly hostile to the Soviet Union. There was no tension between identification with the French for the sake of an integrated Western Europe and dependence on the Americans for security. At that time the French accepted the dependence of Western Europe on the United States in the security field and the US government was a very active proponent of West European integration.

Adenauer's policy was a novel one for a German statesman. It

259

reflected well the bipolar nature of the post-war world in its basic premiss that Germany's traditional central position in Europe had been made obsolete by the division of Europe; a division which now cut Germany in half. Adenauer therefore concluded that the Federal Republic had to make clear that its choice of the West was unwavering and unreserved for only then would the Western powers have an interest in lifting the discriminatory provisions which still weighed on the semi-sovereign Federal Republic. In the long term Adenauer was interested in lifting the restrictions on the sovereignty of the Federal Republic in the field of external and security policy. In the short run it was vitally important to get the restrictions and ceilings laid on German industrial production lifted.

Participation in Western European integration had a series of further benefits for the nascent Federal Republic. It helped restore some of the moral credibility lost by Nazi excesses. It also provided some external support for the new democratic political system because of the high degree of congruence between the values of the new political system and the political goals and values of the European institutions.

There was a long list of advantages to be gained from European integration for the Federal Republic but there was one major obstacle; the division of Germany and the constitutional obligation laid on federal governments to pursue reunification as the primary goal. This obstacle was reinforced by the fact that one-quarter of the population were refugees from the East who might have been expected to ensure that German reunification remained the overwhelming policy imperative of the federal government. In practice, Adenauer was able to neutralize the refugees as a potential focus of opposition to his policy by representing Western European integration as part of a process of strengthening the West in order to 'awe the Russians back to their frontiers'. This policy was shrewdly buttressed by the Equalisation of the Burdens Law of 1951, which compensated refugees financially for lands and property they had lost in the East.

Under Adenauer the Federal Republic was a very consistent supporter of European integration. It agreed to join the Council of Europe despite being initially accorded only associate status. It played a major role in the negotiations which led to the creation of the European Coal and Steel Community in 1952. The ECSC placed the coal and steel industries of the member countries under a common High Authority. Despite some strongly expressed reservations by West German heavy industry, it had Adenauer's enthusiastic support. He was attracted by its supra-national character and its potential for encouraging a Franco-German alliance. It also meant the abolition of the International Authority of the Ruhr. This had been set up in 1948 to control the production and marketing of the Ruhr's coal, coke and steel as a quid pro quo for French agreement to the creation of the Federal Republic.

Adenauer's policy was bitterly opposed by the social democrats. Schumacher was almost as dominant a leader of the SPD as Adenauer was of the CDU. Schumacher's vision, marked by his experiences in Weimar, was decidedly nationalist in tone. Schumacher was against participation in these Western European institutions since he argued that this would freeze the status quo of German division and relegate reunification to a mere aspiration. Schumacher's opposition to European integration was always blunted by the support for it from the trade unions. The unions were naturally attracted by the possibilities of lifting production ceilings and thus making some dent on unemployment which remained high in the early years of the Federal Republic.

The conflict between the government and opposition over European integration reached its highest level of intensity over the question of a German contribution to a proposed European Defence Community. The EDC was proposed by the French when the outbreak of war in Korea increased American pressure to rearm West Germany. The various French proposals were attempts to make the prospect of German rearmament appear less threatening. This essentially involved denying the West Germans the possession of exclusively national forces and setting up federal political arrangements to exercise political control over such armed forces as would be allowed. Adenauer was a keen supporter of the European Defence Community. He was convinced at an early stage that West Germany should rearm in order to demonstrate its identification with the West. In his view the primary need of West Germany, especially after the outbreak of the Korean War, was security against the East. This security could only be provided by the military protection of the United States. A key goal of West German external policy should therefore be to keep the United States committed to this aim by accommodating American views on the uniting of

Western Europe. Adenauer was also attracted to the EDC by its strong federalist elements. It was therefore a major blow to Adenauer's European policy when the EDC was rejected by the French Assembly in August 1954.

Adenauer pursued West German membership of the Common Market and Euratom with great determination. He was prepared after the collapse of the EDC to make significant concessions to the French government since he saw that without these concessions the weak French government of Guy Mollet would not be able to secure French membership of the EEC. By this time the SPD opposition to European integration had disappeared. Schumacher had died in 1952 and been replaced by the more flexible Ollenhauer. By 1955 the return of the Saar to West Germany looked increasingly likely, while reunifications receded into the distance as a practical option. The separation of defence from the agenda of European integration after the collapse of the plans for a European Defence Community removed a major SPD objection to supporting integration. These factors were skilfully manipulated by Jean Monnet who persuaded the SPD leadership to join Jean Monnet's Action Committee for the United States of Europe in 1955. He was also aided in securing SPD support for the idea of a Common Market and Euratom by the support of the West German trade unions and the SPD enthusiasm for Euratom.

There was some domestic opposition to entry into the EEC however. Ludwig Erhard, the Economics Minister, would have preferred a wider free trade area. West German agriculture was firmly opposed to entry. The FDP in opposition after February 1956 also opposed entry, arguing like Erhard in favour of a broader free trade area and reviving the abandoned SPD arguments on the primacy of reunification.

Adenauer was in an immensely strong political position and won an absolute majority in the 1957 Federal election. The strength of this position allowed him to ignore domestic political reservations about the terms of West German membership in the Common Market. There was almost no opposition to West German membership of Euratom.

The unity of Adenauer's European and security policies began to fray in the 1960s in the face of the growing divergence between the foreign and security policies of General de Gaulle and US administrations. Adenauer had much less faith in US policy after the death of John Foster Dulles and his fears about

American unreliability were skilfully exploited by de Gaulle. Adenauer's support for Gaullist policy introduced into his policy an incoherence that it formerly avoided because of Gaullist opposition to the idea of supra-nationalism.

After Adenauer's reluctant retirement in 1963, the CDU/CSU was split between the 'Atlanticists' and the 'Gaullists'. It was essentially a struggle between the 'ins' – Chancellor Erhard, Foreign Minister Schröder and Defence Minister Von Hassel – and the 'outs' – Konrad Adenauer and Franz Josef Strauss, respectively in retirement and in disgrace. The 'outs' however remained party chairmen; Adenauer of the CDU and Strauss of the CSU. The Gaullists carried on a continual guerrilla campaign against the government, accusing it of placing too much emphasis on the Atlantic relationship, of neglecting France and of turning its back on the commitment of supra-nationalism. This conflict persisted between 1963 and 1988 and was only buried by the collapse of the Erhard government. In the Grand Coalition of 1966–9 difficulties and disagreements, including the 'Gaullist' and 'Atlanticist' dispute were simply bracketed out (*ausgeklammert*). The SPD had a long tradition of suspicion of France and there was simply no possibility that the SPD would have agreed to a Gaullist orientation. In any case the conflict had contained an element of shadow boxing since no West German politician would have risked serious conflict with the Americans, given West German security dependence on the United States.

THE EUROPEAN POLICY OF BRANDT AND SCHMIDT

Willy Brandt was preoccupied with *Ostpolitik* in his first administration. By the time of the formation of the second Brandt administration, the dramatic phase of *Ostpolitik* was largely over and he gave more attention to Western European policy. His policy, however, remained incoherent. He advocated European Union but was never able to spell out successfully how it would look in institutional terms. The weaknesses of his European policy became more marked after the oil price rise of 1973 made the Federal government extremely reluctant to utilize its financial resources to help attain the goals it claimed to be committed to.

Helmut Schmidt's style was much more pragmatic than Brandt's. He was hostile to the EC Commission and was strongly in favour of an intergovernmental Europe.

According to Schmidt, Europe and its present condition can only be advanced through the will of statesmen and not through thousands of regulations and hundreds of sessions of the Council of Ministers each year.[1]

Schmidt's initial concern was to try to encourage greater financial and budgetary discipline. To this end he made a number of specific suggestions, e.g. that one of the commissioners be appointed a sort of European Finance Minister and that a European '*Rechnungshof*' (Court of Audit) be created. He also argued that West German financial resources should not be committed to an EEC undertaking without some certainty that tangible policy benefits would be realized. In a study written for the SPD *Präsidium* shortly before he became Chancellor, Schmidt rejected the idea of any major West German financial sacrifice in pursuit of European integration. For Schmidt, Europe was a question of head rather than heart; he remained a *Vernunfteuropaer* (a European by dint of reason). His lack of enthusiasm for a Brussels-centred model of the European community caused some friction with Katherina Focke, the most European of his ministerial team and she was dropped when he formed his second government in 1976.

There was one other major departure from previous SPD policies during the Schmidt Chancellorship. Throughout the preceding two decades the SPD had been much cooler in its attitudes to France than the CDU/CSU. In the Schumacher period the picture had been one of hostility and suspicion exacerbated by, but not restricted to, the Saar issue. In the 1960s the SPD's belated espousal of supra-nationalism had made it very critical of Gaullist attitudes and policies. Paradoxically, Schmidt, a lifelong Anglophile, became very much identified with a European policy of working in tandem with the French after 1974. Schmidt was concerned by what he saw as a failure of US leadership in monetary and security matters and his alliance with France represented an attempt to create a 'zone of stability' in the EC. Its major institutional expression was the launching of the European monetary system in March 1979. The alliance could, in Schmidt's view, only be with France given British difficulties.

Helmut Kohl

The gap between the rhetoric and reality of West German European policy, which had noticeably narrowed under Helmut Schmidt, widened again under Helmut Kohl. Kohl likes to think of himself as Adenauer's political heir and his Europeanist posture is part of that perception. This commitment has been more noticeable at the rhetorical and presentational than at the policy level. The Kohl government, in practice, has rarely given a high priority to European policy. It has shown itself extremely vulnerable to the agricultural sector. West Germany has taken the lead in reintroducing national subsidies for its farmers, in effect partially renationalizing the sector where integration is most advanced. It has also allowed agricultural pressure funnelled through party channels to override general policy goals. Pressure from the agricultural interest has increased during the Kohl years as the European Community has taken the first faltering steps towards the reform of the Common Agricultural Policy. West German farmers have objected especially strongly to the introduction of milk quotas and the level of cereal price agreements. The CSU has an especially close relationship with agriculture and they have pressed the agricultural interest very strongly in coalition negotiations.

In looking at the development of West German European policy, we have concentrated on presenting the broad outlines of that policy. This provides only a partial answer to two key questions. Will West German public opinion continue to display the same high level of commitment to European integration as in the past and will the Federal Republic exercise a leadership role in the EC commensurate with its economic strength?

PUBLIC OPINION

By the late 1950s West German public opinion was overwhelmingly in favour of European integration. European integration offered West Germans a surrogate identity, a passport back to respectability, the lifting of restrictions on German sovereignty; production and access to a very large market for West Germany's export-oriented industry were also important motives. The major disadvantage, the tension with the reunification option, was softened by the all-too-clear difficulties of achieving any progress given the permafrost in which East–West relations were embedded. The consensus at the level of mass public opinion reflected and was encouraged by the attitudes of the major interest groups. Both the BDI and the DGB (see chapter 8) have consistently supported European integration. The German Farmers Union (DBV), after opposing entry, has generally supported integration whilst expressing criticism of particular community initiatives like the ill-fated Mansholt Plan for the reform of agriculture.

The very strong public support for European integration has weakened slightly but perceptibly since the early 1970s. In one sense it is only to be expected that citizens of the prosperous and stable Federal Republic of the 1970s and 1980s should be less enthusiastic about merging its sovereignty than the citizens of the provisional Federal Republic of the 1950s, still close to the shaming experience of the Third Reich and its collapse.

A contingent explanation is provided by the oil price rises of 1973 which brought a new concentration on budgetary questions. Governmental statements on Europe which had hitherto concentrated on the generalized advantages of membership changed to some extent to an emphasis on financial costs and the danger of the Federal Republic being regarded as the 'milk-cow'. The effect of these pronouncements was to make West German opinion much more sensitive to the Federal Republic's 'paymaster' role.

Interest in the community also declined in the 1970s. This was partly a product of detente which focused attention, especially for SPD supporters, on the possibilities inherent in a relaxation of East–West tension rather than concentrating exclusively on Western Europe. There was also a generational shift with young people, who had not experienced the traumas of the 1940s and 1950s, exhibiting less interest in European integration than older age groups. One striking contrast to Britain in West German public opinion is in attitudes towards agricultural surpluses. In a 1984 survey on West German attitudes towards the EC only 5 per cent mentioned over-production and agricultural surpluses as a problem and the most often cited advantage of EC membership was better food supplies.[2]

In West Germany, as elsewhere in the European Community, a great deal of hope was invested in the mobilizing capacity of direct elections to the European Parliament. Both elections have failed dismally in this respect. In 1984 the turnout of 56.8 per cent was over 30 per cent below the normal turnout at Federal elections. An internal paper of the Federal government, commenting on a public opinion survey conducted during the campaign, referred to West German's feelings towards the EC as being 'characterized by considerable inner reserve'.

German European policy at present operates within a mildly positive 'permissive consensus' towards the goal of European integration. Although permissive, this consensus has clear boundaries, especially in relation to German financial contributions. Moreover this opinion is largely passive and, if the policy-making elites, who at present support European integration, were to become disillusioned, then there does not appear to be a broad and deep reservoir of support which could be mobilized against such a change of course.

The contrast between the Federal Republic's economic preponderance and its perceived political role as junior partner of France has often been remarked upon. This situation reflects the shadow of the past which would make it difficult for other EC members, especially France, to accept Germany in a leadership role. The external constraints on German leadership are complemented by deeply ingrained domestic attitudes which see the Federal Republic as the *Musterknabe* (the good boy) of the EC. It is very difficult to see how one can move from that sort of attitude, conditioned by the need to be accepted by other states, to the successful performance of a leadership role.

The Federal Republic is further constrained by a notably loose and reactive set of policy-making instruments. In European policy, as in other policy areas, the obstacles inherent in the pluralistic framework of German institutions can be transcended by a Chancellor who has a strong political base and a firm grip on the administrative machine. Adenauer had a coherent and active European policy because he had an exceptionally strong political base backed up by a brilliant Chancellor's Office which enabled him to dominate the nascent ministries. The only other Chancellor comparable to Adenauer in playing an active role was Helmut Schmidt. Schmidt had a much weaker political base than Adenauer but a complete mastery of policy detail. Schmidt was particularly successful in winning French agreement to his policies and presenting them as Franco-German initiatives.

Helmut Kohl has found it difficult to emulate Adenauer and

Schmidt. In both domestic and European policy the *Ressortprinzip* (departmental principle) has reasserted itself with a vengeance. This was dramatically illustrated in the confusion displayed by West German policy in relation to the Milan Summit in early summer 1985. The basic thrust of the FRG's European policy at the summit was to encourage some progress towards European union and this included *inter alia* support for the greater use of majority voting in the Council of Ministers. This longstanding policy was nevertheless treated with some scepticism by other member states since only the previous month Ignaz Kiechle, the Agriculture Minister, had invoked the veto to protect the West German position on cereal prices. This was the first time a West German minister had made use of the veto in a council session.

Different ministries have pursued conflicting policies and Chancellor Kohl has only been able to articulate a clear and recognizable policy on occasions. He has been much criticized for his failure to mention policy detail and for the weaknesses of his administrative and coordinating staff in the Chancellor's office. The weakness of coordination at the horizontal federal level have now been exacerbated by new difficulties of vertical public coordination. The Single European Act of 1986 required the agreement of the *Länder* for ratification. The *Länder*, especially Bavaria, were concerned by the loss of a number of their competences, particularly on environmental matters, to the European level and pressed for much stronger consultative rights. An agreement was reached in December 1987 providing for formal consultation of the *Länder* where their exclusive powers are affected by EC proposals. A further complication has been the decision of the *Länder* to set up individual representations in Brussels with the attendant danger that the Commission can play them off against the Federal government. This lack of coordination is a serious barrier to developing an active European policy. The sensitivity of German mass and elite opinion to financial contributions to the EC suggests an alliance with Britain and the EC Commission. The strength of the agricultural interest suggests an orientation towards France and the southern states. In fact, different ministers simply pursue conflicting policies. This can be sustained by a very rich economy like the Federal Republic but it is scarcely compatible with playing a leadership role.

THE FEDERAL REPUBLIC, THE UNITED STATES AND THE WESTERN ALLIANCE

The security problem when the Federal Republic came into being was uppermost both in the minds of policy-makers and in the opinion of the wider public. At the level of public opinion fear of the Soviet Union was very intense. One-quarter of the population had fled from areas under Soviet control and sought security in the Federal Republic. Their fears were shared by the indigenous population of the Western zones. The outbreak of the Korean War in 1950 significantly increased these anxieties and parallels were often drawn between the Federal Republic and South Korea. One of the most commonly used phrases in the Federal Republic of the 1950s was '*Wenn die Russen kommen*' (when the Russians come . . .).

The fears of the policy-makers were heightened by the difficulty of defending the Federal Republic against any attack from the east. The Federal Republic was physically on the Iron Curtain and shared a thousand-mile border with its adversary, the GDR. Its waist, the distance between its eastern and western borders, is only 225 kilometers at its narrowest and 480 km at its widest point. This configuration left very little room for retreat and a few initial defeats could lead to the whole territory being overrun. Moreover, two-thirds of the population lived less than 200 km from the eastern border. The sense of vulnerability inherent in this geographic position remains and it was one about which Helmut Schmidt used constantly to remind American policy-makers.

At its inception the Federal Republic had a very large security deficit. Initially, it relied totally on the Western Allies, especially the United States, to make up this deficit. In security terms the Federal Republic was basically a consumer of security and the Western Allies were producers. In an important sense this situation was not unwelcome to West German policy-makers since the Federal Republic did not have to spend on providing security and policy-makers were also aware that security dependence was, initially at least, the price of Germany's acceptance by the West.

The Federal Republic's security was essentially provided by others. Hence, it could neither threaten nor be threatened. Instead of having to embark on an autonomous defense policy – traditionally the most important source of conflict among nations – the Federal Republic could reap the benefits of tutelage.[3]

The outbreak of the Korean War in June 1950 had a clear knock-on effect on American policy in Germany. The stretch of US resources meant that there was heavy pressure on the United States to bring about a situation in which the Federal Republic would make a contribution to its own defence. This policy presented a number of difficulties. The Basic Law had not anticipated rearmament and German domestic opinion was likely to be opposed. Moreover, other Western European states, especially France, were likely to perceive a rearmed Germany as a threat.

Adenauer anticipated a formal American request and unilaterally signalled to the US government in an interview with the *Cleveland Plain Dealer* that he would accede to a request for West German rearmament. Adenauer's calculation was that it was only by being seen to support the West that the Federal Republic would be accepted and sovereignty restored. Adenauer's failure to consult the Cabinet led to the resignation of Dr Gustav Heinemann, the Minister of Defence.

The EDC Episode

The depth of external and internal opposition to German rearmament excluded both the revival of independent German armed forces or an immediate German entry into NATO. Between 1950 and 1954 an attempt was made to make German rearmament more palatable by linking it to various proposals to create a European Defence Community (see above).

The WEU Treaties

The defeat of the EDC put considerable pressure on the West German and US governments to find another formula. The British government, which had refused to commit forces permanently to the EDC, now guaranteed the permanent presence of British troops in West Germany to allay French fears. In the Paris Accords, which set up the Western European Union, the means by which the Federal Republic joined NATO, the Federal Republic renounced its right to develop atomic, biological, or chemical weapons. In return, the other European states agreed to German rearmament and the Federal Republic became the fifteenth member of NATO in May 1955. Its membership of NATO was more complete than those of the other larger European members. Unlike Britain and France, all its forces were committed to NATO. It had no general staff and no independent strategic planning function. This was in a sense the second foundation of NATO which was now redesigned to contain the Federal Republic alongside its pre-existing role of deterring the Soviet Union.

The decision to join NATO and to develop West German military forces provoked considerable opposition both inside and outside the Bundestag. The parliamentary opposition of the SPD stressed the impact entry would have on German unity. It was also involved in the extraparliamentary movement – the *Paulskirche* Movement – which staged a number of massive anti-rearmament demonstrations in 1955.

Despite the evidence of considerable public disquiet, a bill to introduce conscription was passed in 1956 and conscription itself began in 1961. Opposition quickly lost much of its force. The Hungarian uprising of 1956 had a very powerful impact in the Federal Republic, reinforcing demands for more security. In the 1957 election Adenauer won the only absolute majority in the history of the Federal Republic and this victory was seen by both government and opposition as expressing public support for Adenauer's policy on rearmament. The SPD sponsored a large extra-parliamentary opposition to atomic weapons in 1959 when it was decided to provide the Bundeswehr with dual-key tactical nuclear weapons, but withdrew from this movement (*Kampf dem Atomtod*) fairly soon after it was founded.

Despite its own contribution, the Federal Republic continued and continues to rely on the Western Allied to make the major contribution to West German security. In particular, from its inception the Federal Republic has had a very high interest, given the difficulty of defending the Federal Republic, pervasive feelings of insecurity and the implications that any offensive strategy would have for the other half of Germany, in the deterrent value of the American nuclear umbrella. West German membership of NATO was always perceived as part of the price the FRG would have to pay to ensure that the United States remained committed to this deterrent.

In return for West German participation in NATO, the

United States continued to provide security for the Federal Republic, and NATO accepted the view of the Federal Republic that the denial of the German right to self-determination was the major cause of tension in Europe and that any progress towards relaxation of tension had to be based on an acceptable solution to the German question.

It was the breakdown in the US commitment to this sequence – solution of the German problem and then detente – which first began to impose some strain on the relationship in the early 1960s. This had been preceded by some disenchantment with the United States because of what was seen as an insufficiently resolute approach at various points in the Berlin crisis of 1958–61, but especially in terms of the US reaction to the building of the Wall in 1961 which stressed Allied rights rather than German interests. German–American relations became extremely strained when, in the aftermath of the building of the wall, the Kennedy administration began to explore with the Soviet Union the idea that access to West Berlin should be controlled by an international authority which would include East Germany as a member. Adenauer leaked these draft proposals and vigorously attacked the Kennedy administration who responded by requesting the recall of the West German Ambassador in Washington.

American policy towards the Soviet Union generally presented a serious challenge to entrenched German positions which stressed the compatibility of NATO membership and the insistence of the Federal government on the primacy of German reunification. President Kennedy indicated increasingly after the Cuban crisis of 1962 that he was intent on pressing ahead with superpower detente despite lack of progress, even negative developments, on the German question. West German frustration at these policies was skilfully manipulated by de Gaulle who offered the Germans a rival vision of a European bloc with more support for their national aspirations.

This question of a French or American orientation appeared to divide the CDU/CSU between 1962 and 1966 but the differences were more apparent than real. However disappointed West German leaders were at developments in US policy, the dependence of the Federal Republic on the United States to satisfy its elemental security needs was almost total and could not be replaced by France. It was rather a stick with which Adenauer, who had retired unwillingly in 1963, and Franz Josef

Strauss, who had been forced out by the *Spiegel* affair in 1962 (see chapter 3, p. 67) could beat their victorious adversaries, Chancellor Ludwig Erhard, Dr Gerhard Schroeder, the Foreign Minister, and Dr Kai-Uwe Von Hassel, the Defence Minister. Moreover, the SPD, which had been a fierce critic of the dependence on the United States and NATO, signalled in a famous speech by Herbert Wehner on 30 June 1960 that it accepted the defence and security policies of the government.

The new priorities of the United States, emphasizing detente, began to be internalized in West German political debate. They were taken up first and most vigorously by the SPD and the FDP. This theme will be explored more thoroughly in the following chapter but it is important at this point to stress that detente and *Ostpolitik* was to quite a considerable degree motivated by *West-politik*, by the accommodation of the West Germans to the detente policy of the United States. It was in origin less an illustration of the independence than of the dependence of the Federal Republic on the United States.

In the 1950s and 1960s the security policy of the Federal Republic had been characterized by an unequivocal and single-minded endorsement of the concept of deterrence. It was for instance the Germans who were most unsettled by new American strategic concepts like flexible response which were aired during the Kennedy administration.

The advent of the SDP–FDP government did not lead to any lessening of the commitment at governmental level to the deterrence concept. It did mean, however, the introduction of the concept of detente to a central place in governmental thinking. They were not initially rival concepts since NATO policy in the 1970s was committed to both. However, policies stressing the importance of capabilities and of military strength were potentially in tension with policies that emphasized intentions, atmospherics and the reduction of armaments.

These tensions became very visible during the Schmidt chancellorship. Conflict first surfaced on the issue of enhanced radiation weapons, later called the neutron bomb. The Carter administration first suggested the production and stationing of enhanced radiation weapons shortly after Carter became President. Enhanced radiation weapons were, the administration argued, a way of enhancing deterrence since their use appeared more credible than that of the tactical nuclear weapons which were already stationed on the soil of the Federal Republic. For this reason and out of a desire not to cross the United States, Helmut Schmidt supported the idea.

There was very considerable opposition to the proposed policy, however. It was attacked very strongly by Willy Brandt and Egon Bahr, the architects of West Germany's detente policy, and was rejected at the SPD Hamburg Party Conference in November 1977. Public opinion was also extremely hostile. Faced with this opposition, the Schmidt government stressed three elements in its response to US policy. It insisted the decision to produce a nuclear weapon was solely the sovereign decision of the United States. Bonn would accept enhanced radiation weapons on its soil only if all other NATO members agreed and enhanced radiation weapons must not be stationed only in the Federal Republic. The West German government was prepared to accept the deployment of enhanced radiation weapons in the Federal Republic after James Callaghan accepted such deployment for Britain against considerable opposition from his own party. Like Callaghan, Schmidt was therefore greatly angered by Carter's decision to drop the initiative after his allies had incurred considerable political embarrassment.

Intermediate Nuclear Forces (INF)

The divisions and tensions revealed by the disputes surrounding the proposed production and deployment of enhanced radiation weapons widened and deepened. The INF imbroglio began with a speech by Helmut Schmidt to the International Institute for Strategic Studies meeting in London in 1977. Schmidt, like other German defence policy-makers, was worried by a growing imbalance between the capacities of the Warsaw Pact and NATO in medium-range nuclear systems. By 1977 the Soviet Union had deployed some 1,300 medium-range weapons, including the SS20 and 'Backfire' bomber, while NATO only had something under 400 ageing weapons. Schmidt drew attention to this gap and suggested that policy attention be given to dealing with it. 'We must maintain the balance of the full range of deterrence strategy.' Schmidt's initiative was taken up by NATO and in 1979 NATO adopted the so-called twin track decision. The resolution, as noted in chapter 7, envisaged negotiation with the Soviet Union to persuade them to remove their SS20 missiles from Eastern Europe with the threat that, should these negotiations fail, then NATO would deploy intermediate range nuclear missiles including a large number of Pershing 2 and Cruise missiles in the Federal Republic.

The NATO decision provoked a great deal of opposition in the Federal Republic. It gave rise to a large Peace Movement which organized a hectic programme of petitions and demonstrations. More threateningly for Schmidt, there was considerable opposition from within the SPD. It attracted predictable criticism from Egon Bahr and Willy Brandt, who had in the late 1970s become increasingly critical of US policy. Especially worryingly for Schmidt, it attracted very bitter criticism from Herbert Wehner, the leader of the SPD *Bundestagsfraktion*, who complained that the deployment of these weapons would turn the Federal Republic into a kind of stationary aircraft carrier for the United States.

The SPD had opposed nuclear weapons in the late 1950s but the new opposition by significant sections of the SPD had a novel character. In the 1950s the SPD protest was largely a moral one against nuclear weapons. The opposition to the enhanced weapons and, even more clearly, the stationing of Cruise and Pershing 2 missiles, was clearly linked to preservation of detente. Opposition to the stationing of the weapons became increasingly bound up with accusations that the Reagan Presidency had brought detente to an end. Opposition thus continued to increase, particularly as negotiations proved fruitless and plans for deployment went ahead. A demonstration in Bonn against the imminent stationing of the missiles in October 1981 was the largest in history of the Federal Republic and was supported, much to Helmut Schmidt's anger, by almost a quarter of the SPD *Bundestagsfraktion*.

A possible defeat for government policy at the Munich Conference of the SPD in April 1982 was staved off by a compromise which left the decision to a special conference in November 1983. The collapse of the Schmidt government put enormous pressure on the official SPD policy of support for the 'twin track' decision. Initially the move away was very cautious since the party leadership were constrained by the risk that Schmidt would make damaging statements during the 1983 election. After the elections events moved quickly. In June 1983 the SPD party executive stated that the party was in broad agreement with the themes and issues of the Peace Movement and deployment of the missiles was rejected overwhelmingly at a party conference in Cologne in November 1983.

The missiles were in fact installed in early winter 1983 with rather less public protest than had been predicted given the size of the Peace Movement. In the period immediately preceding deployment, Erich Honecker, the East German leader, introduced a new theme in the debate. Since the late 1960s, the SPD and, to a lesser degree, the FDP had argued that the German past laid a special responsibility on the Federal Republic to encourage detente. In a letter to Chancellor Kohl in Autumn 1983, Honecker introduced the concept of a '*Verantwortungsgemeinschaft*', a shared responsibility of both German states to safeguard peace and to ensure that 'war never again starts from German soil'. This tactic was unsuccessful in preventing the Chancellor from supporting deployment but it struck a responsive chord among a wide section of the West German population.

In opposition, the SPD changed the relative weighting it accords to deterrence and detente in its security policy. The special geographical situation of the Federal Republic and the circumstances of its history mean that the perception of the threat from the Soviet Union and the need to deter it by nuclear means was stronger than in the British Labour Party. The SPD therefore never asked for the removal of all Allied nuclear weapons or rejected the overall American nuclear umbrella when it asked for the removal of the Cruise and Pershing missiles. In its revised security programme for the 1987 election it played down the Soviet threat and nuclear deterrence, advocated a reduction in defence spending and the length of national service and in general argued for giving NATO a more explicitly defensive posture while at the same time advocating a reduction in the resources it would have to do this.

In all its security proposals since 1983 the SPD has given increasing weight to detente. It has cultivated relations with the Soviet Union and East Germany, a process it refers to rather grandiosely as 'a second *Ostpolitik*'. In a very unusual move, the SPD agreed to a draft agreement on a chemical-weapons-free zone in Central Europe in June 1985 and it has held discussions with the SED on Palme-type nuclear-free zones in central Europe. The general tenor of its pronouncements has been critical of the United States and, unlike the CDU/CSU, who are concerned to ensure that the United States preserves its level of commitment, SPD plans argue for a greater Europeanization of defence. The special situation of West Berlin and the strongly entrenched position of the Allies in the Federal Republic meant that, unlike the British Labour Party, it did not argue for the removal of US bases. but Oskar Lafontaine, the new Vice-Chairman of the party, and in December 1990 Chancellor-candidate, has been a bitter critic of NATO and nuclear deterrence, and when he became party leader the balance tilted further from deterrence to detente.

The Double Zero Option

The Kohl government was relieved that the level of civil disturbance that accompanied the deployment of the missiles was less than predicted and that there was a relative atrophying of the Peace Movement thereafter. The offer by Mikhail Gorbachev to remove all Soviet intermediate range weapons in return for the removal of the Cruise and Pershing missiles in Western Europe exposed deep divisions in the West German government. Foreign Minister Genscher welcomed the offer as a vindication of the original 'dual track' decision. He was moreover able to point to a positive US response. Genscher's position was supported by the FDP and by the SPD, who welcomed the Soviet proposal as a major contribution to detente.

Initially, it was opposed by Chancellor Kohl and Manfred Wörner, the Minister of Defence. They accorded detente a lesser priority and were much more concerned that such an agreement would presage denuclearization. In their view, given the superiority of the Warsaw Pact in conventional forces, this would leave the Federal Republic exposed and vulnerable to Soviet pressure.

Their position quickly became untenable however. The British government, after some hesitation, indicated a positive attitude to the proposals. This would have left the Federal government as the only government opposing a proposal that appeared to favour detente and one which was supported by the Federal Republic's allies and by its coalition partner the FDP. Internally the CDU/CSU appeared to be isolated and in two state elections, in Hamburg and the Rhineland Palatinate, in mid-May 1987, public disquiet on this issue, especially marked in Hamburg, led to electoral losses for the CDU. Shortly thereafter, the government indicated its agreement with the proposals although it signalled its desire to maintain its own Pershing 1As.

These are ageing tactical nuclear weapons with a dual-key system, i.e. the Americans in practice retain control. This demand was therefore seen as a face-saving gesture rather than a serious attempt to maintain the initial objectives of the CDU/CSU and was eventually abandoned.

Acceptance of the INF Treaty by the Federal government has not led to a harmony of views between the Federal Republic and its major allies on nuclear weapons. The US and British governments would like to move forward towards an agreement on strategic nuclear weapons, i.e. a massive reduction in long range missiles while modernizing tactical nuclear weapons in Europe. These priorities create awkward dilemmas for the Federal government. It remains committed to deterrence and is therefore not opposed in principle to such a modernization. However, it also recognizes that almost all these weapons are sited in or targeted on the Federal Republic and modernization would be likely to increase the already considerable anxieties of the German public. ('The shorter the range, the deader the German,' Volker Rühe.) This 'singularity might well, in the view of the Federal government, undermine the present support for the nuclear deterrent. The Federal government is also worried that a scrapping of strategic nuclear weapons possibly signals an American decoupling from the defence of Western Europe.

THE COSTS AND BENEFITS OF WEST GERMAN DEFENCE

The very high level of dependence on external powers, especially the United States, has carried with it certain costs for the Federal Republic. In the Kennedy era it meant the Federal Republic sometimes felt that its vital national interests were being sacrificed. More recently some Germans have felt that the Republic's vital interest in detente has been sacrificed to superpower tension. A more consistent theme is suspicion and alarm on the part of successive German governments at any changes in US nuclear doctrines. The West German dependence of the US nuclear deterrent and its lack of any independent alternative creates a greater nervousness in this area than is displayed by either Britain or France.

The rewards of the dependence far outweigh the costs. The dependence on the United States for security means that the Federal Republic can have normal relations with its Western

European neighbours which would be very difficult to imagine if the Federal Republic were solely responsible for its own defence. Such a situation would set free potentially unmanageable tensions in Western Europe and would claim a great deal of policy attention from German policy-makers.

The constraints on German policy imposed by this security dependence are not now as narrow as in the past. Contrary to expectations, the Federal Republic was able to maintain the Inner-German micro-detente in the early 1980s at a point when the macro-detente had collapsed.

The economic costs of defence on the basis of dependence on NATO have also been very low – significantly lower than those of Britain.

For the Federal Republic the key allocation issue has not been 'How much do we need to pay for an adequate defence? or 'How much military power do we need in support of our global role?' but, at first, 'How much do we need to contribute to regain sovereignty and to achieve membership in NATO?', and thereafter 'How much do we have to contribute in order to maintain the American guarantee?'[4]

The West German economy has enjoyed a double gain from this relationship. The presence of a large number of foreign troops on West German soil is a direct economic gain and, despite some American unhappiness at the amount it contributes, the Federal Republic still spends significantly less as a proportion of GNP on defence than Britain (table 9.1)

Table 9.1 West German versus UK defence expenditure (1988)

	FRG	UK
Population (m)	61.7	56.8
Defence expenditure (% of GNP)	3[a]	4.9
Standing forces	495,000	320,000

[a] Including Berlin, 3.8 per cent.

10   *Ostpolitik, Deutschlandpolitik* and the Two Germanies

The collapse of the Third Reich led, as we have seen in chapter 2, to the dismemberment not only of the Third Reich but of the previous territorial arrangements. The territories beyond the Oder–Neisse line were occupied by the Soviet Union and Poland and the indigenous German population was expelled at the end of hostilities. The emergence of two states, the Federal Republic and the German Democratic Republic, in 1949 as a result of East–West tension, was even more profound a blow to the idea and reality of a unified Germany. Its most obvious impact was to rob Berlin of its historic role as capital of a unified Germany and to place West Berlin in an extremely precarious position as an eastern outpost of the Federal Republic more than 100 miles inside the German Democratic Republic. Responsibility for Berlin rested not with the Federal Republic but with the three Western Allies.

When the Federal Republic was founded in 1949 great care was taken to stress its provisional character. It was given a 'Basic Law', not a fully fledged constitution, and the Basic Law was not adopted by a referendum, which would have lent it too much legitimacy. The Federal Republic was less than a state in this view and more like a holding company for the rights pertaining to Germany as a whole, meaning Germany within its 1937 boundaries.

In the first few years of the Federal Republic federal politics revolved around the question of what was going to replace it. All the major parties were committed to reunification, a commitment which was raised to a constitutional imperative by its expression in the Preamble to the Basic Law. The major political debate in the first years of the Federal Republic (see chapter 9) was on the relative priority of reunification as against European integration. The CDU/CSU stressed the priority of European integration since it was possible to make progress in this area.

The SPD opposition and some influential voices in the FDP argued that such progress would undercut any chances of later reunification and therefore opposed such moves. At the rhetorical and declaratory level at which the debate was conducted all the participants accepted that the Federal Republic would be transcended by a reunified Germany whether or not this unified Germany was incorporated in a united Western Europe.

From their foundation both German states denied each others' legitimacy. The Federal Republic claimed to be the successor state to the Third Reich and its government also claimed, on the basis of its elected status, an *Alleinvertretungsanspruch* (an exclusive claim) to represent all Germans. For its part, East Germany portrayed the Federal Republic as a product of capitalist restoration, American domination and continuity with the Third Reich.

The two states did not maintain diplomatic relations and contact between them at an official level was very restricted. The main official point of contact was at the level of economics, where an Inter-zonal Trade Agreement providing for free trade between the two parts of Germany was signed at Frankfurt am Main immediately after the creation of the two German states in October 1949. It represented on the West German side a desire to keep the German question open and to soften the edges of the choice that had been imposed. It was also an important interest for the Federal Republic to try and reduce the isolated status of West Berlin. The East German interest in the trade agreement had much more of an economic character. It offered an avenue of access to Western technology, and afforded entry for particular sectors of the East German economy, such as textiles, to an important market. At that time there were also subsidiary political motives as East Germany wished to present itself as the torch-bearer of German unity.

In the first years of the Federal Republic Adenauer pursued a fairly single-minded Western-oriented policy, a policy which, as we have seen, brought the Federal Republic rich dividends in terms of international acceptance in the West. The proposed rearmament of West Germany within the context of EDC was regarded as very threatening by the Soviet Union, however, and in a series of Notes in 1952 the Soviet government appeared to offer the Federal Republic the prospect of a reunified Germany provided it became militarily neutral. A great deal of controversy still surrounds the question as to whether or not in rejecting the Soviet advances in 1952 Adenauer had passed up a real chance of a reunified Germany. It seems unlikely that such a chance existed since even if the Soviet offers were genuine rather than mere delaying tactics, the Western occupying powers, especially the United States, would scarcely have agreed to such a step. Moreover, despite the rhetorical commitment to reunification, very few West Germans, and certainly not the Federal government, would have been prepared to trade their democratic liberties or even their economic prosperity for a reunified Germany. The reunified Germany that they envisaged was basically a territorial extension of the Federal Republic through the collapse of the GDR and the Soviet Empire in Eastern Europe. This perception was strengthened by the uprising in East Germany on 17 June 1953 which had to be suppressed by Russian tanks. How central the notion of the weakness of East Germany was to West German public thinking is illustrated by the fact that 17 June became, and has remained, an official public holiday in West Germany.

With the lifting of occupational status and the attainment of full sovereignty in 1955, the absence of diplomatic relations with the Soviet Union appeared to be a much more pressing problem to West Germany policy-makers. Two issues in particular, the return of the German POWs and the German question seemed to demand the establishment of full diplomatic relations with the Soviet Union. Negotiations took place in October 1955 and diplomatic relations were established. In order to protect its *Alleinvertretungsanspruch* the Federal government promulgated in the same year the Hallstein Doctrine which labelled recognition of the GDR by other states as an unfriendly act. Only the Soviet Union was to be allowed to maintain diplomatic relations with both East and West Germany.

THE BERLIN CRISIS

Reference has already been made to the exposed position of West Berlin. A first attempt by the Soviet Union to exert pressure on West Berlin through a blockade in 1948/9 was defeated by the year-long allied airlift of supplies. A second Berlin crisis was precipitated from 1958 onwards by Kruschev's attempt to play down the four-power presence in Berlin, upgrade the role of East Germany and attenuate the links between West Berlin and the Federal Republic.

West Berlin was a vital interest to the Federal government and Adenauer was disappointed by what he perceived as an absence of resolve in some American reactions. The key development of long-term significance was not, however, a direct result of Kruschev's diplomatic efforts. The collectivization of East German agriculture in 1960 led to a greatly increased rate of flight from the GDR. This flight was largely through Berlin because of its open character, which meant that travel within the city proceeded in a relatively unimpeded fashion. By mid 1961 this flight had reached proportions which made some action by the East German government inevitable. Its response on 13 August 1961 was the building of the Berlin Wall which bisected the city and presented an almost insurmountable barrier to movement by persons between the two states.

The erection of the Berlin Wall had a number of very significant long-term consequences. It was very widely seen in the Federal Republic as indicating the limitations of Adenauer's policy of strength. East Germany would not collapse and a policy of unremitting pressure by the Federal Republic would only make the GDR leadership even more defensive and repressive towards its own population. It was therefore time to rethink West German policy away from an exclusive emphasis on reunification to policies designed to improve the conditions of those actually living within the East German state.

This response was especially marked in Willy Brandt and the Berlin SPD. A year after the erection of the wall, in a series of lectures at Harvard entitled 'The Ordeal of Coexistence', Brandt argued for the abandonment of the policy of confrontation.[1] A year later, in a much publicized speech at Tützing, Brandt's foreign policy alter ego, Egon Bahr, argued for a policy of *'Wandel durch Annäherung'* (change through accommodation). This Bahr/Brandt concept involved transcending the status quo by recognising it, the argument being that some accommodation with East Germany would allow its leadership to pursue a less repressive policy towards its own population. As Governing Mayor of West Berlin, Party Chairman and candidate for the Chancellorship, Brandt was in a very strong position to get the SPD behind his new policy.

The governing coalition of CDU/CSU, and after the 1961 election the FDP, was also affected by the erection of the wall. In the case of the CDU/CSU the change was much less marked than in that of the FDP but even in the CDU/CSU there was a recognition that the previous 'policy of strength' in its original form was unsustainable. The shock to the previous policy represented by the building of the wall was accompanied by a whole series of changes in the external and internal environment of the Federal Republic which cumulatively destroyed the foundations on which the previous policy had rested.

The most important change was in the policy of the US government. The Kennedy administration made it clear that it intended to press for detente with the Soviet Union despite the continued division of Germany. It had been one of Adenauer's early successes that he had obtained the Western Allies' assurance that any detente would be predicated on a solution to the German question. For a short period in the early 1960s, however, there was a great deal of tension between Washington and Bonn; and the German ambassador in Washington, Wilhelm Grewe, made himself so unpopular in Washington that he was replaced.

It became clear that, if the Federal Republic was to preserve its position in the Western Alliance, then it had to make some concessions in relation to its eastern policy. In that sense *Ostpolitik* was essentially an outgrowth of *Westpolitik*.

The other major external factor was the steady consolidation of the East German state. Paradoxically, the confession of weakness that the regime made in 1961 in building the Berlin Wall resulted in a strengthening of the GDR. Having deprived its population of the right to flee, the East German government embarked on a process of liberalization in the economic field. With a population less than one-third of that of the Federal Republic, East Germany became Europe's fifth industrial power and the second industrial trading nation in the Eastern bloc, contributing one-fifth of the Soviet Union's total import requirements by the end of the 1960s. This economic success contributed greatly to the strengthening of the system. A common view at that time was that the East German citizen had proved to be as much of a *homo economicus* as his West German neighbour, and the increased economic success of the 1960s had done something to reconcile him to the system. At the same time the regime stressed the separate and permanent nature of the GDR. In April 1968 East Germany adopted a new constitution that emphasized its distinctness from West Germany and proclaimed it to be a 'Socialist State of the German People', while the Secretariat for All-German Affairs was renamed the Secretariat for West German Affairs. This process of consolidation was a serious challenge to Adenauer's policy, which had held out the hope that a strong and united Western Europe would eventually persuade the Soviet Union to hand over East Germany.

INTERNAL CHANGES

These changes in the external environment were accompanied by significant internal changes. At the elite level there were significant shifts in attitudes. West German industrial leaders, especially in heavy industry, became more concerned about the trade that was being lost by the absence of normal relations with Eastern Europe and they began to encourage the federal government to adopt more flexible attitudes towards *Ostpolitik*.

In the Federal Republic, as we have seen elsewhere, the churches have played an important role in politics, including support for particular foreign policies. Whilst the Roman Catholic Church had been an important source of support to policies of Western European integration, the Protestant Church, reflecting the traditional East–West confessional divide, had been very strongly identified with the cause of German unity. The Protestant Church had been a conspicuously vocal supporter of the West German consensus belief that the Germans had an unrestricted right to self-determination. The importance of the Protestant Church's 'memorandum on the situation of the refugees and the relationship of the German people to their Eastern neighbours' (published in October 1965), which relativized the moral claim of the Germans by stressing that the Poles also had a *Recht auf Heimat* (right to a homeland) was thus, in the words of Karl Kaiser, 'impossible to overemphasize'.[2]

The change in the attitude of the Protestant Church was paralleled by a drastic decline in the bargaining position of the refugees. The refugee vote had been eagerly courted by all parties in the 1950s and was seen as a permanent veto against a recognition of new eastern boundaries. This influential position had been subject to erosion. A refugee party, the *Block der Heimatvertriebenen und Entrechteten*, founded in January 1950, won twenty-seven seats in the 1955 election. The desertion to the CDU of its two most prominent representatives, Kraft and

Oberländer, proved fatal and it was not represented in the Third Bundestag. Another vehicle for the views of the refugees, the *Gesamtdeutsche Partie* (GDP) only polled approximately 2.8 per cent of the votes in 1961. The refugees' hopes of influencing the two major parties were reduced by the death of their most prominent spokesmen, Hans-Christoph Seebohm of the CDU and Wenzel Jaksch in the SPD. Seebohm, despite his undoubted expertise as Transport Minister (continually in office from 1949), was excluded from office in 1965 because his views on *Ostpolitik* had become an embarrassment to the government. More importantly, there was a growing discrepancy between the views of the ageing functionaries of the refugee movements, and those of their sons and daughters and the West German population at large. Although they fought a vigorous rearguard action, they suffered a continual series of reverses from the mid 1960s.

These external and internal developments had a marked effect on popular attitudes in the Federal Republic. Public belief in and concern with reunification and the related issue of the eastern borders, especially the Oder–Neisse line, dropped sharply throughout the 1960s. Kitzinger argued on the basis of his reading of survey data that, by 1969, reunification was considered the most important task of a Federal government by only 6 per cent of the electorate.[3] Even more revealing are the figures cited by Josef Korbel.[4] In 1956 the partition of Germany was considered 'intolerable' by 52 per cent; in 1962 (in the aftermath of the Berlin Wall) by 61 per cent; and in 1963 by 53 per cent. The proportion dropped to 38 per cent in 1965 and 22 per cent in 1966. In 1955, 58 per cent of West Germans polled believed that the United States was in favour of reunification, but in 1969 only 37 per cent thought so.

THE BEGINNINGS OF *OSTPOLITIK*

The beginnings of an *Ostpolitik* were made by the CDU Foreign Minister Gerhard Schroeder, who took up contacts, particularly at trade level, with Eastern European states. This new policy reflected both a response to internal change, especially industrial pressures, and changing American perceptions, of which the most influential were those of Brzezinski, who advocated strengthening contacts with Eastern Europe but isolating the GDR.

To undermine the Eastern European stake in East Germany, the West will have to differentiate sharply between its attitude toward East Germany and toward the rest of Eastern Europe. For East Germany, the policy must be one of isolation; for East Europe, one of peaceful engagement – economic, cultural, and eventually political. Only then will East Germany become a political anachronism on the map of Europe, a source of continuing embarrassment to Moscow, and no longer a source of security to the East Europeans.[5]

Schroeder's policy had two main aims: first, to prevent the Federal Republic from being diplomatically isolated in the West, particularly from the United States, and secondly to isolate East Germany from its neighbours. No great progress was made however since the Hallstein Doctrine prevented the establishment of diplomatic relations with states that also recognized East Germany. In a bid to proceed beyond trade relations, the Federal government launched a peace initiative towards Eastern Europe in March 1966. This initiative centred on a renunciation of force but it met a less than enthusiastic response from Eastern European leaders who pointed both to similar German suggestions in the 1920s and to the fact that no note had been sent to the East German government.

The formation of the Grand Coalition in November 1966 with Brandt as Foreign Minister did lead to a slightly faster rate of change. The Hallstein Doctrine had become more and more costly to maintain. As the number of states multiplied and the international system became less and less bipolar, more and more states were using it as a lever to extract expensive concessions from the Federal government which it was forced to concede in order to maintain a central pillar of its foreign policy. It was also politically costly, due to its very constraining effect on relations with Eastern Europe. In practice the Hallstein doctrine was gradually dropped and relations were established with Yugoslavia and Romania. However, the possibility of any great change was circumscribed by the opposition of the CDU/CSU and the hostile attitude of the Soviet Union, especially after the Czech crisis of 1968.

THE HIGH POINT OF *OSTPOLITIK*

The major treaties establishing a new relationship between the Federal Republic and Eastern Europe which form the core of

Ostpolitik represent the historic achievement of the Brandt Chancellorship. The early days of the Brandt government in 1969 were marked by some fairly dramatic pronouncements, particularly in relation to East Germany. Perhaps the most famous of these was Brandt's reference to 'two states of one German nation', which, whilst stopping short of full international recognition of the GDR, also by implication ruled out, for the foreseeable future, the reunification option. Brandt's government declaration of 1969 was the first not to use the term 'reunification'. This meant that Brandt recognized that the pursuit of a policy based on the primacy of reunification had resulted in the atrophying of contacts between East and West Germany by encouraging the government of the GDR to maintain its defensive posture. Explicit acceptance of the fact that reunification was not practical policy would, it was hoped, enable the East German government to feel free enough to liberalize contacts between the two states and thus strengthen the sense of *Zusammengehörigkeitsgefühl* (feeling of belonging together). Historically, this feeling has not, as Brandt constantly emphasized, depended on living within the same frontiers. In other words, the new government, in the hope of preserving the German nation as a *Kulturnation* (nation defined by culture), refrained from stressing the pursuit of a *Staatsnation* (nation defined by citizenship). The primary goal of *Ostpolitik* was and remained throughout a new relationship with East Germany. The new relationship with the GDR, although central to Brandt's plans, was likely to be the most difficult to achieve and depended on the prior settlement of relations with the Soviet Union.

THE MOSCOW AND WARSAW TREATIES

For the leading figures in the SPD and FDP government, normalization of relations with Eastern Europe was on overriding priority on three main grounds. First, normal relations with Eastern Europe were seen as a precondition for progress on the central plane of German–German relations, including some easing of the Berlin problem. Secondly, it was part of a process of emancipation and would decrease the reliance of the Federal Republic on the Western Allies who hitherto had acted as its interlocutors with Eastern Europe. Finally, there was an important moral dimension symbolized by Willy Brandt's gesture of throwing himself on his knees at the site of the Warsaw Ghetto during his visit in 1970. This moral dimension recognized that German action in Eastern Europe in the Second World War had not only fatally compromised German territorial rights in the area but had been of such a traumatic character that it continued to impose obligations on the Germans to make some sort of recompense. This last view, although widely held in the governing parties, was rejected by the CDU/CSU opposition who pointed to the forcible expulsion of Germans from these areas in 1945 and the repressive role practised by communist governments. In their view the two sets of atrocities cancelled each other out. This argument has re-emerged in the 1980s in a controversy between historians, the so-called '*Historikerstreit*'. The debate centres around those who stress the uniqueness of Nazi atrocities and those mainly identified with the CDU/CSU who reject this whilst not denying the horror of Nazi crimes.[6]

The basic thrust of the new *Ostpolitik* was not only to offer, as the CDU/CSU–FDP government had done in 1966, a renunciation of force, but to buttress this by a recognition of realities, in effect a recognition of existing frontiers in Europe. It was this, of course, which was of key interest to the Soviet and Polish governments.

Negotiations with the Soviet Union and Poland proceeded at an almost dizzy pace after the advent of the social–liberal government in the autumn of 1969. This pace was much criticized by the CDU/CSU and Brandt had continually to ensure that he was not running too far ahead of his allies, particularly the United States, as is clear from the Kissinger memoirs.

There would be no attempt to change this basic course. We would not encourage any particular negotiating strategy. Nor would we comment on specific terms of his negotiation. For this he would have to take responsibility; we would not participate in the German domestic debate, on either side. We would support Brandt's objectives, stay silent on his methods, urge closer consultation with his allies, warn against raising excessive expectations. And we would give him sense of partnership, which was the best assurance against the latent dangers of purely national policy.[7]

The crucial negotiations which led to the Moscow Treaty were carried out on the German side by Egon Bahr between January and May 1970. The so-called 'Bahr Paper', setting out the points of agreement, was leaked in May 1970. The paper anticipated the later Moscow Treaty and in it the Federal government committed itself to respecting the territorial integrity of all European states and the inviolability of their frontiers including the Oder–Neisse line and the demarcation line between the Federal Republic and the GDR. In the Bahr Paper the Federal Republic also committed itself to support the admission of the two German states into the United Nations, whilst not accepting the Soviet demand for full international recognition of the GDR.

The Moscow Treaty itself was negotiated and signed in July/August 1970 by Walther Scheel, the Foreign Minister. The position of the Federal Republic was strengthened in two ways by Scheel. In order to safeguard the long-term position of the Federal government and to quieten domestic opposition, a 'letter on German Unity' was presented to the Soviet government at the signing of the treaty, reaffirming the Federal government's commitment to German unity. Equally significantly, ratification was subject to a successful outcome of four-power negotiations on Berlin – an issue of central concern to the Federal government.

THE QUADRUPARTITE AGREEMENT ON BERLIN

The coupling of the quadrupartite negotiations and the Moscow Treaty gave the Soviet Union an interest in a speedy outcome of the quadrupartite negotiations. Neither German state took part in the negotiations but they were, of course, intensively consulted. The Western position was very largely worked out by the Bonn Group of Western Ambassadors plus the Federal government and the Berlin Senate. After prolonged negotiations the Agreement was signed in 1971. The Western Powers reaffirmed their view that West Berlin was not a constituent part of the Federal Republic while declaring that the ties between West Berlin and the Federal Republic should be strengthened. The key practical provisions of the agreement provided for unimpeded transit of people and goods between West Berlin and the Federal Republic. This was a key interest of West Berlin and the Federal Republic since, without guarantees of unimpeded traffic, West Berlin looked economically doomed in the long term.

The Negotiations with Poland

The key element in the negotiations between the Federal Republic and Poland was the question of the recognition of Poland's western frontiers. The Polish government desired an explicit and unconditional recognition of the frontier line (Oder–Neisse line) established in practice after 1945. The Federal government was unable to meet this demand fully without making ratification impossible. In the event German consciousness of historic guilt weighed heavily on the negotiators and the final formula went very far towards meeting Polish aspirations. In Article I it was stated that the Oder–Neisse line 'shall constitute the western state frontier of the People's Republic of Poland'. The recognition of Poland's western frontier was flanked by provisions for economic and technological cooperation and measures designed to make it easier for citizens of German origin to leave Poland.

The Ratification of the Moscow and Warsaw Treaties

Although public opinion polls consistently demonstrated that *Ostpolitik* was very popular with German voters, the Moscow and Warsaw Treaties were opposed as bitterly by the CDU/CSU as the treaties with the West had been by the SPD in the early 1950s. In a sense this was predictable; any opposition was likely to dwell on the costs and, although Brandt might declare 'nothing has been lost that was not gambled away long ago', some long-established West German positions were being abandoned. There were two other more contingent factors in the CDU/CSU's opposition. The CDU/CSU felt cheated in being deprived of its governmental vocation in 1969 since it was still the largest party in the Bundestag. The SPD–FDP had a tiny majority and a stress on opposition to *Ostpolitik* seemed a way of attracting enough '*Überläufer*' (floor crossers) from the FDP and the SPD. This was a strategy with some hope of success since the FDP Parliamentary Party did contain unreconciled elements and there were also a number of representatives of refugee interests who were prepared to leave the SPD on this issue. It was also an important issue for Franz Josef Strauss and the CSU. After the building of the Berlin Wall, Strauss and his then foreign policy adviser, Klaus Bloemer, suggested policies which were not dissimilar from those of Brandt and Bahr. After his fall from Federal office, and especially after the appearance of the NPD, Strauss changed to a very traditional stance on German unity. Two reasons seem to account for Strauss's change of tack which led to Bloemer's resignation. First, the NPD episode convinced Strauss that the CSU must not leave a gap on its right. Secondly, opposition to *Ostpolitik* offered a way of appealing to the traditionally nationalistic Protestant minority in Bavaria who had hitherto voted FDP but who had deserted in large numbers to the NPD.

The CDU/CSU's objections stressed the necessity of preserving the Germans' right to self-determination and the non-recognition of borders in advance of a peace treaty. Early objections about the negative impact of *Ostpolitik* on West Berlin and on the Western Alliance were largely abandoned after the conclusion of the Berlin Agreements improved the position of Berlin and made clear the commitment of other Western powers to the policy.

By April 1972 the government's majority had all but disappeared and the CDU/CSU increased pressure on the government over the treaties. A joint resolution was agreed in the Bundestag which reaffirmed the right of self-determination, stressed that no recognition of borders could be considered final before a peace treaty and restated the commitment to unity. A constructive vote of no confidence moved by Rainer Barzel on 27 April 1972 failed, although the government by that time could no longer count on a majority. On the basis of the agreed joint resolution, the CDU recommended acceptance of both treaties but this was opposed by the CSU and the CDU/CSU in fact abstained in the ensuing votes on the treaties. The Moscow Treaty was adopted by 248 votes to ten with 238 abstentions and the Warsaw Treaty by 248 votes to seventeen with 231 abstentions. Two days after their acceptance by the Bundestag on 17 May 1972, they were accepted by the Bundesrat and became law a week later. Despite their intransigent opposition, the CDU/CSU accepted the legality of these treaties and did not seek to reverse them after regaining office in 1982.

RELATIONS BETWEEN THE TWO GERMANIES

Despite the prior conclusion of the Moscow and Warsaw

Treaties, the principal aim of *Ostpolitik* remained the transformation of relations with 'the other party of Germany'. Priority was given to agreement with the Soviet Union since it was seen as the ultimate repository of power in Eastern Europe. Moreover the decades of hostility between the two states and the degree to which the legitimacy of the Federal Republic was seen to depend on the lack of legitimacy of the GDR, necessarily meant that it was likely to prove a much more difficult enterprise.

Early meetings were held between Brandt and Stoph, the East German Prime Minister, at Erfurt and Kassel, but the East German leadership proved unresponsive. Closer contacts between the two German states were still perceived as a real danger, a view reinforced by pro-Brandt demonstrations at Erfurt when Brandt took part in meetings there.

Serious progress was made only after the conclusion of the Quadrupartite Agreement in September 1971. The aim of the GDR was to achieve international recognition whilst making as few concessions as possible in opening up the country. The Federal government wanted to ensure the maximum contact with the population of East Germany whilst limiting the degree of recognition in order to preserve the doctrine of common nationality and the special character of relations between the two Germanies. In the event, the Federal Republic had to concede rather more than its eastern neighbour. In the so-called Basic Treaty (*Grundlagenvertrag*) which was concluded just before the Federal election of 19 November 1972, the Federal government did not accord full international recognition to the German Democratic Republic but the difference is wafer thin. Article 3 of the Basic Treaty talks of the inviolability of the existing border and commits both states to unqualified respect for each others' territorial integrity. Article 6 recognizes unconditionally the internal and external sovereignty of both states. Both states agreed to support each other's membership of the United Nations and to establish diplomatic relations with each other, through their representatives would be known as High Commissioners rather than Ambassadors. As in the case of the Moscow Treaty, the Federal government submitted a 'letter on German Unity' to the East German government, restating its traditional position on reunification.

The election of 19 November 1972 was fought out very largely on *Ostpolitik*, and its overwhelming popularity was demonstrated by the massive endorsement of the governing coalition and an unprecedentedly good result for the SPD.

THE CONSTITUTIONAL COURT

The law ratifying the Basic Treaty was passed by the Bundestag on 11 May 1973, by a margin of 268 to 217. On a second reading, the Bundesrat, on 25 May 1973, referred it to the mediation committee (*Vermittlungsauschuss*). Undeterred by the size of the coalition majority in the November 1972 election in which the Basic Treaty had been much discussed, the Bavarian government referred the Basic Treaty to the Federal Constitutional Court. The Bavarian government argued that the Basic Treaty

contravened the constitutional mandate on preserving the political unity of Germany; violated the injunction on reunification; precluded the right of the other part of Germany to accede to the jurisdiction of the Federal Republic's constitution, the Basic Law; was incompatible with the provisions of the Basic Law pertaining to Berlin; contravened the obligation to render protection and assistance to all Germans including those in the GDR.[8]

In the view of the Federal government the Basic Treaty did not contradict the mandate on reunification since the three Western powers remained bound to relate the four-power proviso to Germany as a whole, the treaty adhered to the continued existence of Germany as a legal subject and avoided any qualification of the German Democratic Republic as a foreign entity. In its defence the Federal government argued further that the treaty left the unity of the German nation and German nationality intact; did not imply any recognition of the GDR under international law and left the status of Berlin untouched as established by the Quadrupartite Agreement.

The Court found for the Federal government in its judgment of 31 July 1973. It reaffirmed the government's view that the commitment to reunification was a constitutional imperative, the pursuit of which no Federal government could constitutionally abandon. The means to reach this objective were, however, a matter for the Federal government.

Although the judgement endorsed the treaties, some of the Court's reasoning appeared to be in tension with the treaty.

Whilst the treaty stressed the permanence of the existing arrangements and the inviolability of the frontiers, some of the language of the judgment appeared to call them into question.

It must be clear that present conditions at the border between West and East Germany – the Berlin Wall, barbed wire, death-strips, orders to shoot – are incompatible with the treaty. To this extent the treaty provides grounds in law for the Federal government to do everything within its power to change and do away with these inhuman conditions.[9]

In another statement on the border between East and West Germany, the Court appeared to deny the separate existence of the eastern state and talked about the German/German border as 'similar to those between the *Länder* of the Federal Republic of Germany'.[10] This view rested on the continued invocation of the 'partial identity theory' which asserted a partial identity between the Federal Republic and the German Reich. The Federal Republic represented the continuation of the German Reich within a more restricted territorial area but with a continued responsibility for the area occupied by the Democratic Republic. This is the so-called *Dach* (roof) theory.

The conclusion of the Basic Treaty eased relations between the two German states but did not totally transform them. They remained adversaries; a point vividly demonstrated by the activities of Günter Guillaume, Brandt's personal assistant, who was revealed to be an East German spy in 1974 and whose unmasking led to the resignation of the architect of *Ostpolitik* in May 1974.

The goals of the two governments appeared to show little sign of converging in the next decade and a half. The Federal government regarded the conclusion of the Basic Treaty as a point of departure which it hoped would lead to a whole network of agreements designed to improve communications between the two Germanies and the quality of life of the inhabitants of East Germany. The aim of the GDR government was almost diametrically opposed. The Basic Treaty from its perspective represented the culmination of a long-term policy to secure international acceptance and recognition of the GDR. It had a strong interest in stressing that relations between the two states should be conducted on the basis of the separate and distinct nature of the two societies and that negotiations should not contribute towards convergence. The constraining impact of these conflicting perspectives was somewhat blunted by the economic weakness of East Germany. This weakness meant that the East German government were prepared to conclude agreements on a number of practical matters, especially in relation to transport. Quite often, as in the case of transit motorways to West Berlin, the Federal government paid the costs of building or upgrading roads within East Germany. The Federal government was also very active in purchasing the freedom of East German dissidents.

Trade between the two states continued on a non-tariff basis. This trade was largely financed by the Federal government which provided an interest-free credit line to the East through the 'swing mechanism' which allowed one partner to be overdrawn.

The opposition of the CDU/CSU to the Basic Treaty led many to expect that relations with East Germany would come under strain when they returned to power. This was always unlikely given the importance West Germans attached to contacts with East Germany. What could not have been predicted was that the lead in providing credit to the GDR, which was short of hard currency, would be taken by Franz Josef Strauss who had, as we have seen, been much more militantly opposed to the Basic Treaty than the CDU. The other major development of the early 1980s, referred to in chapter 9, was the change of tack by the East German government who now became keen to stress Pan-German consciousness in opposition to the stationing of US missiles in West Germany.

THE GERMAN NATION DEBATE

Among the numerous questions on which West German politicians, including those outside the consensus like the KPD, were agreed, was that the Federal Republic should not and could not become a nation-state like France or Italy. Its citizens were expected to owe only instrumental loyalty to the West German state; deeper loyalties were to be reserved for a future reunified Germany. As time passed loyalties to the Federal Republic were legitimized by the fact that the anti-communist nature of the state genuinely reflected the views of the majority of its citizens; by free elections, which provided the basis of the Federal Republic's claim to be the sole legitimate representative of the

German people (*Alleinvertretunganspruch*) and by the implicit understanding that acceptance of the Federal Republic would result in a relation of Allied controls and increasing prosperity for the West German economy.

Paradoxically, by the time of the formation of the Grand Coalition, which triggered the first crisis of legitimacy in the Federal Republic with the emergence of both right- and left-wing extra-parliamentary oppositions, the Federal Republic looked like a permanent fixture. Gaullist obstruction had put paid to the idea of a united Europe and reunification looked increasingly unreal.

Against this background the impact of *Ostpolitik* on West German conceptions of identity and nation was both dramatic and ambiguous. A number of authors, most notably Paterson and Schweigler, argued in the early 1970s that the central thrust of *Ostpolitik* with its emphasis on the recognition of realities, especially the reality of the GDR, involved a recognition of the non-provisional nature of the Federal Republic itself.[11] This line of argument asserted that West Germans were increasingly losing their all-German consciousness and developing a West German identity.

The contrary view found expression in the judgement of the Federal Constitutional Court already referred to. Supporters of this view also pointed out that both the Moscow and Basic Treaties were flanked by 'Letters of German Unity' which restated the traditional commitment. Egon Bahr, the architect of *Ostpolitik*, always claimed that his eventual goal was a reunified Germany.

Developments in the eighties were used to support either line of argument. Supporters of the continuance of the German nation thesis pointed to the vigorous restatement of the commitment to eventual reunification by the CDU/CSU in government and the revival of all-German rhetoric by the GDR government in the early 1980s to harness support in West Germany against the stationing of US missiles. Foreign observers, especially in France but also in the United States, were quick to seize on any revival of all-German consciousness and often claimed to find it in some of the pronouncements by the Greens.

Supporters of the West German consciousness school pointed to the unlikelihood of unity. They also pointed to a curious development where West Germans used 'Germany' to mean only the Federal Republic. In football commentaries reference was often made to 'Germany versus the GDR'!

The debate on the issue of identity appeared likely to continue. Any totally unambiguous assertion of a West German identity looked unlikely. It would have been against the Basic Law, and such indications as we have, indicate that it would have come up against the objections of the Federal Constitutional Court. Another major difficulty is that any unambiguous assertion of West German identity left West Berlin vulnerable. It would also ultimately have required a revision of the West German nationality law away from its present basis which automatically grants citizenship to a refugee from East Germany or indeed any of the areas which constituted Germany in 1937. And yet reunification did look increasingly remote and the number of West Germans with an experience of a unified Germany diminished year by year.

The striking feature of travel statistics between West and East, however, was the steep decline in the number of visits by West German citizens after the GDR authorities raised the amount they were required compulsorily to convert into East German

Table 10.1 Travel by citizens of the Federal Republic to East Germany 1967–1985

Year	Total	Year	Total
1967	1,423,000	1976	3,120,000
1968	1,261,000	1978	2,987,000
1969	1,107,000	1979	3,177,000
1970	1,254,000	1980	2,923,000
1971	1,267,000	1981	2,746,000
1972	1,540,000	1982	2,086,000
1973	2,278,000	1983	2,218,000
1974	1,919,000	1984	2,499,000
1975	3,123,000	1985	2,600,000

marks to DM 25 in October 1980 (table 10.1). That such a relatively small sum of money produced such a steep decline suggests the fulfilment of a residual duty rather than a burning all-German consciousness on the part of the citizens of the Federal Republic.

BALANCE SHEET OF *OSTPOLITIK*

In drawing up a balance sheet of *Ostpolitik* we need to consider both its internal and external effects.

Internal Effects

Internally one very clear effect of *Ostpolitik* was to help maintain the SPD in government. *Ostpolitik* was the buckle which united the SPD and FDP, especially in the Brandt/Scheel years of 1969–74, and without it the coalition would have lacked a legitimating formula. *Ostpolitik* was also a very important source of integration within the SPD. Factional strife was a very marked feature of the years between 1969 and 1982 but all the contending wings of the party were agreed on *Ostpolitik* throughout the whole period and defence of the achievements of *Ostpolitik* was often an important reason for continuing to stick together when other issues made continued cooperation difficult. Perhaps the most surprising effect of *Ostpolitik* was that it represented a considerable electoral bonus to the SPD and has often been held to have played a decisive part in the SPD's victory in 1972. Throughout the 1950s and much of the 1960s conventional wisdom assumed in the Federal Republic that recognition of the post-war realities of lost territories would bring electoral punishment. By the time that the *Ostpolitik* of the SPD–FDP government was launched, the pain of recognizing what had been lost by Germany's defeat was overshadowed by the attraction of freer movement to and from the GDR if the treaties were concluded.

External Impact

The West   The conclusion of the complex of treaties at the core of *Ostpolitik* was an important step in the process of emancipation of the Federal Republic from its unilateral dependence on the Western Allies in relation to policy towards Eastern Europe. This was most obviously the case in relation to West Berlin. The Federal Republic continued to depend on the Western Allies to represent its interests in Berlin but the conclusion of the Berlin Agreements in 1971 greatly reduced the occasions for pressure on the Federal government on this issue as the effect of the agreement was to defuse the Berlin Question.

In its origins *Ostpolitik* was *inter alia* the specific West German adaptation to the detente process entered into by the United States and the Soviet Union. In that sense it was a question of making West German policy compatible with US policy in order to prevent the diplomatic isolation of the Federal Republic. The contribution of *Ostpolitik* to the growing international self-confidence of the Federal Republic is well illustrated by the Republic's response to the breakdown of the detente between the superpowers after the Soviet incursion into Afghanistan. The Federal Republic continued to insist on its own priorities in relation to detente. The detente with the Soviet Union was maintained even against specific American wishes, as on the Siberian pipeline issue. The priority given to the maintenance of an Inner-German detente was even more striking. The change of government in 1982 had much less effect than expected not only because Hans-Dietrich Genscher continued to pursue his former policy on detente, but also because the CDU/CSU seemed much more interested in detente, especially inner-German detente, than their pronouncements in opposition might have led one to expect.

The Eastern dimension   There can be little doubt that *Ostpolitik* significantly improved the climate of relations between the Federal Republic and the Eastern European states in general. There can, however, be equally little doubt that relations with the West have a much higher priority, despite the fears of some French and American commentators who are haunted by fears of a Rapallo-like relationship between the Federal Republic and the Soviet Union. This is also true in relation to trade. *Ostpolitik* did help to bring about an increased volume of trade which might be important in some sectors, like steel, but it was very small in relation to West German trade with the West.

The German–German dimension   A central aim of *Ostpolitik* was to make the border more porous, both to improve the quality of life of the population of the GDR and to maintain a *Zusammenge-hoerigkeitsgefuehl* (sense of belonging together) between the populations of the two parts of Germany. These aims were never likely to be realized totally to the satisfaction of the government and public opinion in the Federal Republic. The East German government desired international recognition to help make up for its lack of legitimacy and to increase stability.

Once recognition was gained, it attempted to constrain contact which it perceived as destabilizing through a policy of demarcation (*Abgrenzung*) which sought to emphasize separateness and restrict contacts.

One way it did this was by raising the compulsory daily exchange rate on a number of occasions. Nevertheless, travel did become much easier. Telephone communication also became easier, though the number of telephone calls from East to West is calculated to be about one-fifth of calls from West to East.

This picture began to change dramatically after 1986 and East Germany began to allow its citizens to visit the Federal Republic in large numbers for the first time. Previously visits were restricted to pensioners or visitors on urgent family business. In 1986, however, 573,000 East Germans below retirement age visited the Federal Republic, a figure which was increased to 1.2 million in 1987. The success of the visit by the East German leader Erich Honecker to Bonn in October 1987 led to even easier travel between the two states and it began to look as if Brandt's initial optimism about making the borders more porous might have been right over the long term. These developments helped pave the way for the rush to unification in 1989–90.

11 Conclusion

TOWARDS A THIRD REPUBLIC

In a much admired recent article Peter Katzenstein has written of the emergence of the Third West German Republic.[1] The First Republic lasted from 1949 to 1969 and it can best be understood as a conservative welfare state. Its external policy rested on a total identification with the United States, European integration and a refusal to accept German division as legitimate. The common thread between these policies was the fear of political instability.

The Second Republic lasted from 1969 to 1980 in Katzenstein's view, though 1982 and the change of government seems a more obvious break. The Second Republic is characterized by a growing confidence in the political elite about the stability of the institutions and some move towards a neo-corporatist system through the institutionalization of the role of industry and the labour unions. The counterpart to the stability and consensus suggested by the West German model was its rejection, sometimes violently, by a fairly large section of the educated young on the grounds that it was too stable, too materialistic and too unresponsive to new issues like the environment.

The major change from the First to the Second Republic was in external policy, where *Ostpolitik* reduced the one-sided dependence on the Western Allies and opened up a new set of relationships with Eastern Europe. In particular, the relationship between the Federal Republic and the German Democratic Republic, which had rested on a mutual denial of legitimacy, took on a wholly altered character.

THE THIRD REPUBLIC

The change to a Third Republic was much less clear. The decentralized consensual nature of decision-making in the Federal Republic ensured that governmental change had much less effect than in Britain. Before the governmental change in

1982, there was much talk of a *Wende* (turnaround) but policy and institutional innovation has been limited. The most obvious change has been a very much reduced emphasis on tripartism and the marginalization of the unions in governmental discussion.

The most striking change was not at the governmental level, but at the level of opposition where the formation and electoral success of the Greens has had far-reaching consequences. It has made the system clearly less consensual. Not only do the Greens themselves articulate alternatives, but the need to compete electorally with the Greens has moved the SPD to less consensual positions. Although the Greens have increased dissensus, it could until recently be argued that they might well have increased the already marked stability of the institutions by integrating into the parliamentary system a group who were hitherto alienated.

However, renewed fears about the internal stability of the system were expressed after elections in West Berlin in January 1989 and in Frankfurt in March 1989. The CDU lost badly in both elections, while the SPD increased its share of the poll. Fears about stability were raised by three other features. In both elections extreme right parties, the Republikaner in West Berlin and the NPD in Frankfurt, secured representation. The Greens (known in West Berlin as the Alternative List) increased their share of the vote while the FDP failed to secure representation. Fears about stability arose from projecting these results forward to the 1990 election. If the FDP were to be dragged down by the CDU/CSU it would be unavailable as a coalition partner. It is the preferred partner, not only of the CDU/CSU but of many in the SPD leadership and its absence would mean that the pressure on the SPD to think in terms of a coalition with the Greens, especially after forming a coalition with the Greens in West Berlin, would be very high. The chances of a Red/Green coalition were strengthened by the victory of the 'Realos' over the 'Fundis' in February 1989 in the selection of leadership posts in the Greens. Such a coalition might alienate some of the SPD's traditional support and would imply a greater change in defence and security policy than the SPD leadership is yet ready for. These fears proved groundless. The position of the governing coalition has been immeasurably strengthened by unity whilst that of the SPD and the Greens has been severely weakened by its uncertain response.

Conclusion

THE NEW GERMANY

THE NEW GERMANY

The emergence of a unified Germany on 3 October 1990 changes the terms of the debate on Germany. At the most extreme the alternatives posed are between a new, Fourth Reich and a greater Federal Republic. The traumatic experience of war and defeat between 1939 and 1945 removed the psychological preconditions for a new Fourth Reich. The new Germany will clearly approximate much more to the Federal Republic. Its economy, institutional and constitutional structure will owe almost nothing to East German experience. Some changes, however, will take place. Berlin seems predestined as the new capital, and a capital barely 100 kms from the Polish border has a different mentality from Bonn on the western rim of Germany. The disparity in wealth between the Eastern and Western parts of Germany are very considerable. It will require skilful political management to prevent this becoming a source of instability between a resentful East and a grudging West.

THE GERMAN GULLIVER

> An economic giant but a political dwarf.
> Willy Brandt

The circumstances of the creation of the Federal Republic and the continued fears of its European neighbours meant that its foreign policy was not independently formulated but anchored in the transnational defence and economic structures of NATO and the European Community. In that sense the Federal Republic was, and remained, a Gulliver, a giant bound and tied by a myriad network of Alliance and Community ties. It was also a Gulliver in a second sense in the view of some conservative commentators since its citizens suffered a collective amnesia about the exercise of power. The German tiger of 1870 or 1945 had lost its feral characteristics and become a house cat.

This situation was already changing before unity. In NATO events were conspiring to move the Federal Republic into a much more prominent role. West Germans now occupy a high

proportion of important command positions and Manfred Wörner, the Defence Minister, has succeeded Lord Carrington as
Secretary-General of NATO. More fundamentally, the palpable
strains on the US budget mean that the United States is now
understandably putting more and more pressure on the structural surplus countries of the Federal Republic and Japan to play a
very much increased role in the provision of international public
goods such as security. However, while the external preconditions of a stronger German leadership role in NATO were
present, the public's changing view of the Soviet threat meant
that the internal support for a prominent role in NATO is now
even weaker than in the past.

On a longer time horizon European fears of decoupling of the
United States from Western Europe, and worries about the
impact of demographic trends on the capacity of the Federal
Republic to meet its security commitments, led to tentative
efforts at bilateral cooperation in which the Federal Republic
has played the key role. The most advanced of these initiatives
have been between France and the Federal Republic. Joint
exercises have been held and a joint brigade and a joint Defence
Council have been established. These initiatives are likely to
remain limited, however, since it is unclear that any other states
could provide an equivalent to the nuclear guarantee provided
by the United States.

The German Presidency of the European Community in 1988
coincided with a rise in expectations in some other member
states about the role the Federal Republic could play in the EC.
The ever-increasing costs of subsidizing the Common Agricultural Policy had run ahead of present arrangements to raise the
necessary finance. In any resolution of this problem the Federal
Republic, as easily the largest net contributor, was seen as
playing a key role. In some ways surprisingly, given Kohl's
reputation for weak leadership, the West German incumbency
of the Presidency of the EC was a success and many observers
expect it to provide a platform for an extended German role in
the Community.

THE MAN MOUNTAIN

The Federal Republic's position had probably begun to change
to semiGulliver status under the self-confident Chancellorship

305

of Helmut Schmidt but the biggest change was symbolized by Helmut Kohl's Ten Point Plan of November 1989. West Germany had for some time possessed the lion's share of the resources of power in Europe, but was inhibited from playing a leadership role by the shadow of historical experience. Kohl's self-confident proclamation of the Ten Point Plan indicated the change that was taking place. Germany is now the key ally of the United States while at the same time being the most favoured partner of the USSR. As the Soviet Union has ceased to be able to play the role of the superpower convincingly because of her economic weakness, the immense economic strength of the Federal Republic has conferred on it a status close to that of a superpower.

The position of a unified Germany will be even more powerful and the historical experience of the international consequences of a united Germany is not encouraging. No one is more aware of this than the German political elite, however, and they will continue to ensure that Germany fits into the architecture of an emerging Europe, rather than attempting to overpower it like Bismarck's successors.

Appendix: Statistical Tables

Table A1 *Länder*: Population, area, resources

Länd	Population (31.12.87)	Area km²	Tax yield 1987 (DM m)	Expenditure 1987 (DM m)
Schleswig–Holstein	2,612,000	15,270	6,284	10,270
Hamburg	1,567,000	755	5,788	12,940
Lower Saxony	7,189,000	47,431	17,240	28,049
Bremen	654,000	404	1,820	5,512
North Rhine–Westphalia	16,672,000	34,066	45,196	60,075
Hessen	5,552,000	21,114	16,626	21,714
Rhineland–Palatinate	3,606,000	19,848	8,892	14,066
Baden–Württemberg	9,350,000	35,752	27,653	37,136
Bavaria	11,043,000	70,546	30,202	39,802
Saarland	1,041,000	2,571	2,483	4,569
West Berlin	1,884,000	480	4,305	21,638
Total	61,170,000	248,237	166,489	255,771

Source: *Statistisches Jahrbuch* 1988

Table A2 Public Expenditure 1987

Authority	Tax income (DM m)	Expenditure (DM m)	Share of tax revenue (%)	Borrowings (DM m)
Federation	218,841	270,864	49	440,477
Länder	166,489	255,771	37	311,898
Local authorities	64,849	157,147	14	115,855
Total	450,179	683,782		868,230

Source: *Statistisches, Jahrbuch,* 1988; *Finanzbericht* 1987

Appendix

Table A3 Personnel employed in the public service as of 30 June 1987

Authority	Officials	Employers	Workers	Total
Federation	113,528	89,627	109,911	313,066
Länder	924,000	463,000	162,000	1,549,000
Local authorities	150,000	547,000	295,000	992,000
Federal railways	158,766	5,997	111,364	276,127
Federal post	309,090	29,351	102,079	440,520
Social insurance funds	27,279	187,466	10,496	225,241
Total	1,682,663	1,322,441	790,850	3,795,954

Source: Statistisches Jahrbuch 1988

Activity	1949–53	1953–7	1957–61	1961–5	1965–9	1969–72	1972–6	1976–80	1980–3	1983–7
Bills										
Federal government	445	431	394	368	415	351	461	322	155	280
Bundestag	301	414	207	245	225	171	136	111	58	183
Bundesrat	29	16	5	8	14	24	73	52	38	59
Total	775	861	606	621	654	546	670	485	251	522
Laws	545	511	424	426	461	335	516	354	139	320
Mediation committee										
Convened by:										
Federal government	3	3	3	3	4	2	7	7	3	—
Bundestag	2	3	—	2	1	—	1	1	—	—
Bundesrat	70	59	46	34	34	31	96	69	17	6
Total	75	65	49	39	39	33	104	77	20	6
Measures referred to Mediation Committee and published as laws	63	56	47	35	29	30	89	57	17	6
Bundestag										
Interpellations	160	97	49	34	45	31	23	47	32	175
Kleine Anfrage	355	377	410	308	487	569	483	434	297	1,006
Question time	—	—	—	2	17	8	18	9	12	117
Bundesrat										
Decrees etc.	535	656	519	664	711	445	811	631	343	519
EEC Laws	—	—	28	475	897	685	1,053	666	405	634
Plenary sessions										
Bundestag	282	227	168	198	247	199	259	230	142	256
Bundesrat	116	69	54	50	56	43	55	51	28	52
Committee meetings										
Bundestag	5,474	4,389	2,493	2,986	2,692	1,449	2,223	1,955	1,099	2,305
Bundesrat	1,092	887	718	705	803	650	820	796	436	828
Party group meetings	1,774	1,777	675	727	802	529	718	674	400	900

Source: Statistiches Jahrbuch 1987; Handbuch des Deutsehen Bundestages

Table A5   Horizontal (inter-*Länd*) financial equalization, 1986

Länd	Amount (DM m)	Amount per head of population (DM)
Contributors		
Hamburg	198.9	126.6
Hessen	783.1	141.3
Baden–Württemberg	1,745.6	187.2
	2,727.6	
Recipients		
Schleswig–Holstein	616.2	235.8
Lower Saxony	856.2	118.9
Bremen	445.5	681.2
Rhineland–Palatinate	379.4	105.1
Bavaria	48.3	4.4
Saarland	382.0	366.6
	2,727.6	
Free from equalization		
North Rhine–Westphalia		

Source: *Finanzbericht* 1988

Table A6   Grants-in-aid, 1986

Recipient Länd	Amount (DM m)	%
Schleswig–Holstein	254.6	15.2
Lower Saxony	558.0	33.3
Rhineland–Palatinate	321.7	19.2
Bavaria	293.0	17.4
Saarland	160.8	9.6
Bremen	86.1	5.3
	1,674.2	

Source: *Finanzbericht* 1988

Table A7 Structure of administration as at 1 January 1988

Länd	Government district	Counties (Kreise)			Municipalities (Gemeinden)		
		County boroughs	Rural counties	Total	Total	Members of municipal associations	Municipal associations
Schleswig–Holstein	—	4	11	15	1,131	1,026	119
Hamburg	—	1	—	1	1	—	—
Lower Saxony	4	9	38	47	1,030	744	142
Bremen	—	2	—	2	2	—	—
North Rhine–Westphalia	5	23	31	54	396	—	—
Hessen	3	5	21	26	426	—	—
Rhineland–Palatinate	3	12	24	36	2,303	2,253	163
Baden–Württemberg	4	9	35	44	1,111	922	272
Bavaria	7	25	71	96	2,051	1,068	341
Saarland	—	—	6	6	52	—	—
Total	26	91	237	327	8,503	6,013	1,037

Source: Statistiche Jahrbuch 1988

Notes

Chapter 1

1 W. Paterson and G. Smith, *The West German Model* (London, 1981), Introduction.

Chapter 2

1 Lothar Gall, *Bismarck, the White Revolutionary* (London, 1986).
2 P. G. J. Pulzer, 'The German Party System in the Sixties', *Political Studies*, 19 (1971), 1–17.
3 W. J. Mommsen, 'The German Revolution 1918–1920: Political Revolution and Social Protest Movement', in R. J. Bessel and E. J. Feuchtwanger (eds), *Social Change and Political Development in Weimar Germany* (London, 1981), pp. 21–54.
4 K.-B. Netzband and H. P. Widmaier, *Währungs- und Finanzpolitik der Ara Luther: 1912 bis 1925* (Tübingen, 1964).
5 K. D. Bracher, 'Brünings unpolitische Politik und die Auflösung der Weimarer Republic', *Vierteljahreshefte für Zeitgeschichte*, 19 (1971) 113–23.
6 George Orwell, *Nineteen Eighty-four* (Penguin edition, London, 1954), pp. 211–12.
7 R. J. Overy, *The Nazi Economic Recovery 1932–1938* (London, 1982).
8 A. J. P. Taylor, *The Origins of the Second World War* (Penguin edition, London, 1964), pp. 266–7.
9 Christian Streit, *Keine Kameraden: Die Wehrmacht und die sowjetischen Kriegsgefangenen 1941–1945* (Stuttgart, 1978).
10 Gerh R. Uberschar and Wolfram Wette (eds), *Unternehmen Barbarossa. Der deutsche Uberfall auf die Sowjetunion 1941* (Paderborn, 1985).

Chapter 3

1 E. W. Böckenförde, 'Entstehung und Wandel des Rechtsstaatsbegriffs', *Festschrift für Adolf Arndt* (Tübingen, 1969), pp. 53–76.
2 Wilhelm Bleek, *Von der Kameralausbildung zum Juristenprivileg: Studium, Prüfung und Ausbildung der höheren Beamten des allgemeinen Verwaltungsdienstes in Deutschland im 18. und 19. Jahrhundert* (West Berlin, 1967).

3 Reinhart Koselleck, 'Staat und Gesellschaft in Preussen 1815–1848', in Werner Conze (ed.), *Staat und Gesellschaft im deutschen Vormärz* (Stuttgart, 1962), pp. 79–95; *Preußen zwischen Reform und Revolution. Allgemeines Landrecht, Verwaltung und soziale Bewegung von 1791 bis 1848* (West Berlin, 1967).

4 P. Badura, *Verwaltungsrecht im liberalen und sozialen Rechtsstaat* (Tübingen, 1966), p. 12; W. Rufner, *Formen öffentlicher Verwaltung im Bereich der Wirtschaft* (West Berlin, 1967), p. 52.

5 Ulrich Scheuner, 'Die nationale Revolution. Eine staatsrechtliche Untersuchung', *AöR*, 63 (1934), 166–220, 261–344.

6 Arnold Brecht, *Federalism and Regionalism in Germany: the Division of Germany* (New York, 1945), p. 138.

7 Rudolf Smend, *Verfassung und Verfassungsrecht* (Munich–Leipzig, 1928).

8 *Entscheidungen des Bundesverfassungsgerichts (BVerfGE)*, vol. 7, p. 205.

9 *BVerfGE*, 39, 1, at 44.

10 *BVerfGE*, 2, 1; 5, 85.

11 *BVerfGE*, 39, 334, at 349.

12 Fritz Ossenbühl, *NJW*, 29 (1976/II), 2104.

13 H. H. Hartwich, *Sozialstaatspostulat und gesellschaftlicher Status Quo*, 2nd edn (Opladen, 1977), p. 50.

14 Keith Tribe (ed.), *Social Democracy and the Rule of Law: Otto Kirchheimer, Franz Neumann* (London, 1987).

15 Hans Kelsen, 'The international legal status of Germany to be established immediately upon termination of the war', *American Journal of International Law*, (1944), 689, at 693.

16 *BVerfGE*, 36, 1.

17 Carl Schmitt, 'Die Hüter der Verfassung', *Archiv des öffentlichen Rechts*, new series, 16, (1929), 161–237.

18 Ulrich Scheuner, 'Die überlieferung der deutschen Staatsgerichtsbarkeit im 19. und 20. Jahrhundert', in Christian Starck (ed.), *Bundesverfassungsgericht und Grundgesetz: Festgabe aus Anlass des 25. jährigen Bestehens des Bundesverfassungsgerichts*, I, 37; Bartolomäus, 'Fürst Bismarck und der preussische Richterstand', *Preussische Jahrbücher*, 99 (1900), 178.

19 Simons, 'Das Reichsgericht im Gegenwart und Zukunft', *Deutsche Juristenzeitung*, 29 (1924), 241–6; Letter to Reich Chancellor, Bundesarchiv Koblenz, R431, No. 1211, f. 315; 'Relation of the German Judiciary to the Executive and Legislative Branches', *American Bar Association Journal*, 15 (1929), 762.

20 *BVerfGE*, 20, 162.

21 *BVerfGE*, 39, 334, at 349.

22 *BVerfGE*, 12, 205.

23 Philip Blair, 'Law and Politics in Germany', *Political Studies*, 26 (1978), 348–62.

24 Konrad Hesse, *Grundzüge des Verfassungsrechts der Bundesrepublik Deutschlands*, 13th edn (Tübingen, 1977), p. 13.

Chapter 4

1 *Berliner Morgenpoest*, 6 March 1927.
2 *Deutsche Allgemeine Zeitung*, 26 May 1926; 3 January 1930.
3 Otto Mayer, *Deutsches Verwaltungsrecht*, 3rd edn (Leipzig, 1924), p. 111.
4 Michael Kirn, *Verfassungsumsturz oder Rechtskontinuität. Die Stellung der Jurisprudenz nach 1945 zum Dritten Reich, insbesonderes die Konflikte über die Kontinuität der Beamtenrechte und Art. 131 Grundgesetz* (West Berlin, 1974); *BVerf GE*, 3, 58.
5 Carl Schmitt, 'Die Diktatur des Reichsprädisenten nach Art. 48', *Veröffentlichungen der Vereinigung Staatsrechtslehrer*, new series, 7 (1924), 84.
6 D. P. Kommers, *Judicial Politics in West Germany: A Study of the Federal Constitutional Court* (Beverley Hills, Ca, 1975), p. 24
7 F. K. Fromme, *Von der Weimarer Verfassung zum Bonner Grundgesetz* (Tübingen, 1960), pp. 5–6.
8 Ibid., p. 9.
9 P. Merkl, *Germany Yesterday and Tomorrow* (Oxford, 1965); K. D. Bracher, 'Die Kanzlerdemokratie' in R. Löwenthal and H.-P. Schwarz (eds), *Die zweite Republik: 25 Jahre Bundesrepublik Deutschland – eine Bilanz* (Stuttgart, 1974), pp. 181–200.
10 Carl Schmitt, *Verfassungslehre* (West Berlin, 1954), p. 291.
11 See Ulrich Scheuner, 'Die Anwendung des Art. 48 der Weimarer Reichsverfassung unter den Präsidentschaften von Ebert und Hindenburg', in F. A. Hermans and T. Schieder (eds), *Staat, Wirtschaft und Politik in der Weimarer Republik: Festschrift für Heinrich Brüning* (West Berlin, 1967), pp. 249–86.
12 R. E. M. Irving and W. E. Paterson, 'The Machtwechsel of 1982–3: A Significant Landmark in the Political and Constitutional History of West Germany', *Parliamentary Affairs*, 36 (1983), 417–35.
13 Kurt Shell, 'Extraparliamentary Opposition in Postwar Germany', *Comparative Politics*, 2 (1970), 659; Jillian Becker, *Hitler's Children* (London, 1977); Stefan Aust, *The Baader–Meinhof Group: the inside story of a phenomenon* (London, 1987).
14 Ulrich Scheuner, 'Die Lage des parlamentarischen Regierungssystem in der Bundesrepublik', *Die öffentliche Verwaltung*, 27 (1974), 659.
15 Irving and Paterson, *The Machtwechsel*, p. 426.
16 *BVerfGE*, 62, 1.
17 Konrad Adenauer, *Erinnerungen 1955–1959* (Hamburg, 1969, pp. 502–7.
18 S. Schöne, *Von der Reichskanzlei zum Bundeskanzleramt* (West Berlin, 1968).
19 Conrad, *Aus meiner Dienstzeit: Band IV 1906–1918* (Vienna–Leipzig–Munich, 1923), p. 153.
20 Thomas Eschenburg, *Zur politischen Praxis* (Tübingen, 1970), vol. III, p. 162.

21 L. J. Edinger, *Politics in West Germany*, 2nd edn (Boston, Mass., 1977), pp. 269–70.

22 *Die Zeit*, 17 April 1973. The British Military Governor of North Rhine Province had dismissed Adenauer as Chief Bürgermeister of Cologne on 6 October 1945 and forbade him further political activity: Adenauer, *Erinnerungen 1945–1953* (Hamburg, 1967), pp. 29–34.

23 *Vorwärts*, 15 January 1925.

24 Renate Mayntz, 'West Germany', in William Plowden (ed.), *Advising the Rulers* (Oxford, 1987), p. 13.

25 T. Ellwein, *Das Regierungssystem der Bundesrepublik Deutschland*, 4th edn (Opladen, 1979), p. 371.

26 T. Eschenburg, 'Der bürokratische Rückhalt', in Löwenthal and Schwarz, *Die zweite Republik*, pp. 64–94.

27 Thomas Ellwein and R. Zoll, *Berufsbeamtentum – Anspruch und Wirklichkeit* (Baden-Baden, 1973).

28 Otto Pflanze, *Bismarck and the Development of Germany* (Princeton, NJ, 1963), p. 199.

29 K. H. F. Dyson, *Party, State and Bureaucracy in West Germany* (London, 1977).

30 K. H. F. Dyson, 'Anti-Communism in the Federal Republic of Germany: the case of the Berufsverbot', *Parliamentary Affairs*, 28 (1974–5), 51–68.

31 Geoffrey K. Fry, 'The Thatcher Government, the Financial Management Initiative and the "New Civil Service"', *Public Administration*, 66 (1988), 1–20.

Chapter 5

1 Gerhard Loewenberg, *Parliament in the German Political System* (Ithaca, NY, 1966); 'Parliamentarism in Western Germany: the Functioning of the Bundestag', *American Political Science Review*, 55 (1961), 87–102.

2 Peter Schindler, *Datenhandbuch zur Geschichte des Deutschen Bundestages 1949 bis 1982* (Bonn, 1983), pp. 703–712. Additional statistics are derived from: N. Nienhaus, 'Konsensuale Gesetzgebung im Deutschen Bundestag: Zahlen und Anmerkungen zur 7. bis 9. Wahlperiode', *Zeitschrift für Parlamentsfragen*, 16 (1985), pp. 163–9; Peter Schindler, 'Deutscher Bundestag 1949–1987: Parlaments- und Wahlstatistik', *Zeitschrift für Parlamentsfragen*, 18 (1987), pp. 185–202; *Statistiches Handbuch für die Bundesrepublik Deutschlands*.

3 In 1976 the CSU briefly threatened to dissolve the *Fraktionsgemeinschaft* but this possibility quicky evaporated: Alf Mintzel, 'Der Fraktionszusammenschluß nach Kreuth: Ende einer Entwicklung?', *Zeitschrift für Parlamentsfragen*, 8 (1977), 58–76.

4 Nevil Johnson, 'Questions in the Bundestag', *Parliamentary Affairs*, 16 (1962–3), 22–34.

5 Wilhelm Hennis, 'Die Rolle des Parlaments und die Parteidemok-

ratie', in R. Löwenthal and H.-P. Schwarz (eds), *Die Zweite Republik: 25 Jahre Bundesrepublik Deutschland – Eine Bilanz* (Stuttgart, 1974,), at p. 220.

6   A. J. Burkett, 'Developments in the West German Bundestag in the 1970s', *Parliamentary Affairs*, 34 (1981), p. 291, at p. 300.

7   Hennis, 'Rolle des Parlaments', p. 224.

8   Klaus von Beyme, 'The Role of Deputies in West Germany', in S. Suleiman (ed.), *Parliaments and Parliamentarians*, (New York, 1958), p. 159.

9   *Der Spiegel*, No. 25, 1975, pp. 40–6.

10   *BVerfGE*, 40, 296.

11   *BVerfGE*, 2, 213, at 224; 3, 407, at 412; 4, 115, at 127–8.

12   Ulrich Scheuner, *Die öffentliche Verwaltung*, (1966), p. 513, at p. 517.

13   P. M. Blair, *Federalism and Judicial Review in West Germany* (Oxford, 1981), p. 85.

14   Konrad Hesse, *Grundzüge des Verfassungsrechts der Bundesrepublik*, 13th edn (Tübingen, 1977), p. 98.

15   E. Katzenstein, *Die öffentliche Verwaltung*, (1958), p. 593, at p. 594.

16   P. H. Merkl, *The Origins of the West German Republic* (New York, 1963), pp. 66–78.

17   H. Schneider, 'Die Zustimmung des Bundesrats zu Gesetzen', *Deutsches Verwaltungsblatt*, (1953), 257.

18   *BVerfGE*, 37, 363.

19   Fritz Ossenbühl, 'Die Zustimmung des Bundesrats beim Erlass von Bundesrecht', *Archiv des öffentlichen Rechts*, 99 (1974), 369, at 420–3.

20   *BVerfGE*, 37, 271; [1974] European Court Reports, 491.

Chapter 6

1   Arnold Brecht, *Federalism and Regionalism in Germany: the division of Prussia* (New York, 1945), p. 47. See also: A. J. Zurcher, *The Experiment with Democracy in Central Europe* (New York, 1933).

2   Peter H. Merkl, 'Executive–Legislative Federalism in West Germany', *American Political Science Review*, 53 (1959), pp 732–41.

3   Brecht, *Federalism and Regionalism*, p. 133.

4   J. F. Golay, *The Founding of the Federal Republic of Germany*, 2nd edn (Chicago, 1965), p. 17.

5   Carlo Schmid, 'Bund und Länder' in R. Löwenthal and H.-P. Schwarz (eds), *Die zweite Republik: 25 Jahre Bundesrepublik Deutschland – Eine Bilanz* (Stuttgart, 1974), p. 247.

6   Brecht, *Federalism and Regionalism*, p. 120.

7   *BVerfGE*, 6, 309, at 346.

8   Konrad Hesse, *Grundzüge des Verfassungsrechts der Bundesrepublik Deutschlands*, 13th edn (Tübingen, 1977), p. 89.

9   Golay, *Founding of the FRG*, pp. 55–6.

10   Otto Koellreuter, 'Der Konflict Reich-Thüringen in der Frage der

Polizeikostenzuschüsse', *Archiv des öffentlichen Rechts*, 59 (1931), 68–102; Kurz Häntzschel, ibid., pp. 384–411.

11 *BVerfGE*, 2, 213, at 224.

12 Karl Loewenstein, *Max Weber's Political Ideas in the Perspective of Our Time* (Boston, Mass., 1966), p. 21.

13 *BVerfGE*, 72, 330, at 386.

14 Kommission für die Finanzreform, *Gutachten über die Finanzreform in der Bundesrepublik*, 2nd edn (Bonn, 1966), p. 11.

15 K. H. Neunreiter, 'Politics and Bureaucracy in the West German Bundesrat', *American Political Science Review*, 53 (1959), 713–41, at 726.

16 R. Hellwig, 'Die Rolle der Bundesländer in der Europa Politik', *Europa-Archiv*, 42 (10) (1987), 297–302; Simon Bulmer and William Paterson, 'European Policy-making in the Federal Republic – Internal and External Limits to Leadership', in *The Federal Republic of Germany and the European Community: the Presidency and Beyond* (Europa Union Verlag, 1988), pp. 231–65.

17 K. C. Wheare, *Federal Government*, 4th edn (Oxford, 1963), p. 33.

18 M. J. C. Vile, *The Structure of American Federalism* (Oxford, 1961).

19 C. J. Friedrich, *Trends of Federalism in Theory and Practice* (Princeton, NJ., 1958), p. 47.

Chapter 7

1 P. Pulzer, 'What the 1986 Election did not Solve', in *West European Politics*, vol. 4, no. 2, p. 127.

2 H. D. Klingemann, 'West Germany', in I. Crewe and D. Denver (eds), *Electoral Change in Western Democracies* (London, 1985), p. 49.

3 P. Pulzer, 'West Germany and the Three Party System', *Political Quarterly*, vol. 33 (1962), 414–26.

4 Peter Merkl, 'Allied Strategies of Effecting Political Change and Their Reception in Occupied Germany', *Public Policy*, No. 17, p. 75.

5 Christian Hacke, 'The Christian Democratic Union and the Christian Social Union', in R. Morgan and S. Silvestri (eds), *Moderates and Conservatives in Western Europe* (London, 1985), p. 25.

6 In Arno Scholz, *Turmwachter der Demokratie*, vol. 2, *Reden und Schriften* (Berlin, 1952), p. 33.

7 *Die Zeit*, 22 December 1978.

8 Pulzer, 'West Germany', n. 3.

9 *BVerfGE*, 8, 55ff.

10 *BVerfGE*, 20, 56ff.

11 Kremendahl, *Vertrauenskrise der Parteien* (Berlin, 1978), p. 59.

12 K. Dyson, *Party, State and Bureaucracy* (London, 1977), p. 45.

13 Dyson, ibid.

14 K. Von Beyme, 'The Changing Relations Between Trade Unions and the Social Democratic Party in West Germany', *Government and Opposition*, 13, 1978, p. 409.

Notes

Chapter 8

1 E. J. Horn, 'Germany, a Market Led Process', in F. Duchene and G. Shepherd (eds), *Managing Industrial Change in Western Europe* (London, 1987), pp. 41–75, at pp. 42–3.
2 P. Lawrence, *Managers and Management in West Germany* (London, 1980), p. 15.
3 R. E. M. Irving and W. E. Paterson, 'The West German General Election of 1987', *Parliamentary Affairs*, vol. 40, No. 3, July 1987, pp. 333–56, at p. 334.
4 A. Shonfield, *Modern Capitalism: the Changing Balance of Public and Private Power* (Oxford, 1965), esp. chap. 11.
5 K. Dyson, 'West Germany: The Search for a Rationalist Consensus', in J. Richardson (ed.), *Policy Styles in Western Europe* (London, 1982), p. 19.
6 J. Zysman, *Governments, Markets and Growth* (Oxford, 1983), p. 124.
7 Ibid., p. 264.
8 D. Webber, 'Framework of Government–Industry Relations in the FRG', typescript, University of Sussex, 1985.
9 *Financial Times*, 23 October 1985.

Chapter 9

1 *Frankfurter Allgemeine Zeitung*, 30 October 1975.
2 S. Bulmer and W. E. Paterson, *The Federal Republic of Germany and the European Community* (London, 1987), p. 119.
3 J. Joffe, 'German Defense Policy; Novel Solutions and Enduring Dilemmas', in G. Flynn (ed.), *The Internal Fabric of Western Security* (London, 1981), pp. 63–96, at p. 66.
4 Ibid., pp. 67–8.

Chapter 10

1 W. Brandt, *The Ordeal of Coexistence* (Cambridge, Mass., 1962).
2 K. Kaiser, *German Foreign Policy in Transition* (London, 1968), p. 38.
3 *The Times*, 15 September 1969.
4 J. Korbel, *Detente in Europe* (Princeton, NJ, 1972), p. 247.
5 Z. Brzezinski, *Alternative to Partition: For a broader conception of America's role in Europe* (New York, 1965), p. 139.
6 W. E. Paterson, 'From *Vergangenheitsbewältigung* to the *Historikerstreit*', in R. Woods (ed.), *The Historikerstreit* (Aston, Modern German Studies Association, 1989).
7 H. Kissinger, *The White House Years* (Boston, Mass., 1979), pp. 423–4.
8 For an analysis of the judgment see esp. H. Haftendorn, *Security and Detente: Conflicting priorities in foreign policy* (New York, 1985), pp. 240–1.
9 *BVerfGE*, 31 July 1973.

10   Ibid.
11   W. E. Paterson, 'Foreign Policy and Stability in West Germany', *International Affairs*, July 1973, pp. 413–30; G. Schweigler, *Nationalbewusstsein in der BRD und DDR* (Düsseldorf, 1973).

Chapter 11

1   Peter J. Katzenstein, 'The Third West German Republic: Continuity in Change', *Journal of International Affairs*, 1988, 325–44.

Further Reading

Chapter 2

While there is a wide choice of one-volume histories of modern Germany in English, William Carr's *A History of Germany 1815–1945* (2nd edn, London, Edward Arnold, 1979) provides an analytical narrative of rare power and compression. The need for a guide through the complexities of the Weimar period which takes account of modern learning has now been filled by Eberhard Kolb, *The Weimar Republic* (London, Hutchinson, 1988). There are two classic biographies of Hitler, which complement rather than duplicate each other. Alan Bullock, *Hitler: A Study in Tyranny* (London, Penguin, 1962) was written before the bulk of modern sources were available, but subsequent research has largely confirmed the soundness and acuity of the author's historical insight. Joachim Fest, *Hitler* (London, Penguin, 1977) integrates the social and ideological dimension of National Socialism with political history. A full-blooded structural account of National Socialism may be found in M. Broszat, *Hitler's State* (London, Longmans, 1981).

V. R. Berghahn, *Modern Germany* (2nd edn, Cambridge University Press, 1987) is a remarkable feat of condensation, which covers the period from 1900 to the present day. Edward G. Litchfield (ed.), *Governing Post-War Germany* (Ithaca, NY, Cornell University Press, 1953) is a volume of essays remarkable for the direct personal experience of the authors in the problems of post-war reconstruction. Barbara Marshall, *The Origins of Post-War German Politics* (London, Croom Helm, 1988) provides a concise and accurate introduction. J. F. Golay, *The Founding of the Federal Republic of Germany* (Chicago University Press, 1958) is particularly valuable for its description of the proceedings of the Parliamentary Council. A. Grosser, *Germany in our Time* (London, Penguin, 1971) falls between two stools, in attempting both a post-war history and an analysis of political institutions, but has a sense of perspective, which narrower studies sometimes lack. The classic statement of the changes wrought by the Third Reich is Ralf Dahrendorf's *Society and Democracy in Germany* (Weidenfeld, 1967).

Chapter 3

The indispensable starting-point for the study of the constitution is the text of the Basic Law. The Press and Information Office of the Federal

Republic publish an English translation of the Basic Law, which is available from official sources. A translation of the Basic Law is also contained in S. E. Finer (ed.), *Five Constitutions* (London, Penguin, 1976). H. W. Koch, *A Constitutional History of Germany in the Nineteenth and Twentieth Centuries* (London, Longmans, 1984) is a testimony to the author's deep learning, but veers uneasily between constitutional and general political history, and deals with the post-war period in a rushed and over-summary fashion. K. H. F. Dyson, *The State Tradition in Western Europe* (Oxford, Martin Robertson, 1980) analyses the state on a conceptual and comparative basis, takes on German writers at their own game, and almost wins. For readers of German, Hans Hattenhauer, *Zwischen Hierarchie und Demokratie* (Karlsruhe, C. F. Müller, 1971) constitutes a virtuoso account of the intellectual history of German law. Friedrich Karl Fromme, *Von der Weimarer Verfassung zum Bonner Grundgesetz* (2nd edn, Tübingen, J. C. B. Mohr, 1962) is a fluent and incisive analysis of the Basic Law, which with the passing of time gains rather than loses in authority. D. P. Kommers, *Judicial Politics in West Germany: A Study of the Federal Constitutional Court* (London and Beverly Hills, Ca, Sage, 1975 is a thorough and empirically based study of the Constitutional Court. A short piece, over-reliant on assertion, but containing much of value is Glen Schram, 'Ideology and Politics: the Rechtsstaat Idea in West Germany', *Journal of Politics*, 33 (1971), 133–57.

Chapter 4

Nevil Johnson, *Government in the Federal Republic of Germany* (2nd edn, Oxford, Pergamon Press, 1983) is a densely argued and penetrating account of executive institutions. Renate Mayntz and Fritz W. Scharpf, *Policy-making in the German Federal Bureaucracy* (Amsterdam, Elsevier, 1975) puts policy formulation in context. K. H. F. Dyson, *Party, State and Bureaucracy in West Germany* (Beverly Hills, Ca, Sage, 1977) is a concise and lucid analysis of the bureaucratic culture and interpenetration of party and state machines. Konrad Adenauer, *Memoirs 1945–1959* (London, Weidenfeld and Nicolson, 1965) conveys something of the tireless energy and unswerving sense of direction which the first post-war Chancellor brought to the reconstruction of Germany. R. A. Chaput de Saintonge, *Public Administration in Germany: A Study of Regional and Local Administration in Rheinland-Pfalz* (London, Weidenfeld and Nicolson, 1961) is an unusually readable study, which conveys an authentic feel of how government works.

Chapter 5

Works in English on parliament in West Germany are few. Pride of place must go to Gerhard Loewenberg, *Parliament in the German Political System* (Ithaca, NY, Cornell University Press, 1966). Though overtaken by subsequent events, this is well grounded in history and is a classic study. E. Suleiman (ed.), *Parliament and Parliamentarians* (New York, Holmes and Meier, 1958) has a valuable section on members. V. Bogdanor, *Representatives of the People* (London, Gower, 1985) and J. D. Lees and M. Shaw, *Committees in Legislatures* (London, Macmillan 1980) make cross-national comparisons, but include analysis of the Bundestag.

Chapter 6

There is a thoughtful, general consideration of federalism in W. S. Livingston, *Federalism and Constitutional Change* (Oxford, Oxford University Press, 1956). Geoffrey Sawer, *Modern Federalism* (London, Watts and Co.) has a valuable section on West Germany. Edward L. Pinney, *Federalism, Bureaucracy and Party Politics in Western Germany: the Role of the Bundesrat* (Chapel Hill, NC, University of North Carolina, 1963) shows the pivotal influence of the Bundesrat, but is now very dated. P. M. Blair, *Federalism and Judicial Review in West Germany* (Oxford, Oxford University Press, 1981) deals with the umpiring of the federal system by the Federal Constitutional Court.

Chapter 7

The best general study of West German political parties is S. Padgett and T.Burkett's *Political Parties and Elections in West Germany* (London, C. Hurst, 1986). G. Smith's excellent *Democracy in Western Germany* (3rd edn, Aldershot, Gower, 1986) is centrally concerned with political parties. The standard account of the CDU is G. Pridham's *Christian Democracy in Western Germany* (London, Croom Helm, 1977). The CSU has been exhaustively analysed in A. Mintzel, *Die CSU: Anatomie einer konservativen Partei* (Cologne, Westdeutscher Verlag, 1975).

The SPD has been the subject of a great many articles, especially in *West European Politics*. The standard recent book-length treatment is G. Braunthal, *The West German Social Democrats 1969–82* (Boulder, Colorado, Westview, 1983). Little has appeared as yet in English on the FDP but there is a very good chapter by Christian Soe in H. P. Wallach and G. Romoser (eds), *West German Politics in the mid-Eighties* (New York, Praeger, 1985). On the Greens the most useful treatment is E. Kolinsky (ed.), *The West German Green Party* (Berg, Oxford, 1989). The relationship between parties and movements is analysed in E. Kolinsky, *Parties, Opposition and Society in West Germany* (London, Croom Helm, 1984).

Chapter 8

There is no general account of the political economy of the Federal Republic but it is very well treated in P. Katzenstein's *Policy and Politics in West Germany* (Philadelphia, Temple, 1988). There is also a very good chapter by E. J. Horn in F. Duchene and G. Sheperd, *Managing Industrial Change in Western Europe* (London, F. Pinter, 1987). Government–industry relations are very well analysed in D. Webber, 'Framework of Government–Industry Relations in the Federal Republic', Sussex University Working Paper, Series on Government/Industry Relations, No. 1, 1986. In the first of a series of sectoral studies by British researchers, W. Grant, C. Whitston and W. Paterson look at *Government and the Chemical Industry; A Comparative Case Study of Britain and West Germany* (Oxford, Clarendon, 1989). The trade union movement is well covered in A. Markovits's magisterial, *The Politics of the West German Trade Unions* (Cambridge, Cambridge University Press, 1986).

Chapter 9

The most incisive and reliable account of the foreign policy of the Federal Republic is Helga Haftendorn's *Security and Detente* (New York, Praeger, 1985). The standard analysis of the Federal Republic's relationship with the European Community is S. Bulmer and W. Paterson, *The Federal Republic and the European Community* (London, Unwin Hyman, 1987). The European policy of the SPD is covered in W. E. Paterson, *The SPD and European Integration* (Farnborough, D. C. Heath, 1974). Josef Joffe's essay on West German defence policy in G. Flynn (ed.), *The Internal Fabric of Western Security* (London, Croom Helm, 1981) is by far the best account of West Germany's defence options.

Those who read German should consult Arnulf Baring's *Unser Neuer Grössenwahn* (Stuttgart, 1988) for a spirited analysis of recent developments.

Chapter 10

Helga Haftendorn, *Security and Detente* (New York, Praeger, 1988) provides a reliable and balanced account of the passage of the Eastern Treaties. Angela Stent, *From Embargo to Ostpolitik* (Cambridge, Cambridge University Press, 1981) is a sound study of the interplay of trade and *Ostpolitik* though it is not as comprehensive as the subtitle suggests. R. Tilford's edited collection, *The Ostpolitik and Political Change in Germany* (Farnborough, Gower, 1975) is a useful though now slightly dated study of various aspects of *Ostpolitik*. Gebhard Schweigler's *National Consciousness in Divided Germany* (New York, Sage, 1975) is by far the most interesting contribution to the debate about German versus West German national consciousness.

Further Reading

The variable quality of the articles edited by Edwina Moreton, *Germany Between East and West* (Cambridge, Cambridge University Press, 1987) renders this a less useful book than it might have been. Karl Kaiser's short book *German Foreign Policy in Transition* (London, Oxford University Press, 1968) still repays reading because of the outstanding quality of its analysis.

Index

Abitur, 104–5
abortion legislation 59, 181
Abs, Hermann, 247
absolutism, 22–4, 56
Adenauer, Konrad, 18, 49, 72, 73, 74, 89, 96, 100, 175, 218, 234
  becomes Federal Chancellor, 50, 92–3
  foreign policy, 191–2, 258, 259–63, 267, 270, 271, 272, 281–2, 284
ADF (APO party), 176
administration, 100–6, 149, 152
  delegated and autonomous, 150–4
  Federal-*Land*, 149–50
  indirect state (*Selbstverwaltung*), 108, 141, 150
  structure (1988), 311 Table A7
administrative agreements (*Verwaltungsabkommen*), 168
administrative regulations (*Verwaltungsvorschriften*), 150
AEG, 249
Afghanistan, 300
Africa, North, 41, 255
Agricultural Act (1955), 236
agriculture
  collectivization of East Germany, 283
  in depression (1929), 33
  EC Common Agricultural Policy, 138, 186, 195, 227, 236, 256, 265, 305
  Greens on, 246
  interests, 23, 235–6, 242, 262
  reform of, 266
Agricultural, Ministry of, 236
Albrecht, Ernst, 135
Allgemeiner Deutscher ArbeiterVerein (German General Workers' Association), 199
Alliance of Free Democrats, 6, 7
Alliance for Germany, 6, 7
Alliance 90, 7–9
Allied Control Council, 42, 45, 145
Allied occupation, 1, 2, 42–7
  and centralization of legislation, 153
  and political parties, 173
  territorial reorganization of Germany, 144–5
Allies, 25
  and Berlin, 15, 280

rights of intervention in West Germany, 84
and unification, 15–17
and West German Foreign policy, 259–63, 284
Alsace, 1
Alternative List, West Berlin, *see* Greens
amendments, constitutional, 111
anti-communism, 3, 50–1, 72, 75, 296
anti-semitism, 36–7, 41–2
APO (*Ausserparlamentarische Opposition*), 85, 176, 202: ADF party, 176
Apportionment Law (1971), 155
area-states (*Flachenstaaten*), 147, 161
Arendt, Walter, 243
armed forces, 126, 152
  and NATO, 17
Armed Forces Ombudsman (*Wehrbeauftragter*), 126
Atlantic Alliance, 15
audit offices, 161
Auditor-General for the Federal Republic (*Bundesrechnungshof*), 126
Austria, 1, 4, 19, 39
Austrian Empire, 20, 21
Autobahns, 152

Bad Godesberg Programme (1959), 3, 175–6, 180, 187, 201–2, 210
Baden, 54; *see also* Baden-Württemberg
Baden-Württemberg, 132, 146, 147, 156, 160, 161, 165, 187, 239, 256
Bahr, Egon, 274, 275, 283, 297: 'Bahr Paper', 289–90
Balkans, 41
ballot papers, 182–3 Fig. 7.1
banks, 165
  and industry, 246–50
  role of the 'House Bank', 247–8
Baring, Arnulf, 259
Barzel, Rainer, 117, 193, 292
BASF, 226, 248
Basic Law (*Grundgesetz*), 4, 49, 50, 52
  absence of parliamentary power of self-dissolution, 85–6
  amendments, 63–4, 111
  Article 23 on unification, 6, 9, 10, 11

Basic Law (*Grundgesetz*) – *cont.*
  Article 146 on new constitution, 7, 9–10
  on finance, 154–5
  fundamental principles, 74–6
  legislative categories, 129–30
  legislative process, 111–13
  legitimacy of, 280
  modification of parliamentary system, 80–9
  and rights of *Länder*, 145–6, 147, 148, 152–4
  state organization, 60–4
basic rights, 57–60, 61–3, 76
  'democratic-functional theory', 59–60, 72
  'participation theory', 60
Basic Treaty (*Grundlagenvertrag*) (1972), 66, 74, 293–6
Bastian, Gert, 213
Baum, Gerhart, 250
Bavaria, 45, 54, 132, 145, 146, 156, 160, 161, 165, 187, 239, 256, 268, 292
  CSU in, 174, 178, 194–6
Bavarian government, 31–2, 66, 74, 294
Bavarian Party (*Bayern Partei*), 145, 174, 175, 184, 195
Bayer, 226, 241, 248, 251
Bayerische Volkspartei (BVP), 194
Bebel, August, 199
Berchthold, 91
Bergsdorf, Wolfgang, 192
Berlin, 280
  Allied occupation of, 42
  crisis (1958–61), 272, 282–5
  Four Power Agreement on (1971), 65, 290–2
  'Greater', 64–5
  Soviet blockade (1948/49), 48, 282
  and unification, 304
Berlin, East, 9
Berlin, West, 49, 65, 146, 161, 177, 207, 298
  Alternative List, *see* Greens
  financial position, 158
  and *Ostpolitik*, 299
Berlin Senate, 290
Berlin uprisings (1919), 29
Berlin Wall (1961), 272, 283, 295
  opening up of (1989), 5
Berufsverbot (vocational ban), 60, 108–9
Bethmann-Hollweg, Theobald von, 24, 25, 91
Beyme, Klaus von, 223
Biedenkopf, Kurt, 193, 243
bills, 111–12
  'Experts' Draft', 112

readings, 112
Bismarck, Otto von, 22–4, 67, 120, 180, 199
  federal system, 142–3
  Reich Chancellery, 90–1, 95
Bizone (British and American occupation zones), 47
Blankenhorn, Herbert, 93, 259
Blitzkrieg, 40
Block der Heimatvertriebenen und Entrechteten (refugee party), 285–6
Bloemer, Klaus, 291–2
Blüm, Norbert, 194
Böckler, Hans, 242
Bolshevism, 37
Bonn Group of Western Ambassadors, 290
Bonn Republic, 49, 52, 57, 60, 75, 95–6, 124, 154
bourgeoisie, 19–20
  and political parties, 176
brake theory, and legislative role of Bundesrat, 137
Brandenburg, 10, 19
Brandt, Willy
  as Chancellor (1969–72), 92, 94, 97, 202, 208, 211
  critical of US policy, 274, 275
  European policy, 263
  on FRG, 304
  no confidence vote, 83, 86
  and *Ostpolitik*, 242, 287, 288–9, 291, 293, 295
  as SPD Chairman, 6, 115, 128, 188, 203, 205, 252
  'The Ordeal of Coexistence', 283
Braun, Otto, 80
Brecht, Arnold, 57, 143, 144–5, 147
Bremen, 45, 145, 146, 147, 156, 157, 161, 187, 256
Bremerhaven, 147
Britain, 1
  civil service, 105, 110
  defence expenditure, 279 Table 9.1
  industry in, 246, 247, 248, 257
  nuclear policy, 274, 278
  parliamentary system, 140, 182
  relations with FRG, 30, 268, 270, 274
  and unification, 16, 17
  in WWII, 39, 40, 65
British Labour Party, 201, 237, 243, 276
British North America Act (1867), 129
British occupation zone, 42, 45, 46, 47, 145, 174
broadcasting corporations, 168
Brüning, Heinrich, 33–4
Brussels Pact, *see* West European Union

Brzezinski, Zbigniew, 286
Budget, Federal (1973–80), 228–9
  debate, 118–19
Bulgaria, 25
Bund (Federation), 19, 54, 141
Bundesbank (Federal Bank), 11, 12,
  165, 223, 230
Bundesoberbehörden (Federal higher
  authorities), 98
Bundesrat, 11, 22, 111, 127, 131–8,
  142, 146, 152–3, 170
  allocation of votes after unification,
  11–12
  Committee on European
    Community Affairs, 139
  Committee of *Land* Ministers of
    Justice, 70
  composition, 131
  democratic legitimacy issue, 137–8
  functions, 166–7
  and *Länder* influence, 165–7
  role as upholder of federalism, 134–
  8, 140
  veto powers (1949–87), 131–2, 135–
  7 Table 5.1, 140
  work (1949–87), 309 Table A4
Bundesrepublik Deutschlands (BRD), *see*
  Federal Republic of Germany
  (FRG)
Bundestag, 11, 58, 125–9, 146
  committee system, 119–23
  deputies, 123–4
  election, 85–6
  election of first (1949), 50
  election of speaker, 117
  electoral functions, 69–70
  Eleventh (1989), 120
  Foreign Affairs Committee, Sub-
    Committee (Europe), 139
  functions and organization of, 113–
  18
  interpellation (Grosse Anfrage),
  116, 118
  Judicial Election Committee, 70
  as the legislature, 111, 114
  Ninth (1980–3), 86
  parliamentary group, 115–17
  plenary sessions, 118–19, 125
  protection from dissolution, 85–9
  question time (*Fragestunde*), 119
  role, 63
  Rules of Procedure, 115
  Sixth (1969–72), 86
  work (1949–87), 309 Table A4
Bundestreue (federal comity) doctrine,
  166
Bundesverband der Deutschen Industrie
  (BDI), 121, 232, 233, 266
*Bundesvereinigung der Deutschen
  Arbeitgeberverbände* (BDA), 232–3

Bundeswehr, 17, 271
bureaucracy, 77–8
  relationship with political parties,
  222–3
Bürgermeister, 142, 151, 163
Burgfrieden, 24
Burke, Edmund, 54
Burkett, Tony, 122
business, finance for parties, 217–18
business associations, 232–4
business interests
    (*Mittelstandsvereinigung*), 194
  representation of, 232–6
business tax, 155, 157
Byrnes, James F., 46

cabinet principle, 90, 100–1
cabinet of state secretaries
    (*Ministerialbürokratie*), 96
cabinets
  coalition-based, 101
  size of, 100
Callaghan, James, 274
CAP, *see* EC, Common Agricultural
  Policy
capital investment in West Germany,
  246–50
Carr, Jonathan, 249
Carrington, Lord, 305
Carstens, Karl, 87, 89
Cartel Act (1957), 226
Carter, Jimmy, 273–4
Casablanca Conference (1943), 65
Catholicism, 22, 43, 145, 180, 190,
  194, 195–6, 237, 285
CDU/CSU, 3, 6, 14, 49, 69, 83, 89,
  134, 173
  Catholics in, 145, 180
  on detente issue, 277–8, 300
  dominance (1950s), 175
  election (1987), 186
  on European integration, 280
  Fraktionsgemeinschaft (single party
    group) in Bundestag, 115
  leadership crisis, 303
  opposition to *Ostpolitik*, 287, 289,
  291–2, 296
  relationship, 196–8
  self-employed in, 178
  split between Atlanticists and
    Gaullists, 263
CDU/CSU and SPD, percentage of
  votes (1949–87), 177 Table 7.1
CDU/CSU-FDP coalition (1949–56),
  208
  anti-union policies, 181
CDU/CSU-FDP coalition government
  (1982–9), 87, 94, 165, 209–11,
  229, 244–5, 283–4

Centre Party, Catholic, 22, 27, 49, 174, 180, 190, 217
chambers of commerce, 233
Chancellor, 170
  election of, 84–6
  powers and role of, 81–4
chancellor principle, 90–2: 'guidelines competence', 90–2
chemical industry, 226, 231, 232, 235, 241, 248, 251
  and environmental pressures, 251, 254
Chernobyl disaster, 187, 189, 190, 216, 252, 253
Christian Democratic Union (CDU), 6, 7, 43, 44, 62, 69, 93, 100, 116, 165, 166, 174, 175
  Catholics in, 180, 243
  composition, 190–4
  East German, 6
  Filzokratie campaign, 243
  party groupings, 193–4
  Pentagon group, 193
  'Social Committees', 242
  on social rights, 62
  see also CDU/CSU
Christian Social Union (CSU), 14, 49, 74, 116, 131, 166, 174, 178, 194–6
  Landesgruppe (parliamentary group), 196–7
  see also CDU/CSU
churches, 43
  decline in attendance, 180
  role in politics, 285
  and tax revenues, 157
citizens' initiatives (*Bürgerinitiativen*), 212
citizenship, West of East Germans, 65, 298
city states (*Stadtstaaten*), 147, 161
civil servants, in committee proceedings, 120–1
civil service, 77–8, 102–6
  British, 110
  career, 58, 123–4
  and educational hierarchies, 102
  influence of, 55–6
  and politics, 106–7
  Prussion reforms (1807–11), 102
Civil Service Law (1937), 102–3
  see also Federal Civil Service Law
class voting, patterns of, 178–9
Cleveland Plain Dealer, 270
co-responsibility theory, and legislative role of Bundesrat, 137
Coalition Committee, 91, 101
coalition preferences, 182–4
coalitions, 114
  Weimar, 28
Codetermination Law, 234, 240–1

codetermination (*Mitbestimmung*), 240–1
Cold War, 2, 3, 50, 72
collective bargaining, 233, 238–9
Commerzbank, 247
committee system, 119–23
Common Agricultural Policy, *see under* EC
Common Market, 262; *see also* European Community
communism, in trade unions, 237
Communist Party, new, *see* DKP
Communist Party of Germany (KPD), 26, 32
compensation theory, and legislative role of Bundesrat, 137–8
competition, economic, 226
Competition Law, 234
Concerted Action (1967–77) (*Konzertierte Aktion*), 227–8, 238–9, 239–40
Conradi, Peter, 124
conscription, 126, 271
consensus, 75–6, 107, 117, 128, 169–70, 221–2, 223–4, 266, 267
  erosion of, 245–6, 303
conservatism, 23–4
Consolidation Law (1950), 164
constitution
  possibility of new (Article 146), 7, 9–10
  theory of the, and power of Bundesrat, 137–8
Constitution (1871), 21, 22
Constitution, East German (1949), 10
constitutional political order summarized, 63
constitutionalism, 53–76, 170
construction industry, 247
Continental Gummi Werke, 249
corporatism, in West German system, 239–41
Council of Europe, 260
Council of Experts (*Sachverständigenrat*), 227
Council of People's Representatives, 26
Countercyclical Advisory Council (*Konjunkturrat*), 228
Court for Constitutional Conflicts, 67, 151
courts, 74, 163–4
  federal, 164
  organization of the, 163–4
Courts of Appeal (*Oberlandesgerichte*), 163
Cruise missiles, 205, 276, 277
Crusades, 19
Cuban crisis (1962), 272
Cuno, Chancellor, 31

currency
  reform (1948), 225
  stabilization of (1923), 31
  union (1990), 12–13
Czechoslovakia, 1, 39
  crisis (1968), 287

Dach (roof) theory, 295
Daimler Benz, 248, 249, 254
dairy quotas, 186, 236, 265
dates, 52
de Gaulle, Charles, 262–3, 272
de Maizière, Lothar, 9, 13
decentralization, and federalism, 141–6
defence, 74, 258–79
  civil, 152
  costs and benefits of West German, 278–9
  joint Defence Council with France, 305
Defence Ministry, 149
Dehler, Thomas, 208
democracy, 1–2
  'Chancellor', 81, 210
  direct of Weimar Republic, 63
  leaderless, 79
  legitimacy of, 75–6
  'militant', 60
  'military', 73
  parliamentary, 110
  representative, 1, 63–4
Democratic Awakening (DA), 6, 7
'democratic-functional theory' of basic rights, 59–60, 72
democratization, 45–6, 51–2
departmental principle, 90, 97–8, 268
depression (1929), 172
Deputies Law (1976), 124
deputies (MDBs), 123–4, 213, 219
  constituency and party list, 181–2
detente, 208, 209, 266, 272–8, 284, 300
  see also Ostpolitik
deterrence, 273, 278
Dettling, Wanfried, 192
Deutsche Angestellten-Gewerkschaft (DAG), 104
Deutsche Bank, 246, 247, 248, 249
Deutsche Partei (DP), 47, 49
Deutscher Beamtenbund (DBB), 104
Deutscher Gewerkschaftsbund (DGB), 237–9, 251, 266
  and government, 238–9
  relations with SDP, 242–3
Deutscher Industrie und Handelstag (DIHT), 232, 233–4
Deutschlandpolitik, 280–301
Deutschmark, 6, 48, 229, 254
  introduced (1948), 225

  and Ostmark, 6, 12–13
dictatorship, 36–9, 68
directives (*Weisungen*), 150
directorships, interlocking, 247
dissidents, East German, 4–5, 296
District Courts (*Landgerichte*), 163
districts, 161–2
Ditfurth, Jutta, 215
divorce legislation, 181
DKP (*Deutsche Kommunistische Partei*), 202
Double Zero Option, 277–8
Dresdner Bank, 247
DRP (*Deutsche Rechts Partei*), 174
Dulles, John Foster, 262–3
Dyson, K., 246, 247

East Germany, *see* German Democratic Republic
Eastern bloc countries, relations with West Germany, 66
Ebermann, Thomas, 215
Ebert, Friedrich, 26, 27, 29
EC, Common Agricultural Policy, 138, 186, 195, 227, 236, 256, 265, 305
economic and monetary union, German, 12–15
economic interests, political parties and, 242–6
Economic Reconstruction League (WAV), 174
Economics, Ministry of, 230–1
economy, 48, 225–57, 304, 306
  (1960s), 227–8
  (1973), 228–9
  GDR, 284, 296
  Hitler's policies, 36, 39
  state intervention in, 227–8
  under Allies, 225
  union (1990), 10
  Weimar, 30
Edinger, L. J., 92
education, 98, 148, 161, 165
  of civil servants, 55
Education Council (*Wissenschaftsrat*), 167
Ehmke, 97
Elbe, east, 43
elections
  (1930), 34
  (1932), 35
  (1949–87), 185 Table 7.2
  (1972), 243, 293–4
  (1976, 1980, 1983), 243–4
  (1987), 185–6: parties in, 186–90
  (1989), 303
  (1990) all-German, 13–15
  (1990) East German, 5–9 Table 1.1
  European, 212, 219, 266–7
  political parties and, 181–90

Electoral Law (1920), 28
Electoral Law (1990), 15
electoral patterns, 178–81; *see also* voting
electoral system, all-German, 14–15
five per cent barrier clauses, 14–15
electoral system, West German, 181–4
list system, 181–2
plurality principle, 181–2
electronics industry, 231, 253
Ellwein, T., 102
emergency, internal and external, 85
Emergency Law, 202
Emergency Powers Act (1968), 85
Emergency Tax Decree, Third (1924), 148
Emminger Decree (1924), 163–4
'employees', 102, 103, 104
employers' organization (*Wirtschaftsrat*), 194, 232, 237
Enabling Law (1933), 38, 56, 67–8, 84, 190
energy costs, 228
environmental issues, 206, 212, 215–16, 245
and economic issues, 246
growth of pressures, 250–4
and unification, 13, 17
Environmental Ministry, 252
Equalization of the Burdens Law (1951), 260
Erfurt Programme, 199
Erhard, Ludwig
as Chancellor, 47, 89–90, 92, 93, 97, 131, 165, 192, 263, 273
Economics Minister, 47, 99, 225–6, 262
Ertl, Josef, 99
Erzberger, 28–9, 30, 143
Eschenburg, Thomas, 91–2
Euratom, 262
Europa-Kommission, 139
Europe
Eastern, 15, 287, 300, 302
Southern, 255
Western, integration and FRG, 259–63
European Coal and Steel Community (ECSC), 260–1
European Commission, 17, 138
European Community (EC), 16, 51, 208
environmental powers, 13, 253
FRG role in, 304, 305–6
and the *Länder*, 168–9
and legislation, 138–9
membership of West Germany, 227
and unified Germany, 17
and West German foreign policy, 258

see also EC, Common Agricultural Policy
European Council of Ministers, 138, 268
European Court of Justice, 139, 164
European Defence Community (EDC), 79, 261–2, 270
European legislation, 138–9
European Monetary System, 264
European Parliament, 266
European *Rechnungshof* (Court of Audit), 264
exchange rate, changes in daily, 301
executive, 55, 61, 77–110
constitutional provisions, 79–89
exports, 227, 253

famine (1917), 25
farmers, 235–6
voting, 186, 189
Federal Acts (1815), 19
Federal Assembly, 82
Federal Chancellery (*Bundeskanzlerei*), 4, 95
Federal Chancellors (since 1949), 92–5
Federal Civil Service Law, 103, 105–6
democratic order clause, 109
Federal Constitutional Court, 11, 58, 59, 66–73, 88, 109, 130, 137, 139, 153, 166, 175
and the Basic Treaty, 294–6
on civil service law (1953), 78
decision-making role, 71–3
equality of opportunity for political parties, 14–15
established (1951), 164
on financial equalization, 159
judicial power of review, 66–9, 222
jurisprudence of, 72
Law on (1951, 1971), 69
norm control procedure, 68–9, 71–2, 74, 113
on party financing, 218–19, 220
political effectiveness principle, 72–3
remedies, 70–1
structure and composition, 69–70
Federal Government, 77–110, 146
Federal High Court (*Bundesgerichtshof*), 164
Federal Republic of Germany, (FRG)
comparison of defence expenditure with UK, 279 Table 9.1
foreign policy, 258–79, 304–5
founded (1949), 1, 18, 47–51, 280
leadership role in Europe, 267–8, 304–6
legitimacy of, 293, 296–7
relations with GDR, 5–6, 292–4

and unification, 4–11
and the West, 258–79
the Western Alliance and USA,
    269–78
federal states (*Freistaaten*), 22
federal system, and party system, 133–
    4, 166–7
Federal-*Land* administration, 149–50
Federal-*Land* relations, 164–8
federalism, 141–71
    cooperative, 165–6, 221–2, 232
    and decentralization, 141–6
    financial system of, 154–60
    horizontal, 143
    and the *Länder*, 147–9
    vertical American, 143, 148, 169
    West German quasi-, 169–71
Federation of German Industry
    (BDI), 121, 232, 233, 266
female representation, 216–17
Fette, 242
'final solution' to Jewish problem, 41–
    2
finance, central legislation, 153
Finance, Ministry of, 98–9, 230
Finance Equalization Law (1969,
    amended 1987), 155, 159
Finance Planning Council
    (*Finanzplanungsrat*), 167–8, 228
financial equalization, 12, 155–7:
    (1984), 157 Table 6.1
    horizontal (inter-*Land*) (1986), 310
    Table A5
    influence of *Länder* in, 159–60
financial system of federalism, 154–60
First Republic, West German (1949–
    69), 302
fiscal administration, federal, 152
Fiscal Planning Council
    (*Finanzplanungsrat*), 167–8, 228
Fischer, Joschka, 213–14, 215
Flick affair, 219
Focke, Katharina, 264
Foreign Office, 149, 230
foreign service, 152
foundations, funding political parties,
    219–20
France, 1, 17, 30, 39, 145, 262, 267,
    268, 305
franchise, 172
Franconia, 197
Frankfurt am Main, 281
Frankfurt Coalition (CDU, FDP and
    DP), 47
Frankfurt Documents, 145
Frankfurt Economic Council (1947),
    201
Frankfurt National Assembly, 19–20
Free Democratic Party (FDP), 6, 7, 14,
    44, 49, 83, 89, 92, 94, 101, 116,

166, 173, 174, 175, 177
    election (1987), 189–90
    on European integration, 281
    German Programme (1954), 207
    and *Ostpolitik*, 273, 291, 299
    role in West German party system,
        128, 207–11
    threat to support, 303
Free University of Berlin, 192
Freiburg Theses, 208, 225
Freikorps, 29
Freistaaten (federal states), 22
Freitag, Walter, 242
French Constitutional Charter (1814),
    54
French occupation zone, 42, 47
French Revolution, 65
Frick, 144, 151
Friderichs, 219
Friedrich, C. J., 80
Friedrich Ebert Foundation, 116
Friedrich Naumann Foundation, 116
Friesenhahn, 79
fringe groups, 85
Fromme, F. K., 80

Gall, Lothar, 21
Ganf of Five unions, 239
Gastarbeiter (guest-workers), 255
Gauleiter, 144
Gemeindeverbände (municipal unions),
    163
Genscher, Hans-Dietrich, 7, 17, 87,
    99, 186, 209, 277, 300
German Democratic Party (DDP), 27
German Democratic Republic (GDR),
    4–10, 15, 269
    consolidation of, 284–5
    Constitution (1949), 10
    Constitution (1968), 284–5
    Constitution (1974), 10
    economy, 284
    election (1990), 5–9 Table 1.1
    entry to EC, 17
    founded (1949), 1, 50
    non-recognition of, 66, 286–7
    policy of demarcation (*Abgrenzung*),
        301
    recognition of, 282
    relationship with FDR, 5–6, 292–4,
        304, 306
    and unification, 4–11
    uprising (1953), 282
German economic and monetary
    union, 12–15
German Farmers' Union (*Deutscher
    Bauernverband*) (DVB), 121, 235–
    6, 266
German Federation of Officials, 121
German Forum Party (DFP), 6

German nation debate, 296–8
German National People's Party (DNVP), 28, 32, 33
German People's Party (DVP), 28
German Republic, proclaimed (1918), 26
German Revolution (1918), 27, 29
German Social Union (DSU), 6, 14
German unity, letters on, 290, 293, 297
   see also unification
Germany
   East, *see* German Democratic Republic
   origins of modern, 18–52
   West, *see* Federal Republic of Germany
Gesamtdeutsche Partei (GDP), 286
Gesamtmetall (metal confederation), 233
Gladstone, William Ewart, 28
Globke, Hans, 96–7
Glotz, Peter, 196
GNP
   proportion on defence, 279
   proportion of exports, 227
Goethe, Johann Wolfgang von, 36
Golay, 148–9
Gorbachev, Mikhail, 5, 16, 17, 177, 277
Göttingen, 174
government
   and industry, 230–2
   and opposition, 110, 124–9
   Regierung, 77
government districts (*Regierungsbezirk*), 142
Government of Ireland Act (1920), 129
GPBHE (refugee party), 175
Grand Coalition
   (1928), 28, 33
   (1966–9), 84–5, 101, 117, 176, 202, 208, 263, 287, 297
grants-in-aid, 12, 154, 156: (1986), 310 Table A6
Greens, 116, 122–3, 127, 128, 204, 206–7, 224, 246, 297, 303
   Basis Demokratie, 212–14
   East German, 6, 14
   election (1987), 190
   election (1989), 303
   emerged (1983), 80, 177–8, 211–12, 252
   Fundos (fundamentalists), 215, 303
   Realos (realists), 215, 303
   rotational principle of organization, 213–14
   in West German party system, 214–16

women's issues, 216–17
'zip principle', 190, 216
Grewe, Wilhelm, 93, 284
Groener, General, 26
Grotewohl, Otto, 200
Gscheidle, Kurt, 243
Guillaume, Gunter, 203, 295
Gysi, Grygor, 9

Habsburgs, 1
Hacke, Christian, 192
Hallstein, Walter, 93, 259
Hallstein Doctrine, 282, 287
Hamburg, 45, 59, 145, 146, 156, 160, 161, 168, 187, 188, 215, 256
Hans Seidel Foundation, 116
Heinemann, Gustav, 89, 270
Hennis, Wilhelm, 123
Herrenchiemsee Draft of Basic Law, 49, 67
Hesse, 206, 209
Hesse, Konrad, 148
Hessen, 145, 156, 161, 177
Heuss, Theodor, 89
High Court (*Reichsgericht*), 163
Hilferding, 248
Hindenburg, Paul Von, 25, 26, 29, 33, 35
Historikerstreit, 289
Hitler, Adolf, 1, 31, 34–43, 56, 68, 144
   became Chancellor (1933), 35
   Beer Hall Putsch, Munich (1923), 31–2
   foreign policy, 39–42
   Mein Kampf, 36–7
   policies, 36–9
Höcherl, Hermann, 73
Hoechst, 226, 248
Holy Roman Empire, 19
Honecker, Erich, 5, 276, 301
Horn, E. J., 226
housing, 161, 162
Hugenberg, 33
human rights, 54, 61
Hungarian border issue (1989), 4
Hungarian uprising (1956), 271

identity issue, 296–8
IG Chemie, 239, 251
IG Druck, 239
IG Farben, 226
IG Metall, 238, 239, 241, 244, 251
immigration issue, 255
Imperial Period (1870–1918), 1, 143, 154, 172
Independent Social Democrats (USPD), 26
industrial relations, 233, 239–41
industrial revolution, 20, 246

industry, 2, 195, 206, 226–7
  banks and, 246–50
  and environmental pressures, 250–4
  export orientation, 227, 253
  FRG, 285
  GDR, 284
  government and, 230–2
  interests, 23, 232–6
  Land policies, 165, 256
  party support, 218
  restructuring, 157
  'sun belt' and 'rust belt' states, 239
inflation
  (1923), 31
  (1980–1), 229
integration, European, 258–63, 280
  public opinion on, 265–8
intelligence services, 96
inter-*Land* treaties, 168
Inter-Zonal Trade Agreement, 281
interest groups, 121, 123
Intermediate Nuclear Forces (INF), 198, 274–7
International Institute for Strategic Studies, 204, 274
investment, direct foreign, 254
Iranian Revolution, (1979), 228
Italy, 41

Jaksch, Wenzel, 286
Japan, 253, 305
Jews, extermination of, 36–7, 41–2
Joël, 78
John XXIII, Pope, 180
Joint Tasks (*Gemeinschaftsaufgaben*), 168
judges, 164
Judges Law, 70
Judicature Act (1877), 163
judiciary, 61, 66–73
JUSOS (*Jungsozialisten*), 202–3, 244
Justice, Federal Minister of, 70

Kaiser, Karl, 285
Kaliningrad (Königsberg), 44
Karlsruhe, 66
Katzenstein, Peter, 302
Katzer, Hans, 194
Kelly, Petra, 213, 214
Kelsen, Hans, 65
Kennedy, John F., 272–3, 278, 284
Keynesianism, 227
Khrushchev, Nikita, 282–3
Kiechle, Ignaz, 236, 268
Kiel mutinies, 26
Kierey, Hans-Joachim, 192
Kiesinger, Kurt, 92, 93
Kirchheimer, 200
Kissinger, Henry, 289

Kitzinger, 286
kleindeutsch solution, 21
Klingemann, H. D., 179
Koblenz, 48
Kohl, Helmut
  Chairman of CDU/CSU, 128, 197–8
  as Chancellor, 84, 87, 88, 92, 94–5, 96, 97, 100, 188, 193, 211, 221, 238, 239
  in EC, 305
  European policy, 265, 267–8
  meeting with Gorbachev: (1988), 277; (1990), 16, 17
  Ten Point Plan (1989), 5, 15–16, 306
  and unification, 5–7, 12, 14
Kommandatura, 42
Königsberg, becomes Kaliningrad, 44
Konrad Adenauer Foundation, 116
Korbel, Josef, 286
Korean War, 3, 226, 261, 269, 270
KPD (German Communist Party before 1956), 26, 32, 44, 49, 177, 199, 200, 296
  banned (1956), 60, 69, 72, 173, 175
Kraft, 285
Kreis (district), 162
Krenz, Egon, 5
Kressbronner Kreis, 93
Kulturkampf, 22, 180, 201
Kulturnation, 288

labour
  organization of, 237–9
  refugee, 255
labour costs, 254
labour law, 233
Labour Ministry, 149
Lafontaine, Oskar, 7, 13, 205, 207, 245, 277
Lambsdorff, Otto, 209, 219, 229
Länder, 64, 73, 141, 146–7, 170
  administrative functions, 98
  administrative structure within, 161–3
  civil servants in, 105–6
  constitutional assembly (1948), 48
  constitutions, 147
  democratic legitimation, 143–4
  disputes between, 69
  of East Germany, 10
  and the EEC, 168–9, 268
  established by occupation powers, 44–5
  industries, 146
  interests of, 135
  loss of financial autonomy (1920), 143–4
  new of unified Germany, 6, 11–12
  population, 146

Länder – cont.
  population, area, resources, 307
    Table A1
  relations with federal system, 127,
    147–9, 164–8
  reorganized by Allies, 144–5
  treaties with other *Länder*, 168
  voting allocation in unified
    Germany, 11–12
  voting behaviour, 165
  Weimar, 45
Länderrat, 47
Landkreis, 162
Landtage, 49, 67, 129–31, 153
Lasalle, Ferdinand, 199
law
  Community and national, 138–9
  federal and *Land*, 152–4
  federal and state, 143
  passage of, 112
  and politics, 73–6
  process of making, 223
  supremacy of, 56
  taking effect of, 112–13
Law for the Defence of the Republic,
  31
Lawrence, P., 226–7
laws
  consent, 111, 132–3, 135, 137, 148–
    9, 153, 154
  simple, 111, 132, 133, 135, 153
lawyers' monopoly (*Juristenmonopol*),
  55–6
LDPD, *see* Liberal Democratic Party
Lebensraum strategy, 36–7
Leber, Georg, 243
legal control (*Rechtsmässigkeitskontrolle*),
  150
legislation
  categories of, 129–30
  concurrent, 129–30
  exclusive, 129–30
  framework, 129–30
  passed by all parties, 122–3
  reserved, 129–30
  secondary, 133
legislative process, 111–13, 140
legislature, 111–40
Lehr, Ursula, 221
Leipzig demonstrations (1989), 5
liberal democracy, 2–4, 43
Liberal Democratic Party (LDPD), 6,
  13, 44
liberalism, 19–20, 23–4, 53, 56, 207,
  210–11
liberty, negative, 58–60, 62
Liebknecht, Karl, 22, 26
Liebknecht, Wilhelm, 199
Local Courts (*Amtsgerichte*), 163
local governments, 58, 149–51, 158

local self-government
  (*Selbstverwaltung*), 141
London Conference of the Three
  Western Powers and the Benelux
  countries (1947), 48
London Four Power Conference
  (1947), 48
London Recommendations (1948), 48
Lower Saxony, 132, 145, 156, 161,
  168, 174, 187, 209, 256
Lübeck, 144
Lübke, Heinrich, 89, 90
Lübke Plan (1953), 236
Ludendorff, 25
Lüth judgement (1953), 59
Luther (1926), 83
Lutheranism, 19
Luxemburg, Rosa, 36

Majority Social Democrats (MPSD),
  26, 32
Mann, Thomas, 60
  The Magic Mountain, 51
Mansholt Plan, 266
mark, 31, 226
markets, law on the liberalization of
  (1948), 225–6
Marshall Plan, 52, 201, 226
Marx, Karl, 83
Marxism, 10, 176, 180, 199, 200, 202,
  248
Matthöfer, Hans, 243
Max von Baden, Prince, 25–6
Mayer, Otto, 78
Mecklenburg, 10
Mediation Committee, 112–13, 133, 140
Mende, Erich, 208
Menzel, 131
Merkl, Peter, 143
Metternich system, 19
middle class
  in administration, 55–6
  new, 192
  support for the Greens, 216
  voting, 178–9
  see also bourgeoisie
Milan Summit, (1985), 268
ministers, 99–100, 221
  state, 99–100
ministries, 97–100
  and the Chancellor, 96–7
  Länder, 161
Modrow, Hans, 5, 6, 9
Mollet, Guy, 262
Molotov, Vyacheslav Mikhailovich, 80
Moltke, Helmuth Karl Bernard, Graf
  von, 91
monarchy
  and popular sovereignty, 54
  Prussian, 20–1

Monnet, Jean: Action Committee for the United States of Europe (1955), 262
Monopolkommission, 247, 249
morality
 and law, 56–60
 state power and, 56–7
Morgenthau Plan, 45
Moscow Foreign Ministers' Conference (1947), 48
Moscow Treaty, 288–90
 ratification of, 291–2
Müller, Adam, 54
Müller, Albrecht, 251
Müller, Hermann, 33, 39
Müller-Armack, Alfred, 225
Munich, 146, 196, 256
Munich Conference of Minister-Presidents of *Länder* (1947), 48
Municipalities Decree, (1808), 54
municipalities (*Gemeinden*), 142, 149, 162–3

Napoleon, 19
nation, and the state, 18–21
national socialism, 10, 36–9
 see also Nazi regime
National Socialist German Workers Party (NSDAP), 1, 31, 32, 33, 34–5, 173, 199
nationalism, 43–4
nationality, determinants of, 65
nationality law, West German, 298
Nationality Law (1913), 65
NATO, 65, 206, 258, 279
 dual track decision, 204–5, 274–5
 FRG relations with, 270–9
 FRG role in, 304–5
 and united Germany, 16–17, 305
Natural Law, 54, 75
Navy, 26
Nazi regime, 33, 36–9, 53, 56–7
 debate on crimes, 289
 and municipal autonomy, 144, 151
Nazi-Soviet pact (1939), 44
Nazis, *see* National Socialist German Workers Party
Neue Heimat (trade union housing body), 188, 206, 238
New Centre (*Neue Mitte*), 211
'New Forum', 5
Niederwald, 48, 50
North German Radio, 168
North Rhine-Westphalia, 132, 145, 146, 156, 157, 160, 161, 165, 187, 188, 239, 256
North-South gap in West Germany, 146–7, 160, 169, 256–7
NPD (neo-Nazi party), 176, 292, 303
nuclear energy, 152, 212

nuclear energy industry, 231
 and environmental pressures, 252–3
nuclear weapons, 271, 274–7
 enhanced radiation, 273–4
Nürnberg, 187
NVA (East German army), 17

Oberbürgermeister, 151
Oberländer, 286
occupation, *see* Allied occupation
Occupation Statute, 65, 120
Oder-Neisse line, 1, 280, 286, 290, 291
 and German unity, 16
Offenburg, 187
Öffentlicher Dienst, Transport und Verkehr (ÖTV), 104, 243
Office of the Federal Chancellor (*Bundeskanzleramt*), 95–7, 169
Office for the Protection of the Constitution, 109
'officials', 102, 103, 104
oil price crisis (1973), 228, 263, 266
Ollenhauer, Erich, 202, 262
Operation Barbarossa, 41
opposition
 constructive, 123
 government and, 110, 124–9
Orwell, George, *1984*, 38
Ossenbühl, Fritz, 137–8
Ostmark, 6, 12–13
Ostpolitik, 196, 203, 208, 263, 273, 280–301, 302
 balance sheet of, 299–301
 the beginnings, 286–7
 effect on the West, 299–300
 the German-German dimension, 300–1
 high point, 287–8
 internal effects, 299
 and relations with Eastern Europe, 300
Ottawa Conference (1990), 16
'two plus four' formula, 16
ÖTV (public service union), 104, 243

Pan-German consciousness, 296–7
Paris Accords, 270
parliament
 distribution of seats (1961–7), 184–5 Table 7.3
 role separate from government, 55, 125–9
 'speech', 125
 'work', 125
Parliament, *see* Bundesrat; Reichstag
Parliamentary Council (*Parlamentarischer Rat*), 49–50, 64, 79–80, 82, 84, 102, 131, 145, 148
parliamentary sovereignty, fear of, 79

parliamentary state secretaries, 100
Parteienstaat (party-state), 107
'partial identity theory', 295
participation theory, and legislative
  role of Bundesrat, 137
Parties Law (1967), 219
Party of Democratic Socialism (PDS)
  (formerly Socialist Unity Party), 6,
  9, 14, 15
party districts (*Gaue*), 144
Paterson, W., 3–4, 297
Paulskirche movement, 271
Peace Movement, 205, 275–6, 277
Pershing 2 missiles, 205, 276, 277
Petersburg Abkommen (1950), 74
Phoenix, 249
plenum, 118
pluralism, institutional, 223–4
Pöhl, Karl-Otto, 12
Poland, 1, 16, 42, 280
  invasion of (1939), 40
  negotiations with, 291
  partitioning of, 44
  relations with, 289–90, 291–2
Poles, *Recht auf Heimat*, 285
police, 98, 151, 161, 165
political control
  (*Zweckmässigheitskontrolle*), 150
political economy, FDR, 225–57
political parties, 63, 172–224
  banning of, 69
  development of West German
    system, 173–7
  East German, 6–9 Table 1.1
  and economic interests, 242–6
  and elections, 181–90
  equality of opportunity for, 14–15
  financing of West German, 71, 217–
    20: (1984), 220 Table 7.5
  foundations, 116, 219–20
  freedom of formation, 58–9
  groupings, 193–4
  licensing of, 46, 173
  and making of public policy, 221–4
  patronage functions, 179
  status of, 71
Politburo, 5
politics
  contribution of history to, 51–2
  law and, 73–6
  and unified Germany, 10, 11–12
popes, 180
positivism, 57
Post Office, 152
post-materialism, 179, 204, 206, 251
Potsdam Agreement (1945), 44–6
powers, separation of, 61
POWs, return of German, 282
presidency, 81–3
  since 1949, 89–90

Press and Information Office,
  Federal, 96
pressure groups, power over
  legislation, 121–2
Preuss, Hugo, 28, 67
property, 58
proportional representation, 28, 114,
  172, 181–2, 184
protectionism, 23
Protestant Church, 5
Protestant Working Circle
  (*Evangelischer-Arbeitskreis*), 193–4
Protestantism, 180, 191, 196, 285
Prussia, 1, 19–24, 28, 45, 54, 142,
  144–5, 191
  abolition of, 145
  decentralization, 141–3
  East, 33, 44
  local government, 150–1
  regional coordination of state
    activities, 141–3
Prussian Audit Commission, 126
Prussian General Code of Law (1794),
  54
public expenditure, 126, 228–9
  (1987), 307 Table A2
public law corporation (*öffentlich
  rechtliche Körperschaft*), 108
public law institution (*Anstalt*), 108
public opinion
  on European integration, 265–8
  on reunification, 286
public service, 102–6
  career groups within, 104 Table 4.1
  grades compared with British, 105
  personnel employed (1987), 308
    Table A3
  tripartite division, 102–4
Pulzer, Peter, 175, 186
Pünder, Hermann, 95

'Radicals Decree' (1972), 109
Radunski, Peter, 192
railways, 152
Rainbow Foundation, proposed, 116
Rathenau, 30
Rau, Johannes, 128, 187, 188, 207
Rauschning, Herman
  The Revolution of Nihilism, 37–8
Reagan, Ronald, 275
rearmament issue, 270–4
Rechtsstaat, development of the, 53–
  7, 79
Referentensystem, 96–7
refugees, 173–4, 255, 260
  Chilean, 198
  decline in bargaining position, 285–
  6
  from East Germany, 4–5, 12
  and *Länder*, 145

post WWII, 3
refugees party (GPBHE), 175
regional interests, and political
    alignment, 166–7
Reich
    continuity in FRG, 66, 295
    First (1871), 21–4
Reich Chancellor, 22
Reich Reconstruction Law (1934), 144
Reichskanzlei, 91
Reichsrat, 28, 143
Reichstag, 22–3, 81, 142
Reichstag Fire Decree (1933), 38
religion, and voting behaviour, 179–
    81
religious revival (post 1945), 190–1
Republikaner, 303
Research and Technology, Ministry
    for, 230, 231–2
reunification, 66, 259–63, 280, 281–2,
    286, 288, 297, 298
    achievement of, 11–17, 304
    and the Basic Treaty, 294–6
Reuter, Ernst, 50
Rhine, chemical spillages (1986), 188–
    9, 190, 216, 252
Rhine-Ruhr, 146
Rhineland, 20
Rhineland-Palatinate, 156, 161, 162,
    168
roads, 152, 161, 162
Röhde, Helmut, 243
Romania, 25, 287
Rome, Treaties of, 138
Roosevelt, F. D., 40
Rosenberg, Alfred
    The Myth of the Twentieth Century, 36
Roth, Wolfgang, 244
Ruhr, 20, 189, 243
    French occupation (1923), 31
    International Authority of the, 261
rural subdistricts (*Landkreis*), 142
Russia, 39, 48
    invasion of (1941), 40–2
    see also USSR
Russian occupation zone, 1, 42, 44, 45,
    46, 47, 50, 145
Russian prisoners, 41, 42
Russian Revolution, 25, 172

Saar, 207, 209, 239, 256, 262, 264
Saarland, 9, 147, 156, 157, 162, 187
Saxony, 10, 19, 201; *see also* Lower
    Saxony
Saxony-Anhalt, 10
Schäuble, 97
Scheel, Walther, 89, 208, 290
Schiller, Karl, 227, 240
Schilly, Otto, 214
Schlect, Otto, 249

Schleicher, 35
Schleswig-Holstein, 33, 156, 165, 168,
    205, 256
Schlieffen Plan, 36
Schmid, Carlo, 49, 146
Schmidt, Helmut
    as Chancellor, 84, 87, 92, 94, 96,
        100, 305
    European policy, 263–4
    foreign policy, 267, 269, 273–4
    nuclear policy, 273–5
    and SPD, 117, 203–5, 211, 212, 228,
        238, 250–1, 252–3
    vote of no confidence, 193, 198, 209
Schmitt, Carl, 79, 81
Schnur, Wolfgang, 7
Schonbohm, Wulf Dieter, 192
school system, 58
schools inspectorate, 161
Schroeder, Gerhard, 89, 194, 263,
    273, 286–7
Schumacher, Kurt, 47–8, 200, 261,
    262, 264
Schweigler, G., 297
Second Republic, West German
    (1969–80), 302
security, West German, 258–63, 269–
    79, 305
Seebohm, Hans-Christoph, 286
Septennat, 126
service class, 179
shareholding, 247, 248–9
Shelley, Percy Bysshe, 53
Shonfield, Andrew, 246
Siberian pipeline, 300
Siemens, 231, 232, 235, 256
Silesia, 20
Simons, Walter, 67
Single European Act (1986), 169, 253,
    268
Slavs, elimination of, 36–7
small and medium-sized enterprises,
    231, 234, 254
Smend, Rudolf, 57, 80, 166
Smith, G., 3–4
social changes, 254–7
Social Contract, 54
Social Democratic Party (SPD), 3, 5,
    6–7, 13, 14, 15, 22, 24, 27, 44,
    47–8, 49, 69, 89, 94, 115, 116,
    131, 145–6, 165, 166, 173, 174,
    199–207
    Berlin, 283
    Cologne Conference (1983), 275–6
    election (1987), 187–9
    on European integration, 281
    and foreign policy, 74, 262–3, 273
    in government (1966–82), 202–7
    and the Greens, 245, 251–2
    Hamburg Conference (1977), 274

Social Democratic Party (SDP) – *cont.*
  JUSOS (*Jungsozialisten*), 202–3
  Kampf der Atomtod, 271
  Munich Conference (1982), 275
  nuclear policy, 276
  opposed Hitler's Enabling Law, 38–9
  and *Ostpolitik*, 291, 294, 299
  relations with trade unions, 242–5
  split into MPSD and USPD, 26
  threat to support, 303–4
  working class, 23, 178
  Working Group for Employees' Questions, 244
  see also Bad Godesberg Programme: SPD-FDP coalition
social market economy, 225–9
social rights, 62–3
social union, 13
social welfare state, 63, 74
Socialist Labour Party, 199
Socialist Reich Party, banned, 60
Socialist Unity Party (SED), 5, 6, 9, 10, 47, 48, 200, 276; *see also* Party of Democratic Socialism
South Schleswig Voters' Association, 174
sovereignty, 79, 141, 260
  national and Community, 168–9
Sozial Demokratische Arbeiterpartei (Social Democratic Workers Party), 199
Spartacist League, 26, 29
Späth, Lothar, 303
SPD-FDP coalition (1969–82), 87, 94, 134, 176, 181, 202–4, 208–9
Spiegel, Der, 73
Spiegel affair (1962), 197, 273
SRP (*Sozialistische Reichspartei*), 69
Staatsnation, 288
Stability and Growth Act (1967), 227
Stadtkreis (county borough), 142, 151, 162
Stalin, Joseph, 39, 42, 44
standing conferences, 167–8
'Stasi' (State Security Police), 5, 7
state
  as executive, 77–8
  form of the, 64–6
  and the nation, 18–21
  powers of the, 55–7
  Staat, use of term, 54
state administration (*Staatsverwaltung*), 108
state organization, 60–4
state rights, 147
State Treaty on Economic and Monetary Union (1990), 13
statutes, 61, 68
Statutes, Federal (*Bundesgesetzblatt*), 113, 140

statutory authority, 55
steel industry, 248, 253
Steinkühler, Franz, 244
stock exchange, 246
Stoltenberg, Gerhard, 229
Stoph, 293
Strauss, Franz Josef, 94–5, 186, 193, 197–8, 209, 263, 273
  as Minister President of Bavaria, 115, 128
  opponent of *Ostpolitik*, 196, 291–2, 296
Streibl, Max, 198
Strength Through Joy movement, 39
Stresemann, Gustav, 32, 83
strikes, 233
  (1919–20), 29
  pro-government, 243
  unemployment pay during, 245
Stuttgart, 256
subdistricts (*Kreise*), 142
subsidies, 17, 152
Sudetenland, 1, 196
Supreme Court for Constitutional Conflicts, 67, 151

tariffs, 138
tax reform programme, 160
tax revenues, distribution of, 156–8 Table 6.2
taxes, 152, 154–60
  community, 155, 158, 160
  local yield principle, 155
  undivided, 155
Taylor, A. J. P., 40
teachers, 161, 179
television, commercial, 73
Television Council, 168
Thatcher, Margaret, 110
Third Reich (Hitler), 1, 2–3, 38–42, 172, 280
Third Republic, towards a West German, 302–3
Thuringia, 10, 151, 201
'ticket splitting', 182, 186
trade, 138, 281
  between GDR and FRG, 296
  GDR with USSR, 284
trade unions, 104, 220, 237–9, 261
  Catholics in, 194
  and Concerted Action, 238–41
  industrial (*Industriegewerkschaft*), 237
  marginalization of, 303
  membership and party allegiance, 178
  unitary (*Einheitsgewerkschaft*), 237
Trampert, Rainer, 215
Transition Treaty (1954), 65, 84
transport, 165
treaties (*Staatsverträge*), 168

tripartism, 238, 239–40
Troeger Commission, Report (1967),
  165–6
Turkey, 255

unemployment
  (1925), 30
  (1950s), 226
  (1970s), 181
  (1980s), 229, 239, 245–6
  abolition of, 39
  and *Gastarbeiter*, 255
  in GDR, 13
  shorter working week to combat,
    245
unicameral system, 111, 140
unification (1990), 4–11, 13, 304, 306
  economic and monetary union, 12–
    15
  external factors, 15–17
  negotiations, 9–11
  politics of, 11–12
  see also reunification
United Economic Region (*vereinigtes
  Wirtschaftsgebiet*), 10, 47, 50
  Economic Council, 119–20
United Kingdom, *see* Britain
United Nations, 290, 293
United States of America, 2, 41, 65,
    140, 143, 145, 166, 201, 246, 247
    253, 278, 305
  FRG and the Western Alliance,
    269–78
  policy on German question, 284
  relations with USSR, 289, 300
  security dependency of FRG on,
    258, 259, 261, 263, 271–8
universities, 55, 58, 71, 202, 256
urban subdistricts (*Stadtkreis*), 142
US occupation zone, 42, 44, 46, 47
USPD, 32
USSR, 1, 15, 204–5, 269, 271, 280,
    287, 300
  relations with FRG, 16, 282, 287,
    288–92, 306
  relations with GDR, 10
  relations with USA, 272, 284
  and unification, 15–17

VAT, 12, 155, 156
Vatican, 180
Verantwortungsgemeinschaft (shared
  responsibility in peace
  maintenance), 276
Verband der Chemischen Industrie
  (Chemical Industries
  Association), 232
Versailles, Treaty of (1919), 30, 31,
    34, 39, 172

veto
  absolute, 111
  suspensory, 11, 113, 140
veto powers
  of Bundesrat, 111, 132, 135–7, 140
  of Reichsrat, 143
Vienna Settlement (1815), 19, 54
Vietnam War, 84
'vocational ban' (*Berufsverbot*), 60, 108–
  9
Vogel, Hans-Jochen, 128, 196, 205
Volk
  cultural identity, 19
  Hitler's strategy, 36–7
Volksgerichte, Munich, 32
Volkskammer, 14
Volkspartei, 3
Volkswagen, 241, 249
vom Stein, Freiherr, 54, 55
von Brentano, Heinrich, 259
von Delbruck, Rudolf, 91
Von Hassel, Kai-Uwe, 263, 273
von Heeremann, 236
von Humboldt, Alexander, 55
von Mangoldt, 62
von Mohl, Robert, 54
Von Papen, 35, 78
Von Stauffenberg's Bomb Plot (1944),
  42
von Weisäcker, Richard, 89
vote of no confidence procedure, 118
voting
  class, 178–9
  female, 181
  religious cleavage, 179–81
  after unification, 11–12

wage agreements, 238–9
Waigel, Theo, 198
Wallmann, Walter, 115
Wandel durch Annäherung (change
  through accommodation), 283
war, state of, 85
War of Liberation (1812–14), 19
Wars of Unification (1864, 1866,
  1870–1), 21
Warsaw Ghetto, 289
Warsaw Pact, 274
Warsaw Treaty, 288–90
  ratification of, 291–2
waterways, inland, 152
Weber, Max, 79, 154
Wehner, Herbert, 201–2, 203, 205,
  273, 275
Wehrmacht, 40
Weimar Coalition, 27
Weimar Constitution, 28–9, 56, 64,
  67, 80–1, 141
  Coalition Committee, 91

Weimar National Assembly, 27, 67
Weimar Republic (1919–33), 1–2, 26–
    35, 154, 172
    Reichstags, 86, 119
    weaknesses of, 53, 57, 63
Welcher, Carl Theodor, 54
Wels, Otto, 39
Wertordnung, 57–60
'West German model' of consensus,
    224
West Germany, *see* Federal Republic
    of Germany
West-East travel statistics, 298–9
Western Alliance, USA and FRG,
    269–78
Western European Union, 65, 270–4
Westminster model of parliament,
    123, 125, 140
Westpolitik, 273
Westrick, 97
Wheare, K. C., 169
Wilhelm II, Kaiser, 24
Wirth, Josef, 30
Wirtschaftswunder (economic miracle
    1950s), 225–7
Wolfsburg, 174

women, participation in Green Party,
    214
women's issues, Greens, 216–17
Women's League, 6
worker participation in management,
    240–1
'workers', 102, 103, 104
working class, SPD, 178
works councils (*Betriebsräte*), 241
World War I, 24–6
World War II, 40–2
Wörner, Manfred, 277, 305
Württemberg-Baden, *see* Baden-
    Württemberg
Württemberg-Hohenzollern, *see*
    Baden-Württemberg

Yalta, Treaty of (1945), 42
Young Plan, 33
Yugoslavia, 287

ZDF (*Zweites Deutsches Fernsehen*), 168
Zusammengehörigkeitsgefühl, 288, 300–1
Zweckverbände (special administrative
    associations), 163
Zysman, J., 247